ESSAYS IN SOCIAL HISTORY

Edited
for the Economic History Society

by

M. W. FLINN and T. C. SMOUT

CLARENDON PRESS
OXFORD
1974

Oxford University Press, Ely House, London W.1

GLASGOW NEW YORK TORONTO MELBOURNE WELLINGTON
CAPE TOWN IBADAN NAIROBI DAR ES SALAAM LUSAKA ADDIS ABABA
DELHI BOMBAY CALCUTTA MADRAS KARACHI LAHORE DACCA
KUALA LUMPUR SINGAPORE HONG KONG TOKYO

CASEBOUND ISBN 0 19 877016 2
PAPERBACK ISBN 0 19 877017 0

© *Oxford University Press 1974*

*Printed in Great Britain by
Richard Clay (The Chaucer Press), Ltd.,
Bungay, Suffolk*

Contents

INTRODUCTION — vii

ACKNOWLEDGEMENTS — xiii

1. FROM SOCIAL HISTORY TO THE HISTORY OF SOCIETY — 1
E. J. Hobsbawm, *Birkbeck College, University of London*

2. SOCIOLOGICAL HISTORY: THE INDUSTRIAL REVOLUTION AND THE BRITISH WORKING-CLASS FAMILY — 23
Neil J. Smelser, *University of California, Berkeley*

3. TIME, WORK-DISCIPLINE, AND INDUSTRIAL CAPITALISM — 39
E. P. Thompson

4. CHANGING ATTITUDES TO LABOUR IN THE MID-EIGHTEENTH CENTURY — 78
A. W. Coats, *University of Nottingham*

5. THE FIRST MANCHESTER SUNDAY SCHOOLS — 100
A. P. Wadsworth

6. THE MYTH OF THE OLD POOR LAW AND THE MAKING OF THE NEW — 123
M. Blaug, *Institute of Education, University of London*

7. THE LANGUAGE OF 'CLASS' IN EARLY NINETEENTH-CENTURY ENGLAND — 154
Asa Briggs, *University of Sussex*

8. NINETEENTH-CENTURY TOWNS: A CLASS DIMENSION — 178
J. Foster, *University of Strathclyde*

9. NINETEENTH-CENTURY SOCIAL REFORM: A TORY INTERPRETATION OF HISTORY — 197
Jenifer Hart, *St. Anne's College, Oxford*

10. REASONS FOR THE DECLINE OF MORTALITY IN ENGLAND AND WALES DURING THE NINETEENTH CENTURY — 218
T. McKeown and R. G. Record, *University of Birmingham*

11. TRADE UNIONS AND FREE LABOUR: THE BACKGROUND TO THE TAFF VALE DECISION — 251
J. Saville, *University of Hull*

12. THE POSITION OF WOMEN: SOME VITAL STATISTICS — 277
Richard M. Titmuss

Introduction

THE Economic History Society's purpose in initiating this volume of reprinted essays is to facilitate the study of social history by bringing together
essays at present scattered in journals and symposia of varying degrees of
familiarity and accessibility. Meeting the needs of students in Britain today
carried two broad implications for the planning of the volume. First, while
economic history has been taught in universities, colleges, and schools for
long enough for its study to have broadened out from British economic
history to that of most parts of the developed and developing world, social
history is a relative newcomer to the curriculum and its serious study in
Britain still rarely involves study of Europe, America, or further afield.
Catering primarily for the needs of British students, therefore, implied
concentration on studies of British social history. On the other hand, while
the modern approach to the academic study of social history may not yet
have inspired scholars in all countries, there are nevertheless, as Professor
Hobsbawm's opening essay in this collection illustrates, highly distinguished
schools of social history outside Great Britain; and in deciding to confine this
volume to studies in British social history, the Society and its editors have
reluctantly had to eschew much outstanding work by scholars abroad. The
sharpest deprivation, of course, is the work of the French *Annales* school
of historians, whose trail-blazing comprehensive approach to social history
has undoubtedly been the most exciting influence on social historians
throughout the world during the last few decades. Incidentally, we consider
that Hobsbawm's survey of the nature of, and approaches to, social history
today not only provided the most concise and erudite survey available, but
also made any editorial introduction along similar lines superfluous.

Second, because there is an overwhelming tendency for the modern study
of social history in Britain to concentrate on little more than the last two
hundred years, a conscious, if somewhat reluctant, decision was made to
pander to this chronological concentration in the preparation of this volume.
Given the availability of sources this concentration is understandable. But
so pronounced is it that it would, at present anyway, have been a much
more difficult editorial task to fill a volume with essays of high quality on
periods before the eighteenth century. Time, it is to be hoped, will quickly
remedy this imbalance.

Within these limitations of chronological and spatial coverage the editors
had no difficulty at all in determining their principal guidelines of choice.
Even at the expense of some lack of balance in chronology and subject
distribution, academic merit, they felt, should be the first criterion. Our

initial short list was compiled solely from essays which, in our judgement, were of outstanding quality, and the final choice has not involved any departure from this standard. If, in the process, one or two admirable essays had to be cast aside, it was only on account of the exigencies of space or in the interests of over-all balance. An aspect of this insistence on academic distinction has been a desire to include examples of the work of those we consider to be the outstanding social historians of Britain today.

Other purely practical constraints stood between the editors and an ideally balanced selection. Given the utilitarian function of the volume, we had to decide against the reprinting of essays already reprinted (or, in at least one case, about to be reprinted) elsewhere. These include major essays like H. J. Dyos's study of the London slums in *Victorian Studies*, xi (1967), E. A. Wrigley's pioneering explorations of family reconstitution in *Economic History Review*, 2nd ser. xix (1966) and *Daedalus* (1968), T. McKeown and R. G. Brown on demographic change in eighteenth-century England in *Population Studies*, ix (1955), or any one of several essays that E. J. Hobsbawm has reprinted himself in *Labouring Men* (1964). Secondly, limitations of space prevented the inclusion of larger-scale essays: it was disappointing, for example, on this score not to be able to include A. S. Wohl's brilliant study of the influence of *The Bitter Cry of Outcast London* in *International Review of Social History*, xiii (1968). Thirdly, we have eschewed articles that are predominantly bibliographical: O. R. McGregor's 'The social position of women in England, 1850–1914: a bibliography', *British Journal of Sociology*, vi (1955) would otherwise clearly have been included in this collection. Fourthly, we have avoided articles that are, in effect, previews of books: even work as good as, for example, that of D. Bythell on handloom weavers in *Economic History Review*, 2nd ser. xvii (1964–5), has been left out on this criterion. The partial exception which we have made to this rule is by reprinting Smelser's essay, in effect a postview of some of his ideas in his highly original *Social Change in the Industrial Revolution* (1959). This has the extra virtue of exemplifying the contribution sociology is at last making to social history.

The essays are printed substantially in the form in which the originals appeared, but each living author was invited to make minor alterations or corrections if he or she saw fit. Such changes as have been made are generally very small, though Coats has added a brief postscript in acknowledgement of criticism made of the original paper in the *Economic History Review*.

The editors have appended to all but one article a bibliographical note which tries to take account of the main items that have appeared in its field since the article was first published. It is not comprehensive or critical, but is intended simply as a guide to further study by the student.

The choice of articles eventually made reflects, we believe, the historical development of the subject and prompts some observations on both the present state and the future expectations of our discipline. It was difficult, for instance, to find a wide choice of articles on twentieth-century social history. So far the field has been largely left to sociologists and demographers. The former are largely interested in contemporary problems and content to preface their papers with quick looks over their shoulder at the immediate past: frequently the quality of their glance illustrates Dahrendorf's aphorism that sociologists' history is too often 'invented in order to provide an impressive contrast for contemporary data'. Demographers' work, represented mainly by articles in *Population Studies*, is more satisfactory for the historian: but even here he must be tempted to regard it more as a primary source than as interpretative history, since the figures are expected to speak for themselves (which they seldom do), and there is little perspective. Even those beavers among us, the labour historians, have cut few logs and dammed few streams past 1920: historians of social policy have done a little better, but scarcely carried the story beyond the inter-war years. Altogether, the twentieth century presents an enormous field of untouched material for the social historian: one suspects that it has been neglected not merely because it is recent but also because the tools needed to cultivate it properly are not in plentiful supply in our profession. Knowledge both of relatively sophisticated quantification and of the theoretical concepts of the other social sciences, especially sociology, are probably going to be needed by those who make the significant breakthrough: even now, students seldom receive a thorough training both in these *and* in historical methods in British universities.

Another period in which good work is somewhat thin on the ground is the eighteenth century, especially that part of it which it is fashionable to regard as 'pre-industrial'. The concentration of scholarly effort has quite understandably been on the processes of industrialization itself—economic historians, labour historians, and sociologists alike have been fascinated by what happened to work-patterns, stratification, and the instruments of social control under the impact of the Industrial Revolution. But many, who, interested in significant change, now jostle for elbow-room in studies of the nineteenth century, may, in the future, find more satisfaction in the roots than in the branches. They might with advantage follow the example of E. P. Thompson who, after his classic *Making of the English Working Class*, has turned back to the period before 1790 and, in a series of articles in *Past and Present* and elsewhere, is surveying the scene of the eighteenth century from which so much of import sprang.

Most British social historians, therefore, have written mainly about the nineteenth century. Even within this area, some sectors have been very much better covered than others. The seeds the Webbs sowed have been growing for a long time. Their great descriptive studies on administrative history, for instance, have issued in a modern crop of more analytical works both on the poor law and on other aspects of public policy. It is hard to choose single examples for a work of this nature. Similarly their pioneer works on trade union history have multiplied a hundred-fold, and British labour historians must be the most prolific in the world. Although in the past too much of their work has been either highly tendentious or antiquarian in approach, there are signs that under the sterner and inspiring leadership of such various scholars as Briggs, Hobsbawm, Pelling, and Saville those days are passing.

Other nineteenth-century studies have had a shorter history but scarcely less vigorous life. His colleagues may be forgiven for imagining that urban history sprang from the head of Olympian Dyos as fully armed as Pallas Athene from the head of Zeus. The example of the genre which we reprint, however, is from an author who owes at least as much to Marxist models and sociological method. The boom in urban history is only to be compared with that which accompanied the re-invigoration of historical demography, and which, transformed by the *Annales* school, has been brought in its new guise into this country mainly under the aegis of the Cambridge Group. So far their work has lain mainly outside the nineteenth century and, for various reasons (see above) is unsuitable for this collection. If their brilliance over the field as a whole eclipsed the older tradition rooted in T. H. Marshall and Griffith, the latter nevertheless led to important and underrated work on Victorian demography of the kind reproduced here. Certainly much more work on urban history, demography, and general social structure, using computer-aided record linkage techniques which are particularly appropriate for the nineteenth century, is likely to appear in the course of the next decade: it threatens to form a New Social History as challenging and intimidating to the profession as New Economic History was to our *alter ego*. It will undoubtedly dispose of the comfortable feeling that social history is the last refuge where the innumerate can live undisgraced.

Finally we have, in making our choice, been aware of serious lacunae, or, sometimes, of work being undertaken which has not yet advanced enough to provide sufficiently plentiful examples to choose from. As we have already hinted, we have rather more hope of the usefulness of sociological theory applied by historians to the history even of the nineteenth century than Professor Hobsbawm has (pp. 7–8 below): but Smelser's article remains only the starting-point for a discussion of great intrinsic importance which historians have been slow to take up. Similarly, for all the contemporary interest in women's liberation, it is astonishingly hard to find good articles on the social history of that half of humanity, apart from the one printed here. Children are even more neglected. Much work is being undertaken in doctoral theses and elsewhere on popular religion and recreation, on immigrants and on regional or occupational subcultures: some of it has surfaced as books, but little has appeared in the kind of article we felt clearly justified in reprinting here. With more space, no doubt, we could have been more generous and more representative, but it would have been with a sacrifice of quality about which we should have felt some hesitation.

The really exciting thing, for those of us engaged in teaching the enthusiastic and able students at present going through the universities, is perhaps the future. We have neither of us much doubt that our successors in the next generation, if commissioned to do a similar task for the Economic History Society, will want to print a totally different selection of articles, most of which will have been produced in the next twenty or thirty years. They will no doubt find the present social historians' approach stumbling and old-fashioned, if perhaps meritorious for its day. We would have no reason to complain at that: the first duty of a historian is to leave vigorous children who will devour him, and lo! they are all about us.

Acknowledgements

IN addition to the advice and encouragement of the Publications Committee of the Economic History Society, we would like to acknowledge our debt to colleagues at Edinburgh University, particularly Dr. Michael Anderson, Mrs. Rosalind Mitchison, and Dr. R. J. Morris.

1

From Social History to the
History of Society*

E. J. HOBSBAWM

THIS essay is an attempt to observe and analyse, not to state a personal credo or to express (except where this is clearly stated) the author's preferences and value judgements. I say this at the outset in order to distinguish this essay from others which are defences of or pleas for the kind of history practised by their authors—as it happens social history does not need either at the moment—but also to avoid two misunderstandings especially common in discussions heavily charged with ideology. All discussions about social history are.

The first is the tendency for readers to identify authors with the views they write about, unless they disclaim this identification in the clearest terms and sometimes even when they do so. The second is the tendency to confuse the ideological or political motivations of research, or its utilization, with its scientific value. Where ideological intention or bias produces triviality or error, as is often the case in the human sciences, we happily condemn motivation, method, and result. However, life would be a great deal simpler if our understanding of history were advanced exclusively by those with whom we are in agreement or in sympathy on all public and even private matters. Social history is at present in fashion. None of those who practise it would care to be seen keeping ideological company with all those who come under the same historical heading. Nevertheless, what is more important than to define one's attitude is to discover where social history stands today after two decades of unsystematic if copious development, and whither it might go.

I

The term social history has always been difficult to define, and until recently there has been no great pressure to define it, for it has lacked the institutional and professional vested interests which normally insists on precise demarcations. Broadly speaking, until the present vogue of the subject—

* From *Daedalus*, 100 (winter, 1971), 20–45. Reprinted by permission of the author and the editor of *Daedalus*, Journal of the American Academy of Arts and Sciences.

or at least the name—it was in the past used in three sometimes overlapping senses. First, it referred to the history of the poor or lower classes, and more specifically to the history of the movements of the poor ('social movements'). The term could be even more specialized, referring essentially to the history of labour and socialist ideas and organizations. For obvious reasons this link between social history and the history of social protest or socialist movements has remained strong. A number of social historians have been attracted to the subject because they were radicals or socialists and as such interested in subjects of great sentimental relevance to them.[1]

Second, the term was used to refer to works on a variety of human activities difficult to classify except in such terms as 'manners, customs, everyday life'. This was, perhaps for linguistic reasons, a largely Anglo-Saxon usage, since the English language lacks suitable terms for what the Germans who wrote about similar subjects—often also in a rather super-ficial and journalistic manner—called *Kultur-* or *Sittengeschichte*. This kind of social history was not particularly oriented towards the lower classes—indeed rather the opposite—though the more politically radical practitioners tended to pay attention to them. It formed the unspoken basis of what may be called the residual view of social history, which was put forward by the late G. M. Trevelyan in his *English Social History* (London, 1944) as 'history with the politics left out'. It requires no comment.

The third meaning of the term was certainly the most common and for our purposes the most relevant: 'social' was used in combination with 'economic history'. Indeed, outside the Anglo-Saxon world, the title of the typical specialist journal in this field before the Second World War always (I think) bracketed the two words, as in the *Vierteljahrschrift fuer Sozial u. Wirtschaftsgeschichte*, the *Revue d'Histoire E. & S.*, or the *Annales d'Histoire E. & S.* It must be admitted that the economic half of this com-bination was overwhelmingly preponderant. There were hardly any social histories of equivalent calibre to set beside the numerous volumes devoted to the economic history of various countries, periods, and subjects. There were in fact not very many economic and social histories. Before 1939 one can think of only a few such works, admittedly sometimes by impressive authors (Pirenne, Mikhail Rostovtzeff, J. W. Thompson, perhaps Dopsch), and the monographic or periodic literature was even sparser. Nevertheless, the habitual bracketing of economic and social, whether in the definitions of the general field of historical specialization or under the more specialized banner of economic history, significant.

It revealed the desire for an approach to history systematically different from the classical Rankean one. What interested historians of this kind was the evolution of the economy, and this in turn interested them because of the light it threw on the structure and changes in society, and more especially on the relationship between classes and social groups, as George

Unwin admitted.[2] This social dimension is evident even in the work of the most narrowly or cautiously economic historians so long as they claimed to be historians. Even J. H. Clapham argued that economic history was of all varieties of history the most fundamental because it was the foundation of society.[3] The predominance of the economic over the social in this combination had, we may suggest, two reasons. It was partly owing to a view of economic theory which refused to isolate the economic from social, institutional, and other elements, as with the Marxists and the German historical school, and partly to the sheer headstart of economics over the other social sciences. If history had to be integrated into the social sciences, economics was the one it had primarily to come to terms with. One might go further and argue (with Marx) that, whatever the essential inseparability of the economic and the social in human society, the analytical base of any historical inquiry into the evolution of human societies must be the process of social production.

None of the three versions of social history produced a specialized academic field of social history until the 1950s, though at one time the famous *Annales* of Lucien Febvre and Marc Bloch dropped the economic half of its subtitle and proclaimed itself purely social. However, this was a temporary diversion of the war years, and the title by which this great journal has now been known for a quarter of a century—*Annales: économies, sociétés, civilisations*—as well as the nature of its contents, reflect the original and essentially global and comprehensive aims of its founders. Neither the subject itself, nor the discussion of its problems, developed seriously before 1950. The journals specializing in it, still few in number, were not founded until the end of the 1950s: we may perhaps regard the *Comparative Studies in Society and History* (1958) as the first. As an academic specialization, social history is therefore quite new.

What explains the rapid development and growing emancipation of social history in the past twenty years? The question could be answered in terms of technical and institutional changes within the academic disciplines of social science: the deliberate specialization of economic history to fit in with the requirements of the rapidly developing economic theory and analysis, of which the 'new economic history' is an example; the remarkable and world-wide growth of sociology as an academic subject and fashion, which in turn called for subsidiary historical service-branches analogous to those required by economics departments. We cannot neglect such factors. Many historians (such as the Marxists) who had previously labelled themselves economic because the problems they were interested in were plainly not encouraged or even considered by orthodox general history, found themselves extruded from a rapidly narrowing economic history and accepted or welcomed the title of 'social historians', especially if their mathematics were poor. It is improbable that in the atmosphere of the 1950s and early

1960s someone like R. H. Tawney would have been welcomed among the economic historians had he been a young researcher and not president of the Economic History Society. However, such academic redefinitions and professional shifts hardly explain much, though they cannot be overlooked

Far more significant was the general historization of the social sciences which took place during this period, and may retrospectively appear to have been the most important development within them at this time. For my present purpose it is not necessary to explain this change, but it is impossible to avoid drawing attention to the immense significance of the revolutions and struggles for political and economic emancipation of colonial and semi-colonial countries, which drew the attention of governments, international and research organizations, and consequently also of social scientists, to what are essentially problems of historic transformations.[4] These were subjects which had hitherto been outside, or at best on the margins of, academic orthodoxy in the social sciences, and had increasingly been neglected by historians.

At all events essentially historical questions and concepts (sometimes, as in the case of 'modernization' or 'economic growth', excessively crude concepts) have captured even the disciplines hitherto most immune to history, when not actually, like Radcliffe-Brown's social anthropology, actively hostile to it. This progressive infiltration of history is perhaps most evident in economics, where an initial field of growth economics, whose assumptions, though much more sophisticated, were those of the cookery book ('Take the following quantities of ingredients *a* through *n*, mix and cook, and the result will be the take-off into self-sustained growth'), has been succeeded by the growing realization that factors outside economics also determine economic development. In brief, it is now impossible to pursue many activities of the social scientist in any but a trivial manner without coming to terms with social structure and its transformations: without the history of societies. It is a curious paradox that the economists were beginning to grope for some understanding of social (or at any rate not strictly economic) factors at the very moment when the economic historians, absorbing the economists' models of fifteen years earlier, were trying to make themselves look hard rather than soft by forgetting about everything except equations and statistics.

What can we conclude from this brief glance at the historical development of social history? It can hardly be an adequate guide to the nature and tasks of the subject under consideration, though it can explain why certain more or less heterogeneous subjects of research came to be loosely grouped under this general title, and how developments in other social sciences prepared the ground for the establishment of an academic theory specially demarcated as such. At most it can provide us with some hints, at least one of which is worth mentioning immediately.

A survey of social history in the past seems to show that its best practitioners have always felt uncomfortable with the term itself. They have either, like the great Frenchmen to whom we owe so much, preferred to describe themselves simply as historians and their aim as 'total' or 'global' history, or as men who sought to integrate the contributions of all relevant social sciences in history, rather than to exemplify any one of them. Marc Bloch, Fernand Braudel, Georges Lefebvre are not names which can be pigeon-holed as social historians except in so far as they accepted Fustel de Coulanges' statement that 'History is not the accumulation of events of all kinds which occurred in the past. It is the science of human societies.'

Social history can never be another specialization like economic or other hyphenated histories because its subject matter cannot be isolated. We can define certain human activities as economic, at least for analytical purposes, and then study them historically. Though this may be (except for certain definable purposes) artificial or unrealistic, it is not impracticable. In much the same way, though at a lower level of theory, the old kind of intellectual history which isolated written ideas from their human context and traced their filiation from one writer to another is possible, if one wants to do that sort of thing. But the social or societal aspects of man's being cannot be separated from the other aspects of his being, except at the cost of tautology or extreme trivialization. They cannot, for more than a moment, be separated from the ways in which men get their living and their material environment. They cannot, even for a moment, be separated from their ideas, since their relations with one another are expressed and formulated in language which implies concepts as soon as they open their mouths. And so on. The intellectual historian may (at his risk) pay no attention to economics, the economic historian to Shakespeare, but the social historian who neglects either will not get far. Conversely, while it is extremely improbable that a monograph on Provençal poetry will be economic history or one on inflation in the sixteenth century intellectual history, both could be treated in a way to make them social history.

II

Let us turn from the past to the present and consider the problems of writing the history of society. The first question concerns how much societal historians can get from other social sciences, or indeed how far their subject is or ought to be merely the science of society in so far as it deals with the past. This question is natural, though the experience of the past two decades suggests two different answers to it. It is clear that social history has since 1950 been powerfully shaped and stimulated, not only by the professional structure of other social sciences (for example, their specific course requirements for university students), and by their methods and techniques, but also by their questions. It is hardly too much to say that the recent efflores cence of studies in the British Industrial Revolution, a subject once grossly neglected by its own experts because they doubted the validity of the concept of industrial revolution, is due primarily to the urge of economists (doubtless in turn echoing that of governments and planners) to discover how industrial revolutions happen, what makes them happen, and what socio-political consequences they have. With certain notable exceptions, the flow of stimulation in the past twenty years has been one way. On the other hand, if we look at recent developments in another way, we shall be struck by the obvious convergence of workers from different disciplines towards socio-historical problems. The study of millenial phenomena is a case in point, since among writers on these subjects we find men coming from anthropology, sociology, political science, history, not to mention students of literature and religions—though not, so far as I am aware, economists. We also note the transfer of men with other professional formations, at least temporarily, to work which historians would consider historical—as with Charles Tilly and Neil Smelser from sociology, Eric Wolf from anthropology, Everett Hagen and Sir John Hicks from economics.

Yet the second tendency is perhaps best regarded not as convergence but as conversion. For it must never be forgotten that if nonhistorical social scientists have begun to ask properly historical questions and to ask historians for answers, it is because they themselves have none. And if they have sometimes turned themselves into historians, it is because the practising members of our discipline, with the notable exception of the Marxists and others—not necessarily *Marxisants*—who accept a similar problematic, have not provided the answers.[5] Moreover, though there are now a few social scientists from other disciplines who have made themselves sufficiently expert in our field to command respect, there are more who have merely applied a few crude mechanical concepts and models. For every *Vendée* by a Tilly, there are, alas, several dozen equivalents of Rostow's *Stages*. I leave aside the numerous others who have ventured into the difficult territory of historical source material without an adequate knowledge of the hazards they are likely to encounter there, or of the means of avoiding and overcoming them. In brief, the situation at present is one in which historians, with all their willingness to learn from other disciplines, are required to teach rather than to learn. The history of society cannot be written by applying the meagre available models from other sciences; it requires the construction of adequate new ones—or, at least (Marxists would argue), the development of existing sketches into models.

This is not, of course, true of techniques and methods, where the historians are already net debtors to a substantial extent, and will, or at least ought, to go even more heavily and systematically into debt. I do not wish to discuss this aspect of the problem of the history of society, but a point or two can be made in passing. Given the nature of our sources, we can hardly advance much beyond a combination of the suggestive hypothesis and the apt anecdotal illustration without techniques for the discovery, the statistical grouping, and handling of large quantities of data, where necessary with the aid of division of research labour and technological devices, which other social sciences have long developed. At the opposite extreme, we stand in equal need of the techniques for the observation and analysis in depth of specific individuals, small groups, and situations, which have also been pioneered outside history, and which may be adaptable to our purposes—for example, the participant observation of the social anthropologists, the inter-view-in-depth, perhaps even psychoanalytical methods. At the very least these various techniques can stimulate the search for adaptations and equivalents in our field, which may help to answer otherwise impenetrable questions.[6]

I am much more doubtful about the prospect of turning social history into a backward projection of sociology, as of turning economic history into retrospective economic theory, because these disciplines do not at present provide us with useful models or analytical frameworks for the study of long-run *historical* socio-economic transformations. Indeed the bulk of their thinking has not been concerned with, or even interested in, such changes, if we except such trends as Marxism. Moreover, it may be argued that in important respects their analytical models have been developed systematic-ally, and most profitably, by abstracting from historical change. This is notably true, I would suggest, of sociology and social anthropology.

The founding fathers of sociology have indeed been more historically minded than the main school of neoclassic economics (though not neces-sarily than the original school of classical political economists), but theirs is an altogether less developed science. Stanley Hoffmann has rightly pointed to the difference between the 'models' of the economists and the 'checklists' of the sociologists and anthropologists.[7] Perhaps they are more than mere checklists. These sciences have also provided us with certain visions, patterns of possible structures composed of elements which can be permuted and combined in various ways, vague analogues to Kekulé's ring glimpsed at the top of the bus, but with the drawback of unverifiability. At their best such structural-functional patterns may be both elegant and heuristically use-ful, at least for some. At a more modest level, they may provide us with use-ful metaphors, concepts, or terms (such as 'role'), or convenient aids in ordering our material.

Moreover, quite apart from their deficiency as models, it may be argued that the theoretical constructions of sociology (or social anthropology) have been most successful by excluding history, that is, directional or oriented change.[8] Broadly speaking, the structural-functional patterns illuminate what societies have in common in spite of their differences, whereas our problem is with what they have not. It is not what light Lévi-Strauss's Amazonian tribes can throw on modern (indeed on any) society, but on how humanity got from the cavemen to modern industrialism or post-industrialism, and what changes in society were associated with this progress, or necessary for it to take place, or consequential upon it. Or, to use another illustration, it is not to observe the permanent necessity of all human societies to supply themselves with food by growing or otherwise acquiring it, but what happens when this function, having been overwhelmingly fulfilled (since the neolithic revolution) by classes of peasants forming the majority of their societies, comes to be fulfilled by small groups of other kinds of agricultural producers and may come to be fulfilled in nonagricultural ways. How does this happen, and why? I do not believe that sociology and social anthropology, however helpful they are incidentally, at present provide us with much guidance.

On the other hand, while I remain sceptical of most current economic theory as a framework of the historical analysis of societies (and therefore of the claims of the new economic history), I am inclined to think that the possible value of economics for the historian of society is great. It cannot but deal with what is an essentially dynamic element in history, namely the process—and, speaking globally and on a long time-scale, progress—of social production. In so far as it does it has, as Marx saw, historical development built into it. To take a simple illustration: the concept of the 'economic surplus', which the late Paul Baran revived and utilized to such good effect,[9] is patently fundamental to any historian of the development of societies, and strikes me as not only more objective and quantifiable, but also more primary, speaking in terms of analysis, than, say, the dichotomy *Gemeinschaft–Gesellschaft*. Of course Marx knew that economic models, if they are to be valuable for historical analysis, cannot be divorced from social and institutional realities, which include certain basic types of human communal or kinship organization, not to mention the structures and assumptions specific to particular socio-economic formations or cultures. And yet, though Marx is not for nothing regarded as one of the major founding fathers of modern sociological thought (directly and through his followers and critics), the fact remains that his major intellectual project *Das Kapital* took the form of a work of economic analysis. We are required neither to agree with his conclusions nor his methodology. But we would be unwise to neglect the practice of the thinker who, more than any other, has defined or suggested the set of historical questions to which social scientists find themselves drawn today.

III

How are we to write the history of society? It is not possible for me to produce a definition or model of what we mean by society here, or even a checklist of what we want to know about its history. Even if I could, I do not know how profitable this would be. However, it may be useful to put up a small and miscellaneous assortment of signposts to direct or warn off future traffic.

(1) The history of society is *history;* that is to say it has real chronological time as one of its dimensions. We are concerned not only with structures and their mechanisms of persistence and change, and with the general possibilities and patterns of their transformations, but also with what actually happened. If we are not, then (as Fernand Braudel has reminded us in his article on 'Histoire et longue durée'[10]) we are not historians. *Conjectural* history has a place in our discipline, even though its chief value is to help us assess the possibilities of present and future, rather than past, where its place is taken by *comparative* history; but actual history is what we must explain. The possible development or nondevelopment of capitalism in imperial China is relevant to us only in so far as it helps to explain the actual fact that this type of economy developed fully, at least to begin with, in one and only one region of the world. This in turn may be usefully contrasted (again in the light of general models) with the tendency for other systems of social relations—for example, the broadly feudal—to develop much more frequently and in a greater number of areas. The history of society is thus a collaboration between general models of social structure and change and the specific set of phenomena which actually occurred. This is true whatever the geographical or chronological scale of our inquiries.

(2) The history of society is, among other things, that of specific units of people living together and definable in sociological terms. It is the history of societies as well as of human society (as distinct from, say, that of apes and ants), or of certain types of society and their possible relationships (as in such terms as 'bourgeois' or 'pastoral' society), or of the general development of humanity considered as a whole. The definition of a society in this sense raises difficult questions, even if we assume that we are defining an objective reality, as seems likely, unless we reject as illegitimate such statements as 'Japanese society in 1930 differed from English society'. For even if we eliminate the confusions between different uses of the word 'society', we face problems (*a*) because the size, complexity, and scope of these units varies, for example, at different historical periods or stages of development; and (*b*) because what we call society is merely one set of human interrelations among several of varying scale and comprehensiveness into which people are classifiable or classify themselves, often simultaneously and with overlaps. In extreme cases such as New Guinea or Amazon tribes, these various sets may define the same group of people, though this is in fact rather improbable. But normally this group is congruent neither with such relevant sociological units as the community, nor with certain wider systems of relationship of which the society forms a part, and which may be functionally essential to it (like the set of economic relations) or nonessential (like those of culture).

Christendom or Islam exist and are recognized as self-classifications, but though they may define a *class* of societies sharing certain common characteristics, they are not societies in the sense in which we use the word when talking about the Greeks or modern Sweden. On the other hand, while in many ways Detroit and Cuzco are today part of a single system of functional interrelationships (for example, part of one economic system), few would regard them as part of the same society, sociologically speaking. Neither would we regard as one the societies of the Romans or the Han and those of the barbarians who formed, quite evidently, part of a wider system of interrelationships with them. How do we define these units? It is far from easy to say, though most of us solve—or evade—the problem by choosing some outside criterion: territorial, ethnic, political, or the like. But this is not always satisfactory. The problem is more than methodological. One of the major themes of the history of modern societies is the increase in their scale, internal homogeneity, or at least in the centralization and directness of social relationships, the change from an essentially pluralist to an essentially unitary structure. In tracing this, problems of definition become very troublesome, as every student of the development of national societies or at least of nationalisms knows.

(3) The history of societies requires us to apply, if not a formalized and elaborate model of such structures, then at least an approximate order of research priorities and a working assumption about what constitutes the central nexus or complex of connections of our subject, though of course these things imply a model. Every social historian does in fact make such assumptions and hold such priorities. Thus I doubt whether any historian of eighteenth-century Brazil would give the Catholicism of that society analytical priority over its slavery, or any historian of nineteenth-century Britain would regard kinship as being as central a social nexus as he would in Anglo-Saxon England.

A tacit consensus among historians seems to have established a fairly common working model of this kind, with variants. One starts with the material and historical environment, goes on to the forces and techniques of production (demography coming somewhere in between), the structure of the consequent economy—divisions of labour, exchange, accumulation, distribution of the surplus, and so forth—and the social relations arising from these. These might be followed by the institutions and the image of society and its functioning which underlie them. The shape of the social structure is thus established, the specific characteristics and details of which in so far as they derive from other sources, can then be determined, most likely by comparative study. The practice is thus to work outwards and upwards from the process of social production in its specific setting. Historians will be tempted—in my view rightly—to pick on one particular relation or relational complex as central and specific to the society (or type of society) in question, and to group the rest of the treatment around it—for example, Bloch's 'relations of interdependence' in his *Feudal Society*, or those arising out of industrial production, possibly in industrial society, certainly in its capitalist form. Once the structure has been established, it must be seen in its historical movement. In the French phrase 'structure' must be seen in 'conjuncture', though this term must not be taken to exclude other, and possibly more relevant, forms and patterns of historical change. Once again the tendency is to treat economic movements (in the broadest sense) as the backbone of such an analysis. The tensions to which the society is exposed in the process of historic change and transformation then allow the historian to expose (1) the general mechanism by which the structures of society simultaneously tend to lose and re-establish their equilibria, and (2) the phenomena which are traditionally the subject of interest to the social historians, for example, collective consciousness, social movements, the social dimension of intellectual and cultural changes, and so on.

My object in summarizing what I believe—perhaps wrongly—to be a widely accepted working plan of social historians is not to recommend it, even though I am personally in its favour. It is rather the opposite: to suggest that we try and make the implicit assumptions on which we work explicit and to ask ourselves whether this plan is in fact the best for the formulation of the nature and structure of societies and the mechanisms of their historic transformations (or stabilizations), whether other plans of work based on other questions can be made compatible with it, or are to be preferred to it, or can simply be superimposed to produce the historical equivalent of those Picasso portraits which are simultaneously displayed full-face and in profile.

In brief, if as historians of society we are to help in producing—for the benefit of all the social sciences—valid models of socio-historic dynamics, we shall have to establish a greater unity of our practice and our theory, which at the present stage of the game probably means in the first instance to watch what we are doing, to generalize it, and to correct it in the light of the problems arising out of further practice.

IV

Consequently, I should like to conclude by surveying the actual practice of social history in the past decade or two, in order to see what future approaches and problems it suggests. This procedure has the advantage that it fits in both with the professional inclinations of a historian and with what little we know about the actual progress of sciences. What topics and problems have attracted most attention in recent years? What are the growing-points? What are the interesting people doing? The answers to such questions do not exhaust analysis, but without them we cannot get very far. The consensus of workers may be mistaken, or distorted by fashion or

—as is obviously the case in such a field as the study of public disorder—
by the impact of politics and administrative requirements, but we neglect
it at our peril. The progress of science has derived less from the attempt to
define perspectives and programmes *a priori*—if it did we should now be
curing cancer—than from an obscure and often simultaneous convergence
upon the questions worth asking and, above all, those ripe for an answer.
Let us see what has been happening, at least in so far as it is reflected in the
impressionistic view of one observer.

Let me suggest that the bulk of interesting work in social history in the
past ten or fifteen years has clustered around the following topic or complexes
of questions:

(1) Demography and kinship
(2) Urban studies in so far as these fall within our field
(3) Classes and social groups
(4) The history of 'mentalities' or collective consciousness or of 'culture'
    in the anthropologists' sense
(5) The transformation of societies (for example, modernization or indus-
    trialization)
(6) Social movements and phenomena of social protest.

The first two groups can be singled out because they have already institutionalized themselves as fields, regardless of the importance of their subject
matter, and now possess their own organization, methodology, and system
of publications. Historical demography is a rapidly growing and fruitful
field, which rests not so much on a set of problems as on a technical innovation in research (family reconstitution) that makes it possible to derive
interesting results from material hitherto regarded as recalcitrant or exhausted
(parish registers). It has thus opened a new range of sources, whose characteristics in turn have led to the formulation of questions. The major interest
for social historians of historical demography lies in the light it sheds on
certain aspects of family structure and behaviour, on the life-curves of
people at different periods, and on intergenerational changes. These are important though limited by the nature of the sources—more limited than the
most enthusiastic champions of the subject allow, and certainly by themselves
insufficient to provide the framework of analysis of 'The World We Have
Lost'. Nevertheless, the fundamental importance of this field is not in question, and it has served to encourage the use of strict quantitative techniques.
One welcome effect—or side-effect—has been to arouse a greater interest in
historical problems of kinship structure than social historians might have
shown without this stimulus, though a modest demonstration effect from
social anthropology ought not to be neglected. The nature and prospects
of this field have been sufficiently debated to make further discussion
unnecessary here.

Urban history also possesses a certain technologically determined unity. The individual city is normally a geographically limited and coherent unit, often with its specific documentation and even more often of a size which lends itself to research on the Ph.D. scale. It also reflects the urgency of urban problems which have increasingly become the major, or at least the most dramatic, problems of social planning and management in modern industrial societies. Both these influences tend to make urban history a large container with ill-defined, heterogeneous, and sometimes indiscriminate contents. It includes anything about cities. But it is clear that it raises problems peculiarly germane to social history, at least in the sense that the city can never be an analytical framework for economic macrohistory (because economically it must be part of a larger system), and politically it is only rarely found as a self-contained city state. It is essentially a body of human beings living together in a particular way, and the characteristic process of urbanization in modern societies makes it, at least up to the present, the form in which most of them live together. The technical, social, and political problems of the city arise essentially out of the interactions of masses of human beings living in close proximity to one another; and even the ideas about the city (in so far as it is not a mere stage-set for the display of some ruler's power and glory) are those in which men—from the Book of Revelation on—have tried to express their aspirations about human communities. Moreover, in recent centuries it has raised and dramatized the problems of rapid social change more than any other institution. That the social historians who have flocked into urban studies are aware of this need hardly be said.[11] One may say that they have been groping towards a view of urban history as a paradigm of social change. I doubt whether it can be this, at least for the period up to the present. I also doubt whether many really impressive global studies of the larger cities of the industrial era have so far been produced, considering the vast quantity of work in this field. However, urban history must remain a central concern of historians of society, if only because it brings out—or can bring out—those specific aspects of societal change and structure with which sociologists and social psychologists are peculiarly concerned.

The other clusters of concentration have not so far been institutionalized, though one or two may be approaching this stage of development. The history of classes and social groups has plainly developed out of the common assumption that no understanding of society is possible without an understanding of the major components of all societies no longer based primarily on kinship. In no field has the advance been more dramatic and—given the neglect of historians in the past—more necessary. The briefest list of the most significant works in social history must include Lawrence Stone on the Elizabethan aristocracy, E. Le Roy Ladurie on the Languedoc peasants, Edward Thompson on the making of the English working class, Adeline

Daumard on the Parisian bourgeoisie; but these are merely peaks in what is already a sizeable mountain range. Compared to these the study of more restricted social groups—professions, for instance—has been less significant.

The novelty of the enterprise has been its ambition. Classes, or specific relations of production such as slavery, are today being systematically considered on the scale of a society, or in intersocietal comparison, or as general types of social relationship. They are also now considered in depth, that is, in all aspects of their social existence, relations, and behaviour. This is new, and the achievements are already striking, though the work has barely begun—if we except fields of specially intense activity, such as the comparative study of slavery. Nevertheless, a number of difficulties can be discerned, and a few words about them may not be out of place.

(1) The mass and variety of material for these studies is such that the pre-industrial artisan technique of older historians is plainly inadequate. They require co-operative teamwork and the utilization of modern technical equipment. I would guess that the massive works of individual scholarship will mark the early phases of this kind of research, but will give way on the one hand to systematic co-operative projects (such as the projected study of the Stockholm working class in the nineteenth century)[12] and on the other hand to periodic (and probably still single-handed) attempts at synthesis. This is evident in the field of work with which I am most familiar, the history of the working class. Even the most ambitious single work—E. P. Thompson's—is no more than a great torso, though it deals with a rather short period. (Jürgen Kuczynski's titanic *Geschichte der Lage der Arbeiter unter dem Kapitalismus*, as its title implies, concentrates only on certain aspects of the working class.)

(2) The field raises daunting technical difficulties, even where conceptual clarity exists, especially as regards the measurement of change over time—for example, the flow into and out of any specified social group, or the changes in peasant landholdings. We may be lucky enough to have sources from which such changes can be derived (for example, the recorded genealogies of the aristocracy and gentry as a group) or from which the material for our analysis may be constructed (for example, by the methods of historical demography, or the data on which the valuable studies of the Chinese bureaucracy have been based). But what are we to do, say, about Indian castes, which we also know to have contained such movements, presumably intergenerational, but about which it is so far impossible to make even rough quantitative statements?

(3) More serious are the conceptual problems, which have not always been clearly confronted by historians—a fact which does not preclude good work (horses can be recognized and ridden by those who can't define them), but which suggests that we have been slow to face the more general problems of social structure and relations and their transformations. These in

turn raise technical problems, such as those of the possibly changing speci-
fication of the membership of a class over time, which complicates quantitative study. It also raises the more general problem of the multi-dimensionality
of social groups. To take a few examples. There is the well-known Marxian
duality of the term 'class'. In one sense it is a general phenomenon of all
post-tribal history, in another a product of modern bourgeois society; in one
sense almost an analytical construct to make sense of otherwise inexplicable
phenomena, in another a group of people actually seen as belonging together in their own or some other group's consciousness, or both. These
problems of consciousness in turn raise the question of the language of class
—the changing, often overlapping, and sometimes unrealistic terminologies
of such contemporary classification[13] about which we know as yet very little
in quantitative terms. (Here historians might look carefully at the methods
and preoccupations of social anthropologists, while pursuing—as L. Girard
and a Sorbonne team are doing—the systematic quantitative study of socio-
political vocabulary.)[14]

Again, there are degrees of class. To use Theodore Shanin's phrase,[15] the
peasantry of Marx's 18th Brumaire is a 'class of low classness', whereas
Marx's proletariat is a class of very high, perhaps of maximal 'classness'.
There are the problems of the homogeneity or heterogeneity of classes; or
what may be much the same, of their definition in relation to other groups
and their internal divisions and stratifications. In the most general sense,
there is the problem of the relation between classifications, necessarily static
at any given time, and the multiple and changing reality behind them.

(4) The most serious difficulty may well be the one which leads us directly
towards the history of society as a whole. It arises from the fact that class
defines not a group of people in isolation, but a system of relationships, both
vertical and horizontal. Thus it is a relationship of difference (or similarity)
and of distance, but also a qualitatively different relationship of social function, of exploitation, of dominance/subjection. Research on class must therefore involve the rest of society of which it is a part. Slave-owners cannot be
understood without slaves, and without the nonslave sectors of society. It
might be argued that for the self-definition of the nineteenth-century European middle classes the capacity to exercise power over people (whether
through property, keeping servants, or even—via the patriarchal family
structure—wives and children), and of not having direct power exercised
over themselves, was essential. Class studies are therefore, unless confined
to a deliberately restricted and partial aspect, analyses of society. The most
impressive—like Le Roy Ladurie's—therefore go far beyond the limits of
their title.

It may thus be suggested that in recent years the most direct approach to
the history of society has come through the study of class in this wider
sense.[16] Whether we believe that this reflects a correct perception of the

nature of post-tribal societies, or whether we merely put it down to the current influence of *Marxisant* history, the future prospects of this type of research appear bright.

In many ways the recent interest in the history of 'mentalities' marks an even more direct approach to central methodological problems of social history. It has been largely stimulated by the traditional interest in 'the common people' of many who are drawn to social history. It has dealt largely with the individually inarticulate, undocumented, and obscure, and is often indistinct from an interest in their social movements or in more general phenomena of social behaviour, which today, fortunately, also includes an interest in those who fail to take part in such movements—for example, in the conservative as well as in the militant or passively socialist worker.

This very fact has encouraged a specifically dynamic treatment of culture by historians, superior to such studies as those of the 'culture of poverty' by anthropologists, though not uninfluenced by their methods and pioneering experience. They have been not so much studies of an aggregate of beliefs and ideas, persistent or not—though there has been much valuable thought about these matters, for example, by Alphonse Dupront[17]—as of ideas in action and, more specifically, in situations of social tensions and crisis, as in Georges Lefebvre's *Grande Peur*, which has inspired so much subsequent work. The nature of sources for such study has rarely allowed the historian to confine himself to simple factual study and exposition. He has been obliged from the outset to construct models, that is, to fit his partial and scattered data into coherent systems, without which they would be little more than anecdotal. The criterion of such models is or ought to be that its components should fit together and provide a guide to both the nature of collective action in specifiable social situations and to its limits.[18] Edward Thompson's concept of the 'moral economy' of pre-industrial England may be one such; my own analysis of social banditry has tried to base itself on another.

In so far as these systems of belief and action are, or imply, images of society as a whole (which may be, as occasion arises, images either seeking its permanence or its transformation), and in so far as these correspond to certain aspects of its actual reality, they bring us closer to the core of our task. In so far as the most successful such analyses have dealt with traditional or customary societies, even though sometimes with such societies under the impact of social transformation, their scope has been more limited. For a period characterized by constant, rapid, and fundamental change, and by a complexity which put society far beyond the individual's experience or even conceptual grasp, the models derivable from the history of culture have probably a diminishing contact with the social realities. They may not even any longer be very useful in constructing the pattern of aspiration of modern society ('what society ought to be like'). For the basic change brought about by the Industrial Revolution in the field of social thought has been to substitute a system of beliefs resting on unceasing *progress* towards aims which can be specified only as a *process*, for one resting on the assumption of permanent order, which can be described or illustrated in terms of some concrete social model, normally drawn from the past, real or imaginary. The cultures of the past measured their own society against such specific models; the cultures of the present can measure them only against possibilities. Still the history of 'mentalities' has been useful in introducing something analogous to the discipline of the social anthropologists into history, and its usefulness is very far from exhausted.

I think the profitability of the numerous studies of social conflict, ranging from riots to revolutions, requires more careful assessment. Why they should attract research today is obvious. That they always dramatize crucial aspects of social structure because they are here strained to the breaking-point is not in doubt. Moreover, certain important problems cannot be studied at all except in and through such moments of eruption, which do not merely bring into the open so much that is normally latent, but also concentrate and magnify phenomena for the benefit of the student, while—not the least of their advantages—normally multiplying our documentation about them. To take a simple example: How much less would we know about the ideas of those who normally do not express themselves commonly or at all in writing but for the extraordinary explosion of articulateness which is so characteristic of revolutionary periods, and to which the mountains of pamphlets, letters, articles, and speeches, not to mention the mass of police reports, court depositions, and general inquiries, bear witness? How fruitful the study of the great, and above all the well-documented, revolutions can be is shown by the historiography of the French Revolution, which has been studied longer and more intensively perhaps than any period of equal brevity, without visibly diminishing returns. It has been, and still remains, an almost perfect laboratory for the historian.[19]

The danger of this type of study lies in the temptation to isolate the phenomenon of overt crisis from the wider context of a society undergoing transformation. This danger may be particularly great when we launch into comparative studies, especially when moved by the desire to solve problems (such as how to make or stop revolutions), which is not a very fruitful approach in sociology or social history. What, say, riots have in common with one another (for example, 'violence') may be trivial. It may even be illusory, in so far as we may be imposing an anachronistic criterion, legal, political, or otherwise, on the phenomena—something which historical students of criminality are learning to avoid. The same may or may not be true of revolutions. I am the last person to wish to discourage an interest in such matters, since I have spent a good deal of professional time on them.

However, in studying them we ought to define the precise purpose of our interest clearly. If it lies in the major transformations of society, we may find, paradoxically, that the value of our study of the revolution itself is in inverse proportion to our concentration on the brief moment of conflict. There are things about the Russian Revolution, or about human history, which can only be discovered by concentrating on the period from March to November 1917 or the subsequent Civil War; but there are other matters which cannot emerge from such a concentrated study of brief periods of crisis, however dramatic and significant.

On the other hand, revolutions and similar subjects of study (including social movements) can normally be integrated into a wider field which does not merely lend itself to, but requires, a comprehensive grasp of social structure and dynamics: the short-term social transformations experienced and labelled as such, which stretch over a period of a few decades or generations. We are dealing not simply with chronological chunks carved out of a continuum of growth or development, but with relatively brief historic periods during which society is reoriented and transformed, as the very phrase 'industrial revolution' implies. (Such periods may of course include great political revolutions, but cannot be chronologically delimited by them.) The popularity of such historically crude terms as 'modernization' or 'industrialization' indicates a certain apprehension of such phenomena.

The difficulties of such an enterprise are enormous, which is perhaps why there are as yet no adequate studies of the eighteenth-nineteenth century industrial revolutions as social processes for any country, though one or two excellent regional and local works are now available, such as Rudolf Braun on the Zurich countryside and John Foster on early nineteenth-century Oldham.[20] It may be that a practicable approach to such phenomena can be at present derived not only from economic history (which has inspired studies of industrial revolution), but from political science. Workers in the field of the prehistory and history of colonial liberation have naturally been forced to confront such problems, though perhaps in an excessively political perspective, and African studies have proved particularly fruitful, though recent attempts to extend this approach to India may be noted.[21] In consequence the political science and political sociology dealing with the modernization of colonial societies can furnish us with some useful help.

The analytical advantage of the colonial situation (by which I mean that of *formal* colonies acquired by conquest and directly administered) is that here an entire society or group of societies is sharply defined by contrast with an outside force, and its various internal shifts and changes, as well as its reactions to the uncontrollable and rapid impact of this force, can be observed and analysed as a whole. Certain forces which in other societies are internal, or operate in a gradual and complex interaction with internal elements of that society, can here be considered for practical purposes and in the short run as entirely external, which is analytically very helpful. (We shall not of course overlook the distortions of the colonial societies—for example, by the truncation of their economy and social hierarchy—which also result from colonization, but the interest of the colonial situation does not depend on the assumption that colonial society is a replica of non-colonial.)

There is perhaps a more specific advantage. A central preoccupation of workers in this field has been nationalism and nation-building, and here the colonial situation can provide a much closer approximation to the general model. Though historians have hardly yet come to grips with it, the complex of phenomena which can be called national(ist) is clearly crucial to the understanding of social structure and dynamics in the industrial era, and some of the more interesting work in political sociology has come to recognize it. The project conducted by Stein Rokkan, Eric Allardt, and others on 'Centre Formation, Nation-Building and Cultural Diversity' provides some very interesting approaches.[22]

The 'nation', a historical invention of the past two hundred years, whose immense practical significance today hardly needs discussion, raises several crucial questions of the history of society, for example, the change in the scale of societies, the transformation of pluralist, indirectly linked social systems into unitary ones with direct linkages (or the fusion of several pre-existing smaller societies into a larger social system), the factors determining the boundaries of a social system (such as territorial–political), and others of equal significance. To what extent are these boundaries objectively imposed by the requirement of economic development, which necessitate as the locus of, for example, the nineteenth-century-type industrial economy a territorial state of minimum or maximum size in given circumstances?[23] To what extent do these requirements automatically imply not only the weakening and destruction of earlier social structures, but also particular degrees of simplification, standardization, and centralization—that is, direct and increasingly exclusive links between 'centre' and 'periphery' (or rather 'top' and 'bottom')? To what extent is the 'nation' an attempt to fill the void left by the dismantling of earlier community and social structures by inventing something which could function as, or produce symbolic substitutes for, the functioning of a consciously apprehended community or society? (The concept of the 'nation-state' might then combine these objective and subjective developments.)

The colonial and ex-colonial situations are not necessarily more suitable bases for investigating this complex of questions than is European history, but in the absence of serious work about it by the historians of nineteenth- and twentieth-century Europe, who have been hitherto—including the Marxists—rather baffled by it, it seems likely that recent Afro-Asian history may form the most convenient starting-point.

V

How far has the research of recent years advanced us towards a history of society? Let me put my cards on the table. I cannot point to any single work which exemplifies the history of society to which we ought, I believe, to aspire. Marc Bloch has given us in *La Société féodale*, a masterly, indeed an exemplary, work on the nature of social structure, including both the consideration of a certain type of society and of its actual and possible variants, illuminated by the comparative method, into the dangers and the much greater rewards of which I do not propose to enter here. Marx has sketched out for us, or allows us to sketch for ourselves, a model of the typology and the long-term historical transformation and evolution of societies which remains immensely powerful and almost as far ahead of its time as were the Prolegomena of Ibn Khaldun, whose own model, based on the interaction of different types of societies, has of course also been fruitful, especially in prehistory, ancient, and oriental history. (I am thinking of the late Gordon Childe and Owen Lattimore.) Recently there have been important advances towards the study of certain types of society—notably those based on slavery in the Americas (the slave-societies of antiquity appear to be in recession) and those based on a large body of peasant cultivators. On the other hand the attempts to translate a comprehensive social history into popular synthesis strike me so far as either relatively unsuccessful or, with all their great merits, not the least of which is stimulation, as schematic and tentative. The history of society is still being constructed. I have in this essay tried to suggest some of its problems, to assess some of its practice, and incidentally to hint at certain problems which might benefit from more concentrated exploration. But it would be wrong to conclude without noting, and welcoming, the remarkably flourishing state of the field. It is a good moment to be a social historian. Even those of us who never set out to call ourselves by this name will not want to disclaim it today.

NOTES

1. See the remarks of A. J. C. Rueter in *IX Congrès international des sciences historiques* (Paris, 1950), i. 398.

2. R. H. Tawney, *Studies in Economic History* (London, 1927), pp. xxiii, 33–4, 39.

3. J. H. Clapham, *A Concise Economic History of Britain* (Cambridge, 1949), introduction.

4. Two quotations from the same document (Economic and Social Studies Conference Board, *Social Aspects of Economic Development*, Istanbul, 1964) may illustrate the divergent motivations behind this new pre-occupation. By the Turkish president of the board: 'Economic development or growth in the economically retarded areas is the most important question which confronts the world today ... Poor countries have made of this issue of development a high ideal. Economic development is to them associated with political independence and a sense of sovereignty.' By Daniel Lerner:

'A decade of global experience with social change and economic development lies behind us. The decade has been fraught with efforts, in every part of the world, to induce economic development without producing cultural chaos, to accelerate economic growth without subverting political stability' (xxiii, 1).

5. Sir John Hicks's complaint is characteristic: 'My "theory of history" ... will be a good deal nearer to the kind of thing that was attempted by Marx ... Most of [those who believe ideas can be used by historians to order their material, so that the general course of history can be fitted into place] ... would use the Marxian categories, or some modified version of them; since there is so little in the way of an alternative version that is available, it is not surprising that they should. It does, nevertheless, remain extraordinary that one hundred years after *Das Kapital*, after a century during which there have been enormous developments in social science, so little else should have emerged.' *A Theory of Economic History* (Oxford, 1969), pp. 2–3.

6. Thus Marc Ferro's sampling of the telegrams and resolutions sent to Petrograd in the first weeks of the February revolution of 1917 is plainly the equivalent of a retrospective public opinion survey. One may doubt whether it would have been thought of without the earlier development of opinion research for nonhistorical purposes. M. Ferro, *La Révolution de 1917* (Paris, 1967).

7. At the conference on New Trends in History, Princeton, N.J., May 1968.

8. I do not regard such devices for inserting direction into societies as 'increasing complexity' as historical. They may, of course, be true.

9. P. Baran, *The Political Economy of Growth* (New York, 1957), chap. 2.

10. For an English version of this important article, see *Social Science Information*, 9 (February 1970), 145–74.

11. Cf. 'At stake in a broader view of urban history is the possibility of making the societal process of urbanization central to the study of social change. Efforts should be made to conceptualize urbanization in ways that actually represent social change.' Eric Lampard in Oscar Handlin and John Burchard, *The Historians and the City* (Cambridge, Mass., 1963), p. 233.

12. This work is in progress under the direction of Professor Sven-Ulric Palme at the University of Stockholm.

13. For the possible divergences between reality and classification, see the discussions about the complex socio-racial hierarchies of colonial Latin America. Magnus Mörner, 'The History of Race Relations in Latin America', in L. Foner and E. D. Genovese, *Slavery in the New World* (Englewood Cliffs, N.J., 1969), p. 221.

14. See A. Prost, 'Vocabulaire et typologie des familles politique', *Cahiers de lexicologie*, xiv (1969).

15. T. Shanin, 'The Peasantry as a Political Factor', *Sociological Review*, 14 (1966), 17.

16. Class has long been the central preoccupation of social historians. See, for example, A. J. C. Rueter in *IX Congrés international des sciences historiques*, i, 298–9.

17. A Dupront, 'Problèmes et méthodes d'une histoire de la psychologie collective', *Annales: É.S.C.* 16 (January–February 1961), 3–11.

18. By 'fitting together' I mean establishing a systematic connection between different, and sometimes apparently unconnected, parts of the same syndrome—for example, the beliefs of the classic nineteenth-century liberal bourgeoisie in both individual liberty and a patriarchal family structure.

19. We look forward to the time when the Russian Revolution will provide historians with comparable opportunities for the twentieth century.

20. R. Braun, *Industrialisierung und Volksleben* (Erlenbach-Zurich, 1960); *Sozialer und kultureller Wandel in einem ländlichen Industriegebiet ... im 19. und 20. Jahrhundert* (Erlenbach-Zurich, 1965). J. O. Foster, *Class Struggle and the Industrial Revolution* (London, 1974).

21. Eric Stokes, who is doing this, is conscious of applying the results of work in African history. E. Stokes, 'Traditional Resistance Movements and Afro-Asian Nationalism: The Context of the 1857 Mutiny-Rebellion in India', *Past and Present*, 48 (1970).

22. *Centre Formation, Nation-Building and Cultural Diversity: Report on a Symposium Organized by UNESCO* (duplicated draft, n.d.). The symposium was held 28 Aug.–1 Sept. 1968.

23. Though capitalism has developed as a global system of economic interactions, in fact the real units of its development have been certain territorial–political units—British, French, German, U.S. economies—which may be due to historic accident but also (the question remains open) to the necessary role of the state in economic development, even in the era of the purest economic liberalism.

2

Sociological History:
The Industrial Revolution and the
British Working-Class Family*

NEIL J. SMELSER

IN this essay I am constrained to pursue two objectives. The first is to explore some of the general relations between sociological and historical analysis—how these are similar, how they are different, and how they might contribute something to one another. This objective raises many philosophical and methodological problems. The second objective, more empirical (it does not matter whether we call it sociological or historical for the moment), is to give an account of the causes, character, and consequences of the changes in working-class family life in Great Britain during the Industrial Revolution.

Each objective is important, and it is tempting to discuss them separately because there is a scholarly literature on each issue. There exists, on the one hand, a vast literature on the history of the working classes and their condition of life; much of this literature does not deal directly with the family, but those sources on child and female labour involve the family. There exists, on the other hand, a great proliferation of discussions on the general relations between history and sociology.[1] The first type of literature is interesting and provocative, but I shall resist the temptation to discuss the historical materials directly, if for no other reason than that as a sociologist I would like to do something more than dwell on things historians know more about than I. I shall also refrain from adding my bit on the general relations between sociology and history for several reasons. First, I am not sufficiently conversant with the literature of the philosophy of history. Second, that part of the literature I do know runs the danger of drifting into

* From *Essays in Sociological Exploration* (New York, 1968), pp. 76–91. Revised version of a paper delivered at the annual meetings of American Sociological Association, Los Angeles, Aug. 1963; and at the Pacific Coast Meetings of the American Historical Association, San Francisco, Aug. 1963. The paper appeared in *The Journal of Social History*, 1 (1967), 18–35. Copyright 1967 by Peter N. S. Fearns. Reprinted by permission of the author and the editor.

uninformative abstractions, and I have no good reason to believe that my own ideas would not meet the same fate. Finally, I believe that so great is the variety of activities that go under the name 'sociological analysis' (and the same is probably true of what is called 'historical analysis') that any general attempt to relate them to one another would have to be couched in so many qualifications that the statements would lose general interest.

What I shall try to do is to bring the two traditions of scholarship I have outlined into some new relation. I shall proceed by examining a few general problems that arose in my own attempt to apply sociological theory to history. I shall thus avoid 'straight' history and explicit and methodological discussion of the relations between sociology and history. I shall discuss some general issues, but hopefully only those that come alive in conducting actual research that involved applying a theoretical model from sociology to a well-worked historical era. The results of my research have appeared in a book entitled *Social Change in the Industrial Revolution*.[2] I shall summarize parts of this work in this paper, but I shall try to focus more on general issues.

THE MODEL OF STRUCTURAL DIFFERENTIATION

The thing that set my research off most from what many historians do is that I approached the Industrial Revolution as a case illustration of an explicit, formal conceptual model drawn from the general tradition of sociological thought. Stated in very general terms, this model says that under conditions of social disequilibrium, the social structure will change in such a way that roles previously encompassing many different types of activities become more specialized; the social structure, that is, becomes more complex and differentiated. It was this abstract, analytic model—the details of which I shall spell out presently—that generated problems for me, not the period of the Industrial Revolution as such. I might well have chosen industrial change in another country and another period, or even an instance of rapid social change in which industrialization did not occupy a significant place.

The intellectual roots of the model of differentiation are very diverse. They can be located, for example, in Adam Smith's conceptions of the division of labour, Karl Marx's theory of the development of industrial capitalism, Herbert Spencer's principles of differentiation and integration, Emile Durkheim's theory of the social aspects of the division of labour, and, more recently, the work of Talcott Parsons and his associates on role differentiation and personality development.[3] In varying degree all these men were cognizant of the forces that went into the Industrial Revolution, and some of them have had something to say about this historical era. But it is also important to note that many of the essential features of the model I used arose not from the analysis of the Industrial Revolution—indeed, not from the study of industrial change at all—but from the study of experimental small groups, learning, and personality adjustment, and so on.

I have implied that when posing questions sociologists and historians differ in that the former rely on models and the latter do not. This is not literally correct. The very act of posing a question about a historical period implies that the investigator—whether he be sociologist or historian—regards a certain range of facts as more relevant to his purposes than other facts. It follows from this that all historical analysis is bound to be selective. Moreover, the manner in which the investigator poses his question reveals that he brings to history certain preoccupations, hunches, hypotheses, and general notions about human conduct, however implicit these might be. Historical selectivity, viewed in this way, emerges as an essential ingredient of all historical analysis, necessary if we are to avoid writing about all aspects of all historical facts at once. A model formalizes this selectivity. As a conceptual apparatus, it states that if a given number of conditions are combined in a certain way, a definite historical outcome is to be expected. It makes as explicit as possible the exact dimensions of the historical problem, the explanations, and the underlying assumptions. In the light of these considerations, it is more nearly correct to say that both sociologists and historians employ models in their interpretations of history, but that they differ in the degree to which these are made formal and explicit.

What is the character of the model of structural differentiation? As indicated, its most general feature rests on the well-known sociological principle that as a society develops, its social structure becomes more complex. This perspective is contained in Adam Smith's famous formulation that as an economy grows its division of labour increases in complexity. This principle is clear enough in the case of the economic division of labour. But as a general sociologist I was operating with an extended formulation, namely, that rapid social development involves the same increasing complexity of structure in other institutions as well—in education, religion, politics, the family, and so on. For example, in the pre-industrial family of a craftsman, the parents themselves are responsible for teaching the child minimum occupational skills, as well as for his emotional moulding during his early years. When a growing economy places demands for greater literacy and more technical skills, the pressure is for this multifunctional family to give way to a new, more complex set of social arrangements. Structurally distinct educational institutions appear, and the family begins to surrender some of its previous training functions to these new institutions; having lost these functions, accordingly, the family becomes more specialized, focusing relatively more on emotional conditioning in the early childhood years and relatively less on its former economic and educational functions. This process of increasing specialization is called *structural differentiation*.

Another feature of the model is that differentiation does not happen automatically. It occasions a great deal of pain and dislocation for people, and it destroys many traditions that are likely to be held sacred; consequently it brings on a flurry of protest, uncertainty, groping, and experimentation before new, more differentiated units actually appear. Differentiation therefore produces conflict and social disorganization, which is likely to jeopardize social stability.

The model has been broken into a formal seven-step sequence which recapitulates analytically the process of structural differentiation:

Step 1 Dissatisfaction with the performance of incumbents of an institutionalized role, or with the organization of the role itself. In the economic sphere an example would be dissatisfaction with the level of profits, or with inefficiencies in a marketing system. In the family sphere an example would be dissatisfaction with a family's inability to earn a living wage in a particular occupational endeavour.

Step 2 Symptoms of disturbance reflecting this dissatisfaction, which are manifested in expressions of anxiety, hostility, and fantasy. For those sectors of society under pressure to change there is a sense of threatened loss or decay, perhaps generalized into prophecies of gloom. A great deal of scapegoating and conflict between agents of change and traditional and vested interests is also found in this stage. Finally, in the face of dissatisfactions, tendencies to glorify the past or build utopian visions of the future also flourish. Sometimes these symptoms of disturbance congeal into an ideology, in the name of which one or more social movements arise.

Step 3 Handling and channelling the symptoms of disturbance. This step is a first-line response to the disturbances just outlined. The agencies of social control—the police, the courts, the press, community leaders, etc. —are activated, in an effort to prevent the symptoms of disturbance from threatening social stability. These handling and channelling processes constitute a holding operation before any structural change actually occurs.

Step 4 Encouragement of new ideas to deal with the supposed sources of dissatisfaction. Here the energy unleashed in the expression of symptoms of disturbance begins to be turned more in the direction of positive change. This is the stage of investigating what cultural resources might be brought to bear on the sources of dissatisfaction.

Step 5 Attempts to specify institutional forms that will ease the supposed sources of dissatisfaction. Here the process of change moves from the general to the specific, from ideas and notions to concrete proposals for innovation. In the economic sphere this might involve the proposal to reorganize labour around a new invention. In the social sphere it might involve the entertainment of legislation to ease a social problem.

Step 6 Attempts to establish new institutional forms. Here the 'innovator' takes over from the 'inventor'; and here the new, differentiated element of social structure makes its appearance. Attempts are now made to implement the ideas and suggestions of the previous two steps. In the economic sphere, the entrepreneur sets up new firms and thus meets the test of the market. In another sphere the legislature actually passes laws and thus meets the test of public support. In this step, successful innovations are greeted with an extraordinary burst of rewards—for example, huge profits or public goodwill.

Step 7 The new institutional forms are consolidated as permanent features of the social structure.

The general consequence of a large number of interrelated sequences of differentiation just outlined is a vast social upheaval, resulting in the emergence of a much more complex, specialized organization of the social structure. The purpose of the model is to permit the investigator of a historical period in flux to disentangle and analyse the many separate social processes that are proceeding apace.

What is the methodological status of this model? First, it is an abstract heuristic device rather than a simple empirical generalization. It may be likened to the economists' supply–demand scheme for a perfectly competitive market—a theoretical construct which is seldom if ever found in pure form empirically, but which permits us to interpret a wide variety of empirical situations. Second, it is a middle-range theory of change rather than a grand theoretical account of the history of a whole civilization. While resting on Spencer's notion of differentiation, for instance, the model lacks the concomitant of Spencer's theory—the notion that the over-all direction of multiple processes of differentiation is from a military to an industrial society. The model of structural differentiation does not involve any specific claims as to a particular type of society as a point of beginning or a particular type of society as a point of termination. It is thus an 'open-ended' model. Third, the model of structural differentiation is not a single-factor theory of change. Rather, it is a combination of a large number of assertions and assumptions about the relations among social phenomena (many of which do not hold universally but which are useful for purposes of analysis). The utility of this model, to repeat, is to unravel and analyse the bewildering tangle of happenings that present themselves in periods of rapid social change.

What are some of the assumptions on which the model is based? A central assumption is that, as a matter of psychological fact, people come to be disturbed about inadequate performance in roles; another assertion is that the intial manifestation of this disturbance is anxiety, anger, and fantasy. Both of these assertions, while widely applicable empirically, are certainly questionable as psychological universals. Another assumption is that the social-control operations referred to in Step 3 will always 'work', and that symptoms of disturbance—tendencies to violence, social movements, perhaps even threats to political legitimacy—will in fact be contained. Empirically this is a very questionable assumption; the frequency of violent outbursts and successful revolutionary movements in human history testifies to its limitations. Yet still we retain the assumption. Why? Because in the analysis of complex processes of change it is necessary to employ convenient fictions as working assumptions to simplify the multiplicity of sources of historical variations. If the convenient fictions become too fictional, of course, they lose their convenience, for they cease to apply to *any* historical situation. Furthermore, the convenient fiction (e.g., success of social-control operations) may be useful in one historical setting (e.g., parliamentary Britain) but not in another (e.g., parliamentary Iraq). Yet as I hope to indicate later, we may capitalize on this limitation. For purposes of more extensive comparative historical analysis, we may relax these rigid, limited, but workable assumptions and allow them to become a source of variation; and then we can ask, for instance, what happens when social control breaks down in different ways.

THE APPLICATION OF THE MODEL TO
THE INDUSTRIAL REVOLUTION

Up to this point I have depicted the many relations that compose the model of structural differentiation in completely general terms, without reference to any definite historical period or problem. This is an important thing to do, but it constitutes only half the job of sociological history. At this analytic level, the model may be criticized logically in terms of its consistency; it may be assessed aesthetically in terms of its elegance or simplicity; and it may be viewed in terms of its imaginativeness or originality. But its utility for interpreting history is unknown. To determine this utility, the investigator must turn to the laborious tasks of historical analysis. He must translate the general concepts and relations into historically specific terms. He must track down the best historical sources to ascertain the degree to which the hypothesized connections among events hold. He must render as careful and objective a judgement as possible on whether the historical record lends support to the relations posited in the model. And if history proves embarrassing by not conforming to the model sequences, he must be prepared to return to the model and modify it in the light of his researches.

In bringing the model of structural differentiation to the Industrial Revolution, I proceeded by attempting to ascertain the degree to which the general relations of the model were replicated in many different institutional contexts. The two major spheres of application were the changes occurring in the industrial sector of society and those occurring in the family life of workers employed in industry. To make my application manageable, I chose the cotton-textile industry, the leader in the British Industrial Revolution. On the industrial side, I analysed the organizational changes in domestic and factory industry arising from the introduction of the various inventions—the jenny, the water-frame, the mule, the steam-engine, and the power-loom. For each I traced the course of indices such as economic organization, profits, capital investment, prices, and so on, as data to assess the workability of the model. On the family side, I traced the changes in family structure of workers in the cotton industry. In addition I applied the model to changes in other structures that were intimately tied to the family's security—friendly societies, trade unions, savings banks, and co-operative societies. I shall now summarize the application of the model to the changing structure of family life between 1770 and 1840, with particular reference to the 'factory question', the agitation to limit hours, and factory legislation.

It is widely accepted that the sources of pressure on the family of the working classes lay in the demands imposed by the new urban, industrial environment of the late eighteenth and early nineteenth centuries. Yet this environment did not exert its pressure very early in the Industrial Revolution; nor did it exert its pressure in the ways commonly supposed. In fact, it appears that the traditional British working-class family survived the first fifty years of the Industrial Revolution quite remarkably intact and without much protest. Yet these were the gloomiest years from the standpoint of wages, hours, and working conditions. It was only when the industrial and urban changes began to affect the traditional relations *within* the family that really furious protest and disturbance began. Let me elaborate these points.

The typical pre-industrial textile family was an economic unit. The father normally was a weaver and he was assisted by his older sons, whom he apprenticed to the trade. The mother spun on the distaff or spinning wheel; she was assisted by the younger children, and she taught her daughters how to spin. The father was the main breadwinner, the wife and children auxiliary workers.

Between 1770 and 1790 the major technological innovations in the cotton industry were the spinning-jenny and the water-frame. The jenny was initially installed in the home and run by an adult male, with the wife and children occupying subsidiary roles. The jenny raised the wage-level of the family, but it did not disturb the traditional relations among its members. For the water-frame, which was set up in manufactories instead of homes, a different set of family arrangements evolved. According to the very limited information that is available, masters preferred to hire whole families as units—and actually did so—because of their more reliable work habits. Another adaptation was to set up cottages near the manufactory and put out cotton to be worked up in the home, where domestic duties kept adult women. As indicated, some of the child labour in the manufactories was supervised by parents; in addition, however, the water-frame manufactories made widespread use of parish apprentices, or children without any family, who were shipped from workhouse to manufactory to work. With the exception of parish apprentices, the historical record shows that the initial phase of the Industrial Revolution did not seriously alter the traditional relations between family members.

Between 1790 and 1820 a number of sweeping changes came over the cotton industry. The mule thoroughly displaced the jenny and surpassed the water-frame in production. When yoked to steam, moreover, the machines moved from mills on country streams into factories in the crowded centres of population, especially Manchester and Salford and the surrounding towns. In these decades the factories came to approximate to their modern form. Yet when we examine the internal structure of the factory, we find a tenacity of the traditional family-patterns. Typically the skilled spinner was allowed by the master to hire his own assistants (two or three in number in these years), and typically he hired his wife, children, or nephews, and apprenticed sons and nephews to the trade. Most of the trade-union regulations of the day *required* that he restrict his apprentices to these relatives. So within the anonymous city and impersonal factory an anchor of tradition persisted; and the working-class family, at least in this sector of industry, was not under pressure to relinquish a significant portion of its traditional functions of apprenticeship and economic co-operation.

In the middle 1820s and 1830s a number of historical trends continued and a number of new developments materialized. The centralization of industry in urban Lancashire, the concentration of population in this county, and the increase in size of the factories all proceeded apace. From the standpoint of immediate pressures on the family, however, two technological changes were apparently of much greater consequence. One was in spinning, the other in weaving. In spinning the 1820s brought a much larger and more productive variety of mule. This meant lower piece-rates but higher weekly wages for spinners; it also meant a possibility of technological unemployment because of the larger mules' greater productivity, even though the industry as a whole was continuing to expand. In addition, the larger mules called for a multiplication of assistants to the spinner. Whereas in the period between 1810 and 1820 two or three assistants per spinner were required, estimates in the early 1830s ranged from four to nine per spinner. This development immediately undermined the family-apprentice system, for a spinner would seldom have enough children of his own to fill these positions. He was forced to let in outsiders. Furthermore, the multiplication of assistants threatened in the long run to glut the market with too many skilled spinners.

The advent of the power-loom aggravated these threats. For the hand-loom weaving family—already in a sick trade by the 1820s—the power-loom brought new hardships. The advance of the power-loom was most dramatic in the late 1820s and early 1830s. It drove down weavers' wages even more, and increased the pressure on weavers to send their children into the factories. But in the power-loom factories the team necessary to man the looms did not permit parental supervision of children at work. From all sides in the late 1820s, then, the pressures were to split the parent from his child, both on the factory premises and in the surviving domestic industries. It was in these years, 1825–35, that the question of child labour became critical, not because of any deterioration in the hours and working conditions for children (indeed, these aspects appear to have been improving in that decade) but because the social environment of the child was changing.

So much for the pressures on the family life of the factory workers in the Industrial Revolution. What can now be said about the timing and content of the symptoms of disturbance arising from these circumstances?

In the first fifty years of the Industrial Revolution, 1770–1820, there were many manifestations of protest among the working classes in the textile industry. Yet most of these came from representatives of the pre-industrial order, especially hand-spinners and handloom weavers. In the last three decades of the eighteenth century, the new machines in the mills and manufactories were periodically attacked; the most serious outburst was the wholesale destruction of machinery in Lancashire in 1779. In all these cases the opposition came from domestic workers and was directed towards factory machinery. The handloom weavers participated in a long parade of disturbances beginning with petitions for support in the 1790s and ending with their active involvement in the violent aspects of the Chartist movement in the 1840s. Their history in this half-century is one of alternatively appealing for assistance, bursting into violence, embracing a variety of utopian schemes, and failing in sporadic attempts to organize into trade unions.

The new factory proletariat presents a study in contrast with the surviving domestic workers. Between 1770 and 1800 the factory-workers were almost completely quiescent. Between 1800 and 1820 they engaged in a number of strikes, but these were mainly for higher wages in periods of brisk trade. As far as can be ascertained, the factory operatives were almost entirely passive with respect to the factory legislation of 1802 and 1819. Furthermore, according to the best available records, factory operatives were scarcely involved in the Luddite disturbances and played a secondary role in the popular disturbances between 1816 and 1819. According to the thesis here offered, the quiescence of the factory operatives is traceable to the persistence of certain fundamental family relations in the factory setting. In many ways their lot was hard and their adjustments many; but these family traditions were being preserved. The pressures on the surviving domestic workers, by contrast, were to abandon a total traditional way of life.

In the 1820s, however, the factory operatives were drawn into massive protest against the progress of the Industrial Revolution for the first time. Beginning about 1820, increasing in intensity through the 1820s, and culminating in the gigantic outburst in Ashton-under-Lyne in 1830–1, the Lancashire spinners launched one strike after another against the enlarged mules and their accompanying piece-rate reductions. Most of these strikes failed. The records of the Lancashire trade unions in this decade show the spinners' increasing apprehension over the apprenticeship problem. It is my interpretation that these strikes and the other efforts of the unions were aimed at halting the flood of children into the industry, at guarding against threatened technological unemployment, and at protecting the traditional economic relationship between parent and child.

This interpretation is strengthened by examining the factory operatives' role in the agitation to limit hours of labour in the cotton industry. As indicated, they were quite passive on this question in the first several decades of the nineteenth century. But towards the end of the period of unsuccessful strikes against the enlarged mules, the factory-workers became embroiled in the factory agitation. This agitation reached explosive proportions between 1831 and 1833. The factory movement was accompanied by many extravagant claims concerning the effects of machinery and the factory on the health of the children, the morals of the factory population, and so on. But if we examine the more immediate aims and behaviour of the factory operatives in this agitation and after the Factory Act of 1833, it becomes apparent that their objectives were very similar to what they had been in the strikes against improved machinery in the 1820s—to halt the flood of children into the industry, and to continue the link between parent and child. Let me illustrate.

Between 1831 and 1833 the factory operatives insisted on a ten-hour day for children, knowing that this would probably mean a ten-hour day for adults as well. They apparently wished to reduce their own hours and maintain the link between the labour of children and adults. In fact, when the Factory Act of 1833 was passed, limiting children's hours to eight and suggesting a relay system for young children, the operatives were not satisfied. In fact, Nassau Senior commented after the passage of this Act that the operatives were 'far more vehement for a ten hours' bill [for all labour] than before'.[4] Their further agitation, *after* factory legislation had been passed, makes sense according to the present interpretation. For, indeed, the Factory Act of 1833, with its relay system and its eight-hour limitation, worked to further weaken the link between parents' and children's labour (a tendency already set in motion by the enlarged mules). In short, the pressures to differentiate the economic aspects from the other aspects of family life were augmented by the Factory Act of 1833.

What form did the operatives' agitation take after 1833? In late 1833 some factory operatives formed a furtive little movement called the Society for National Regeneration, one objective of which was to call for a universal eight-hour day. This movement failed after several months of existence, terminated by a feeble strike. Then, in 1835, factory operatives began to hold meetings throughout Lancashire to call for a universal twelve-hour day, which would extend the hours of children, who had been limited to eight hours for several years. And again in 1837 the workers agitated for a universal ten-hour day, including ten hours for children. These last two agitations embarrassed the supporters of factory legislation in Parliament, for it appeared that the workers themselves were indifferent to the length of the children's working day and to their health and morals. Finally, between 1833 and 1837, despite the efforts of the government, it was apparent that both masters and operatives were willing to evade the Factory Act of 1833 by working children more than eight hours. All these signs point towards a strong desire on the part of the operatives to maintain the traditional link between parent and child on the factory premises.

We have now covered the first steps of the process of differentiation—pressures on the family generating dissatisfactions and symptoms of disturbance arising from these pressures. The remainder of the sequence of structural differentiation is found in the history of the factory legislation itself. In the period of explosive agitation for the Ten-Hour Day (1831–3), the demonstrations, petitions, and the rest were permitted but contained by the authorities. And before long, the government moved to establish investigatory machinery to inquire into the factory question. The Sadler Committee of 1832, and its supersession by the Factory Commission of 1833, mark the attempts of the government to ascertain the facts of the factory question, to entertain suggestions and recommendations, and to make its proposals for action to Parliament. These parliamentary activities constitute Steps 4 and 5 of the sequence of differentiation—entertainment of ideas and suggestions for implementation.

With the Factory Act of 1833 Parliament opted in favour of pushing the family towards the future. By splitting the hours of child labour from those of adults, they augmented the pressures already being exerted by the technological improvements. In addition, the Commission recommended and Parliament adopted an educational provision—that the factories provide schools for children for several hours a day while adults presumably continued at work. This educational provision also marked a line of structural differentiation—to give a rudimentary schooling to children meant that some of the training responsibilities of the undifferentiated family were being turned over to a separate social organization.

Yet even though the Factory Act of 1833 completed, as it were, a number of pressures towards structural differentiation, the story of factory legislation was not yet finished. A number of separate forces had come to bear on the family in the 1820s and 1830s, all of which operated to remove some of its economic and training functions from it. These forces were in the technological advances of the spinning and weaving branches, the impact of these changes on the domestic handloom weaving population, and the legislative enactment of Parliament in 1833. Yet the success of these forces, success evident already by 1833, posed a new, serious problem for the family: if the link between parent and child on the factory premises was broken, *and* if masters still insisted on working adults the full twelve-hour day, what then became of the family? So long as many 'domestic' functions such as discipline and even some recreation and play could be carried out in the factory, the length of the working day was not so critical from the standpoint of performing the various family functions. But if the children were to be separated from the parents during the working day, the home took on a new significance. This need to reconstitute the family in the home, once it was broken up in the factory, lay behind the pressures to reduce the hours of all labour and establish the 'normal working day' for adults during the fifteen years following 1833. The final factory legislation of the late 1840s and early 1850s, establishing the ten-hour day, then, completed the differentiation of the working-class family—involving a clearer split between home and factory, a split between the economic and other aspects of the parent–child relationship, and a surrender of some of the family's training functions to an embryonic educational system.

SOME METHODOLOGICAL PROBLEMS

Such, in brief outline, is my account of the major events surrounding the changing structure of the family life of the cotton operatives during the first few generations of the Industrial Revolution. To conclude, I should like first to mention a few specific methodological problems that arise in applying the model of differentiation and second to raise the more general question of how necessary or helpful it is to use a formal model in interpreting history.

One methodological problem concerns the difficult task of deciding when an historical fact is an 'instance' of one of the general categories of the model. For example, in applying the model to industrial growth, I classified entrepreneurial decisions as an instance of institutional innovation; in applying it to the changing structure of the family I classified certain acts of Parliament—such as the Factory Acts—as instances of institutional innovation; in applying it to the rise of new forms of trade unions I took the passage of union regulations as an instance of institutional innovation. The question that the investigator must face in these kinds of operations is the following: By what criterion are these three historical events—an entrepreneurial decision, an act of the legislature, and an enactment of a union regulation—assigned to the same general category? My answer in this case was that each involves a commitment of resources to a selected line of social action. But even this criterion is a bit vague, and in the case of other general categories, the criteria for moving from general concepts to historical events are even less satisfactory. I might add, however, that this particular method-ological problem is not limited to the application of theoretical models to history; it is a problem that arises, even though not always explicitly, every time an investigator—historian or sociologist—attempts to apply a generic term to historical events.

A second methodological problem concerns the location of appropriate historical data when bringing a relatively novel approach—such as struc-tural differentiation—to history. In many cases the investigator asks ques-tions for which there are no data; this is particularly true for questions about the family, an intimate institution for which records are not generally kept, especially in the working classes. In other cases the investigator must revisit primary sources that have already been combed over, since other investigators have not necessarily been sensitive to data that are brought into question by the novel approach. And in still other cases, the investi-gator is forced to reinterpret many secondary sources radically, since the questions he is asking are so different from those asked by writers of past accounts; such reinterpretation, it goes without saying, is a very risky practice.

A third and very important methodological problem concerns what to do when the theoretical model does not seem to work. Suppose, for instance, that the investigator discovers a clear instance of differentiation that de-velops without any accompanying symptoms of disturbance; in this case Steps 2 and 3 are skipped. Suppose, to take another example, Step 2 brings an array of disturbances that are not contained by the agencies of social control, but generalize into widespread social conflict, leading ultimately to a collapse of the governmental regime in the face of violent revolution. Here we have a case of something that begins like differentiation, but ends as something very different; clearly the model does not apply. The tempta-tion of the investigator, enamoured as he is with his model, is to generate some *ad hoc* explanation every time the model does not appear to fit the facts. He can say that there were special historical circumstances at hand— for example, that the Napoleonic Wars influenced the process of change, or that the factory agitation was influenced by the simultaneous agitation to reform Parliament. However tempting it is to indulge in these asides, it is illegitimate from the standpoint of the application of theory to history. For if the investigator generates *ad hoc* explanations for all the exceptions, he is making an *appearance* of applying the model, but he is in actuality ap-pealing to all kinds of extraneous, theoretically irrelevant factors to account for instances that are potentially embarrassing for the model.

I feel the presence of historical exceptions to a general theoretical model signalizes the end for further theoretical development. The investigator should admit his embarrassment but capitalize on it. When a process that looks very much as though it is starting out as an orderly process of differentiation suddenly turns into an uncontrolled disturbance, the theoretically interesting question is the following: Given the apparent fact that the process of differentiation and the development of uncontrolled disturbance have some but not all factors in common, what are the conditions that push the process towards one outcome or the other? By asking such a question the investigator is likely to end up with a second model. But so much the better. It is more difficult, but more profitable, to build systematic accounts of exceptions than to explain each one away as it arises.

WHY APPLY A MODEL?

In closing, let me ask a few rude questions of myself. Was it necessary to use a general model for this study of labour history? Assuming for the moment that the study has some merit as a piece of historical analysis, could not the same connections have been traced by an historian without benefit of the model? If so, what are the gains, if any, that accrue from approaching history in the theoretically selfconscious way I did? These questions raise the problem of the general utility of formal, explicit models in interpreting history.

It is true that it is not essential to have a model to arrive at the empirical conclusions I did about the Industrial Revolution. A social historian, proceeding inductively and without the model of structural differentiation, might well have made similar assertions about the causes of factory agitation. His conclusions might not have been shrouded in such general terms as mine, but the content would have been the same. Any advantages that arise from applying this model—or any model—to history must be other than that a sociologist with a model can discover historical truths that an historian without one cannot. What, then, are the advantages?

A first advantage is specific to social history, and, within that, specific to the problem of explaining the content and timing of social disturbances such as violent outbursts and social movements. My impression of the work of social historians is that as a rule their explanations of these kinds of events often rest on oversimple causal assumptions—for example that economic misery or political repression alone will provoke such disturbances. For a variety of reasons such explanations are inadequate.[5] The model of structural differentiations, while acknowledging the role of these factors, incorporates them into a systematically organized framework containing other social variables. It is my conviction that the model of differentiation offers a superior explanation. But above and beyond this assertion—the validity of which can be established only on the basis of theoretical debate and empirical research—it is true that the model of differentiation introduces a number of determinants of social disturbances that have hitherto been relatively neglected by social historians. The first advantage of using a generalized model, then, is that it is likely to suggest new causal connections among historical events.

A second advantage, alluded to earlier, concerns the discipline that a formal model imposes on historical explanation. If an historical investigator is operating within a very loose and implicit interpretative framework, it is a simple matter for him to introduce new factors and explanations on an *ad hoc* basis when the main interpretative thrust appears to be losing its force. In so far as this is done, historical analysis is weakened. If the investigator is operating with a definite model, he, too, may engage in subtly smuggling in factors and explanations that are not part of the model. But in so far as his model is formal and explicit, it is much easier to identify the lax eclecticism that arises from relying on *ad hoc* explanations as the occasion demands.

A third advantage of framing historical explanations within a general model appears when we wish to consider comparative cases. If we restrict our interest to British society in the late eighteenth and early nineteenth centuries, there is no advantage in using a language more general than that necessary to describe events in that setting. However, if we wish to trace the impact of industrial change more generally—in France, the United States, and India, for example—it is necessary to employ categories general enough to encompass phenomena in highly diverse social settings. The use of a general model to interpret a specific historical case, then, facilitates systematic comparisons with other cases.

Finally, using an abstract model to account for specific historical changes permits the investigator to relate his results more readily to other types of knowledge. As I indicated, the model of structural differentiation has its roots partly in the study of institutional change, partly in experimental small-group research, and partly in the study of personality changes. To frame the model in sufficiently general terms that it can be applied to these diverse settings allows the relations among phenomena in one setting to be translated into analogous relations in other settings. These various relations are confirmed or rejected, of course, not by analogy but by independent empirical investigations in each setting. But the presence of a model does facilitate the exchange and generalization of different kinds of empirical knowledge.

BIBLIOGRAPHICAL NOTE

The social historian will want to compare this with recent empirical work on the history of the family, particularly in the textile districts of Britain. M. Anderson, *The Family in Nineteenth-Century Lancashire* (Cambridge, 1971) is important in this respect, and has implications not in agreement with Smelser's model. Frances Collier, *The Family Economy of the Working Classes* (Manchester, 1964) is also about Lancashire at this period. P. Laslett and R. Wall (edd.), *Household and Family in Past Time* (Cambridge, 1972) is a major compendium of historical studies on the family in Britain and elsewhere. M. Anderson (ed.), *Sociology of the Family* (London, 1971) is a book of introductory readings of relevance to historians and sociologists alike, and D. A. Sweetser, 'The effect of industrialisation on intergenerational solidarity', *Rural Sociology*, 31 (1966), 156–70, is theoretically interesting in the context of the Smelser paper. The whole field is expanding fast, and *The Family in Historical Perspective: an International Newsletter* (begun in 1972) endeavours to keep scholars in touch with the latest research and publications.

NOTES

1. For a brief commentary on the general relations between the two disciplines, see Smelser, *Essays in Sociological Explanation*, pp. 34–7.

2. London and Chicago, 1959.

3. The relevant works are Adam Smith, *Inquiry into the Nature and Causes of the Wealth of Nations* (1776); Karl Marx, *Capital* (1867); Herbert Spencer, *The Principles of Sociology* (1876); Emile Durkheim, *The Division of Labor in Society* (1893); Talcott Parsons, Robert F. Bales, *et al.*, *Family Socialization and Interaction Process* (New York, 1955).

4. Nassau Senior, *Letters on the Factory Act as It Affects the Cotton Manufacture* (London, 1837), p. 19.

5. See *Social Change in the Industrial Revolution*, chap. 14.

3

Time, Work-Discipline, and Industrial Capitalism*

E. P. THOMPSON

Tess ... started on her way up the dark and crooked lane or street not made for hasty progress; a street laid out before inches of land had value, and when one-handed clocks sufficiently subdivided the day. *Thomas Hardy*.

I

IT is commonplace that the years between 1300 and 1650 saw within the intellectual culture of Western Europe important changes in the apprehension of time.[1] In the *Canterbury Tales* the cock still figures in his immemorial role as nature's timepiece : Chauntecleer—

> Caste up his eyen to the brighte sonne,
> That in the signe of Taurus hadde yronne
> Twenty degrees and oon, and somwhat moore,
> He knew by kynde, and by noon oother loore
> That it was pryme, and crew with blisful stevene....

But although 'By nature knew he ech ascensioun/Of the equynoxial in thilke toun', the contrast between 'nature's' time and clock time is pointed in the image—

> Wel sikerer was his crowyng in his logge
> Than is a clokke, or an abbey orlogge.

This is a very early clock : Chaucer (unlike Chauntecleer) was a Londoner, and was aware of the times of Court, of urban organization, and of that 'merchant's time' which Jacques Le Goff, in a suggestive article in *Annales*, has opposed to the time of the medieval church.[2]

I do not wish to argue how far the change was due to the spread of clocks from the fourteenth century onwards, how far this was itself a symptom of a new Puritan discipline and bourgeois exactitude. However we see it, the change is certainly there. The clock steps on to the Elizabethan stage, turn-

* From *Past and Present, a journal of historical studies*, 38 (Dec. 1967), 56–97. World copyright The Past and Present Society, Corpus Christi College, Oxford. Reprinted by permission of the author and the Society.

ing Faustus's last soliloquy into a dialogue with time: 'the stars move still,
time runs, the clock will strike'. Sidereal time, which has been present since
literature began, has now moved at one step from the heavens into the home.
Mortality and love are both felt to be more poignant as the 'Snayly motion
of the mooving hand'[3] crosses the dial. When the watch is worn about the neck
it lies in proximity to the less regular beating of the heart. The conventional
Elizabethan images of time as a devourer, a defacer, a bloody tyrant, a
scytheman, are old enough, but there is a new immediacy and insistence.[4]

As the seventeenth century moves on the image of clock-work extends,
until, with Newton, it has engrossed the universe. And by the middle of the
eighteenth century (if we are to trust Sterne) the clock had penetrated to
more intimate levels. For Tristram Shandy's father—'one of the most regular
men in everything he did ... that ever lived'—'had made it a rule for many
years of his life,—on the first Sunday night of every month ... to wind up
a large house-clock, which we had standing on the back-stairs head'. 'He
had likewise gradually brought some other little family concernments to the
same period', and this enabled Tristram to date his conception very exactly.
It also provoked *The Clockmaker's Outcry against the Author*:

> The directions I had for making several clocks for the country are counter-
> manded; because no modest lady now dares to mention a word about winding-up
> a clock, without exposing herself to the sly leers and jokes of the family ... Nay,
> the common expression of street-walkers is, 'Sir, will you have your clock
> wound up?'

Virtuous matrons (the 'clockmaker' complained) are consigning their clocks
to lumber rooms as 'exciting to acts of carnality'.[5]

However, this gross impressionism is unlikely to advance the present
inquiry: how far, and in what ways, did this shift in time-sense affect labour
discipline, and how far did it influence the inward apprehension of time of
working people? If the transition to mature industrial society entailed a
severe restructuring of working habits—new disciplines, new incentives, and
a new human nature upon which these incentives could bite effectively—
how far is this related to changes in inward notation of time?

II

It is well known that among primitive peoples the measurement of time
is commonly related to familiar processes in the cycle of work or of domestic
chores. Evans-Pritchard has analysed the time-sense of the Nuer: 'The daily
timepiece is the cattle clock, the round of pastoral tasks, and the time of day
and the passage of time through a day are to a Nuer primarily the succession
of these tasks and their relation to one another.'

Among the Nandi an occupational definition of time evolved covering
not only each hour, but half hours of the day—at 5.30 in the morning the

oxen have gone to the grazing-ground, at 6 the sheep have been unfastened, at 6.30 the sun has grown, at 7 it has become warm, at 7.30 the goats have gone to the grazing-ground, etc.—an uncommonly well-regulated economy. In a similar way terms evolve for the measurement of time intervals. In Madagascar time might be measured by 'a rice-cooking' (about half an hour) or 'the frying of a locust' (a moment). The Cross River natives were reported as saying 'the man died in less than the time in which maize is not yet completely roasted' (less than fifteen minutes).[6]

It is not difficult to find examples of this nearer to us in cultural time. Thus in seventeenth-century Chile time was often measured in 'credos': an earthquake was described in 1647 as lasting for the period of two credos; while the cooking-time of an egg could be judged by an Ave Maria said aloud. In Burma in recent times monks rose at daybreak 'when there is light enough to see the veins in the hand'.[7] The *Oxford English Dictionary* gives us English examples—'pater noster wyle', 'miserere whyle' (1450), and (in the *New English Dictionary* but not the *Oxford English Dictionary*) 'pissing while'— a somewhat arbitrary measurement.

Pierre Bourdieu has explored more closely the attitudes towards time of the Kabyle peasant (in Algeria) in recent years: 'An attitude of submission and of nonchalant indifference to the passage of time which no one dreams of mastering, using up, or saving ... Haste is seen as a lack of decorum combined with diabolical ambition'. The clock is sometimes known as 'the devil's mill'; there are no precise meal-times; 'the notion of an exact appointment is unknown; they agree only to meet "at the next market"'. A popular song runs:

It is useless to pursue the world, No one will ever overtake it.[8]

Synge, in his well-observed account of the Aran Islands, gives us a classic example:

While I am walking with Michael someone often comes to me to ask the time of day. Few of the people, however, are sufficiently used to modern time to understand in more than a vague way the convention of the hours and when I tell them what o'clock it is by my watch they are not satisfied, and ask how long is left them before the twilight.[9]

The general knowledge of time on the island depends, curiously enough, upon the direction of the wind. Nearly all the cottages are built ... with two doors opposite each other, the more sheltered of which lies open all day to give light to the interior. If the wind is northerly the south door is opened, and the shadow of the door-post moving across the kitchen floor indicates the hour; as soon, however, as the wind changes to the south the other door is opened, and the people, who never think of putting up a primitive dial, are at a loss ...

When the wind is from the north the old woman manages my meals with fair regularity; but on the other days she often makes my tea at three o'clock instead of six ...[10]

Such a disregard for clock time could of course only be possible in a crofting and fishing community whose framework of marketing and administration is minimal, and in which the day's tasks (which might vary from fishing to farming, building, mending of nets, thatching, making a cradle or a coffin) seem to disclose themselves, by the logic of need, before the crofter's eyes.[11] But his account will serve to emphasize the essential conditioning in differing notations of time provided by different work-situations and their relation to 'natural' rhythms. Clearly hunters must employ certain hours of the night to set their snares. Fishing and seafaring people must integrate their lives with the tides. A petition from Sunderland in 1800 includes the words 'considering that this is a seaport in which many people are obliged to be up at all hours of the night to attend the tides and their affairs upon the river'.[12] The operative phrase is 'attend the tides': the patterning of social time in the seaport follows *upon* the rhythms of the sea; and this appears to be natural and comprehensible to fishermen or seamen: the compulsion is nature's own.

In a similar way labour from dawn to dusk can appear to be 'natural' in a farming community, especially in the harvest months: nature demands that the grain be harvested before the thunderstorms set in. And we may note similar 'natural' work-rhythms which attend other rural or industrial occupations: sheep must be attended at lambing time and guarded from predators; cows must be milked; the charcoal fire must be attended and not burn away through the turfs (and the charcoal burners must sleep beside it); once iron is in the making, the furnaces must not be allowed to fail.

The notation of time which arises in such contexts has been described as task-orientation. It is perhaps the most effective orientation in peasant societies, and it remains important in village and domestic industries. It has by no means lost all relevance in rural parts of Britain today. Three points may be proposed about task-orientation. First, there is a sense in which it is more humanly comprehensible than timed labour. The peasant or labourer appears to attend upon what is an observed necessity. Second, a community in which task-orientation is common appears to show least demarcation between 'work' and 'life'. Social intercourse and labour are intermingled— the working-day lengthens or contracts according to the task—and there is no great sense of conflict between labour and 'passing the time of day'. Third, to men accustomed to labour timed by the clock, this attitude to labour appears to be wasteful and lacking in urgency.[13]

Such a clear distinction supposes, of course, the independent peasant or craftsman as referent. But the question of task-orientation becomes greatly more complex at the point where labour is employed. The entire family economy of the small farmer may be task-orientated; but within it there may be a division of labour, and allocation of roles, and the discipline of an employer–employed relationship between the farmer and his children. Even here time is beginning to become money, the employer's money. As soon as actual hands are employed the shift from task-orientation to timed labour is marked. It is true that the timing of work can be done independently of any time-piece—and indeed precedes the diffusion of the clock. Still, in the mid-seventeenth century substantial farmers calculated their expectations of employed labour (as did Henry Best) in 'dayworkes'—'the Cunnigarth, with its bottomes, is 4 large dayworkes for a good mower', 'the Spellowe is 4 indifferent dayworkes', etc.;[14] and what Best did for his own farm, Markham attempted to present in general form:

A man ... may mow of Corn, as Barley and Oats, if it be thick, loggy and beaten down to the earth, making fair work, and not cutting off the heads of the ears, and leaving the straw still growing one acre and a half in a day: but if it be good thick and fair standing corn, then he may mow two acres, or two acres and a half in a day; but if the corn be short and thin, then he may mow three, and sometimes four Acres in a day, and not be overlaboured....[15]

The computation is difficult, and dependent upon many variables. Clearly, a straightforward time-measurement was more convenient.[16]

This measurement embodies a simple relationship. Those who are employed experience a distinction between their employer's time and their 'own' time. And the employer must *use* the time of his labour, and see it is not wasted: not the task but the value of time when reduced to money is dominant. Time is now currency: it is not passed but spent.

We may observe something of this contrast, in attitudes towards both time and work, in two passages from Stephen Duck's poem, 'The Thresher's Labour'. The first describes a work-situation which we have come to regard as the norm in the nineteenth and twentieth centuries:

> From the strong Planks our Crab-Tree Staves rebound,
> And echoing Barns return the rattling Sound.
> Now in the Air our knotty Weapons Fly;
> And now with equal Force descend from high:
> Down one, one up, so well they keep the Time,
> The *Cyclops* Hammers could not truer chime....
> In briny Streams our Sweat descends apace,
> Drops from our Locks, or trickles down our Face.
> No intermission in our Works we know;
> The noisy Threshall must for ever go.
> Their Master absent, others safely play;
> The sleeping Threshall doth itself betray.
> Nor yet the tedious Labour to beguile,
> And make the passing Minutes sweetly smile,
> Can we, like Shepherds, tell a merry Tale?
> The Voice is lost, drown'd by the noisy Flail....
>
> Week after Week we this dull Task pursue,
> Unless when winnowing Days produce a new;
> A new indeed, but frequently a worse,
> The Threshall yields but to the Master's Curse:

He counts the Bushels, counts how much a Day,
Then swears we've idled half our Time away.
Why look ye, Rogues! D'ye think that this will do?
Your Neighbours thresh as much again as you.

This would appear to describe the monotony, alienation from pleasure in labour, and antagonism of interests commonly ascribed to the factory system. The second passage describes the harvesting:

At length in Rows stands up the well-dry'd Corn,
A grateful Scene, and ready for the Barn.
Our well-pleas'd Master views the Sight with joy,
And we for carrying all our Force employ.
Confusion soon o'er all the Field appears,
And stunning Clamours fill the Workmens Ears;
The Bells, and clashing Whips, alternate sound,
And rattling Waggons thunder o'er the Ground.
The Wheat got in, the Pease, and other Grain,
Share the same Fate, and soon leave bare the Plain:
In noisy Triumph the last Load moves on,
And loud Huzza's proclaim the Harvest done.

This is, of course, an obligatory set-piece in eighteenth-century farming poetry. And it is also true that the good morale of the labourers was sustained by their high harvest earnings. But it would be an error to see the harvest situation in terms of direct responses to economic stimuli. It is also a moment at which the older collective rhythms break through the new, and a weight of folklore and of rural custom could be called as supporting evidence as to the psychic satisfaction and ritual functions—for example, the momentary obliteration of social distinctions—of the harvest-home. 'How few now know', M. K. Ashby writes, 'what it was ninety years ago to get in a harvest! Though the disinherited had no great part of the fruits, still they shared in the achievement, the deep involvement and joy of it.'[17]

III

It is by no means clear how far the availability of precise clock time extended at the time of the industrial revolution. From the fourteenth century onwards church clocks and public clocks were erected in the cities and large market towns. The majority of English parishes must have possessed church clocks by the end of the sixteenth century.[18] But the accuracy of these clocks is a matter of dispute; and the sundial remained in use (partly to set the clock) in the seventeenth, eighteenth, and nineteenth centuries.[19]

Charitable donations continued to be made in the seventeenth century (sometimes laid out in 'clockland', 'ding dong land', or 'curfew bel land') for the ringing of early morning bells and curfew bells.[20] Thus Richard Palmer of Wokingham (Berks) gave, in 1664, lands in trust to pay the sexton to ring the great bell for half an hour every evening at eight o'clock and every morning at four o'clock, or as near to those hours as might be, from 10 September to 11 March in each year 'not only that as many as might live within the sound might be thereby induced to a timely going to rest in the evening, and early arising in the morning to the labours and duties of their several callings, (things ordinarily attended and rewarded with thrift and proficiency)....' but also so that strangers and others within sound of the bell on winter nights 'might be informed of the time of night, and receive some guidance into their right way'. These 'rational ends', he conceived, 'could not but be well liked by any discreet person, the same being done and well approved of in most of the cities and market-towns, and many others places in the kingdom ...' The bell would also remind men of their passing, and of resurrection and judgement.[21] Sound served better than sight, especially in growing manufacturing districts. In the clothing districts of the West Riding, in the Potteries, (and probably in other districts) the horn was still used to awaken people in the mornings.[22] The farmer aroused his own labourers, on occasion, from their cottages; and no doubt the knocker-up will have started with the earliest mills.

A great advance in the accuracy of household clocks came with the application of the pendulum after 1658. Grandfather clocks begin to spread more widely from the 1660s, but clocks with minute hands (as well as hour hands) only became common well after this time.[23] As regards more portable time, the pocket watch was of dubious accuracy until improvements were made in the escapement and the spiral balance-spring was applied after 1674.[24] Ornate and rich design was still preferred to plain serviceability. A Sussex diarist notes in 1688: 'bought ... a silver-cased watch, wch cost me *31i* ... This watch shewes ye hour of ye day, ye month of ye year, ye age of ye moon, and ye ebbing and flowing of ye water; and will goe 30 hours with one winding up.'[25]

Professor Cipolla suggests 1680 as the date at which English clock- and watch-making took precedence (for nearly a century) over European competitors.[26] Clock-making had emerged from the skills of the blacksmith,[27] and the affinity can still be seen in the many hundreds of independent clockmakers, working to local orders in their own shops, dispersed through the market-towns and even the large villages of England, Scotland, and Wales in the eighteenth century.[28] While many of these aspired to nothing more fancy than the work-a-day farmhouse longcase clock, craftsmen of genius were among their numbers. Thus John Harrison, clock-maker and former carpenter of Barton-on-Humber (Lincs.), perfected a marine chronometer, and in 1730 could claim to have 'brought a Clock to go nearer the truth, than can be well imagin'd, considering the vast Number of seconds of Time there is in a Month, in which space of time it does not vary above one second ... I am sure I can bring it to the nicety of 2 or 3 seconds in a year.'[29]

And John Tibbot, a clockmaker in Newtown (Mon.), had perfected a clock in 1810 which (he claimed) seldom varied more than a second over two years.[30] In between these extremes were those numerous, shrewd, and highly capable craftsmen who played a critically important role in technical innovation in the early stages of the industrial revolution. The point, indeed, was not left for historians to discover: it was argued forcibly in petitions of the clock- and watch-makers against the assessed taxes in February 1798. Thus the petition from Carlisle:

... the cotton and woollen manufactories are entirely indebted for the state of perfection to which the machinery used therein is now brought to the clock and watch makers, great numbers of whom have, for several years past ... been employed in inventing and constructing as well as superintending such machinery. ...[31]

Small-town clock-making survived into the nineteenth century, although from the early years of that century it became common for the local clock-maker to buy his parts ready-made from Birmingham, and to assemble these in his own work-shop. By contrast, watch-making, from the early years of the eighteenth century was concentrated in a few centres, of which the most important were London, Coventry, Prescot, and Liverpool.[32] A minute sub-division of labour took place in the industry early, facilitating large-scale production and a reduction in prices: the annual output of the industry at its peak (1796) was variously estimated at 120,000 and 191,678, a substantial part of which was for the export market.[33] Pitt's ill-judged attempt to tax clocks and watches, although it lasted only from July 1797 to March 1798, marked a turning-point in the fortunes of the industry. Already, in 1796, the trade was complaining at the competition of French and Swiss watches; the complaints continue to grow in the early years of the nineteenth century. The Clockmakers' Company alleged in 1813 that the smuggling of cheap gold watches has assumed major proportions, and that these were sold by jewellers, haberdashers, milliners, dressmakers, French toy-shops, per-fumers, etc., 'almost entirely for the use of *the upper classes of society*'. At the same time, some cheap smuggled goods, sold by pawnbrokers or travel-ling salesmen, must have been reaching the poorer classes.[34]

It is clear that there were plenty of watches and clocks around by 1800. But it is not so clear who owned them. Dr. Dorothy George, writing of the mid-eighteenth century, suggests that 'labouring men, as well as artisans, frequently possessed silver watches', but the statement is indefinite as to date and only slightly documented.[35] The average price of plain longcase clocks made locally in Wrexham between 1755 and 1774 ran between £2 and £2 15s. 0d.; a Leicester price-list for new clocks, without cases, in 1795 runs between £3 and £5. A well-made watch would certainly cost no less.[36] On the face of it, no labourer whose budget was recorded by Eden or David Davies could have meditated such prices, and only the best-paid urban artisan. Recorded time (one suspects) belonged in the mid-century still to the gentry, the masters, the farmers and the tradesmen; and perhaps the intricacy of design, and the preference for precious metal, were in deliberate accentuation of their symbolism of status.

But, equally, it would appear that the situation was changing in the last decades of the century. The debate provoked by the attempt to impose a tax on all clocks and watches in 1797–8 offers a little evidence. It was perhaps the most unpopular and it was certainly the most unsuccessful of all of Pitt's assessed taxes:

> If your Money he take—why your Breeches remain;
> And the flaps of your Shirts, if your Breeches he gain;
> And your Skin, if your Shirts; and if Shoes, your bare feet.
> Then, never mind TAXES—*We've beat the Dutch fleet!*[37]

The taxes were of 2s. 6d. upon each silver or metal watch; 10s. upon each gold one; and 5s. upon each clock. In debates upon the tax, the statements of ministers were remarkable only for their contradictions. Pitt declared that he expected the tax to produce £200,000 per annum:

In fact, he thought, that as the number of houses paying taxes is 700,000, and that in every house there is probably one person who wears a watch, the tax upon watches only would produce that sum.

At the same time, in response to criticism, ministers maintained that the ownership of clocks and watches was a mark of luxury. The Chancellor of the Exchequer faced both ways: watches and clocks 'were certainly articles of convenience, but they were also articles of luxury ... generally kept by persons who would be pretty well able to pay ...' 'He meant, however, to exempt Clocks of the meaner sort that were most commonly kept by the poorer classes.'[38] The Chancellor clearly regarded the tax as a sort of Lucky Bag; his guess was more than three times that of Pitt:

GUESSWORK TABLE

Articles	Tax	Chancellor's estimate	Would mean
Silver and metal watches	2s. 6d.	£100,000	800,000 watches
Gold watches	10s. 0d.	£200,000	400,000 „
Clocks	5s. 0d.	£300,000 or £400,000	c. 1,400,000 clocks

His eyes glittering at the prospect of enhanced revenue, Pitt revised his definitions: a *single* watch (or dog) might be owned as an article of convenience—more than this were 'tests of affluence'.[39]

Unfortunately for the quantifiers of economic growth, one matter was left out of account. The tax was impossible to collect.[40] All householders were ordered, upon dire pains, to return lists of clocks and watches within their houses. Assessments were to be quarterly: 'Mr. Pitt has very proper ideas of the remaining finances of the country. The *half-crown* tax upon watches is appointed to be collected *quarterly*. This is grand and dignified. It gives a man an air of consequence to pay *sevenpence halfpenny* to support *religion, property,* and *social order*.'[41]

In fact, the tax was regarded as folly; as setting up a system of espionage; and as a blow against the middle class.[42] There was a buyer's strike. Owners of gold watches melted down the covers and exchanged them for silver or metal.[43] The centres of the trade were plunged into crisis and depression.[44] Repealing the Act in March 1798, Pitt said sadly that the tax *would* have been productive much beyond the calculation orginally made; but it is not clear whether it was his own calculation (£200,000) or the Chancellor of the Exchequer's (£700,000) which he had in mind.[45]

We remain (but in the best of company) in ignorance. There were a lot of time-pieces about in the 1790s: emphasis is shifting from 'luxury' to 'convenience'; even cottagers may have wooden clocks costing less than twenty shillings. Indeed, a general diffusion of clocks and watches is occurring (as one would expect) at the exact moment when the industrial revolution demanded a greater synchronization of labour.

Although some very cheap—and shoddy—time-pieces were beginning to appear, the prices of efficient ones remained for several decades beyond the normal reach of the artisan.[46] But we should not allow normal economic preferences to mislead us. The small instrument which regulated the new rhythms of industrial life was at the same time one of the more urgent of the new needs which industrial capitalism called forth to energize its advance. A clock or watch was not only useful; it conferred prestige upon its owner, and a man might be willing to stretch his resources to obtain one. There were various sources, various occasions. For decades a trickle of sound but cheap watches found their way from the pickpocket to the receiver, the pawnbroker, the public house.[47] Even labourers, once or twice in their lives, might have an unexpected windfall, and blow it on a watch: the militia bounty,[48] harvest earnings, or the yearly wages of the servant.[49] In some parts of the country Clock and Watch Clubs were set up—collective hire-purchase.[50] Moreover, the time-piece was the poor man's bank, an investment of savings: it could, in bad times, be sold or put in hock.[51] 'This 'ere ticker,' said one Cockney compositor in the 1820s, 'cost me but a five-pun note ven I bort it fust, and I've popped it more than twenty times, and had more than forty poun' on it altogether. It's a garjian haingel to a fellar, is a good votch, ven you're hard up'.[52]

Whenever any group of workers passed into a phase of improving living standards, the acquisition of time-pieces was one of the first things noted by observers. In Radcliffe's well-known account of the golden age of the Lancashire handloom weavers in the 1790s the men had 'each a watch in his pocket' and every house was 'well furnished with a clock in elegant mahogany or fancy case'.[53] In Manchester fifty years later the same point caught the reporter's eye:

No Manchester operative will be without one a moment longer than he can help. You see, here and there, in the better class of houses, one of the old-fashioned metallic-faced eight-day clocks; but by far the most common article is the little Dutch machine, with its busy pendulum swinging openly and candidly before all the world.[54]

Thirty years later again it was the gold double watch-chain which was the symbol of the successful Lib–Lab trade-union leader; and for fifty years of disciplined servitude to work, the enlightened employer gave to his employee an engraved gold watch.

IV

Let us return from the time-piece to the task. Attention to time in labour depends in large degree upon the need for the synchronization of labour. But in so far as manufacturing industry remained conducted upon a domestic or small workshop scale, without intricate subdivision of processes, the degree of synchronization demanded was slight, and task orientation was still prevalent.[55] The putting-out system demanded much fetching, carrying, waiting for materials. Bad weather could disrupt not only agriculture, building, and transport, but also weaving, where the finished pieces had to be stretched on the tenters to dry. As we get closer to each task, we are surprised to find the multiplicity of subsidiary tasks which the same worker or family group must do in one cottage or workshop. Even in larger workshops men sometimes continued to work at distinct tasks at their own benches or looms, and—except where the fear of the embezzlement of materials imposed stricter supervision—could show some flexibility in coming and going.

Hence we get the characteristic irregularity of labour patterns before the coming of large-scale machine-powered industry. Within the general demands of the week's or fortnight's tasks—the piece of cloth, so many nails or pairs of shoes—the working day might be lengthened or shortened. Moreover, in the early development of manufacturing industry, and of mining, many mixed occupations survived: Cornish tinners who also took a hand in the pilchard fishing; Northern lead-miners who were also smallholders; the village craftsmen who turned their hands to various jobs, in building, carting, joining; the domestic workers who left their work for the harvest; the Pennine small-farmer/weaver.

It is in the nature of such work that accurate and representative time-budgets will not survive. But some extracts from the diary of one methodical farming weaver in 1782–3 may give us an indication of the variety of tasks. In October 1782 he was still employed in harvesting and threshing, alongside his weaving. On a rainy day he might weave $8\frac{1}{2}$ or 9 yards; on 14

October he carried his finished piece, and so wove only 4¾ yards; on the 23rd he 'worked out' till 3 o'clock, wove two yards before sun set, 'clouted [mended] my coat in the evening'. On 24 December 'wove 2 yards before 11 o'clock. I was laying up the coal heap, sweeping the roof and walls of the kitchen and laying the muck miding [midden?] till 10 o'clock at night'. Apart from harvesting and threshing, churning, ditching and gardening, we have these entries:

January 18, 1783:	'I was employed in preparing a Calf stall & Fetching the Tops of three Plain Trees home which grew in the Lane and was that day cut down & sold to john Blagbrough.'
January 21st:	'Wove 2¾ yards the Cow having calved she required much attendance'. (On the next day he walked to Halifax to buy a medicine for the cow.)

On 25 January he wove 2 yards, walked to a nearby village, and did 'sundry jobbs about the lathe and in the yard & wrote a letter in the evening'. Other occupations include jobbing with a horse and cart, picking cherries, working on a mill dam, attending a Baptist association and a public hanging.[56]

This general irregularity must be placed within the irregular cycle of the working week (and indeed of the working year) which provoked so much lament from moralists and mercantilists in the seventeenth and eighteenth centuries. A rhyme printed in 1639 gives us a satirical version:

> You know that Munday is Sundayes brother;
> Tuesday is such another;
> Wednesday you must go to Church and pray;
> Thursday is half-holiday;
> On Friday it is too late to begin to spin;
> The Saturday is half-holiday agen.[57]

John Houghton, in 1681, gives us the indignant version:

When the framework knitters or makers of silk stockings had a great price for their work, they have been observed seldom to work on Mondays and Tuesdays but to spend most of their time at the ale-house or nine-pins ... The weavers, 'tis common with them to be drunk Monday, have their head-ache on Tuesday, and their tools out of order on Wednesday. As for the shoemakers, they'll rather be hanged than not remember St. Crispin on Monday ... and it commonly holds as long as they have a penny of money or pennyworth of credit.[58]

The work pattern was one of alternate bouts of intense labour and of idleness, wherever men were in control of their own working lives. (The pattern persists among some self-employed—artists, writers, small farmers, and perhaps also with students—today, and provokes the question whether it is not a 'natural' human work-rhythm.) On Monday or Tuesday, according to tradition, the hand-loom went to the slow chant of *Plen-ty of Time, Plen-ty of Time*: on Thursday and Friday, *A day t'lat, A day t'lat*.[59] The temptation to lie in an extra hour in the morning pushed work into the evening, candle-lit hours.[60] There are few trades which are not described as honouring Saint Monday: shoemakers, tailors, colliers, printing workers, potters, weavers, hosiery workers, cutlers, all Cockneys. Despite the full employment of many London trades during the Napoleonic Wars, a witness complained that 'we see Saint Monday so religiously kept in this great city ... in general followed by a Saint Tuesday also'.[61] If we are to believe 'The Jovial Cutlers', a Sheffield song of the late eighteenth century, its observance was not without domestic tension:

> How upon a good Saint Monday,
> Sitting by the smithy fire,
> Telling what's been done o't Sunday,
> And in cheerful mirth conspire,
>   Soon I hear the trap-door rise up,
>   On the ladder stands my wife:
>   'Damn thee, Jack, I'll dust thy eyes up,
>   Thou leads a plaguy drunken life;
>   Here thou sits instead of working,
>   Wi' thy pitcher on thy knee;
>   Curse thee, thou'd be always lurking.
>   And I may slave myself for thee.'

The wife proceeds, speaking 'with motion quicker/Than my boring stick at a Friday's pace', to demonstrate effective consumer demand:

> 'See thee, look what stays I've gotten,
> See thee, what a pair o' shoes;
> Gown and petticoat half rotten,
> Ne'er a whole stitch in my hose ...'

and to serve notice of a general strike:

> 'Thou knows I hate to broil and quarrel,
> But I've neither soap nor tea;
> Od burn thee, Jack, forsake thy barrel,
> Or nevermore thou'st lie wi' me'.[62]

Saint Monday, indeed, appears to have been honoured almost universally wherever small-scale, domestic, and outwork industries existed; was generally found in the pits; and sometimes continued in manufacturing and heavy industry.[63] It was perpetuated, in England, into the nineteenth—and, indeed, into the twentieth[64]—centuries for complex economic and social reasons. In some trades, the small masters themselves accepted the institution, and employed Monday in taking-in or giving-out work. In Sheffield, where the cutlers had for centuries tenaciously honoured the Saint, it had become 'a settled habit and custom' which the steel-mills themselves honoured (1874): 'This Monday idleness is, in some cases, enforced by the fact that Monday is the day that is taken for repairs to the machinery of the great steel-works.'[65] Where the custom was deeply established, Monday was the day set aside for marketing and personal business. Also, as Duveau suggests of French workers, 'le dimanche est le jour de la famille, le lundi celui de l'amitié'; and as the nineteenth century advanced, its celebration was something of a privilege of status of the better-paid artisan.[66]

It is, in fact, in an account by 'An Old Potter' published as late as 1903 that we have some of the most perceptive observations on the irregular work-rhythms which continued on the older pot-banks until the mid-century. The potters (in the 1830s and 1840s) 'had a devout regard for Saint Monday'. Although the custom of annual hiring prevailed, the actual weekly earnings were at piece-rates, the skilled male potters employing the children, and working, with little supervision, at their own pace. The children and women came to work on Monday and Tuesday, but a 'holiday feeling' prevailed and the day's work was shorter than usual, since the potters were away a good part of the time, drinking their earnings of the previous week. The children, however, had to prepare work for the potter (for example, handles for pots which he would throw), and all suffered from the exceptionally long hours (fourteen and sometimes sixteen hours a day) which were worked from Wednesday to Saturday: 'I have since thought that but for the reliefs at the beginning of the week for the women and boys all through the pot-works, the deadly stress of the last four days could not have been maintained.' 'An Old Potter', a Methodist lay preacher of Liberal-Radical views, saw these customs (which he deplored) as a consequence of the lack of mechanization of the pot-banks; and he argued that the same indiscipline in daily work influenced the entire way of life and the working-class organizations of the Potteries. 'Machinery means discipline in industrial operations.'

If a steam engine had started every Monday morning at six o'clock, the workers would have been disciplined to the habit of regular and continuous industry ... I have noticed, too, that machinery seems to lead to habits of calculation. The Pottery workers were woefully deficient in this matter; they lived like children, without any calculating forecast of their work or its result. In some of the more northern counties this habit of calculation has made them keenly shrewd in many conspicuous ways. Their great co-operative societies would never have arisen to such immense and fruitful development but for the calculating induced by the use of machinery. A machine worked so many hours in the week would produce so much length of yarn or cloth. Minutes were felt to be factors in these results, whereas in the Potteries hours, or even days at times, were hardly felt to be such factors. There were always the mornings and nights of the last days of the week, and these were always trusted to make up the loss of the week's early neglect.[67]

This irregular working rhythm is commonly associated with heavy week-end drinking: Saint Monday is a target in many Victorian temperance tracts. But even the most sober and self-disciplined artisan might feel the necessity for such alternations. 'I know not how to describe the sickening aversion which at times steals over the working man and utterly disables him for a longer or shorter period, from following his usual occupation', Francis Place wrote in 1829; and he added a footnote of personal testimony:

For nearly six years, whilst working, when I had work to do, from twelve to eighteen hours a day, when no longer able, from the cause mentioned, to continue working, I used to run from it, and go as rapidly as I could to Highgate, Hampstead, Muswell-hill, or Norwood, and then 'return to my vomit' ... This is the case with every workman I have ever known; and in proportion as a man's case is hopeless will such fits more frequently occur and be of longer duration.[68]

We may, finally, note that the irregularity of working day and week were framed, until the first decades of the nineteenth century, within the larger irregularity of the working year, punctuated by its traditional holidays, and fairs. Still, despite the triumph of the Sabbath over the ancient saints' days in the seventeenth century,[69] the people clung tenaciously to their customary wakes and feasts, and may even have enlarged them both in vigour and extent.[70] But a discussion of this problem, and of the psychic needs met by such intermittent festivals, must be left to another occasion.

How far can this argument be extended from manufacturing industry to the rural labourers? On the face of it, there would seem to be unrelenting daily and weekly labour here: the field labourer had no Saint Monday. But a close discrimination of different work situations is still required. The eighteenth- (and nineteenth-) century village had its own self-employed artisans, as well as many employed in irregular task work.[71] Moreover, in the unenclosed countryside, the classical case against open-field and common was in its inefficiency and wastefulness of time, for the small farmer or cottager:

... if you offer them work, they will tell you that they must go to look up their sheep, cut furzes, get their cow out of the pound, or, perhaps, say they must take their horse to be shod, that he may carry them to a horse-race or cricket-match. (Arbuthnot, 1773.)

In sauntering after his cattle, he acquires a habit of indolence. Quarter, half, and occasionally whole days are imperceptibly lost. Day labour becomes disgusting.... (Report on Somerset, 1795.)

When a labourer becomes possessed of more land than he and his family can cultivate in the evenings ... the farmer can no longer depend on him for constant work.... (*Commercial & Agricultural Magazine*, 1800.)[72]

To this we should add the frequent complaints of agricultural improvers as to the time wasted, both at seasonal fairs, and (before the arrival of the village shop) on weekly market-days.[73]

The farm-servant, or the regular wage-earning field labourer, who worked, unremittingly, the full statute hours or longer, who had no common rights or land, and who (if not living-in) lived in a tied cottage, was undoubtedly subject to an intense labour discipline, whether in the seventeenth or the nineteenth century. The day of a ploughman (living-in) was described with relish by Markham in 1636: '... the Plowman shall rise before four of the clock in the morning, and after thanks given to God for his rest, & prayer for the success of his labours, he shall go into his stable ...' After cleansing the stable, grooming his horses, feeding them, and preparing his tackle, he might breakfast (6–6.30 a.m.), he should plough until 2 p.m. or 3 p.m.; take half an hour for dinner; attend to his horses etc. until 6.30 p.m., when he might come in for supper:

> ... and after supper, hee shall either by the fire side mend shooes both for himselfe and their Family, or beat and knock Hemp or Flax, or picke and stamp Apples or Crabs, for Cyder or Verdjuyce, or else grind malt on the quernes, pick candle rushes, or doe some Husbandly office within doors till it be full eight a clock....

Then he must once again attend to his cattle and ('giving God thanks for benefits received that day') he might retire.[74]

Even so, we are entitled to show a certain scepticism. There are obvious difficulties in the nature of the occupation. Ploughing is not an all-the-year-round task. Hours and tasks must fluctuate with the weather. The horses (if not the men) must be rested. There is the difficulty of supervision: Robert Loder's accounts indicate that servants (when out of sight) were not always employed upon their knees thanking God for their benefits: 'men can worke yf they list & soe they can loyter'.[75] The farmer himself must work exceptional hours if he was to keep all his labourers always employed.[76] And the farm-servant could assert his annual right to move on if he disliked his employment.

Thus enclosure and agricultural improvement were both, in some sense, concerned with the efficient husbandry of the time of the labour-force. Enclosure and the growing labour-surplus at the end of the eighteenth century tightened the screw for those who were in regular employment; they were faced with the alternatives of partial employment and the poor law, or submission to a more exacting labour discipline. It is a question, not of new techniques, but of a greater sense of time-thrift among the improving capitalist employers. This reveals itself in the debate between advocates of regularly-employed wage-labour and advocates of 'taken-work' (i.e. labourers employed for particular tasks at piece-rates). In the 1790s Sir Mordaunt Martin censured recourse to taken-work 'which people agree to, to save themselves the trouble of watching their workmen: the consequence is, the work is ill done, the workmen boast at the ale-house what they can spend in "a waste against the wall", and make men at moderate wages discontented.'

'A Farmer' countered with the argument that taken-work and regular wage-labour might be judiciously intermixed:

Two labourers engage to cut down a piece of grass at two shillings or half-a-crown an acre; I send, with their scythes, two of my domestic farm-servants into the field; I can depend upon it, that their companions will keep them up to their work; and thus I gain ... the same additional hours of labour from my domestic servants, which are voluntarily devoted to it by my hired servants.[77]

In the nineteenth century the debate was largely resolved in favour of weekly wage-labour, supplemented by task-work as occasion arose. The Wiltshire labourer's day, as described by Richard Jeffries in the 1870s, was scarcely less long than that described by Markham. Perhaps in resistance to this unremitting toil he was distinguished by the 'clumsiness of his walk' and 'the deadened slowness which seems to pervade everything he does'.[78]

The most arduous and prolonged work of all was that of the labourer's wife in the rural economy. One part of this—especially the care of infants—was the most task-orientated of all. Another part was in the fields, from which she must return to renewed domestic tasks. As Mary Collier complained in a sharp rejoinder to Stephen Duck:

> ... when we Home are come,
> Alas! we find our Work but just begun;
> So many Things for our Attendance call,
> Had we ten Hands, we could employ them all.
> Our Children put to Bed, with greatest Care
> We all Things for your coming Home prepare:
> You sup, and go to Bed without delay,
> And rest yourselves till the ensuing Day;
> While, we alas! but little Sleep can have,
> Because our froward Children cry and rave....
>
> In ev'ry Work (we) take our proper Share;
> And from the Time that Harvest doth begin
> Until the Corn be cut and carry'd in,
> Our Toil and Labour's daily so extreme,
> That we have hardly ever *Time to dream*.[79]

Such hours were endurable only because one part of the work, with the children and in the home, disclosed itself as necessary and inevitable, rather than as an external imposition. This remains true to this day, and, despite school times and television times, the rhythms of women's work in the home are not wholly attuned to the measurement of the clock. The mother of young children has an imperfect sense of time and attends to other human tides. She has not yet altogether moved out of the conventions of 'pre-industrial' society.

V

I have placed 'pre-industrial' in inverted commas: and for a reason. It is true that the transition to mature industrial society demands analysis in sociological as well as economic terms. Concepts such as 'time-preference' and the 'backward sloping labour supply curve' are, too often, cumbersome attempts to find economic terms to describe sociological problems. But, equally, the attempt to provide simple models for one single, supposedly-neutral, technologically-determined, process known as 'industrialization' (so popular today among well-established sociological circles in the United States)[80] is also suspect. It is not only that the highly developed, and technically alert, manufacturing industries (and the way of life supported by them) of France or England in the eighteenth century can only by semantic torture be described as 'pre-industrial'. (And such a description opens the door to endless false analogies between societies at greatly differing economic levels.) It is also that there has never been any single type of 'the transition'. The stress of the transition falls upon the whole culture: resistance to change and assent to change arise from the whole culture. And this culture includes the systems of power, property relations, religious institutions, etc., inattention to which merely flattens phenomena and trivializes analysis. Above all, the transition is not to 'industrialism' *tout court* but to industrial capitalism or (in the twentieth century) to alternative systems whose features are still indistinct. What we are examining here are not only changes in manufacturing technique which demand greater synchronization of labour and a greater exactitude in time-routines in *any* society; but also these changes as they were lived through in the society of nascent industrial capitalism. We are concerned simultaneously with time-sense in its technological conditioning, and with time-measurement as a means of labour exploitation.

There are reasons why the transition was peculiarly protracted and fraught with conflict in England: among those which are often noted, England's was the first Industrial Revolution, and there were no Cadillacs, steel mills, or television sets to serve as demonstrations as to the object of the operation. Moreover, the preliminaries to the industrial revolution were so long that, in the manufacturing districts in the early eighteenth century, a vigorous and licensed popular culture had evolved, which the propagandists of discipline regarded with dismay. Josiah Tucker, the Dean of Gloucester, declared in 1745 that 'the *lower* class of people' were utterly degenerated. Foreigners (he sermonized) found 'the *common people* of our *populous cities* to be the most *abandoned*, and *licentious* wretches on earth':

Such brutality and insolence, such debauchery and extravagance, such idleness, irreligion, cursing and swearing, and contempt of all rule and authority ... Our people are *drunk with the cup of liberty*.[81]

The irregular labour rhythms described in the previous section help us to understand the severity of mercantilist doctrines as to the necessity for holding down wages as a preventative against idleness and it would seem to be not until the second half of the eighteenth century that 'normal' capitalist wage incentives begin to become widely effective.[82] The confrontations over discipline have already been examined by others.[83] My intention here is to touch upon several points which concern time-discipline more particularly. The first is found in the extraordinary Law Book of the Crowley Iron Works. Here, at the very birth of the large-scale unit in manufacturing industry, the old autocrat, Crowley, found it necessary to design an entire civil and penal code, running to more than 100,000 words, to govern and regulate his refractory labour force. The preambles to Orders Number 40 (the Warden at the Mill) and 103 (Monitor) strike the prevailing note of morally-righteous invigilation. From Order 40:

I having by sundry people working by the day with the connivence of the clerks been horribly cheated and paid for much more time than in good conscience I ought and such hath been the baseness & treachery of sundry clerks that they have concealed the sloath & negligence of those paid by the day....

And from Order 103:

Some have pretended a sort of right to loyter, thinking by their readiness and ability to do sufficient in less time than others. Others have been so foolish to think bare attendance without being imployed in business is sufficient.... Others so impudent as to glory in their villany and upbrade others for their diligence....

To the end that sloath and villany should be detected and the just and diligent rewarded, I have thought meet to create an account of time by a Monitor, and do order and it is hereby ordered and declared from 5 to 8 and from 7 to 10 is fifteen hours, out of which take $1\frac{1}{2}$ for breakfast, dinner, etc. There will then be thirteen hours and a half neat service....

This service must be calculated 'after all deductions for being at taverns, alehouses, coffee houses, breakfast, dinner, playing, sleeping, smoking, singing, reading of news history, quarelling, contention, disputes or anything forreign to my business, any way loytering'.

The Monitor and Warden of the Mill were ordered to keep for each day employee a time-sheet, entered to the minute, with 'Come' and 'Run'. In the Monitor's Order, verse 31 (a later addition) declares:

And whereas I have been informed that sundry clerks have been so unjust as to reckon by clocks going the fastest and the bell ringing before the hour for their going from business, and clocks going too slow and the bell ringing after the hour for their coming to business, and those two black traitors Fowell and Skellerne have knowingly allowed the same; it is therefore ordered that no person upon the account does reckon by any other clock, bell, watch or dyall but the Monitor's, which clock is never to be altered but by the clock-keeper....

The Warden of the Mill was ordered to keep the watch 'so locked up that it may not be in the power of any person to alter the same'. His duties also were defined in verse 8:

Every morning at 5 a clock the Warden is to ring the bell for beginning to work, at eight a clock for breakfast, at half an hour after for work again, at twelve a clock for dinner, at one to work and at eight to ring for leaving work and all to be lock'd up.

His book of the account of time was to be delivered in every Tuesday with the following affidavit:

This account of time is done without favour or affection, ill-will or hatred, & do really believe the persons above mentioned have worked in the service of John Crowley Esq the hours above charged.[84]

We are entering here, already in 1700, the familiar landscape of disciplined industrial capitalism, with the time-sheet, the time-keeper, the informers, and the fines. Some seventy years later the same discipline was to be imposed in the early cotton mills (although the machinery itself was a powerful supplement to the time-keeper). Lacking the aid of machinery to regulate the pace of work on the pot-bank, that supposedly formidable disciplinarian, Josiah Wedgwood, was reduced to enforcing discipline upon the potters in surprisingly muted terms. The duties of the Clerk of the Manufactory were:

To be at the works the first in the morning, & settle the people to their business as they come in,—to encourage those who come regularly to their time, letting them know that their regularity is properly noticed, & distinguishing them by repeated marks of approbation, from the less orderly part of the workpeople, by presents or other marks suitable to their ages, &c.

Those who come later than the hour appointed should be noticed, and if after repeated marks of disapprobation they do not come in due time, an account of the time they are deficient in should be taken, and so much of their wages stopt as the time comes to if they work by wages, and if they work by the piece they should after frequent notice be sent back to breakfast-time.[85]

These regulations were later tightened somewhat: 'Any of the workmen forceing their way through the Lodge after the time alow'd by the Master forfeits 2/-d.'[86] and McKendrick has shown how Wedgwood wrestled with the problem at Etruria and introduced the first recorded system of clocking-in.[87] But it would seem that once the strong presence of Josiah himself was withdrawn the incorrigible potters returned to many of their older ways.

It is too easy, however, to see this only as a matter of factory or workshop discipline, and we may glance briefly at the attempt to impose 'time-thrift' in the domestic manufacturing districts, and its impingement upon social and domestic life. Almost all that the masters *wished* to see imposed may be found in the bounds of a single pamphlet, the Rev. J. Clayton's *Friendly Advice to the Poor*, 'written and publish'd at the Request of the late and present Officers of the Town of Manchester' in 1755. 'If the *sluggard hides his hands* in his bosom, rather than applies them to work; if he spends his Time in Sauntring, impairs his Constitution by Laziness, and dulls his Spirit by Indolence ...' then he can expect only poverty as his reward.

The labourer must not loiter idly in the market-place or waste time in marketing. Clayton complains that 'the Churches and Streets [are] crowded with Numbers of Spectators' at weddings and funerals, 'who in spight of the Miseries of their Starving Condition ... make no Scruple of wasting the best Hours in the Day, for the sake of gazing ...' The tea-table is 'this shameful devourer of Time and Money'. So also are wakes and holidays and the annual feasts of friendly societies. So also is 'that slothful spending the Morning in Bed'. 'The necessity of early rising would reduce the poor to a necessity of going to Bed betime; and thereby prevent the Danger of Midnight revels.' Early rising would also 'introduce an exact Regularity into their Families, a wonderful Order into their Oeconomy'.

The catalogue is familiar and might equally well be taken from Baxter in the previous century. If we can trust Bamford's *Early Days*, Clayton failed to make many converts from their old way of life among the weavers. Nevertheless, the long dawn chorus of moralists is a prelude to the quite sharp attack upon popular customs, sports, and holidays which was made in the last years of the eighteenth century and the first years of the nineteenth.

One other nonindustrial institution lay to hand which might be used to inculcate 'time-thrift': the school. Clayton complained that the streets of Manchester were full of 'idle ragged children; who are not only losing their Time, but learning habits of gaming', etc. He praised charity schools as teaching Industry, Frugality, Order and Regularity: 'the Scholars here are obliged to rise betimes and to observe Hours with great Punctuality.'[88] William Temple, when advocating, in 1770, that poor children be sent at the age of four to work-houses where they should be employed in manufactures and given two hours' schooling a day, was explicit about the socializing influence of the process:

> There is considerable use in their being, somehow or other, constantly employed at least twelve hours a day, whether they earn their living or not; for by these means, we hope that the rising generation will be so habituated to constant employment that it would at length prove agreeable and entertaining to them....[89]

Powell, in 1772, also saw education as a training in the 'habit of industry'; by the time the child reached six or seven it should become 'habituated, not to say naturalized to Labour and Fatigue'.[90] The Revd. William Turner, writing from Newcastle in 1786, recommended Raikes' schools as 'a spectacle of order and regularity', and quoted a manufacturer of hemp and flax in Gloucester as affirming that the schools had effected an extraordinary change: 'they are ... become more tractable and obedient, and less quarrelsome and revengeful.'[91] Exhortations to punctuality and regularity are written into the rules of all the early schools: 'Every scholar must be in the school-room on Sundays, at nine o'clock in the morning, and at half-past one in the afternoon, or she shall lose her place the next Sunday, and walk last.'[92] Once within the school gates, the child entered the new universe of disciplined time. At the Methodist Sunday Schools in York the teachers were fined for unpunctuality. The first rule to be learned by the scholars was: 'I am to be present at the School ... a few minutes before half-past nine o'clock. ...' Once in attendance, they were under military rule: 'The Superintendent shall again ring,—when, on a motion of his hand, the whole School rise at once from their seats;—on a second motion, the Scholars turn;—on a third, slowly and silently move to the place appointed to repeat their lessons,—he then pronounces the word "Begin". ...'[93]

The onslaught, from so many directions, upon the people's old working habits was not, of course, uncontested. In the first stage, we find simple resistance.[94] But, in the next stage, as the new time-discipline is imposed, so the workers begin to fight, not against time, but about it. The evidence here is not wholly clear. But in the better-organized artisan trades, especially in London, there is no doubt that hours were progressively shortened in the eighteenth century as combination advanced. Lipson cites the case of the London tailors whose hours were shortened in 1721, and again in 1768: on both occasions the mid-day intervals allowed for dinner and drinking were also shortened—the day was compressed.[95] By the end of the eighteenth century there is some evidence that some favoured trades had gained something like a ten-hour day.

Such a situation could only persist in exceptional trades and in a favourable labour market. A reference in a pamphlet of 1827 to 'the English system of working from 6 o'clock in the morning to 6 in the evening'[96] may be a more reliable indication as to the general expectation as to hours of the mechanic and artisan outside London in the 1820s. In the dishonourable trades and outwork industries hours (when work was available) were probably moving the other way.

It was exactly in those industries—the textile mills and the engineering workshops—where the new time-discipline was most rigorously imposed that the contest over time became most intense. At first some of the worst masters attempted to expropriate the workers of all knowledge of time. 'I worked at Mr. Braid's mill,' declared one witness:

> There we worked as long as we could see in summer time, and I could not say at what hour it was that we stopped. There was nobody but the master and the master's son who had a watch, and we did not know the time. There was one man who had a watch ... It was taken from him and given into the master's custody because he had told the men the time of day. ...[97]

A Dundee witness offers much the same evidence:

> ... in reality there were no regular hours: masters and managers did with us as they liked. The clocks at the factories were often put forward in the morning and back at night, and instead of being instruments for the measurement of time,

they were used as cloaks for cheatery and oppression. Though this was known amongst the hands, all were afraid to speak, and a workman then was afraid to carry a watch, as it was no uncommon event to dismiss any one who presumed to know too much about the science of horology.[98]

Petty devices were used to shorten the dinner hour and to lengthen the day. 'Every manufacturer wants to be a gentleman at once', said a witness before Sadler's Committee:

and they want to nip every corner that they can, so that the bell will ring to leave off when it is half a minute past time, and they will have them in about two minutes before time ... If the clock is as it used to be, the minute hand is at the weight, so that as soon as it passes the point of gravity, it drops three minutes all at once, so that it leaves them only twenty-seven minutes, instead of thirty.[99]

A strike-placard of about the same period from Todmorden put it more bluntly: 'if that piece of dirty suet, "old Robertshaw's engine-tenter", do not mind his own business, and let ours alone, we will shortly ask him how long it is since he received a gill of ale for running 10 minutes over time.'[100] The first generation of factory workers were taught by their masters the importance of time; the second generation formed their short-time committees in the ten-hour movement; the third generation struck for over-time or time-and-a-half. They had accepted the categories of their employers and learned to fight back within them. They had learned their lesson, that time is money, only too well.[101]

VI

We have seen, so far, something of the external pressures which enforced this discipline. But what of the internalization of this discipline? How far was it imposed, how far assumed? We should, perhaps, turn the problem around once again, and place it within the evolution of the Puritan ethic. One cannot claim that there was anything radically new in the preaching of industry or in the moral critique of idleness. But there is perhaps a new insistence, a firmer accent, as those moralists who had accepted this new discipline for themselves enjoined it upon the working people. Long before the pocket watch had come within the reach of the artisan, Baxter and his fellows were offering to each man his own interior moral time-piece.[102] Thus Baxter, in his *Christian Directory*, plays many variations on the theme of Redeeming the Time: 'use every minute of it as a most precious thing, and spend it wholly in the way of duty.' The imagery of time as currency is strongly marked, but Baxter would seem to have an audience of merchants and of tradesmen in his mind's eye: 'Remember how gainful the Redeeming of Time is ... in Merchandize, or any trading; in husbandry or any gaining course, we use to say of a man that hath grown rich by it, that he hath made use of his Time.'[103]

Oliver Heywood, in *Youth's Monitor* (1689), is addressing the same audience:

> Observe exchange-time, look to your markets; there are some special seasons, that will favour you in expediting your business with facility and success; there are nicks of time, in which, if your actions fall, they may set you forward apace: seasons of doing or receiving good last not always; the fair continues not all the year....[104]

The moral rhetoric passes swiftly between two poles. On the one hand, apostrophes to the brevity of the mortal span, when placed beside the certainty of Judgement. Thus Heywood's *Meetness for Heaven* (1690):

> Time lasts not, but floats away apace; but what is everlasting depends upon it. In this world we either win or lose eternal felicity. The great weight of eternity hangs on the small and brittle thread of life ... This is our working day, our market time ... O Sirs, sleep now, and awake in hell, whence there is no redemption.

Or, from *Youth's Monitor* again: time 'is too precious a commodity to be undervalued ... This is the golden chain on which hangs a massy eternity; the loss of time is unsufferable, because irrecoverable.'[105] Or from Baxter's *Directory*:

> O where are the brains of those men, and of what metal are their hardened hearts made, that can idle and play away that Time, that little Time, that only Time, which is given them for the everlasting saving of their souls?[106]

On the other hand, we have the bluntest and most mundane admonitions on the husbandry of time. Thus Baxter, in *The Poor Man's Family Book* advises: 'Let the time of your Sleep be so much only as health requireth; For precious time is not to be wasted in unnecessary sluggishness': 'quickly dress you': 'and follow your labours with constant diligence.'[107] Both traditions were extended, by way of Law's *Serious Call*, to John Wesley. The very name of 'the Methodists' emphasizes this husbandry of time. In Wesley also we have these two extremes—the jabbing at the nerve of mortality, the practical homily. It was the first (and not hell-fire terrors) which sometimes gave an hysterical edge to his sermons, and brought converts to a sudden sense of sin. He also continues the time-as-currency imagery, but less explicitly as merchant or market-time: 'See that ye walk circumspectly, says the Apostle ... redeeming the time; saving all the time you can for the best purposes; buying up every fleeting moment out of the hands of sin and Satan, out of the hands of sloth, ease, pleasure, worldly business....' Wesley who never spared himself, and until the age of eighty rose every day at 4 a.m. (he ordered that the boys at Kingswood School must do the same), published in 1786 as a tract his sermon on *The Duty and Advantage of Early Rising*: 'By *soaking* ... so long between warm sheets, the flesh is as it were parboiled, and becomes soft and flabby. The nerves, in the mean time, are quite unstrung.' This reminds us of the voice of Isaac Watts's Sluggard. Wherever Watts looked in nature, the 'busy little bee' or the sun rising at his 'proper hour', he read the same lesson for unregenerate man.[108] Alongside the Methodists, the Evangelicals took up the theme. Hannah More contributed her own imperishable lines on 'Early Rising':

> Thou silent murderer, Sloth, no more
> My mind imprison'd keep;
> Nor let me waste another hour
> With thee, thou felon Sleep.[109]

In one of her tracts, *The Two Wealthy Farmers*, she succeeds in bringing the imagery of time-as-currency into the labour-market:

When I call in my labourers on a Saturday night to pay them, it often brings to my mind the great and general day of account, when I, and you, and all of us, shall be called to our grand and awful reckoning ... When I see that one of my men has failed of the wages he should have received, because he has been idling at a fair; another has lost a day by a drinking-bout ... I cannot help saying to myself, Night is come; Saturday night is come. No repentance or diligence on the part of these poor men can now make a bad week's work good. This week is gone into eternity.[110]

Long before the time of Hannah More, however, the theme of the zealous husbandry of time had ceased to be particular to the Puritan, Wesleyan, or Evangelical traditions. It was Benjamin Franklin, who had a life-long technical interest in clocks and who numbered among his acquaintances John Whitehurst of Derby, the inventor of the 'tell-tale' clock, who gave to it its most unambiguous secular expression:

Since our Time is reduced to a Standard, and the Bullion of the Day minted out into Hours, the Industrious know how to employ every Piece of Time to a real Advantage in their different Professions: And he that is prodigal of his Hours, is, in effect, a Squanderer of Money. I remember a notable Woman, who was fully sensible of the intrinsic Value of *Time*. Her Husband was a Shoemaker, and an excellent Craftsman, but never minded how the Minutes passed. In vain did she inculcate to him, *That Time is Money*. He had too much Wit to apprehend her, and it prov'd his Ruin. When at the Alehouse among his idle Companions, if one remark'd that the Clock struck Eleven, *What is that*, says he, *among us all?* If she sent him Word by the Boy, that it had struck Twelve; *Tell her to be easy, it can never be more.* If, that it had struck One, *Bid her be comforted, for it can never be less.*[111]

The reminiscence comes directly out of London (one suspects) where Franklin worked as a printer in the 1720s—but never, he reassures us in his *Autobiography*, following the example of his fellow-workers in keeping Saint Monday. It is, in some sense, appropriate that the ideologist who provided Weber with his central text in illustration of the capitalist ethic[112] should come, not from that Old World, but from the New—the world which was to invent the time-recorder, was to pioneer time-and-motion study, and was to reach its apogee with Henry Ford.[113]

VII

In all these ways—by the division of labour; the supervision of labour; fines; bells and clocks; money incentives; preachings and schoolings; the suppression of fairs and sports—new labour habits were formed, and a new time-discipline was imposed. It sometimes took several generations (as in the Potteries), and we may doubt how far it was ever fully accomplished: irregular labour-rhythms were perpetuated (and even institutionalized) into the present century, notably in London and in the great ports.[114]

Throughout the nineteenth century the propaganda of time-thrift continued to be directed at the working people, the rhetoric becoming more debased, the apostrophes to eternity becoming more shop-soiled, the homilies more mean and banal. In early Victorian tracts and reading-matter aimed at the masses, one is choked by the quantity of the stuff. But eternity has become those never-ending accounts of pious death-beds (or sinners struck by lightning), while the homilies have become little Smilesian snippets about humble men who by early rising and diligence made good. The leisured classes began to discover the 'problem' (about which we hear a good deal today) of the leisure of the masses. A considerable proportion of manual workers (one moralist was alarmed to discover) after concluding their work were left with

several hours in the day to be spent nearly as they please. And in what manner ... is this precious time expended by those of no mental cultivation? ... We shall often see them just simply annihilating those portions of time. They will for an hour, or for hours together ... sit on a bench, or lie down on a bank or hillock ... yielded up to utter vacancy and torpor ... or collected in groups by the road side, in readiness to find in whatever passes there occasions for gross jocularity; practising some impertinence, or uttering some jeering scurrility, at the expense of persons going by....[115]

This, clearly, was worse than Bingo: nonproductivity, compounded with impertinence. In mature capitalist society all time must be consumed, marketed, put to *use*; it is offensive for the labour force merely to 'pass the time'.

But how far did this propaganda really succeed? How far are we entitled to speak of any radical restructuring of man's social nature and working habits? I have given elsewhere some reasons for supposing that this discipline was indeed internalized, and that we may see in the Methodist sects of the early nineteenth century a figuration of the psychic crisis entailed.[116] Just as the new time-sense of the merchants and gentry in the Renaissance appears to find one expression in the heightened awareness of mortality, so, one might argue, the extension of this sense to the working people during the Industrial Revolution (together with the hazard and high mortality of the time) helps to explain the obsessive emphasis upon death in sermons and tracts whose consumers were among the working-class. Or (from a positive stand-point) one may note that as the industrial revolution proceeds, wage incentives and expanding consumer drives—the palpable rewards for the productive consumption of time and the evidence of new 'predictive' attitudes to the future[117]—are evidently effective. By the 1830s and 1840s it was commonly observed that the English industrial worker was marked off from his fellow Irish worker, not by a greater capacity for hard work, but by his regularity, his methodical paying-out of energy, and perhaps also by a repression, not of enjoyments, but of the capacity to relax in the old, uninhibited ways.

There is no way in which we can quantify the time-sense of one, or of a million, workers. But it is possible to offer one check of a comparative kind. For what was said by the mercantilist moralists as to the failures of the eighteenth-century English poor to respond to incentives and disciplines is often repeated, by observers and by theorists of economic growth, of the peoples of developing countries today. Thus Mexican paeons in the early years of this century were regarded as an 'indolent and child-like people'. The Mexican mineworker had the custom of returning to his village for corn planting and harvest: 'His lack of initiative, inability to save, absences while celebrating too many holidays, willingness to work only three or four days a week if that paid for necessities, insatiable desire for alcohol—all were pointed out as proof of a natural inferiority.' He failed to respond to direct day-wage incentives, and (like the eighteenth-century English collier or tinner) responded better to contract and sub-contract systems: 'Given a contract and the assurance that he will get so much money for each ton he mines, and that it doesn't matter how long he takes doing it, or how often he sits down to contemplate life, he will work with a vigour which is remarkable.'[118] In generalization supported by another study of Mexican labour conditions, Wilbert Moore remarks: 'Work is almost always task-orientated in non-industrial societies ... and ... it may be appropriate to tie wages to tasks and not directly to time in newly developing areas.'[114]

The problem recurs in a dozen forms in the literature of 'industrialization'. For the engineer of economic growth, it may appear as the problem of absenteeism—how is the Company to deal with the unrepentant labourer on the Cameroons plantation who declares: 'How man fit work so, any day, any day, weh'e no take absen'? No be 'e go die?' ('How could a man work like that, day after day, without being absent? Would he not die?')[120]

... the whole mores of African life, make a high and sustained level of effort in a given length of working day a greater burden both physically and psychologically than in Europe.[121]

Time commitments in the Middle East or in Latin America are often treated somewhat casually by European standards; new industrial workers only gradually become accustomed to regular hours, regular attendance, and a regular pace of work; transportation schedules or the delivery of materials are not always reliable. . . .[122]

The problem may appear as one of adapting the seasonal rhythms of the countryside, with its festivals and religious holidays, to the needs of industrial production:

> The work year of the factory is necessarily in accord with the workers' demands, rather than an ideal one from the point of view of most efficient production. Several attempts by the managers to alter the work pattern have come to nil. The factory comes back to a schedule acceptable to the Cantelano.[123]

Or it may appear as it did in the early years of the Bombay cotton-mills, as one of maintaining a labour force at the cost of perpetuating inefficient methods of production—elastic time-schedules, irregular breaks and meal-times, etc. Most commonly, in countries where the link between the new factory proletariat and their relatives (and perhaps landholdings or rights to land) in the villages are much closer—and are maintained for much longer—than in the English experience, it appears as one of disciplining a labour force which is only partially and temporarily 'committed' to the industrial way of life.[124]

The evidence is plentiful, and, by the method of contrast, it reminds us how far we have become habituated to different disciplines. Mature industrial societies of all varieties are marked by time-thrift and by a clear demarcation between 'work' and 'life'.[125] But, having taken the problem so far, we may be permitted to moralize a little, in the eighteenth-century manner, ourselves. The point at issue is not that of the 'standard of living'. If the theorists of growth wish us to say so, then we may agree that the older popular culture was in many ways otiose, intellectually vacant, devoid of quickening, and plain bloody poor. Without time-discipline we could not have the insistent energies of industrial man; and whether this discipline comes in the form of Methodism, or of Stalinism, or of nationalism, it will come to the developing world.

What needs to be said is not that one way of life is better than the other, but that this is a place of the most far-reaching conflict; that the historical record is not a simple one of neutral and inevitable technological change, but is also one of exploitation and of resistance to exploitation; and that values stand to be lost as well as gained. The rapidly growing literature of the sociology of industrialization is like a landscape which has been blasted by ten years of moral drought: one must travel through many tens of thousands of words of parched a-historical abstraction between each oasis of human actuality. Too many of the Western engineers of growth appear altogether too smug as to the gifts of character-reformation which they bring in their hands to their backward brethren. The 'structuring of a labour force', Kerr and Siegel tell us:

... involves the setting of rules on times to work and not work, on method and amount of pay, on movement into and out of work and from one position to another. It involves rules pertaining to the maintenance of continuity in the work process ... the attempted minimization of individual or organised revolt, the provision of view of the world, of ideological orientations, of beliefs. . . .[126]

Wilbert Moore has even drawn up a shopping list of the 'pervasive values and normative orientations of high relevance to the goal of social development'—'these changes in attitude and belief are "necessary" if rapid economic and social development is to be achieved':

Impersonality: judgement of merit and performance, not social background or irrelevant qualities.
Specificity of relations in terms of both context and limits of interaction.
Rationality and problem-solving.
Punctuality.
Recognition of individually limited but systematically linked interdependence.
Discipline, deference to legitimate authority.
Respect for property rights. . . .

These, with 'achievement and mobility aspirations', are not, Professor Moore reassures us,

suggested as a comprehensive list of the merits of modern man ... The 'whole man' will also love his family, worship his God, and express his aesthetic capacities. But he will keep each of these other orientations 'in their place'.[127]

It need cause no surprise that such 'provision of ideological orientations' by the Baxters of the twentieth century should be welcome to the Ford Foundation. That they should so often appear in publications sponsored by UNESCO is less easily explained.

VIII

It is a problem which the peoples of the developing world must live through and grow through. One hopes that they will be wary of pat, manipulative models, which present the working masses only as an inert labour force. And there is a sense, also, within the advanced industrial countries, in which this has ceased to be a problem placed in the past. For we are now at a point where sociologists are discussing the 'problem' of leisure. And a part of the problem is: how did it come to be a problem? Puritanism, in its marriage of convenience with industrial capitalism, was the agent which converted men to new valuations of time; which taught children even in their infancy to improve each shining hour; and which saturated men's minds with the equation, time is money.[128] One recurrent form of revolt within Western industrial capitalism, whether bohemian or beatnik, has often taken the form of flouting the urgency of respectable time-values. And the interesting question arises: if Puritanism was a necessary part of the work ethos which enabled the industrialized world to break out of the poverty-stricken economies of the past, will the Puritan valuation of time begin to decompose as the pressures of poverty relax? Is it decomposing already? Will men begin to lose that restless urgency, that desire to consume time purposively, which most people carry just as they carry a watch on their wrists?

If we are to have enlarged leisure, in an automated future, the problem is not 'how are men going to be able to *consume* all these additional time-units of leisure?' but 'what will be the capacity for experience of the men who have this undirected time to live?' If we maintain a Puritan time-valuation, a commodity-valuation, then it is a question of how this time is put to *use*, or how it is exploited by the leisure industries. But if the purposive notation of time-use becomes less compulsive, then men might have to re-learn some of the arts of living lost in the industrial revolution: how to fill the interstices of their days with enriched, more leisurely, personal and social relations; how to break down once more the barriers between work and life. And hence would stem a novel dialectic in which some of the old aggressive energies and disciplines migrate to the newly-industrializing nations, while the old industrialized nations seek to rediscover modes of experience forgotten before written history begins:

... the Nuer have no expression equivalent to 'time' in our language, and they cannot, therefore, as we can, speak of time as though it were something actual, which passes, can be wasted, can be saved, and so forth. I do not think that they ever experience the same feeling of fighting against time or of having to co-ordinate activities with an abstract passage of time because their points of reference are mainly the activities themselves, which are generally of a leisurely character. Events follow a logical order, but they are not controlled by an abstract system, there being no autonomous points of reference to which activities have to conform with precision. Nuer are fortunate.[129]

Of course, no culture reappears in the same form. If men are to meet both the demands of a highly-synchronized automated industry, and of greatly enlarged areas of 'free time', they must somehow combine in a new synthesis elements of the old and of the new, finding an imagery based neither upon the seasons nor upon the market but upon human occasions. Punctuality in working hours would express respect of one's fellow-workmen. And unpurposive passing of time would be behaviour which the culture approved.

It can scarcely find approval among those who see the history of 'industrialization' in seemingly neutral but, in fact, profoundly value-loaded terms, as one of increasing rationalization in the service of economic growth. The argument is at least as old as the industrial revolution. Dickens saw the emblem of Thomas Gradgrind ('ready to weigh and measure any parcel of human nature, and tell you exactly what it comes to') as the 'deadly statistical clock' in his observatory, 'which measured every second with a beat like a rap upon a coffin-lid'. But rationalism has grown new sociological dimensions since Gradgrind's time. It was Werner Sombart who—using the same favourite image of the Clock-maker—replaced the God of mechanical materialism by the Entrepreneur: 'If modern economic rationalism is like the mechanism of the clock, someone must be there to wind it up'.[130] The universities of the West are today thronged with academic clocksmiths, anxious to patent new keys. But few have, as yet, advanced as far as Thomas Wedgwood, the son of Josiah, who designed a plan for taking the time and work-discipline of Etruria into the very workshops of the child's formative consciousness:

My aim is high—I have been endeavouring some master stroke which should anticipate a century or two upon the large-paced progress of human improvement. Almost every prior step of its advance may be traced to the influence of superior characters. Now, it is my opinion, that in the education of the greatest of these characters, not more than one hour in ten has been made to contribute to the formation of those qualities upon which this influence has depended. Let us suppose ourselves in possession of a detailed statement of the first twenty years of the life of some extraordinary genius; what a chaos of perceptions! ... How many hours, days, months have been prodigally wasted in unproductive occupations! What a host of half formed impressions & abortive conceptions blended into a mass of confusion. ...

In the best regulated mind of the present day, had not there been, & is not there some hours every day passed in reverie, thought ungoverned, undirected?[131]

Wedgwood's plan was to design a new, rigorous, rational, closeted system of education: Wordsworth was proposed as one possible superintendent. His response was to write *The Prelude*—an essay in the growth of a poet's consciousness which was, at the same time, a polemic against—

> The Guides, the Wardens of our faculties,
> And Stewards of our labour, watchful men
> And skilful in the usury of time,
> Sages, who in their prescience would controul
> All accidents, and to the very road
> Which they have fashion'd would confine us down,
> Like engines. ...[132]

For there is no such thing as economic growth which is not, at the same time, growth or change of a culture; and the growth of social consciousness, like the growth of a poet's mind, can never, in the last analysis, be planned.

BIBLIOGRAPHICAL NOTE

This essay stands by itself, and nothing published since 1968 has carried the subject much further. On the general business of inculcating new work-disciplines in the British Industrial Revolution see Sidney Pollard, *The Genesis of Modern Management* (London, 1965), especially chapter 5 and the sources cited therein. The influence of upbringing on discipline is considered in M. W. Flinn, 'Social theory and the industrial revolution', in T. Burns and S. B. Saul (edd.), *Social Theory and Economic Change* (London, 1967). Otherwise perhaps the best follow-up is the early chapters in E. P. Thompson's own notable book, *The Making of the English Working Class* (London, 1964).

NOTES

1. Lewis Mumford makes suggestive claims in *Technics and Civilization* (London, 1934), esp. pp. 12–18, 196–9: see also S. de Grazia, *Of Time, Work, and Leisure* (New York, 1962), Carlo M. Cipolla, *Clocks and Culture 1300–1700* (London, 1967), and Edward T. Hall, *The Silent Language* (New York, 1959).

2. J. le Goff, 'Au Moyen Âge: temps de l'Église et temps du marchand'. *Annales, E.S.C.* 15 (1960); and the same author's 'Le temps du travail dans le "crises" du XIVᵉ siècle: du temps médiéval au temps moderne', *Le Moyen Âge*, 69 (1963).

3. M. Drayton, 'Of his Ladies not Coming to London', *Works*, ed. J. W. Hebel (Oxford, 1932), iii. 204.

4. The change is discussed Cipolla, op. cit.; Erwin Sturzl, *Der Zeitbegriff in der Elisabethanischen Literatur* (Wiener Beitrage zur Englischen Philologie, lxix, Wien–Stuttgart, 1965); Alberto Tenenti, *Il Senso della Morte e l'amore della vita nel rinascimento* (Milan, 1957).

5. Anon. *The Clockmaker's Outcry against the Author of . . . Tristram Shandy* (London, 1760), pp. 42–3.

6. E. E. Evans-Pritchard, *The Nuer* (Oxford, 1940), pp. 100–4; M. P. Nilsson, *Primitive Time Reckoning* (Lund, 1920), pp. 32–3, 42; P. A. Sorokin and R. K. Merton, 'Social Time: a Methodological and Functional Analysis', *Amer. Jl. Sociol.* 42 (1937); A. I. Hallowell, 'Temporal Orientation in Western Civilization and in a Pre-Literate Society', *Amer. Anthrop.*, new ser. 39 (1937). Other sources for primitive time reckoning are cited in H. G. Alexander, *Time as Dimension and History* (Albuquerque, 1945), p. 26, and Beate R. Salz, 'The Human Element in Industrialization', *Econ. Devel. and Cult. Change*, 4 (1955), esp. pp. 94–114.

7. E. P. Salas, 'L'Evolution de la notion du temps et les horlogers à l'époque coloniale au Chili', *Annales E.S.C.* 21 (1966), p. 146; *Cultural Patterns and Technical Change*, ed. M. Mead (New York, UNESCO, 1953), p. 75.

8. P. Bourdieu, 'The attitude of the Algerian peasant toward time', in *Mediterranean Countrymen*, ed. J. Pitt-Rivers (Paris, 1963), pp. 55–72.

9. Cf. ibid. 179: 'Spanish Americans do not regulate their lives by the clock as Anglos do. Both rural and urban people when asked when they plan to do something, give answers like: "Right now, about two or four o'clock".'

10. J. M. Synge, *Plays, Poems, and Prose* (London, 1941), p. 257.

11. The most important event in the relation of the islands to an external economy in Synge's time was the arrival of the steamer, whose times might be greatly affected by tide and weather. See Synge, *The Aran Islands* (Dublin, 1907), pp. 115–6.

12. Public Rec. Off., W.O. 40/17. It is of interest to note other examples of the recognition that seafaring time conflicted with urban routines: the Court of Admiralty was held to be always open, 'for strangers and merchants, and seafaring men, must take the opportunity of tides and winds, and cannot, without ruin and great prejudice attend the solemnity of courts and dilatory pleadings' (see E. Vansittart Neale, *Feasts and Fasts* [London, 1845], p. 249), while in some Sabbatarian legislation an exception was made for fishermen who sighted a shoal off-shore on the Sabbath day.

13. Henri Lefebvre, *Critique de la vie quotidienne* (Paris, 1958), ii, pp. 51–6, prefers a distinction between 'cyclical time'—arising from changing seasonal occupations in agriculture—and the 'linear time' of urban, industrial organization. More suggestive is Lucien Febvre's distinction between 'Le temps vécu et le temps-mesure', *La Problème de l'incroyance au XVIe siècle* (Paris, 1947), p. 431. A somewhat schematic examination of the organization of tasks in primitive economies is in Stanley H. Udy, *Organisation of Work* (New Haven, Conn., 1959), chap. 2.

14. *Rural Economy in Yorkshire in 1641 ... Farming and Account Books of Henry Best*, ed. C. B. Robinson (Surtees Society, xxxiii, 1857), pp. 38–9.

15. G. M., *The Inrichment of the Weald of Kent* (10th edn., London, 1660), chap. 12: 'A generall computation of men, and cattel's labours: what each may do without hurt daily', pp. 112–18.

16. Wage assessments still, of course, assumed the statute dawn-to-dusk day, defined, as late as 1725, in a Lancashire assessment: 'They shall work from five in the morning till betwixt seven and eight at the night, from the midst of March to the middle of September'—and thereafter 'from the spring of day till night', with two half hours for drinking, and one hour for dinner and (in summer only) half hour for sleep: 'else, for every hour's absence to defaulk a penny': *Annals of Agriculture*, xxv (London, 1796).

17. M. K. Ashby, *Joseph Ashby of Tysoe* (Cambridge, 1961), p. 24.

18. For the early evolution of clocks, see Carlo M. Cipolla, *Clocks and Culture, passim*; A. P. Usher, *A History of Mechanical Inventions* (rev. edn., Cambridge, Mass., 1962), chap 7; Charles Singer *et al.* (edd.), *A History of Technology* (Oxford, 1956), iii, chap. 24; R. W. Symonds, *A History of English Clocks* (Harmondsworth, Middlesex, 1947), pp. 10–16, 33; E. L. Edwards, *Weight-driven Chamber Clocks of the Middle Ages and Renaissance* (Altrincham, 1965).

19. See M. Gatty, *The Book of Sun-diales* (rev. edn. London, 1900). For an example of a treatise explaining in detail how to set time-pieces by the sundial, see John Smith, *Horological Dialogues* (London, 1675). For examples of benefactions for sun-dials, see C. J. C. Beeson, *Clockmaking in Oxfordshire* (Banbury Hist. Assn., 1962), pp. 76–8; A. J. Hawkes, *The Clockmakers and Watchmakers of Wigan, 1650–1850* (Wigan, 1950), p. 27.

20. Since many early church clocks did not strike the hour, they were supplemented by a bell-ringer.

21. *Charity Commissioners Reports* (1837/8), vol. xxxii, pt. 1, p. 224; see also H. Edwards, *A Collection of Old English Customs* (London, 1842), esp. pp. 223–7; S. O. Addy, *Household Tales* (London, 1895), pp. 129–30; *County Folk-Lore, East Riding of Yorkshire*, ed. Mrs. Gutch (London, 1912), pp. 150–1, *Leicestershire and Rutland*, ed. C. J. Bilson (London, 1895), pp. 120–1; C. J. C. Beeson, op. cit., p. 36; A. Gatty, *The Bell* (London, 1848), p. 20; P. H. Ditchfield, *Old English Customs* (London, 1896), pp. 232–41.

22. H. Heaton, *The Yorkshire Woollen and Worsted Industries* (Oxford, 1965), p. 347. Wedgwood seems to have been the first to replace the horn by the bell in the Potteries: E. Meteyard, *Life of Josiah Wedgwood* (London, 1865), i. 329–30.

23. W. I. Milham, *Time and Timekeepers* (London, 1923), pp. 142–9; F. J. Britten, *Old Clocks and Watches and Their Makers* (6th edn. London, 1932), p. 543; E. Bruton, *The Longcase Clock* (London, 1964), chap. 9.

24. Milham, op. cit. 214–26; C. Clutton and G. Daniels, *Watches* (London, 1965); F. A. B. Ward, *Handbook of the Collections illustrating Time Measurement* (London, 1947), p. 29; Cipolla, op. cit., p. 139.

25. Edward Turner, 'Extracts from the Diary of Richard Stapely', *Sussex Archaeological Collections*, 2 (1899), 113.

26. See the admirable survey of the origin of the English industry in Cipolla, op. cit. 65–9.

27. As late as 1697 in London the Blacksmith's Company was contesting the monopoly of the Clockmakers (founded in 1631) on the grounds that 'it is well known that they are the originall and proper makers of clocks &c. and have full skill and know-

ledge therein ...': S. E. Atkins and W. H. Overall, *Some Account of the Worshipful Company of Clockmakers of the City of London* (London, 1881), p. 118. For a village blacksmith-clockmaker see J. A. Daniell, 'The Making of Clocks and Watches in Leicestershire and Rutland', *Transactions of Leicestershire Archaeological Society*, 27 (1951), p. 32.

28. Lists of such clockmakers are in F. J. Britten, op. cit.; John Smith, *Old Scottish Clockmakers* (Edinburgh, 1921); and I. C. Peate, *Clock and Watch Makers in Wales* (Cardiff, 1945).

29. Records of the Clockmaker's Company, London Guildhall Archives, 6026/1. See (for Harrison's chronometer) F. A. B. Ward, op. cit. 32.

30. I. C. Peate, 'John Tibbot, Clock and Watch Maker', *Montgomeryshire Collections*, xlviii, pt. 2 (Welshpool, 1944), p. 178.

31. *Commons Journals*, liii. 251. The witnesses from Lancashire and Derby gave similar testimonies: ibid. 331, 335.

32. Centres of the clock- and watch-making trade petitioning against the tax in 1798 were: London, Bristol, Coventry, Leicester, Prescot, Newcastle, Edinburgh, Liverpool, Carlisle, and Derby: *Commons Journals*, liii. 158, 167, 174, 178, 230, 232, 239, 247, 251, 316, It was claimed that 20,000 were engaged in the trade in London alone, 7,000 of these in Clerkenwell. But in Bristol only 150 to 200 were engaged. For London, see M. D. George, *London Life in the Eighteenth Century* (London, 1925), pp. 173–6; Atkins and Overall, op. cit. 269; *Morning Chronicle*, 19 Dec. 1797; *Commons Journals*, liii. 158. For Bristol, ibid. 332. For Lancashire, *Victoria County History of Lancashire* (London, 1908), ii. 366–7. The history of the eighteenth-century watch trade in Coventry appears to be unwritten.

33. The lower estimate was given by a witness before the committee on watchmaker's petitions (1798): *Commons Journals*, liii. 328—estimated annual home consumption 50,000, export 70,000. See also a similar estimate (clocks and watches) for 1813, Atkins and Overall, op. cit. 276. The higher estimate is for watch-cases marked at Goldsmiths Hall—silver cases, 185,102 in 1796, declining to 91,346 in 1816—and is in the *Report of the Select Committee on the Petitions of Watchmakers, P.P.* 1817, vi and 1818, ix, pp. 1, 12.

34. Atkins and Overall, op. cit. 302, 308—estimating (excessively?) 25,000 gold and 10,000 silver watches imported, mostly illegally, per annum; and Anon., *Observations on the Art and Trade of Clock and Watchmaking* (London, 1812), pp. 16–20.

35. M. D. George, op. cit. 70. Various means of time-telling were of course employed without clocks: the engraving of the wool-comber in *The Book of English Trades* (London, 1818), p. 438 shows him with an hour-glass on his bench; threshers measured time as the light from the door moved across the barn floor; and Cornish tinners measured it underground by candles (information from Mr. J. G. Rule).

36. I. C. Peate, 'Two Montgomeryshire Craftsmen', *Montgomeryshire Collections*, 48, pt. 1 (Welshpool, 1944), p. 5; J. A. Daniell, op. cit. 39. The average price of watches exported in 1792 was £4: *P.P.* 1818, ix, p. 1.

37. 'A loyal Song', *Morning Chronicle*, 18 Dec. 1797.

38. The exemptions in the Act (37 Geo. II, c. 108, cl. xxi, xxii and xxiv) were (*a*) for one clock or watch for any householder exempted from window and house tax (i.e. cottager), (*b*) for clocks 'made of wood, or fixed up wood, and which clocks are usually sold by the respective makers thereof at a price not exceeding the sum of 20s ...', (*c*) Servants in husbandry.

39. *Morning Chronicle*, 1 July 1797; *Craftsman*, 8 July 1797; *Parl. Hist.*, xxxiii, *passim*.

40. In the year ending 5 Apr. 1798 (three weeks after repeal) the tax had raised £2,600: *P.P.*, ciii, Accounts and papers (1797–98), xlv, 933 (2) and 933 (3).

41. *Morning Chronicle*, 26 July 1797.

42. One indication may be seen in the sluggardly collection of arrears. Taxes imposed, July 1797: receipts, year ending Jan. 1798—£300. Taxes repealed, Mar. 1798: arrears received, year ending Jan. 1799, £35,420; year ending Jan. 1800, £14,966. *P.P.*, cix, Accounts and Papers (1799–1800), li, pp. 1009 (2) and 1013 (2).

43. *Morning Chronicle*, 16 Mar. 1798; *Commons Journals*, liii. 328.

44. See petitions, cited in note 32 above; *Commons Journals*, liii. 327–33; *Morning Chronicle*, 13 Mar. 1798. Two-thirds of Coventry watch-makers were said to be unemployed: ibid., Dec. 1797.

45. *Craftsman*, 17 Mar. 1798. The one achievement of the Act was to bring into existence—in taverns and public places—the 'Act of Parliament Clock'.

46. Imported watches were quoted at a price as low as 5s. in 1813: Atkins and Overall, op. cit. 292. See also note 38 above. The price of an efficient British silver pocket watch was quoted in 1817 (*Committee on Petitions of Watchmakers, P.P.*, 1817, vi) at two to three guineas; by the 1830s an effective metal watch could be had for £1: D. Lardner, *Cabinet Cyclopaedia* (London, 1834), iii. 297.

47. Many watches must have changed hands in London's underworld: legislation in 1754 (27 Geo. II, c. 7) was directed at receivers of stolen watches. The pickpockets of course continued their trade undeterred: see, e.g. *Minutes of Select Committee to Inquire into the State of the Police of the Metropolis* (1816), p. 437—'take watches; could get rid of them as readily as anything else ... It must be a very good patent silver watch that fetched £2; a gold one £5 or £6'. Receivers of stolen watches in Glasgow are said to have sold them in quantities in country districts in Ireland (1834): see J. E. Handley, *The Irish in Scotland, 1798–1845* (Cork, 1943), p. 253.

48. 'Winchester being one of the general rendezvous for the militia volunteers, has been a scene of riot, dissipation and absurd extravagance. It is supposed that nine-tenths of the bounties paid to these men, amounting to at least £20,000 were all spent on the spot among the public houses, milliners, watch-makers, hatters, &c. In mere wantonness Bank notes were actually eaten between slices of bread and butter': *Monthly Magazine*, September, 1799.

49. Witnesses before the Select Committee of 1817 complained that inferior wares (sometimes known as 'Jew watches') were touted in country fairs and sold to the gullible at mock auctions: *P.P.*, 1817, vi, pp. 15–16.

50. Benjamin Smith, *Twenty-four Letters from Labourers in America to their Friends in England* (London, 1829), p. 48: the reference is to parts of Sussex—twenty people clubbed together (as in a Cow Club) paying 5s. each for twenty successive weeks, drawing lots each for one £5 time-piece.

51. *P.P.*, 1817, vi, pp. 19, 22.

52. [C. M. Smith], *The Working Man's Way in the World* (London, 1853), pp. 67–8.

53. W. Radcliffe, *The Origin of Power Loom Weaving* (Stockport, 1828), p. 167.

54. *Morning Chronicle*, 25 Oct. 1849. But in 1843 J. R. Porter, *The Progress of the Nation*, iii, p. 5 still saw the possession of a clock as 'the certain indication of prosperity and of personal respectability on the part of the working man'.

55. For some of the problems discussed in this and the following section, see especially Keith Thomas, 'Work and Leisure in Pre-Industrial Societies', *Past and Present*, no. 29 (Dec. 1964). Also C. Hill, 'The Uses of Sabbatarianism', in *Society and Puritanism in Pre-Revolutionary England* (London, 1964); E. S. Furniss, *The Position of the Laborer in a System of Nationalism* (Boston, Mass., 1920: repr. New York, 1965); D. C. Coleman, 'Labour in the English Economy of the Seventeenth Century', *Econ. Hist. Rev.* 2nd ser. 8 (1955–6); S. Pollard, 'Factory Discipline in the Industrial Revolution', *Econ. Hist. Rev.* 2nd ser. 16 (1963–4); T. S. Ashton, *An Economic History of England in the Eighteenth Century* (London, 1955), chap. 7; W. E. Moore, *Industrialization and Labor* (New York, 1951); and B. F. Hoselitz and W. E. Moore, *Industrialization and Society* (UNESCO, 1963).

56. MS. diaries of Cornelius Ashworth of Wheatley, in Halifax Reference Library; see also T. W. Hanson, 'The Diary of a Grandfather', *Trans. Halifax Antiquarian Society*, 1916. M. Sturge Henderson, *Three Centuries in North Oxfordshire* (Oxford, 1902), pp. 133–46, 103, quotes similar passages (weaving, pig-killing, felling wood, marketing) from the diary of a Charlbury weaver, 1784, etc., but I have been unable to trace the original. It is interesting to compare time-budgets from more primitive peasant economies, e.g. Sol Tax, *Penny Capitalism—a Guatemalan Indian Economy* (Washington, 1953), pp. 104–5; George M. Foster, *A Primitive Mexican Economy* (New

York, 1942), pp. 35–8; M. J. Herskovits, *The Economic Life of Primitve Peoples* (New York, 1940), pp. 72–9; Raymond Firth, *Malay Fishermen* (London, 1946), pp. 93–7.

57. *Divers Crab-Tree Lectures* (1639), p. 126, cited in John Brand, *Observations on Popular Antiquities* (London, 1813), i. 459–60. H. Bourne. *Antiquitates Vulgares* (Newcastle, 1725), pp. 115 f. declares that on Saturday afternoons in country places and villages 'the Labours of the Plough Ceast, and Refreshment and Ease are over all the Village'.

58. J. Houghton, *Collection of Letters* (London, 1683 edn.), p. 177, cited in Furniss, op. cit. 121.

59. T. W. Hanson, op. cit. 234.

60. J. Clayton, *Friendly Advice to the Poor* (Manchester, 1755), p. 36.

61. *Report of the Trial of Alexander Wadsworth against Peter Laurie* (London, 1811), p. 21. The complaint is particularly directed against the Saddlers.

62. *The Songs of Joseph Mather* (Sheffield, 1862), pp. 88–90. The theme appears to have been popular with ballad-makers. A Birmingham example, 'Fuddling Day, or Saint Monday' (for which I am indebted to Mr. Charles Parker) runs:

> Saint Monday brings more ills about,
> For when the money's spent,
> The children's clothes go up the spout,
> Which causes discontent;
> And when at night he staggers home,
> He knows not what to say,
> A fool is more a man than he
> Upon a fuddling day.

63. It was honoured by Mexican weavers in 1800: see Jan Bazant, 'Evolution of the textile industry of Puebla, 1544–1845', *Comparative Studies in Society and History*, 8 (1964), 65. Valuable accounts of the customs in France in the 1850s and 1860s are George Duveau, *La Vie ouvrière en France sous le Second Empire* (Paris, 1946), pp. 242–8, and P. Pierrard, *La Vie ouvrière à Lille sous le Second Empire* (Paris, 1965), pp. 165–6. Edward Young, conducting a survey of labour conditions in Europe, with the assistance of U.S. consuls, mentions the custom in France, Belgium, Prussia, Stockholm, etc., in the 1870s: E. Young, *Labour in Europe and America* (Washington, D.C., 1875), pp. 576, 661, 674, 685, &c.

64. Notably in the pits. An old Yorkshire miner informs me that in his youth it was a custom on a bright Monday morning to toss a coin in order to decide whether or not to work. I have also been told that 'Saint Monday' is still honoured (1967) in its pristine purity by a few coopers in Burton-on-Trent.

65. E. Young, op. cit. 408–9 (Report of U.S. Consul). Similarly, in some mining districts, 'Pay Monday' was recognized by the employers, and the pits were only kept open for repairs: on Monday, only 'dead work is going on', *Report of the Select Committee on the Scarcity and Dearness of Coal, P.P.*, 1873, x, QQ 177, pp. 201–7.

66. Duveau, op. cit. 247. 'A Journeyman Engineer' (T. Wright) devotes a whole chapter to 'Saint Monday' in his *Some Habits and Customs of the Working Classes* (London, 1867), esp. pp. 112–16, under the mistaken impression that the institution was 'comparatively recent', and consequent upon steam power giving rise to 'a numerous body of highly skilled and highly paid workmen'—notably engineers!

67. 'An Old Potter', *When I was a Child* (London, 1903), pp. 16, 47–9, 52–4, 57–8, 71, 74–5, 81, 185–6, 191. Mr. W. Sokol, of the University of Wisconsin, has directed my attention of many cases reported in the *Staffordshire Potteries Telegraph* in 1853–4, where the employers succeeded in fining or imprisoning workers who neglected work, often on Mondays and Tuesdays. These actions were taken on the pretext of breach of contract (the annual hiring), for which see Daphne Simon, 'Master and Servant', in *Democracy and the Labour Movement*, ed. J. Saville (London, 1954). Despite this campaign of prosecutions, the custom of keeping Saint Monday is still noted in the *Report of the Children's Employment Commission, P.P.*, 1863, xviii, pp. xxvii xxviii.

68. F. Place, *Improvement of the Working People* (1834), pp. 13–15: Brit. Mus.,

Add. MS. 27825. See also John Wade, *History of the Middle and Working Classes* (3rd edn., London, 1835), pp. 124–5.

69. See C. Hill, op. cit.

70. Clayton, op. cit. 13, claimed that 'common custom has established so many Holy-days, that few of our manufacturing work-folks are closely and regularly employed above two-third parts of their time.' See also Furniss, op. cit. 44–5, and the abstract of my paper in the *Bulletin of the Society for the Study of Labour History*, no. 9, 1964.

71. 'We have four or five little farmers ... we have a bricklayer, a carpenter, a blacksmith, and a miller, all of whom ... are in a very frequent habit of drinking the King's health ... Their employment is unequal; sometimes they are full of business, and sometimes they have none; generally they have many leisure hours, because ... the hardest part [of their work] devolves to some men whom they hire ...', 'A Farmer', describing his own village (see note 77 below), in 1798.

72. Cited in J. L. and B. Hammond, *The Village Labourer* (London, 1920), p. 13; E. P. Thompson, *The Making of the English Working Class* (London, 1963), p. 220.

73. See e.g. *Annals of Agriculture*, 26 (1796), 370 n.

74. G. Markham, *The Inrichment of the Weald of Kent* (10th edn., London, 1660), pp. 115–17.

75. Attempting to account for a deficiency in his stocks of wheat in 1617, Loder notes: 'What should be the cause herof I know not, but it was in that yeare when R. Pearce & Alce were my servants, & then in great love (as it appeared too well) whether he gave it my horses ... or how it went away, God onely knoweth.' *Robert Loder's Farm Accounts*, ed. G. E. Fussell (Camden Soc., 3rd ser. liii, 1936), pp. 59, 127.

76. For an account of an active farmer's day, see William Howitt, *Rural Life of England* (London, 1862), pp. 110–11.

77. Sir Mordaunt Martin in *Bath and West and Southern Counties Society, Letters and Papers* (Bath, 1795), vii. 109; 'A Farmer', 'Observations on Taken-Work and Labour', *Monthly Magazine*, Sept. 1798, May 1799.

78. R. Jeffries, *The Toilers of the Field* (London, 1892), pp. 84–8, 211–12.

79. Mary Collier, now a Washer-woman, at Petersfield in Hampshire, *The Woman's Labour: an Epistle to Mr. Stephen Duck; in Answer to his late Poem, called The Thresher's Labour* (London, 1739), pp. 10–11.

80. See examples below, notes 126 and 127, and the valuable critique by Andre Gunder Frank, 'Sociology of Development and Underdevelopment of Sociology', *Catalyst* (Buffalo, N.Y., Summer 1967).

81. J. Tucker, *Six Sermons* (Bristol, 1772), pp. 70–1.

82. The change is perhaps signalled at the same time in the ideology of the more enlightened employers: see A. W. Coats, 'Changing attitudes to labour in the mid-eighteenth century', *Econ. Hist. Rev.* 2nd ser. 11 (1958–9), reprinted as chap. 4 in the present work.

83. See Pollard, op. cit.; N. McKendrick, 'Josiah Wedgwood and Factory Discipline', *Hist. Journal* 4 (1961); also Thompson, op. cit. 356–74.

84. Order 103 is reproduced in full in *The Law Book of the Crowley Ironworks*, ed. M. W. Flinn (Surtees Soc., clxvii, 1957). See also Law Number 16, 'Reckonings'. Order Number 40 is in the 'Law Book', Brit. Mus., Add. MS. 34555.

85. MS. instructions, *c.* 1780, in Wedgwood MSS. (Barlaston), 26.19114.

86. 'Some regulations and rules made for this manufactory more than 30 years back', dated *c.* 1810, in Wedgwood MSS. (Keele University), 4045.5.

87. A 'tell-tale' clock is preserved at Barlaston, but these 'tell-tales' (manufactured by John Whitehurst of Derby from about 1750) served only to ensure the regular patrol and attendance of night-watchmen, etc. The first printing time-recorders were made by Bundy in the U.S.A. in 1885. F. A. B. Ward, op. cit. 49; also T. Thomson's *Annals of Philosophy*, 6 (1815), 418–19; 7 (1816), 160; Charles Babbage, *On the Economy of Machinery and Manufacturers* (London, 1835), pp. 28, 40; E. Bruton, op. cit. 95–6.

88. Clayton, loc. cit. 19, 42–3.

89. Cited in Furniss, op. cit. 114.

90. Anon. [Powell], *A View of Real Grievances* (London, 1772), p. 90.

91. W. Turner, *Sunday Schools Recommended* (Newcastle, 1786), pp. 23, 42.

92. *Rules for the Methodist School of Industry at Pocklington, for the instruction of Poor Girls in Reading, Sewing, Knitting, and Marking* (York, 1819), p. 12.

93. *Rules for the Government, Superintendence, and Teaching of the Wesleyan Methodist Sunday Schools, York* (York, 1833). See also Harold Silver, *The Concept of Popular Education* (London, 1965), pp. 32–42; David Owen, *English Philanthrophy, 1660–1960* (Cambridge, Mass., 1965), pp. 23–7.

94. The best account of the employers' problem is in S. Pollard, *The Genesis of Modern Management* (London, 1965), chap. 5, 'The Adaptation of the Labour Force'.

95. E. Lipson, *The Economic History of England* (6th edn., London, 1956), iii. 404–6. See e.g. J. L. Ferri, *Londres et les Anglais* (Paris, An xii), i. 163–4. Some of the evidence as to hours is discussed in G. Langenfelt, *The Historic Origin of the Eight Hours Day* (Stockholm, 1954).

96. *A Letter on the Present State of the Labouring Class in America,* by an intelligent Emigrant at Philadelphia (Bury, 1827).

97. Alfred [S. Kydd], *History of the Factory Movement* ... (London, 1857), i. 283, quoted in P. Mantoux, *The Industrial Revolution in the Eighteenth Century* (London, 1948), p. 427.

98. Anon: *Chapters in the Life of a Dundee Factory Boy* (Dundee, 1887), p. 10.

99. *P.P.,* 1831–32, xv, pp. 177–8. See also the example from the Factory Commission (1833) in Mantoux, op. cit. 427.

100. Placard in my possession.

101. For a discussion of the next stage, when the workers had learned 'the rules of the game', see E. J. Hobsbawm, *Labouring Men* (London, 1964), chap. 17, 'Custom, Wages and Work-load'.

102. John Preston used the image of clock-work in 1628: 'In this curious clocke-worke of religion, every pin and wheel that is amisse distempers all': *Sermons Preached before His Majestie* (London, 1630), p. 18. Cf. R. Baxter, *A Christian Directory* (London, 1673), i. 285: 'A wise and well skilled Christian should bring his matters into such order, that every ordinary duty should know his place, and all should be ... as the parts of a Clock or other Engine, which must be all conjunct, and each right placed.'

103. Ibid. i. 274–5, 277.

104. *The Whole Works of the Rev. Oliver Heywood* (Idle, 1826), v. 575.

105. Ibid. v. 286–7, 574; see also p. 562.

106. Baxter, op. cit. i. 276.

107. R. Baxter, *The Poor Man's Family Book* (6th edn., London, 1697), pp. 290–1.

108. *Poetical Works of Isaac Watts, D.D.* (Cooke's Pocket edn., London, [1802]), pp. 224, 227, 232. The theme is not new, of course: Chaucer's Parson said: 'Sleepinge longe in quiete is eek a great norice to Lecherie'.

109. H. More, *Works* (London, 1830), ii. 42. See also p. 35, 'Time'.

110. Ibid. iii. 167.

111. *Poor Richard's Almanac,* Jan. 1751, in *The Papers of Benjamin Franklin,* ed. L. W. Labaree and W. J. Bell (New Haven, Conn., 1961), iv. 86–7.

112. Max Weber, *The Protestant Ethic and the Spirit of Capitalism* (London, 1930), pp. 48–50 and *passim.*

113. Ford commenced his career repairing watches: since there was a difference between local time and standard railroad time, he made a watch, with two dials, which kept both times—an ominous beginning: H. Ford, *My Life and Work* (London, 1923), p. 24.

114. There is an abundant literature of nineteenth-century dockland which illustrates this. However, in recent years the casual labourer in the ports has ceased to be a 'casualty' of the labour market (as Mayhew saw him) and is marked by his preference for high earnings over security: see K. J. W. Alexander, 'Casual Labour and Labour Casualties', *Transactions of the Institute of Engineers and Shipbuilders in Scotland* (Glasgow, 1964). I have not touched in this paper on the new occupational time-tables introduced in industrial society—notably night-shift workers (pits, railways, etc.): see

the observations by 'Journeyman Engineer' [T. Wright], *The Great Unwashed* (London, 1868), pp. 188–200; M. A. Pollock (ed.), *Working Days* (London, 1926), pp. 17–28; Tom Nairn, *New Left Review*, no. 34 (1965), p. 38.

115. John Foster, *An Essay on the Evils of Popular Ignorance* (London, 1821), pp. 180–5.

116. Thompson, op. cit., chaps. 11 and 12.

117. See the important discussion of forecasting and predictive attitudes and their influence upon social and economic behaviour, in P. Bourdieu, op. cit.

118. Cited in M. D. Bernstein, *The Mexican Mining Industry, 1890–1950* (New York, 1964), chap 7; see also M. Mead, op. cit. 179–82.

119. W. E. Moore, *Industrialization and Labor* (Ithaca, N.Y., 1951), p. 310, and pp. 44–7, 114–22.

120. F. A. Wells and W. A. Warmington, *Studies in Industrialization: Nigeria and the Cameroons* (London, 1962), p. 128.

121. Ibid. 170. See also pp. 183, 198, 214.

122. Edwin J. Cohn, 'Social and Cultural Factors affecting the Emergence of Innovations', in *Social Aspects of Economic Development* (Economic and Social Studies Conference Board, Istanbul, 1964), pp. 105–6.

123. Manning Nash, 'The Recruitment of Wage Labor and the Development of New Skills', *Annals of the American Academy*, 305 (1956), 27–8. See also Manning Nash, 'The Reaction of a Civil-Religious Hierarchy to a Factory in Guatemala', *Human Organization*, 13 (1955), 26–8, and B. Salz, op. cit. (note 6 above), pp. 94–114.

124. W. E. Moore and A. S. Feldman (edd.) *Labor Commitment and Social Change in Developing Areas* (New York, 1960). Useful studies of adaptation and of absenteeism include W. Elkan, *An African Labour Force* (Kampala, 1956), esp. chaps. 2 and 3; and F. H. Harbison and I. A. Ibrahim, 'Some Labor Problems of Industrialization in Egypt', *Annals of the American Academy*, 305 (1956), 114–29. M. D. Morris, *The Emergence of an Industrial Labor Force in India* (Berkeley, Calif., 1965) discounts the seriousness of the problems of discipline, absenteeism, seasonal fluctuations in employment, etc., in the Bombay cotton mills in the late nineteenth century, but at many points his arguments appear to be at odds with his own evidence: see pp. 85, 97, 102; see also C. A. Myers, *Labour Problems in the Industrialization of India* (Cambridge, Mass., 1958), chap. 3, and S. D. Mehta, 'Professor Morris on Textile Labour Supply', *Indian Economic Journal*, 1, no. 3 (1954), 333–40. Professor Morris's 'The Recruitment of an Industrial Labor Force in India, with British and American Comparisons', *Comparative Studies in Society and History*, 2 (1960) flattens and misunderstands the British evidence. Useful studies of an only partially 'committed' labour force are G. V. Rimlinger, 'Autocracy and the early Russian Factory System', *Jour. Econ. Hist.*, 20 (1960) and T. V. Von Laue, 'Russian Peasants in the Factory', ibid. 21 (1961).

125. See G. Friedmann, 'Leisure and Technological Civilization', *Int. Soc. Science Jour.* 12 (1960), 509–21.

126. C. Kerr and A. Siegel, 'The Structuring of the Labor Force in Industrial Society: New Dimensions and New Questions', *Industrial and Labor Relations Review*, 2 (1955), 163.

127. E. de Vries and J. M. Echavarria (edd.), *Social Aspects of Economic Development in Latin America* (UNESCO, 1963), p. 237. See also my review of W. E. Moore, *Man, Time and Society* (New York, 1963), in *Peace News*, 26 June 1964.

128. Suggestive comments on this equation are in Lewis Mumford and S. de Grazia, cited note 1 above; Paul Diesing, *Reason in Society* (Urbana, Ill., 1962), pp. 24–8; Hans Meyerhoff, *Time in Literature* (Berkeley, Calif., 1955), pp. 106–19.

129. E. Evans-Pritchard, op. cit. 103.

130. 'Capitalism', *Encyclopaedia of the Social Sciences* (New York, 1953 edn.), iii. 205.

131. Thomas Wedgwood to William Godwin, 31 July 1797, published in David Erdman's important article, 'Coleridge, Wordsworth, and the Wedgwood Fund', *Bulletin of the New York Public Library*, 60 (1956).

132. *The Prelude* (London, 1805 edn.), book v, lines 377–83. See also draft in *Poetical Works of William Wordsworth*, ed. E. de Selincourt and Helen Darbishire (Oxford, 1959), v. 346.

4

Changing Attitudes to Labour in the Mid-Eighteenth Century*

A. W. COATS

I

In recent years there have been several valuable contributions to the study of doctrinal developments in the transition from 'mercantilist' to 'classical' economics.[1] The present article is designed to suggest the need for a substantial revision of the accepted view of the attitude to labour in the literature of British economics during this transitional era.

Edgar Furniss's excellent pioneer study of eighteenth-century labour doctrines, *The Position of the Labourer in a System of Nationalism*[2] was, in certain respects, distinctly unhistorical: for instance, in the author's condemnation of 'mercantilist' theoretical fallacies, and his inadequate treatment of the socio-economic background and the temporal evolution of attitudes to labour. In chapter 7 of his volume[3] he distinguished between three distinct conceptions of the standard of living considered appropriate to the labourers, selecting his examples from a period of some eighty-odd years in which there were substantial changes in the predominant tone of economic ideas. 'A large group of writers,' Furniss claimed, agreed with William Temple, the Wiltshire clothier, that wages should provide for current physical needs and no more, even for old age. The majority view, however, as represented by Sir Walter Harris, Josiah Tucker, and Jacob Vanderlint, was that real wages should be slightly higher in England than abroad, while a few liberal forerunners of later thought, such as Dudley North, Bishop Berkeley, and David Hume, advocated an improvement of living standards as an end in itself.

Such a classification is obviously inflexible, and Furniss seriously underestimated the importance of the last, minority viewpoint, which was receiving increasing support from the 1750s. Before the mid-century almost all British economic writers agreed that wages must be kept low, since a rise in money-wage rates would increase the cost and reduce the competitiveness of our manufactured exports. Furthermore, owing to the incorrigible idle-

* From *Economic History Review*, 2nd. ser. 11 (1958), 35–51. Reprinted by permmission of the author and the Economic History Society.

ness of most labourers, it was considered advisable to keep up the prices of provisions, so that the pressure of necessity would compel the workers to be industrious. Even in the first half of the eighteenth century, however, some writers were unwilling to give wholehearted approval to this doctrine, and their views met with increasing support from the 1750s. It was conceded that not all the workers were idle and dissolute, and that if too many of them were, it was largely the result of circumstances beyond their control. There was a greater appreciation of the hardships faced by the industrious labourer in times of high prices—a comparatively rare occurrence in the second quarter of the century[4]—and, more heretical still, it was increasingly argued that a policy of depressing wage levels in order to enforce constant and arduous toil would destroy the incentive to effort, and reduce the labouring class to despair. High wages, it was frequently asserted, would act not merely as a stimulus to effective demand, as Daniel Defoe had so insistently argued,[5] but also as a reward for skill and an inducement to further effort, so that the economy in general would benefit as well as the individual worker. Despite continued concern with the moral and economic consequences of luxury consumption, increased spending by the lower classes was not merely becoming accepted as inevitable, but was welcomed as contributing to the preservation of an equitable and stable social order, and even as an aid to the dissemination of political democracy. Adam Smith's famous proposition that 'no society can surely be flourishing or happy, of which the far greater part of the members are poor and miserable' is characteristic of the new outlook,[6] and he was not the first economist to assert that 'consumption is the sole end and purpose of all production',[7] or that 'the high price of labour ... is the very thing in which public opulence consists'.[8] Nor is it sufficient to dismiss these anticipations of later thought as the dreams of misty-eyed idealists or the aberrant ravings of cranks. Support for these views came from some of the most profound thinkers and acute observers of their day, and was consistent with a general movement of thought affecting philosophy: the influence of the Enlightenment on the growth of sympathy for the oppressed classes, religion—particularly in the decline of the Puritan conception of the shamefulness of poverty and the rise of Methodism—and literature, in the emergence of romanticism and sentimentalism. It is, therefore, worth examining this neglected aspect of economic thought in some detail, in order to indicate its development and assess its precise significance.

Within the limits of a single article it is impossible to demonstrate that a more 'sympathetic' attitude to the labourer predominated in the economic writings of the period 1750–76. Instead, attention will be concentrated upon the arguments of those favouring an improvement in the standard of living, for the complexity of the issues involved has been underestimated.[9]

II

The first[10] eighteenth-century writer to argue explicitly that a rise in real wages would stimulate an increase in the labourer's effort was Jacob Vanderlint.[11] Historians of doctrine have noted his proposal to increase the money supply with the object of stimulating the demand for agricultural products, but the significance of his desire to reduce money wages by 25 per cent and the price of necessaries by 50 per cent has been generally overlooked.[12] Like the classical economists, Vanderlint regarded human wants as virtually insatiable,[13] maintaining that 'the working people can and will do a great deal more work than they do, if they were sufficiently encouraged. For I take it for a maxim, that the people of no class will ever want industry, if they don't want encouragement.' As proof of this proposition, Vanderlint cited the occasion of 'a time of general mourning for a Prince [which] necessarily requires abundance of goods to be made in a very short time, ... and we know the weavers, dyers, taylors, etc. do at such times work almost night and day, only for the encouragement of somewhat better pay and wages, which an extraordinary demand for any goods is necessarily connected with'.[14]

It would be legitimate to follow the usual practice of modern writers, who either ignore Vanderlint's plea for increased real wages or dismiss it as an exception to the general rule, but for two singular circumstances: the appearance, in the year after the publication of Vanderlint's pamphlet, of the first part of Bishop Berkeley's *Querist*, which contained a somewhat analogous call for an improvement in the labourer's living standards; and the existence of Malachy Postlethwayt's plagiarism of the above-quoted passages from Vanderlint's text.

The *Querist*[15] embodied a comprehensive series of proposals for stimulating the underdeveloped economy of Ireland, including the suggestion that the Irish peasants would be more industrious if their wants were better supplied.[16] Berkeley not only referred to the degrading and discouraging effects of very low living standards, an idea which, according to Furniss, 'had already gained some support',[17] but added that if the labourer's wants were given priority over the luxuries and conveniences of the rich, the nation in general would benefit.[18] Berkeley's proposals for dealing with the problem of idleness included the enforcement of 'temporary servitude';[19] but his hostility towards the lazy and recalcitrant did not prevent him from adopting a sympathetic and understanding attitude towards the generality of labourers. Moreover, he was fully aware of the need to overcome the main contemporary obstacle to an increase in labour effort—the situation where, as Furniss says, the labourer 'is caught fast in the clutch of custom and rigid tradition. ... Where a rigid standard of living, embracing not much more than the necessaries of physical subsistence, obtains, any increase in wages will result in an immediate diminution in labour hours.'[20] Berkeley's solution was in accordance with that advanced by a growing number of writers in the third quarter of the century, namely, to raise the labourers' living standards and thereby create a new pattern of wants and the desire to satisfy them.

Postlethwayt, on the other hand, represents an entirely different case. It is well known that his numerous works included many passages borrowed from other writers, but his 'indebtedness' to Vanderlint seems to have passed unnoticed hitherto. This is surprising, for the above quoted extracts are reproduced in *Britain's Commercial Interest Explained and Improved* (1757), which one authority has called 'by all odds Postlethwayt's most important contribution to economic literature'.[21] Paragraphs stolen from Vanderlint cannot, of course, be accepted unquestioningly as representing Postlethwayt's own attitude to labour, and it is easy to discover passages in his works in which he advocated low wages.[22] Nevertheless, he frequently appeared as an outspoken defender of the labourer against the familiar charges of idleness and improvidence. In a famous extract quoted by Karl Marx in *Das Kapital*,[23] Postlethwayt attacked those who 'contend for the perpetual slavery of the working people of this kingdom: they forget the vulgar adage, all work and no play.'

Even though the workers refused to work six days if they could maintain themselves in five, this did not mean that necessaries should be heavily taxed.

Have not the English boasted of the ingenuity and dexterity of her working artists and manufacturers, which have hitherto given credit and reputation to British wares in general? What has this been owing to? To nothing more probably, than the relaxation of the working people in their own way ... And if they had not unbendings, we may presume they would pine away, and become enervated as well in body as marred in understanding. And what sort of workmanship could we expect from such hard-driven animals.[24]

These arguments go beyond the earlier patriotic defence of the English worker. When taken together with his borrowings from Vanderlint, his assertion of the superiority of the native artisan over his foreign rival in respect of industriousness and ingenuity, and his recognition of the key role of mechanical devices in the development of competitive efficiency[25], it is clear that Postlethwayt belongs with those later writers who advocated a rise in living standards as an incentive to effort.

David Hume's contribution to the emergence of a new attitude towards the labourer resembled his contribution to the general transition from 'mercantilist' to 'classical' economics,[26] for although he did not explicitly advocate an increase of real wages as a means of spurring the labourer to greater effort, his analysis indirectly lent considerable support to this viewpoint. The most direct reference to the problem in Hume's writings suggests that he favoured moderate taxes on necessaries as a means of stimulating the labourer's effort, since he argued that 'in years of scarcity, if it be not extreme, ... the poor labour more, and really live better, than in years of great plenty, when they indulge themselves in idleness and riot.'[27] This statement, however, was almost immediately followed by a warning that 'exorbitant taxes, like extreme necessity, destroy industry, by producing despair; and ... 'tis to be feared that taxes, all over *Europe*, are multiplying to such a degree, as will intirely crush all art and industry.'[28]

This proviso exemplified Hume's habit of adding a particular qualification to any general proposition, a practice which makes it misleading simply to characterize him as an advocate of moderate hardship as the state of affairs most conducive to the labourer's well-being.[29] Indeed, it can be argued that the main weight of Hume's case was against any attempt to restrict the expansion of the labourer's wants and the improvement of his living standards, and this argument is reinforced by an examination of his psychological theory.

When he discussed the psychological basis of economic activity,[30] as in other parts of his writings, Hume presented both sides of the question. But while he made passing reference to the influence of 'necessity, which is the great spur to industry and invention',[31] he paid more attention to the need to provide incentives to all forms of economic activity. 'It is a violent method and in most cases impracticable, to oblige the labourer to toil, in order to raise from the land more than what subsists himself and family. Furnish him with manufactures and commodities, and he will do it of himself.'[32]

Professor Rotwein has recently concluded that Hume rejected the widely held view that the best way to create a disposition towards industry was to enforce an endless repetition of toil, since he believed that human beings responded more effectively to variety and the challenge of difficulty. Whereas earlier writers 'commonly viewed indulgence in the pleasures of idleness as the fulfilment of a natural craving, Hume recognises it as symptomatic of frustration—that is as an attempt to compensate through pleasure for the want of liveliness resulting from a thwarting of the design for interesting action.'[33] Historians of economic doctrine have long recognized that one aspect of the transition from 'mercantilism' to 'classical' economics was a growing belief in the efficacy of individual freedom in economic affairs. It could be argued that insights of the kind provided by Hume's psychological theory made a significant contribution to the willingness of upper-class writers to concede that the labourer, too, might be responsive to economic incentives.[34]

Although he did not explicitly advocate raising real wages as a means of stimulating effort, Hume's sympathetic discussion of the labourer's predicament may well have influenced other writers to adopt this view. One such writer was Nathaniel Forster, whose *Enquiry into the Causes of the Present High Price of Provisions* (1767), bears unmistakeable traces of

Hume's influence.[35] Forster castigated those who contended that 'the poor will be industrious only in the degree that they are necessitous' for propounding 'a doctrine as false, as it is inhuman'[36] and warned that the deliberate imposition of artificial burdens on the labourer would, instead of stimulating them, drive him to 'desperation and madness'.[37] Of a case in Norwich, when a rise in wages followed 'upon some particular occasion of an extraordinary demand for goods' he admitted that some persons might have worked less. But this would only

be the consequence of a sudden rise of wages with a few idle worthless fellows ... the really industrious would never be less so from any extraordinary encouragement given to industry. And I cannot but think it as good a general maxim as ever was advanced, that the sure way of engaging a man to go through a work with vigour and spirit is, to ensure him a taste of the sweets of it.

When labourers appeared unresponsive to incentives, this was attributable to 'the fluctuating state of most manufactures and trades, and the consequent fluctuation of wages [so that] the masters and their workmen are unhappily in a perpetual state of war with each other.'[38]

Perhaps the most considered and thoroughgoing defence of wage increases as a means of stimulating the effort of labour to be published in the period 1750–75 came from two writers whose contributions appear to have passed almost entirely unnoticed.[39] Both asserted that wages had not kept pace with rising prices and taxes, and complained that insult had been added to this injurious state of affairs, for 'those unhappy, distressed, oppressed and useful people have become the objects of abuse throughout the kingdom'.[40] Neither author was blind to the weaknesses of the labouring classes; both admitted the charge of intemperance, but they strongly attacked the government's attempt to profit from this weakness. Mortimer wanted to reduce the number and hours of opening of taverns, while his anonymous predecessor protested that the Walpole administration had encouraged 'dissipation and even intemperance ... for the sake of raising taxes ... making, moreover, their indulgence in vice the means of impelling them to excessive labour.'[41] Both writers cited and enlarged upon Hume's treatment of the labour problem, drawing the conclusions implied but not explicitly stated in Hume's analysis. The author of the *Considerations on the Policy* accepted the view of Petty and Sir William Temple that some degree of necessity was 'requisite to create a spirit of industry', but after quoting Hume's warning of the dangers of attempting to oppress the labouring classes he added that Hume 'might have looked to his own country for proof, that mere necessity will not always do ... what may be effected by encouragement'. It was the opportunity for gain provided by the Union with England, not the pressure of necessity, that had aroused Scottish manufactures and trade from their former lethargy, making the people responsive to economic incentives. In words strongly reminiscent of Hume's *Essays* he concluded that 'it is ...

more a turn of mind than multiplied necessities that induces men to become industrious, which will be better excited by encouragement than compulsion.'[42]

In his *Elements of Commerce*, Thomas Mortimer carefully reviewed the various proposals advanced by earlier writers who had considered the labour problem, before firmly supporting those who favoured raising real wages as the best method of encouraging industry. Mortimer denied that the enforcement of labour would ensure an improved quality of work. When a labourer is

> oppressed by the combined plagues of dearness of provisions, incessant labour and low wages, ... indifference will take place of emulation, and thus the main springs of industry will be destroyed ... he will carry his industry no further, than to procure [his family] temporary and partial relief; and out of the little he earns by constant labour, he will retain a reserve, to purchase the cup of oblivion, to enable him to forget, for a few hours occasionally, the galling yoke of double bondage, to a hard hearted, mercenary master, and a numerous, distressed family.
>
> Can it be expected, that the labour or industry of a person so situated, will be equal to that of him, who is generously paid, in a degree proportioned to the advantages derived from his ingenuity, close application, or hard bodily labour; ... In the one case, you must be satisfied with the common drudgery of an enervated slave; in the other, you may expect new efforts of ingenuity, extraordinary exertions of abilities, and every good effect of a mind at peace, and a body in the vigour of health ...
>
> Will any man, after this, pretend to say, that manufactures can be perfect, (the only way for them to prosper), where provisions are high, and labour low; by which all encouragement is taken away from the poor fabricator?[43]

As Mortimer's bulky volume was designed as an instruction manual for 'young gentlemen of fortune' who were to take up commerce as their profession, he proceeded to enunciate the general principles to be derived from his discussion. These were that wages should be proportioned to the price of provisions; that they should be high enough to encourage marriages, give the worker a prospect of self-improvement, and a surplus for occasional ease and plenty; that wages duly proportioned to the profits of the work would guarantee speedy and careful performance, and would discourage idleness and vice unless these were general throughout society or encouraged by the government; and that wages should never be paid in an alehouse.[44] Taken together, these principles virtually amounted to a code of 'fair labour practices' that was far removed from the prevalent tone of the writings dealing with the labourer in the first half of the century.

The writers quoted above constitute but a small sample of those who, in the period under review, defended the labouring poor against the charges of idleness and dissipation and protested against the enforced hardships caused by rising prices. By the late 1760s the literature on this subject had attained considerable proportions, and it was no longer true, as Furniss has asserted, that 'even the most compassionate was inclined toward the opinion that life had been too easy for the working-man; that discipline had been un-wisely relaxed, and that [the labourer's] character had suffered from an absence of a necessity for his industry.'[45] Much of this literature lacks inter-est beyond the confines of the immediate problem of rising prices; some of the pamphlets published were positively puerile, and others represented partisan efforts to lay the blame on the luxury of the rich, the government's debt policy, the engrossing of farms, the middlemen, or the corn bounty.[46] Partisanship, however, does not invalidate these writings as evidence of a change in the contemporary attitude towards the labourer's difficulties, and while many authors still supported the doctrine of the utility of poverty, there was some justification for Mortimer's claim that 'the advocate of the poor has one advantage on his side, he cannot be suspected of selfish views',[47] at least when he was not himself a member of the labouring class.

To say that the post-1750 writings demonstrated an increasingly sympa-thetic attitude towards the poor is, however, vague, for this 'sympathy' in-cluded a variety of views expressed with widely differing degrees of analytical subtlety. Some writers who expressed concern at the prevalence of 'hard times' made no reference whatsoever to wage levels, while others would clearly have opposed any scheme to raise wages for fear of damaging the export trade.[48] Not all those who recognized that low wages operated as a deterrent to effort favoured raising real or money wages as an incentive.[49] But whether they contributed systematic treatises or ephemeral pamphlets, many contemporary authors were, consciously or unconsciously, groping their way towards the concept of an optimum wage level—one which would reconcile the interests of the agricultural producers, the exporters of manu-factures, and the wage-earners themselves. The interests of the latter were considered not merely for humanitarian reasons, but also because it was becoming evident to all but the most prejudiced observers that the policy of allowing the wage-earner to be squeezed by rising prices had serious draw-backs, and that its continuance might lead to large-scale emigration or social disturbances.[50]

Needless to say, these attempts to define the 'optimal' level of wages met with little success, often merely amounting to a re-statement of the problem in different terms;[51] and the repeated assertion that wages should be 'propor-tioned to the price of provisions' was of little help until an effort was made to define the absolute level at which this proportionality was to be secured. On this matter there were clear differences of opinion,[52] partly because of the difficulty of allowing for regional and occupational variations, and partly because of the different criteria in terms of which the optimum was to be defined. The agriculturalists, for example, insisted that the prices of pro-visions should not be unduly depressed, and in this group Arthur Young occupied a leading role, not only because of the volume and influence of his writings, but also because of his strenuous efforts to measure the optimum level of wages.[53] Young reproduced page after page of data on family budgets, wages, and prices in different areas, and while it would be foolish to expect perfect consistency from one who wrote so extensively in defence of a sectional interest his arguments may be summarized in the following propositions:

(i) Existing variations in prices and wages conclusively proved that the price of provisions did not determine the price of labour.

(ii) Therefore, a guarantee of 'reasonable' prices to the farmer did not necessarily entail a high level of money wages.

(iii) Owing to the labourer's inherent idleness, high prices were necessary to ensure unremitting effort.

(iv) But as the cost of manufactures was determined by the quality and quantity of work performed as well as the wage rate, it was 'impossible, therefore, to assert, that our manufacturers are undersold, *because* of their high price of labour'.[54]

The second and third propositions presumably require no amplification; the underlying reasoning is obvious. The first and fourth propositions, however, are of considerable interest, both in relation to Young's own position, and to the general contemporary view of the role of labour in an expanding economy. Young was bound to reject the subsistence theory of wages (proposition i): it was incompatible with his desire for high food-prices[55] and low wages, and he undoubtedly considered that his statistical evidence afforded overwhelming support for his case. Yet he did not deny that food prices and wage rates often moved together,[56] and he appeared to be advocating proportionality between prices and wages at a high absolute level. Young is usually regarded as an advocate of low wages,[57] but there are passages in his tours indicating that he recognized the advantages of rising wages under certain circumstances;[58] and although it would be misleading to suggest that he believed in the existence of a casual relationship between high wages and industriousness, it is significant that in his *Political Arithmetic* (1774), the volume which purported to demonstrate the 'first principles' distilled from the information collected on his tours, he categorically stated that dear labour, plentiful employment, rising living standards, and increasing population were the inevitable concomitants of prosperity.[59]

The argument in Young's *Political Arithmetic* does not justify his inclusion as a supporter of high wages as an incentive to effort—in view of his inconsistencies his support would in any case be of doubtful value. But when taken in conjunction with his admission that high wages did not necessarily entail high labour costs (proposition iv)—a distinction drawn by several writers in the period[60]—it is clear that Young had moved some way from the early eighteenth-century view that low wages were essential to national prosperity towards the high-wage doctrine of the *Wealth of Nations*.[61]

Apart from a few isolated advocates of a 'high wage economy',[62] most British economists before 1750 regarded low wages as an essential precondition of the maintenance of a high volume of exports, although the plea that the British workman should enjoy a higher standard of living than that of his continental counterpart[63] represented a tacit admission that successful competition in foreign markets did not require that home wage levels should be equal to or lower than foreign wage levels. By contrast, in the third quarter of the century there was growing support for the view that high wages and rising living standards were not merely compatible with, but were even a necessary concomitant of the prosperity of our domestic and exported manufactures. An attempt will now be made to suggest some of the reasons for this change.

From the analytical viewpoint, incomparably the most significant reason why economic writers after 1750 were less concerned than their predecessors with the high level of British wages was the growing appreciation that high money wages did not necessarily mean high labour costs. The distinction between the productivity and the money cost of labour appears to have been generally overlooked in the earlier period; but after 1750 half a dozen writers explicitly referred to it,[64] some of them including it as an essential part of a systematic body of reasoning, while the distinction was implicit in the works of numerous other authors. Surprisingly enough, those who advocated raising living standards as an incentive to effort did not explicitly state that this inducement would, if a significant increase in productivity occurred, lead to a reduction of effective labour costs per unit of output, although this was an obvious corollary of their general reasoning. Nevertheless, increasing attention was being paid to the kill,[65] quality, and quantity of the labour performed by the English artisan, as well as to the level of money wages. It is no coincidence, though it is difficult to decide whether this was a cause or a consequence of the growing 'sympathy' towards the labourer, that favourable comparisons were being made between the British worker and his continental rivals—even the Dutch, who had so frequently been held up as a model of industry and frugality by the late seventeenth- and early eighteenth-century writers.[66] If, as some were prepared to maintain, the English workman was superior to foreign workers, his higher money wages and living standards might be viewed not simply as a just recompense for his superiority, but even as a guarantee of the preservation of this differential. This is surely one reason for the widespread acknowledgement that low wages could act as a disincentive, and the increasing acceptance of the desirability of a 'high-wage economy'.

Another reason for the diminished concern over our high wage level was the growing importance attached to mechanical devices. It has recently been argued that in seventeenth-century England the possibilities of increasing output by the introduction of improved techniques were very limited, a state of affairs which helps to account for the importance attached to quantitative increases in the labour supply.[67] By the 1750s however, a much wider range of mechanical appliances had become available, and the writers of this period demonstrated a correspondingly enhanced interest in the effects of labour-saving innovations. In discussing this topic they were primarily concerned with the employment effects of such devices, and some insisted that if the net effect of an innovation were a reduction of total employment it should not be adopted.[68] The majority view, however, was optimistic, and several writers attached crucial importance to labour-saving innovations as a means of reducing production costs in both agriculture and manufacturing, and thereby increasing employment and sales, both at home and abroad.[69] Of course machinery was not advocated because it would facilitate the payment of higher wages. But the growing awareness of the efficacy of mechanical aids undoubtedly reinforced the arguments of those who feared that falling real wages would have harmful effects on the labour force, while the increasing importance of capital outlays may have tended to reduce the former emphasis on wage reductions as the principal method of reducing total costs.

IV

The change in the attitude to labour in the mid-eighteenth century was not confined to such matters as wages, incentives, and mechanical aids, but formed part of a generalized conception of the labourer's role in the process of economic and social development, and an attempt will now be made to place the foregoing discussion in its wider setting. An approach to this broader view may be made via a brief examination of the attitude to luxury consumption in the period 1750–75.

Mandeville's *Fable of the Bees*[70] had already enforced a shocked reappraisal of the economic consequences of luxury in the 1720s and 30s, and the growing impact of the 'doctrine of beneficial luxury' can be traced up to Hume's 'synthesis' of the theory in the mid-century.[71] The earlier belief in the 'utility of poverty' was obviously incompatible with support for any substantial increase in the labourer's consumption, but it did not necessarily follow that the later writers who advocated raising real wages as an incentive to effort supported luxurious consumption by the labourer.[72] Moreover, it is doubtful whether there was any favourable trend in the post-1750 attitude towards luxury on the part of the public in general: indeed, there were bitter complaints of current excesses, perhaps the most famous being John Brown's

Estimate of the Manners and Principles of the Times (1757), which went through six editions in six months.

Like other social critics of the day, Brown blamed the upper classes for the prevalent luxury, which brought no benefit to the poor, whose money wages rose in accordance with the prices of provisions only after they had been driven by 'the last necessity and want' to commit public disturbances.[73] Many of Brown's contemporaries regarded luxury as a leading cause of present discontents and drew gloomy parallels between eighteenth-century England and the periods immediately preceding the decay of ancient empires. There were numerous references to the dangers of a growing concentration of national wealth, and to the economic, social, and political instability of a country where a great gap existed between rich and poor. Concern at this prospect inspired various egalitarian proposals, and appeals for more equal distribution of wealth[74] or a wider diffusion of property[75] became frequent enough to constitute a characteristic feature of contemporary literature, although some authors cautiously observed that their schemes for ameliorating the condition of the lower orders would not disrupt the social hierarchy.[76] In this context the customary praise of the merchant assumed a sociological significance in addition to its familiar economic connotation. Many writers valued the contribution of 'middling people' to the preservation of 'a gradual and easy transition from rank to rank'[77] and such references assumed a kind of self-congratulatory patriotism after Montesquieu's eulogy of the English constitution.

Among the economic writers, however, a more qualified approach to luxury consumption was winning acceptance, partly through the influence of David Hume,[78] and many admitted that an increased availability of the comforts and conveniences as well as the necessities of life could operate as a powerful stimulus to industry by all ranks of society. Few persons argued that the workers should consume large quantities of the superfluities of life; but as the difficulty of defining the term luxury was acknowledged, it is reasonable to include those who favoured raising real wages as an incentive to effort among the supporters of the view that the workers should be allowed to benefit from the growing output of consumer's goods.[79] Some writers maintained that luxury consumption was an inevitable and harmless or even desirable consequence of economic progress, but the majority recognized that it might easily extend beyond the point at which it operated as a stimulus to industry. Accordingly they proposed that the government should act to prevent any excess, even though this was 'a matter of great delicacy, and requires a nice judgment'.[80]

The influence of luxury and the role of the labourer were often examined in conjunction with one another in contemporary efforts to define the conditions most conducive to a continuously high rate of economic progress. It was widely believed that Britain afforded just the right balance between the extremes of plenty and hardship and thus provided the challenge of 'difficulty' needed to stimulate the response of energy, industry and innovation (Hume's 'quick march of the spirits').[81] But although the process of development was well under way, there were many pitfalls in the path to prosperity—such as the emergence of a luxurious leisured class, a rapidly rising price level, a burdensome level of debts and taxes, and the pressure of rising living costs on the labouring classes—and appropriate policies were required to counteract these dangers.

Different writers naturally visualized the process in widely different terms, and Brown's theory of 'stages' of development was only one of the more crude attempts to develop the widespread notion that the current prosperity presaged eventual economic and social decay, an idea fostered by the popularity of classical analogies in contemporary historiography. The most sophisticated theory of economic development was that presented by Sir James Steuart, in his *Inquiry into the Principles of Political Economy* (1767).[82] In the primitive stage, according to Steuart, luxury played an initiating role, for the growth of new wants stimulated increased effort and output, and improved consumption standards for all ranks of society constituted an essential condition of progress. But in the intermediate or 'mature' stage, rising population, food-prices, and wages undermined the export trade, and attempts to restrict luxury and to reduce production costs, either by utilizing mechanical devices or by stimulating the workers' effort and ingenuity, could not indefinitely postpone the day when home products were undersold by goods from less advanced countries. Consequently, in the final stage, self-sufficiency should be the object of policy, with an expanding consumption of domestic luxuries to offset the decline in export sales. Thus, despite his emphasis on rising living standards as the initial impulse to economic expansion, Steuart regarded a high wage level as the factor ultimately setting limits to this process.

In this respect Steuart agreed with Hume, who, before his conversion by Josiah Tucker, had contended that a rich country would eventually be unable to withstand the competition of a poor country, because the former would experience a rise in prices and costs resulting from a favourable balance of trade and an inflow of specie.[83] Tucker successfully controverted this view, insisting that the rich country could preserve its superiority over the poorer nation owing to its greater efficiency and its possession of great capital, extensive correspondence, skilful expedients of facilitating labour, dexterity, industry etc.'[84] With respect to the position of the labourer, Tucker claimed that 'the higher wages of the rich country, and the greater scope and encouragement given for the exertion of genius, industry, and ambition, will naturally determine a great many men of spirit and enterprise to forsake their own poor country, and settle in the richer',[85] so that there was no necessary reason why high wages should act as an obstacle to continuous economic expansion. Elsewhere in his writings Tucker advocated wage reductions and appeared as a bitter critic of the idleness and immorality of the English worker;[86] but in his discussion with Hume he indirectly lent powerful theoretical support to the arguments of those who viewed high wages and rising living standards for the labourer as a necessary and desirable feature of economic development. In this respect, perhaps unwittingly, his theory represented the closest approximation to that of Adam Smith, who regarded a high level of wages and a rapid growth of national wealth as inevitably associated.[87]

POSTSCRIPT

Richard C. Wiles attempts to show that what I, and other scholars, regarded as 'typical post-1750' was 'actually common earlier in the period of later English mercantilism'.[88] He presented the views of a number of authors who regarded high wages as (i) 'a bell-wether of economic prosperity'; (ii) conducive to growth in consumption and a resultant "brisk circulation" '; or (iii) 'not inconsistent with low and competitive prices'. He therefore concluded that support for 'a higher wage level' was 'a widespread view—or at least one that was under rather intense discussion': that 'the belief in the desirability of a low and competitive wage level for expanding exports does not seem to fit the last decade of the seventeenth and first half of the eighteenth century as well it would the English economic thought of fifty or one hundred years earlier'; and consequently that 'the rise of more "liberal" mercantilist views upon labour and wages after 1750 is, in reality, a consolidation of opinions and concepts that were already accepted by many authors in the period under discussion'.[89]

These are substantial claims, and in the present context it is obviously impossible either to do justice to Professor Wiles's paper or to defend my own, if indeed such defence is required. The interpretation of 'mercantilist' economic ideas is a subtle and delicate task. Textual exegesis is a time- and space-consuming undertaking; in the absence of acceptable methods of quantification there can be legitimate disagreements as to what is 'typical' or 'representative'; and even more important, and more generally neglected, is the almost irresistible temptation to read modern analytical subtleties into the emphemeral, unsophisticated, and sometimes flatly inconsistent economic writings of yesteryear. While the twentieth-century commentator cannot be expected to jettison his inherited intellectual equipment, he may to some extent need to become a primitive in order fully to understand the primitives.[90]

Given these circumstances it will be fairer to Professor Wiles if I merely state that, while not fully accepting his conclusions, I welcome his effort to draw attention to earlier high wage advocates, most of whom were mentioned either in my article or in the works of the other commentators cited therein.

Professor Wiles rightly emphasized the statements in category (iii) above, for I understated the importance of cost-saving and labour-saving innovations in pre-1750 writings. I was mainly concerned with labour incentives, labour effort, and the standard of living, and while explicitly dismissing the high versus low wage issue as 'a serious oversimplification', I emphasized the broader aspects of contemporary attitudes to labour.[91] Whether Professor Wiles's citations add up to a 'theory' of wages which forms part of 'an entire body of doctrine' that characterizes 'later mercantilism',[92] is another matter.

A. W. COATS

BIBLIOGRAPHICAL NOTE

Apart from a stimulating examination by Jacob Viner of 'Man's economic status' in James L. Clifford (ed.), *Man versus Society in 18th-century Britain* (Cambridge, 1968), the most significant addition to the literature in this field is Richard C. Wiles, 'The theory of wages in later English Mercantilism', *Econ. Hist. Rev.*, 2nd ser. 21 (1968). This article offered a direct criticism of certain points in the essay reprinted here, and Professor Coats has written a brief comment on these criticisms in the Postscript printed above.

NOTES

1. See, for example, the works by Grampp, Hutchinson, Low, and Rotwein referred to below.
2. New York, 1920.
3. Especially pp. 178 ff.
4. For a recent discussion of this period see G. E. Mingay, 'The Agricultural Depression, 1730–50', *Econ. Hist. Rev.* 8, no. 3 (1956), 323–38.
5. Cf. his *Complete English Tradesman*, i (1726), 386–7, ii (1732), pt. 1, 138–9, 144–5, and *A Plan of the English Commerce* (1730), pp. 20, 102–3.
6. *Wealth of Nations* (Everyman Ed.), i. 70. Cf. N. Forster, *An Enquiry into the Causes of the Present High Price of Provisions* (1767), pp. 62–3, and M. Postlethwayt, *Britain's Commercial Interest Explained and Improved* (1757), ii. 367.
7. Smith, op. cit. ii. 155. Cf. J. Vanderlint, *Money Answers All Things* (1734), pp. 67, 120, 140.
8. Smith, op. cit. ii. 155. Cf. Forster, op. cit. 62–3.
9. To regard the issue merely as a dispute between the advocates of high or low wages, as is implied in Miss Gilboy's otherwise valuable discussion of luxury consumption and incentives, *Wages in Eighteenth-Century England* (Cambridge, Mass., 1934), chap. 9, is a serious oversimplification.
10. Although Defoe acknowledged that high wages were accompanied by increased labour effort and skill (e.g. *Plan*, op. cit., pp. 32 ff.) he regarded high wages as a consequence of trade expansion rather than a means of raising labour productivity. Defoe was, of course, no slave to consistency. He denied the possibility of raising the living standards of the lowest paid workers (ibid. 232), while the whole tone of this work and his *Complete English Tradesman* directly conflicted with the hostility to the labourers expressed in *Giving Alms No Charity* (1704), and *The Behaviour of Servants* (1724). His later views may conceivably reflect his experiences on his tours, e.g. the famous case of Halifax: *Tour* (Everyman edn.), ii. 193–5. In this respect his inconsistencies resemble those of a later traveller, Arthur Young, see above pp. 85–87.

11. A timber merchant of Dutch extraction, Vanderlint appears to have written only one tract, *Money Answers All Things* (London, 1734). For the few known biographical details see the *Dictionary of National Biography*, xx. 102.

12. Vanderlint, op. cit. 86. Although Furniss admitted that Vanderlint's advocacy of high wages represented a fundamental break with the 'doctrine of the social utility of hard times' (op. cit. 127), he nevertheless omitted Vanderlint's name from the list of those who sought to improve the labourer's lot (ibid. 185), apparently because Vanderlint regarded wages as normally 'settled and constituted of the price of victuals and drink' (*Money Answers All Things*, pp. 6, 43, 140).

13. Ibid. 82: 'The wants of mankind are full as great, as both their abilities, and the earth too, are capable of supplying; whence it follows, that any want of employment or trade amongst the people is solely owing to this, that we have not land enough in use to employ and support them.'

14. Ibid. 122. This example was repeated by Postlethwayt (above p. 81). It is of incidental interest to note that an Act of 1768, raising statutory wage levels, included an allowance for abnormally high wages at a time of general mourning. See D. George, *London Life in the Eighteenth Century* (London, 1925), p. 206.

15. George Berkeley's, *The Querist*, was published in Dublin and London in 1735–7, in three parts, and reprinted several times in the 1750s, cf. *The Works of George Berkeley, Bishop of Cloyne*, ed. A. A. Luce and T. E. Jessop (London, 1953), vi. 89–93. All subsequent references are to this edition.

There is no evidence of any connection between Berkeley and Vanderlint. The latter's tract was partly inspired by the consequences of 'the extraordinary rise of victuals a few years ago' (op. cit. 1), probably referring to 1728–9. For a penetrating analysis of Berkeley's views see T. W. Hutchison's article 'Berkeley's *Querist* and its Place in the Economic Thought of the Eighteenth Century', *The British Journal for the Philosophy of Science*, 4, no. 3 (1953), 52–77. The present writer is grateful to Professor Hutchison for many helpful comments and suggestions in connection with this study.

16. *The Querist*, Query no. 20: 'Whether the creating of wants be not the likeliest way to produce industry in a people? And whether, if our peasants were accustomed to eat beef and wear shoes, they would not be more industrious?' Cf. no. 350: 'Whether the way to make men industrious be not to let them taste the fruits of their industry?'

17. Furniss, op. cit., 127. Cf. *Querist*, no. 61: 'Whether nastiness and beggary do not, on the contrary, extinguish all such ambition, making men listless, hopeless, and slothful?'

18. Ibid. no. 168. Cf. no. 59: 'Whether to provide plentifully for the poor be not feeding the root, the substance whereof will shoot upwards into the branches, and cause the top to flourish?'

19. Ibid. nos. 382 and 384.

20. Furniss, op. cit. 234–5. Characteristically, he attributes this situation to the 'rigid policies of nationalism' and the absence of any 'prospect of rising in the social scale', rather than to contemporary economic conditions. See also T. W. Hutchison's illuminating comments, op. cit. 55–8.

21. Professor E. A. J. Johnson, *Predecessors of Adam Smith* (New York, 1937), p. 196. The above-quoted passages from Vanderlint, p. 122, appear in *Britain's Commercial Interest*, i. 43–4. In fact p. 1 of Postlethwayt's 'systematically' constructed treatise is almost entirely drawn from Vanderlint, much of it consisting of word-for-word copying—an instructive commentary on Postlethwayt's method of 'integration' (Johnson, op. cit. 205).

22. Such inconsistencies are hardly surprising in a man who, like Defoe (above, note 10) and Arthur Young (below, notes 53–61) wrote prolifically. In Postlethwayt's case it would be somewhat easier to reconcile these discrepancies, for he usually advocated constant or rising real wages, but reduced money wages—as he believed that a low-wage economy could always undersell a high-wage economy (cf. *Great Britain's True System* (1757), p. 158).

23. Karl Marx, *Capital* (Everyman edn., 1930) i. 279.

24. From the Preliminary Discourse to his *Universal Dictionary* (4th edn., written

1766, published 1774), p. xiv. For a similar argument expressed from a more hostile viewpoint see Anon., *Remarks upon the Serious Dissuasive from an intended Subscription for Continuing the Races* (1733) quoted in A. P. Wadsworth and J. de L. Mann, *The Cotton Trade and Industrial Lancashire 1600–1780* (Manchester, 1931), p. 392 n.

25. Below, note 69.

26. Johnson, op. cit., p. 163, remarks that Hume 'expressed ideas which *when further developed* brought about the disintegration of the whole body of ideas which ... [he] was presenting.' (Italics in original.)

27. David Hume, *Writings on Economics*, ed. Rotwein (London, 1955), p. 85 n. In the next sentence Hume cited 'the year 1740, when bread and provisions of all kinds were very dear' as an example. This supports the interpretation that Hume was mainly concerned here with the effects of *short-term* fluctuations in the harvests, whereas his general discussion of the progress of commerce and 'refinement in the arts' suggests that he favoured *long-term* improvements in the labourer's living standards. Ibid. 21–3. For other attempts to distinguish between the long-run and the short-run below, note 38.

28. Ibid. 85 n. (Italics in original.) This entire footnote last appeared, during Hume's lifetime, in the 1768 edition of his essays. Did its subsequent deletion reflect a change in Hume's views, possibly under the influence of contemporary protests against the depressing effects of rising prices on living standards?

29. Furniss, op. cit. 122–3.

30. On this subject I am indebted to Professor Rotwein's analysis in the introduction to his new edition of Hume's economic writings, op. cit., pp. xxxii–liii. He effectively refutes Schumpeter's dogmatic assertion, *History of Economic Analysis* (New York, 1954) p. 447, n. 4, that Hume's 'economics has nothing whatsoever to do with either his psychology or his philosophy'.

31. Op. cit. 17–18.

32. Ibid. 12; cf. p. 146: 'The most natural way, surely, of encouraging husbandry, is, first, to excite other kinds of industry, and thereby afford the labourer a ready market for his commodities, and a return of such goods as may contribute to his pleasure and enjoyment. This method is infallible and universal ...' Also p. 15.

33. Ibid. p. xlix. Cf. Adam Smith, *Lectures on Justice Police Revenue and Arms, 1763* (ed. Cannan, Oxford 1896), p. 179: 'Man is an anxious animal, and must have his care swept off by something that can exhilarate the spirits.' For a remarkable confirmation of Hume's insight see the extracts from Francis Place, *Improvement of the Working People* (1834), p. 15 (quoted by D. George, op. cit. 208–9). Admittedly Place was referring to the late eighteenth century, but this state of affairs was doubtless also true of the mid-century.

34. Many subsequent writers quoted Hume's views on the worker's psychology or employed similar terminology, e.g. J. Massie, *A Plan for the Establishment of Charity Houses* (1758), p. 50; and above, p. 84. This change of attitude was not, however, solely the product of a new theory; it was intimately bound up with contemporary socio-economic changes. Limitations of space preclude a discussion of this topic here.

35. Despite its title, Forster's treatise was no mere broadside fired off in haste, but an extensive and detached analysis of a wide range of economic problems. He explicitly quoted Hume on credit (p. 32), taxes (p. 50) and trade (pp. 127–8, 197), and his whole treatment of luxury (pp. 40–8) and the labour problem (pp. 55–63, under the heading 'Of Taxes') was highly reminiscent of Hume, though he denied that the poor lived better in dear than in cheap years. In many respects Forster's position represented a half-way stage between Hume and Adam Smith. Like them, and other defenders of the poor, Forster quoted extensively from such writers as Mirabeau, Montesquieu and Rousseau, and it would be interesting to trace the French contribution to the discussion.

36. Forster, op. cit. 55.

37. Ibid. 58.

38. Ibid. 60–1. Forster's distinction between the beneficial effects of a stimulus to

incentives in conditions of relative stability and the undesirable repercussions of 'sudden' increases in wages was a significant anticipation of the classical view, as embodied in J. R. McCulloch, *Essay on ... the Condition of the Labouring Classes* (1826), pp. 155, 158. McCulloch argued that although rising real wages and living standards usually led to an improvement in the worker's habits and productivity, a 'sudden and transitory' increase of wages might be followed by a growth of absenteeism, idleness and dissipation. For similar views see Sir W. Harris, *Remarks on the Affairs and Trade of England and Ireland* (1691), p. 53; R. Wallace, *A Dissertation on the Numbers of Mankind* (1753), pp. 151–2; and Kames, *Sketches in the History of Man* (1788 edn.), ii. 393.

39. Anon., *Considerations on the Policy, Commerce, and Circumstances of the Kingdom* (1771), and Thomas Mortimer, *The Elements of Commerce, Politics and Finances* (1772).

40. Anon., *Considerations on the Policy*, p. 44. Also p. 196.

41. Ibid. 57–8.

42. Ibid. 156, 174–5, 177–8. For Hume's views see Rotwein, op. cit., p. xliii. Mortimer referred to Hume's discussion (on pp. 67–8), and also cited Sir James Steuart in support of his arguments (on p. 97). Steuart's position is considered above, pp. 90–1.

43. Mortimer, op. cit. 90–1. For similar views see Francis Moore, *Considerations on the Exorbitant Price of Provisions* (1773), pp. 69–70, 80–1.

44. Ibid. 97–8. The first and third of these principles were, strictly speaking, incompatible.

45. Furniss, op. cit. 137. See also his remarks on Arthur Young's acceptance of the doctrine of the utility of poverty on p. 120: 'it is difficult to see how [his conclusions] could have been avoided by any patriotic writer of his day whose observation had convinced him of a general tendency in all branches of the labouring population towards indolence in the face of rising wages, unless he had been endowed with a much clearer perception of the causes contributing to produce this result than may reasonably be expected of the eighteenth-century theorist.' To demonstrate that a number of writers did in fact perceive these causes is one of the aims of the present article.

46. Prominent among the partisans was William Temple, the Wiltshire clothier, whose oft-quoted attacks on the poor originated in a 1738 wage-dispute (*The Case as It Now Stands Between the Clothiers, Weavers, and other Manufacturers*, 1738), and were reiterated in his later writings, *A Vindication of Commerce and the Arts* (1758), and *An Essay on Trade and Commerce* (1770). Similarly Arthur Young invariably waxed enthusiastic over the beneficial effects of high food-prices on the labourer's effort when he was defending the corn bounty, e.g. *The Expediency of a Free Exportation of Corn* (1770), pp. 5–23, and *The Farmer's Letters* (3rd edn., 1771), i. 185–6. The author of *Considerations on the Policy* complained that Young wanted the labourer 'to toil and starve, for the benefit of landed men, farmers, and jobbers', p. 112, also 297–8. In reply, Young called him a 'supercilious coxcomb'.

For a valuable discussion of the corn-law literature see D. G. Barnes, *A History of the English Corn Laws* (London, 1930), chap. 3.

47. Op. cit. 87.

48. For example, Anon., *Propositions for Improving the Manufactures, Agriculture and Commerce of Great Britain* (1763), pp. 45, 53–4; Anon., *The Causes of the Dearness of Provisions Assigned* (1766), p. 43; Anon., *The Occasion of the Dearness of Provisions, and the Distress of the Poor* (1767), pp. 8, 27–8; [Soame Jenyns], *Thoughts on the Causes and Consequences of the Present High Price of Provisions* (1767), pp. 19, 21; Anon., *An Answer to a Pamphlet entitled, Thoughts on the Causes and Consequences of the Present High Price of Provisions* (1768), pp. 13, 15.

49. For example, Anon., *Considerations on the Effects which the Bounties Granted on Exported Corn, Malt and Flour, have on the Manufactures of the Kingdom* (1768), attacked as 'wicked' and 'dangerous' the policy of 'starving the useful into excessive toil in order to enable the useless to indulge themselves in all kinds of idleness and profusion', but advocated 'punishments *in terrorem*' for the idle (p. 24), and made no reference to wage increases. For similar views see *Considerations on the Present High*

Price of Provisions and the Necessaries of Life (1764), pp. 20–1; *The Occasion of the Dearness of Provisions* pp. 8, 28, 32, and F. Moore, op. cit. 69–70.

50. The following is a sample of those who feared (*a*) large-scale emigration or (*b*) riots by workers who had been driven to desperation; *Considerations on the Present High Price of Provisions* (1764), pp. 21, 22 (*a*) and (*b*); Postlethwayt, *Universal Dictionary*, loc. cit., p. xxii (*a*); Anon., *Gentleman's Magaine* (1766), p. 525 (*a*); *The Occasion of the Dearness of Provisions*, p. 36 (*a*); Forster, op. cit. 59 (*b*); *Considerations on the Effects which the Bounties … have*, p. 23 (*a*) and (*b*); *Considerations on the Policy* (1771), p. 46 (*a*) and (*b*); Moore, op. cit. 24, 78–9 (*a*) and (*b*); Anon., *Gent's Mag.* (1774), p. 314 (*a*). The Editor of this journal observed (1766, p. 525) that those who chose to emigrate would 'return with a better mind', since conditions were worse abroad. Professor W. D. Grampp's view that the mercantilist writers 'hardly ever expressed the fear of insubordination turning into sedition' is, therefore, not true of the period under review. See 'The Liberal Elements in English Mercantilism', *The Quarterly Journal of Economics*, 66. 484. A general account of food riots at this time is given in Barnes, loc. cit.

51. One writer defined the objective as 'to make the life of the poor as comfortable and easy, as is consistent with the ends of government, and the exercise and promotion of industry': *Essays on Several Subjects* (1769), p. 150; another merely stated the dilemma that if provisions were 'too dear the poor cannot live; if too cheap, they will not work': *An Appeal to the Public* (1767), p. 14; also *An Essay on the Causes of the Present High Price of Provisions* (1773), p. 1.

A more careful attempt to define the problem occurred in Mildmay, *The Laws and Policy of England* (1765), pp. 22–5: we should incite industry by the 'allurement of profit' which meant high wages; but this encourages idleness and reduces sales, whereas 'low wages will be a discouragement to any work at all.' Therefore he concluded that we must 'enable our poor to work … upon more moderate terms' by ensuring 'a general cheapness of provisions' while allowing the native worker to enjoy a higher standard of life than his continental counterpart.

52. The writer of *The Occasion of the Dearness of Provisions*, who specified actual figures, sought a wage level high enough to 'allow our manufacturers to obtain a comfortable subsistence, with a reasonable industry' (p. 32) and yet low enough to enable us to compete in foreign markets. On pp. 27–34 he disputed the figures and the 'unjust invectives' against the poor contained in *A Letter to an M.P. on the Present Distresses of the Poor* (1767), by J.W.

53. Perhaps the best discussion of this problem appeared in the 3rd edn. of the *Farmer's Letters* (1771), i. 178 ff. It was based largely on information collected during his tours; e.g. *Northern Tour* (1768), iv, Letters 39 and 40. The remarks in the text are, of course, confined to Young's pre-1776 writings.

54. *Political Essays Concerning the State of the British Empire* (1772), p. 206. See also his *Expediency of a Free Exportation*, p. 25, where he remarked that the notion that the high price of labour ruined our manufactures was a 'vulgar error', an expression identical to that used by Josiah Tucker in his privately printed *Elements of Commerce* (1755). For a discussion of Tucker's views see above, pp. 90–1.

55. Young was, however, sometimes surprisingly inconsistent on this point. Although in *The Expediency of a Free Exportation*, p. 42, he held that it was essential to 'keep the products of the earth at a regular price, and the higher the better', in his *Political Essays* (1772), p. 220, he argued in favour of reducing the price of provisions, provided that provisions and labour were 'kept in balance'.

56. In *The Expediency of a Free Exportation*, p. 27, he observed that 'although the rates of labour … are not decided by those of necessaries; to be in exact proportion to each other; yet in all countries, where provisions are very dear, labour must be dearer than in other countries, where provisions are very cheap.' Cf. *Political Essays*, p. 205: 'Labour must rise with the necessaries of life.'

57. For example the oft-quoted passage that 'every one but an idiot knows, that the lower classes must be kept poor or they will never be industrious', *Eastern Tour* (1771), iv. 361.

58. For example *Northern Tour* (1768), i. 196: 'In a word, idle people are converted by degrees into industrious hands; youths are brought forward to work; even boys perform their share, and women at the prospect of great wages clap their hands with cheerfulness and fly to the sickle. Thus a new race of the industrious, is by degrees created.'

59. *Political Arithmetic; Containing Observations on the Present State of Great Britain; and the Principles of her Policy in the Encouragement of Agriculture* (1774), pp. ix, 61–2, 66, 68, 73–4. See also his *Expediency of a Free Exportation*, p. 28, where he asserted that 'such an high price of provisions, as must be attended by an high price of labour, is absolutely requisite for the prosperity of manufactures.'

60. Below, note 64.

61. Op. cit. ii. 155.

62. The list is usually confined to John Cary, Dudley North, and Daniel Defoe.

63. Furniss, op. cit. 183.

64. To date I have discovered only one pre-1750 mention of this distinction: Anon., *Considerations on the Bill for A General Naturalization* (1748), p. 71. Passing references to it are made in the following works: P. Murray, *Thoughts on Money, Circulation and Paper Currency* (1758), pp. 29–30; Anon., *Propositions for Improving the Manufactures etc.* (1763), pp. 32, 110–11. More systematic use of this distinction appears in Joseph Harris, *An Essay Upon Money and Coins* (1757), Pt. 1. p. 17 n. Adam Smith, *Lectures*, op. cit., p. 165, and *An Early Draft of the Wealth of Nations* (1763), reproduced in W. R. Scott, *Adam Smith as Student and Professor* (Glasgow, 1937), pp. 331–2; in A. Young, *Political Essays*, pp. 205–6, and *Northern Tour*, iv. 556; and also in Josiah Tucker's *Four Tracts on Political and Commercial Subjects* (2nd edn. 1774), (written in 1748) pp. 34–6, where it formed an integral part of his argument that a rich country with high wages and an efficient labour force could always undersell a poor country with low wages.

It is significant that Defoe (*Plan of the English Commerce*, pp. 40–2) did not argue that the highly paid British labourer could work cheaper than a Frenchman, but that his products would command a higher price because of their superior quality.

65. On this topic see Johnson, op. cit., chap. 13.

66. For earlier references to the Dutch see Furniss, op. cit., pp. 23, 101. For favourable comparisons between British and continental workers see J. Harris, loc. cit.; *Propositions for Improving the Manufactures*, pp. 31–2, 110–11; Postlethwayt, *Universal Dictionary* (4th edn.), p. xiv (but contrast this, written in 1766, with *Great Britain's True System* [1757], pp. 160, 219–21); Anon., *Considerations on the Policy*, p. 195; Young, *Political Essays*, pp. 205–6; Mortimer, *Elements of Commerce*, p. 89.

67. D. C. Coleman, 'Labour in the English Economy of the Seventeenth Century', *Econ. Hist. Rev.* 8, no. 3 (1956), 287. To say of this period that 'qualitative improvement', was 'virtually impossible' seems to be an overstatement of the case.

68. Arthur Young quotes several British and continental writers holding this view in his *Political Essays*, pp. 209–19. To his list we may add Mortimer, op. cit. 104–5, and Forster, op. cit. 20–1 n., who believed that most labour-saving devices would not reduce employment. Mildmay, op. cit. 42–3, argued that machines must be introduced even though they were likely to reduce employment, while Sir James Steuart, *An Inquiry into the Principles of Political Economy* (1767), i, bk. i, chap. 19 (*Works* [1805 edn.] pp. 160–5) maintained that the adverse employment effects would be temporary.

69. In this group we may include Tucker, op. cit. 30; Postlethwayt, especially *Britain's Commercial Interest*, ii, 377–8, 420–1; Adam Smith, *An Early Draft of the Wealth of Nations*, p. 332; Mildmay, loc. cit.; Anon., *Gents. Mag.* (1766), p. 572; Steuart, op. cit. i, bk. 2, 390–2; Young, loc. cit.; F. Moore, *Considerations on the Exorbitant Price*, p. 82. Postlethwayt opposed the introduction of machinery in agriculture, whereas Young was mainly concerned with this sphere. To Steuart, innovations in agriculture would release labour for industrial expansion. (See Johnson, op cit. 203, n. 147.)

70. Ed. F. B. Kaye (Oxford 1924). For an excellent account of the economic theory of luxury and the influence of Mandeville's arguments see pp. xciv–xcviii, cxxxvi-cxxxix.

71. Johnson, op. cit. 293, 295–7. See also Rotwein, op. cit. 19–32.

72. This is attributable to the prevalent moral objections to luxury, to the fears of imported luxuries, and to the customary identification of the labourer's consumption in terms of necessaries (e.g. Vanderlint, above, p. 80). Even Arthur Young, whose opposition to the labourer's consumption of tea and other luxuries is notorious, occasionally advocated substantial increases in the consumption of necessaries (e.g. *Political Essays*, p. 111).

73. Brown, op. cit. 195–6. According to his general theory, in the first stage of economic development only necessities were produced; in the second, happy and populous stage, there were conveniences; while in the final stage wealth brought 'superfluity, avarice, effeminate refinement, and loss of principle'.

74. The following writers desired a more equal distribution of wealth or warned against the dangers of excessive inequality: Berkeley, *Querist*, no. 204; Hume op. cit., p. 15; W. Hazeland, *A View of the Manner in which Trade and Civil Liberty Support each Other* (1756), pp. 9–10, 20–1; Joseph Harris, op. cit., pt. 1, 70 fn., pt. 2, 116–17; Postlethwayt, *Great Britain's True System*, pp. 138–9, 157; S. Fawconer, *An Essay on Modern Luxury* (1765), p. 438; Mildmay. op. cit. 124; Forster op. cit. 11, 40–1; Steuart, *Inquiry*, ii. 155–6, advocated on 'equable' not an equal distribution; Anon., *Considerations on the Effects which the Bounties*, etc., pp. 23–4; [Soame Jenyns], *Thoughts*, p. 23, believed a redistribution of wealth would solve current problems, but rejected it as 'unjust and unlawful'; Anon., *An Answer to a Pamphlet entitled Thoughts*, etc., p. 13; Anon., *Considerations on the Exportation of Corn, Wherein the Principal Arguments*, etc. (1770), pp. 56–7; Anon., *An Inquiry into the Connection between the present Price of Provisions and the Size of Farms*, etc. (1773), pp. 45–6.

75. This was usually designed to improve the agricultural situation, see Vanderlint, op. cit. 101, 103–4, 154; Postlethwayt, *Britain's Commercial Interest*, i. 35–7; Wm. Bell, *A dissertation ... What Causes Principally contribute to render a Nation Populous* (1756), p. 27 (Hume, too, argued that equality of property aided population growth, op. cit. 128–31); Anon., *Observations on the Number and Misery of the Poor* (1765), pp. 14, 31–3. In addition there were innumerable complaints of the evil consequences of the engrossing of farms.

76. For example, Anon., *An Answer to a Pamphlet*, p. 12, denied that he was a 'leveller'; while Richard Woodward, *An Argument in Support of the Right of the Poor in the Kingdom of Ireland to a National Provision* (1768), pointed out, in his Advertisement to the Reader, that he had 'inculcated the reasonableness of their subordination in society, and their obligation to obedience.' Similarly F. Moore, op. cit. 70. The desire to preserve the existing social hierarchy, though usually unstated, was implied in most of the contemporary writings on the poor.

77. J. Harris, op. cit. pt. 1, 70 n. See also, Vanderlint, op. cit. 101; Hume, op. cit. 28–9, 98–9; Forster, op. cit., 41; Anon., *An Inquiry into the Late Mercantile Distresses in Scotland and England*, etc. (1772), pp. 120, 123, 128. Many other instances could be cited.

78. Op. cit. 19–21, 30–2. See also Johnson, op. cit. 168–170.

79. In discussing luxury, few writers clearly specified the social and economic classes to which their observations applied. Moreover, the distinction between luxuries, comforts, and conveniences was changing over time. It is, therefore, debatable whether, apart from a few instances (e.g. Postlethwayt, *Great Britain's True System*, p. 237; Forster, op. cit. 38), a defence of the labourer's consumption of tea (e.g. *Gents. Mag.* [1773], p. 60—with the Editor's approval) and meat (e.g. Postlethwayt, *Universal Dictionary* [4th edn.] p. xxxvi; *Gents. Mag.* [1767], pp. 112–13; Mortimer, op. cit. 97–8, where he quoted Steuart in support) should be included in this category.

80. J. Harris, op. cit., pt. 1, 29. Cf. Postlethwayt, *Britain's Commercial Interest*, i. 35–7; Mildmay, op. cit. 123–4; Forster, op. cit. 42, 51.

81. For Hume's views on this point see Rotwein (ed.), chap. 2.

82. Steuart, *Inquiry*, (*Works*, 1805 ed.) bk. ii, chap. 19. The position of labour in this process is outlined in chaps. 11, 17 and 18. Steuart believed the lowest-paid workers should receive 'ample subsistence where no degree of superfluity is implied', and

argued on grounds of humanity and policy against restricting this standard too vigorously (ibid., chap. 21). Recognizing the dangers of a very uneven distribution of wealth (ii. 155) he did not consider modern luxury excessive (ibid. 170) and maintained that drunkenness was decreasing (i. 372).

83. For the materials relevant to this discussion see Rotwein, op. cit., pp. lix, lxxvii, 199–205. Also J. M. Low, 'An Eighteenth Century Controversy in the Theory of Economic Progress', *The Manchester School*, 20 (1952), 311–30.

84. Rotwein, op. cit. 200. These are Hume's words, from a letter to Lord Kames, through whom the debate with Tucker was conducted. Hume's retraction apparently did not cause any change in his attitude to labour, and Kames adhered to Hume's original position. Cf. *Sketches*, i. 147–8. Their contemporary, John Millar, accepted Tucker's views. Cf. *Origin of the Distinction of Ranks* (1806 edn.) p. xlviii.

85. *Four Tracts*, p. 32.

86. Furniss, op. cit. 184, fn. 3.

87. *Wealth of Nations*, pp. 61–2. It is highly probable that the exchange between Hume and Tucker influenced the arguments of Smith's *magnum opus*. For an intermediate stage in the development of his views see *An Early Draft of the Wealth of Nations*, loc. cit. Cf. *Lectures*, op. cit. 165.

88. Richard C. Wiles, 'The Theory of Wages in Later English Mercantilism', *Econ. Hist. Rev.*, 2nd ser. 21 (1968), 114.

89. Ibid. 115, 126.

90. For further discussion of these matters see my article, 'The Interpretation of Mercantilist Economics: some historiographical problems' and the rejoinder by William R. Allen in *History of Political Economy*, 5 (1973), 485–98.

91. See above, p. 79, n. 9, and the companion piece 'Economic Thought and Poor Law Policy', *Econ. Hist. Rev.*, 2nd ser. 13 (1960), 39–51.

92. Op. cit. 115.

5

The First Manchester Sunday Schools*

A. P. WADSWORTH

In August 1786, the magistrates for the Salford Hundred of Lancashire meeting at quarter sessions passed a long resolution deploring what would now be called a crime wave. They recited how 'idle, disorderly and dangerous persons of all descriptions' were wandering about, and how the 'commission of offences hath increased to an alarming degree.' They called for more vigilance in the reporting of crime, more activity by the constables, more 'privy searches', closer control of public houses and 'houses of evil fame'. They ended with this paragraph:

That where Sunday Schools have been opened, their good effects have been plainly perceived in the orderly and decent Comportment of the Youth who are instructed therein. That it is therefore most earnestly to be wished that those virtuous Citizens who have begun this good work, would continue their efforts to forward it, with that Zeal and Perseverance that its great Importance requires; and that if these Institutions should become established throughout the Kingdom, there is good reason to hope they will produce an happy change in the general Morals of the People, and thereby render the Severities of Justice less frequently necessary.[1]

Why should the magistrates have linked Sunday schools with the repression of crime and the regulation of public houses? The answer is that the Sunday schools, then in Lancashire just two years old, were a new social discovery. They seemed to the mind of the time to be a new revelation of how crime could be prevented. The magistrates were not thinking of Sunday schools as religious institutions, branches of church organization, fields for devoted personal Christian service. They were thinking in practical terms of the schools as rescue agencies, as a means of reforming the lives and characters of the uneducated masses—the main source of crime and threats to property. This was the way all their contemporaries looked on them. The Sunday schools in Manchester, started in 1784, were fairly typical in being in their origins a town's effort, undenominational and managed by a committee on which both Church and Dissent sat. They were the product of a

* From *Bulletin of the John Rylands Library*, 33 (1951), 299–326. A lecture delivered in the John Rylands Library on 13 Dec. 1950. Reprinted by permission of the John Rylands Library.

quite remarkable wave of Puritan reform in which the prudential motives were uppermost.

The promoters of the schools most often sought support on this ground that they were a form of social insurance. This was the easiest and the cheapest way to civilize the poor, to make them less dangerous to society, to render them more useful workers and, incidentally, to save their souls. As the Manchester Committee put it, 'They call in a sense of religious obligation to the aid of industry.' Yet it was out of this movement that there came one of the main strands of English popular education and one of the main branches of the work of the churches in the nineteenth century. The story is a familiar one but it is worth retelling for the light it throws on the enormous change in thought that has taken place on the subject of popular and religious education.

The Sunday school movement was not the first attempt to secure social stability through simple Bible teaching. The eighteenth century had opened with a movement with the same aim, that for setting up of charity and subscription schools. This, co-ordinated after 1699 by the Society for the Promotion of Christian Knowledge, spread all over the country in a remarkable way. As its historian has said, it happily combined 'the new method of associated philanthropy and the new device of joint-stock finance'[2] It was built up largely on the thesis that the poor could be reformed and kept in their due place in society by instruction in Bible and catechism. For all the early enthusiasm the vitality of the movement in England hardly outlasted the reigns of Anne and George I, though in Wales it was active longer and its effects were more lasting. The association of charity schools with places of worship did, however, survive, but they touched only a handful of children. Manchester in 1784 had charity schools connected with each of the five Anglican churches and with Cross Street Chapel.[3]

The charity school movement had not been unchallenged on its merits. There was acrimonious debate whether the children of the poor should be educated at all. In the great stirring of thought during the English Revolution of 1640–60 there had seemed to be hope that the ideal of a system of popular education, aided by the State, might be realized. The hope faded away, as do so many dreams of educational advance under the stress of war. The economic theory that came to dominate the popular mind was harsh. What Defoe called 'the great law of subordination' prevailed. Was not education a bad thing because it might set people above themselves? As late as 1763 a writer could argue:

The charity school is another universal nursery of idleness; nor is it easy to conceive or invent anything more destructive to the interests and very foundation principles of a nation entirely dependent on its trade and manufactures than the giving an education to the children of the lowest class of her people that will make them contemn those drudgeries for which they were born.[4]

These ideas died hard. The charity school movement had had to fight against them in England, though less fiercely in Wales, while in Scotland they were largely rejected. The movement certainly had not made what we should think extravagant claims. Isaac Watts, one of the great controversialists on the side of the schools, had explained that their aim was 'to teach the duties of humility and submission to superiors', and of 'diligence and industry in their business'. The children's clothes, the school uniform of the charity schools, were, he said, 'of the coarsest kind, and of the plainest form, and thus they are sufficiently distinguished from children of the better rank, and they ought to be so distinguished'. There was, he declared, 'no ground for charity children to grow vain and proud of their rayment when it is but a sort of livery'.[5] We shall meet with these ideas again. Still the charity schools did teach a few children to read and write and satisfied the philanthropic instinct. But even they got bogged down, first in Jacobitism, then in the eternal struggle between Church and Dissent.

Then, in the early eighties, quite suddenly, the Sunday school movement flashed over the country. One wonders whether any social reform movement had ever before spread with equal rapidity through England. It was one of the first unconscious triumphs of the press. The precise parentage of Sunday schools is disputed and hardly matters. It seems a fairly obvious thing to collect a few children together on a Sunday (their only free day), teach them to read, catechize them, and see they go to church. Doubtless it occurred to quite a number of good people up and down the country. But the kindling spark of the national movement was undoubtedly the effort of Robert Raikes at Gloucester. He was a printer and the proprietor of the *Gloucester Journal*, a well-disposed, prosperous man interested in prison reform among other good works. He was a humane man, yet also a prudent man. When he described in his paper the alarming mortality in Gloucester gaol he could not forbear adding: 'It were well if those unthinking people who now enjoy but abuse their life and liberty to the violation of the law and the detriment of society, would reflect on the danger of infection and the other miseries that await them in a crowded prison.' And, again: 'Could unhappy wretches see the misery that awaits them in a crowded gaol they would surely relinquish the gratifications that reduce them to such a state of wretchedness.'[6]

So too, on that famous morning in 1780, the reform of morals was uppermost in his mind when he heard of the misbehaviour of the child workers of the Gloucester pin factory.

'Ah, sir', said the woman to whom I was speaking, 'could you take a view of this part of the town on a Sunday, you would be shocked indeed; for then the street is filled with multitudes of these wretches, who, released that day from employment, spend their time in noise and riot, playing at "chuck", and cursing and swearing in a manner so horrid as to convey to any serious mind an idea of hell, rather than any other place.'[7]

How, he wondered, to take these 'wretches' off the streets? So he hit on his plan 'to check the deplorable profanation' of the Sabbath, arranged with four keepers of dame schools to open on a Sunday, and teach children reading and the Church catechism, for a shilling a day. A schoolmaster-clergyman, Thomas Stock, joined and superintended their spiritual welfare.

The schools, or rather classes, for each teacher had about twenty children, spread in Gloucester and by the autumn of 1783 there were between 200 and 300 scholars. It was then that the movement was introduced to a wider world. On 3 November 1783, Raikes published the following in his paper:

Some of the clergy in different parts of this county, bent upon attempting a reform among the children of the lower class, are establishing Sunday-Schools, for rendering the Lord's day subservient to the ends of instruction, which has hitherto been prostituted to bad purposes. Farmers, and other inhabitants of the towns and villages, complain that they receive more injury to their property on the Sabbath than all the week besides: this, in a great measure, proceeds from the lawless state of the younger class, who are allowed to run wild on that day, free from every restraint. To remedy this evil, persons duly qualified are employed to instruct those that cannot read; and those that may have learnt to read are taught the catechism and conducted to church. By thus keeping their minds engaged, the day passes profitably, and not disagreeably. In those parishes where the plan has been adopted, we are assured that the behaviour of the children is greatly civilised. The barbarous ignorance in which they had before lived being in some degree dispelled, they begin to give proofs that those persons are mistaken who consider the lower orders of mankind incapable of improvement, and therefore think an attempt to reclaim them impracticable, or, at least, not worth the trouble.[8]

The paragraph went the round of the papers, for in those days scissors and paste were not the least important of the journalist's implements. Eighty or ninety per cent of a country paper's news content was 'lifted' from the London papers, and the London papers reciprocated by drawing freely on what little original matter the country journals had. This press publicity, modest and unobtrusive by present standards, set the movement going. For instance, Richard Townley of Belfield, a small squire and magistrate at Rochdale,[9] must have written immediately, on seeing a reprint of Raikes's paragraph, to the Mayor of Gloucester, who passed the letter on to Raikes. Raikes replied on 25 November with a long account, from which we have quoted. Townley sent it on 26 December to Harrop's *Manchester Mercury*, with a note saying that he had Raikes's permission 'for publishing it in such County Journals or Newspapers, as I shall judge proper'.[10] A little later he returned to the attack with highly practical proposals. The magistrates, he suggested, should approve Mr. Raikes's ideas and recommend the churchwardens and overseers within their districts to set up schools. These could be supported by fines imposed for Sabbath breaking and cursing and swearing, by an annual collection at places of worship, and by donations. He even suggested that the collectors at the church door should have 'Bags, large Purses, or small Straw Baskets instead of the open Boxes commonly used' so as not to leave the giver open to 'impertinent Observation'.[11]

All this had its fruits in Lancashire, and Townley's letter-writing may also have been the genesis of the Yorkshire movement which was well begun by May. Leeds had then 1,800 scholars; Huddersfield and Dewsbury followed[12] and by 18 July Wesley, then at Bingley, could note: 'I find these schools springing up wherever I go'. Lancashire was a little later than Yorkshire, but by August there was great activity. On 10 August the Manchester movement was announced (there were already some schools there); on 17 August Hollinwood reported a gift of spelling books from Mr. Raikes; on 24 August schools were reported to have been set up at Rochdale and Bury.[13] From now on, for the next few years, you can hardly turn over a newspaper without finding little paragraphs about the setting up of Sunday schools, always it appears with miraculous results.[14] It would be hard without many quotations to illustrate the naïve enthusiasm with which they were launched. Magistrates and bishops gave their blessing. The king and queen showed their interest. Raikes became a national figure and basked in the sun of royal approbation. Fanny Burney, fixing up the arrangements for him to be received by the king and queen, has left her impressions of the estimable man:

> Mr. Raikes is not a man that without a previous disposition towards approbation I should have admired. He is somewhat too flourishing, somewhat too forward, somewhat too volatile; but he is worthy, benevolent, good-natured, and good-hearted, and therefore the overflowing of successful spirits and delighted vanity must meet with some allowance.

Raikes had indeed started something greater than he knew and the effects overwhelmed him. His innocuous paragraph had led to a national movement patronized by great and small. And, as is always the way, the indefatigable good of London had started a national undenominational society (in 1785) to spread a national plan.[15] Why should not Raikes have been a little bumptious when Adam Smith could tell him: 'No plan has promised to effect a change of manners with equal ease and simplicity since the days of the Apostles.' And had not Wesley, with slightly more chronological caution, said: 'I verily think these schools are one of the noblest specimens of charity which have been set on foot in England since the time of William the Conqueror.' In these two *dicta*—of the economist and of the enthusiast— the leading strains of thought meet: the Sunday schools were a utilitarian plan for reforming morals and so securing property; they were also a charity satisfying the Christian instinct of benevolence. Their peculiar attractiveness lay in their combination of the two.

In this remarkable movement Manchester took a high place and we must now turn to see how it organized itself.

Manchester (with Salford) had then a population of between 50,000 and 60,000—say about that of Bury or Lancaster today. But it was growing fast. It had been about 25,000 in 1750; it was to be 100,000 by 1800. This expansion, mostly the result of immigration, produced terrible overcrowding and jerry-building. The people lived in a close-packed area, badly paved, largely unsewered, badly lit. Local government services were rudimentary, indeed by modern standards hardly existent. Of educational provision there was hardly any. By 1784 Manchester had seen only the beginnings of the factory system. But everyone was conscious of the feverish industrial expansion and of the growing preponderance of what was called the 'manufacturing poor' or, as they were later to be known, the 'working classes'. The French Revolution had yet to cast its spell but the middle classes were already uneasy. There was a rising standard of living, showing itself in things like tea-drinking, the use of wheaten instead of oat bread, and absenteeism from work, which it was hard for the rich to understand. The working classes seemed to be becoming luxurious and to be less content to accept their due subordination in society. And, of course, there was a good deal of actual demoralization and occasional turbulence in this new raw urban society, addicted to all the brutish pleasures and amusements of the English eighteenth century. The materialistic arguments for Sunday schools had an intelligible basis. Then also we must allow for the genuine philanthropic and humanitarian impulses which moved even such a utilitarian community and had already founded the infirmary and dispensary and the lunatic hospital, and were soon to found a lying-in hospital, a humane society, and the 'Stranger's Friend' for people outside the poor law.

The Manchester Sunday School movement was formally launched on 10 August 1784, with an advertisement in the papers[16] by the boroughreeve and constables commending 'An Address to the Public on Sunday Schools'. This began in the usual way:

The Neglect of it [education] is one principal Cause of the Misery of Families, Cities and Nations: Ignorance, Vice and Misery, being constant Companions. The hardest Heart must melt at the melancholy Sight of such a Multitude of Children, both Male and Female, in this Town, who live in gross Ignorance, Infidelity, and habitual Profanation of the Lord's Day. What Crowds fill the Streets! tempting each other to Idleness, Play, Lewdness, and every other Species of Wickedness. . . . To attempt a remedy is laudable and divine.

It passed on to recite the example of 'the clergyman of Stroud' (it is curious that Raikes was not mentioned) and of another at Leeds, and then described the Leeds plan. That town was divided into 7 divisions, and had 26 schools, 44 or 45 masters, and over 2,000 scholars.

> As it is not customary for children to play in the morning and lest too much confinement should weary them, they enter the school at one o'clock in the afternoon and are kept in till the evening comes, according to the time of the year, being only permitted to ask out, or go one by one. They are conducted by their respective masters to Church; part of them goes to the three churches at three o'clock, the rest to evening prayers at six o'clock in their turns. They are instructed in reading, writing, and the principles of Christianity.

A form of prayer was used, and 'inquisitors' were to be appointed to visit the schools. Funds were to be raised by a house to house collection. The masters were paid 2*s.*, 1*s.* 6*d.*, or 1*s.* a Sunday according to their qualifications. The 'schools' (that is, rooms in houses, etc.) were hired at 30*s.*, 21*s.*, or 15*s.* a year.

This was broadly the plan that came to be adopted in Manchester. Already by 10 August a number of schools had been set up in Manchester and these were to be made part of a general movement. A subscription book was left open at the Exchange Coffee House. By 21 September there were 25 schools, attended by nearly 1,800 children[17] On 24 September a town's meeting was held with the lord of the manor, Sir John Parker Mosley, in the chair, and an imposing and representative committee was appointed, with the Revd. John Bennett of St. Mary's as secretary.[18] Manchester was then predominantly Anglican but both Church and Dissent were on the committee. The town was divided into five districts (there were five Anglican churches), each with a subcommittee. (Salford was not tackled for two years.) The first duty was to overhaul the existing schools and to turn away the children under six. By December the Collegiate Church district had seven different rooms in use, St. John's four, St. Mary's three, St. Ann's two, and St. Paul's ten. The main committee met monthly and exercised its control over the schools by visitors, three of whom were chosen each month to inspect the schools and make reports. Children had to present a subscriber's recommendation and 'no subscriber shall recommend any children whose parents may be supposed capable or able to send them to any other school'. Hours of attendance were: October to February, 9 to 12 and 1 to 4; March to September, 9 to 12, 2 to 5. Children were to attend the nearest school in their district, except that Dissenters 'may prefer a more distant Master of their own persuasion'. The visitors were to regulate the time and mode of attendance at divine service. Masters were to be paid 1*s.* 6*d.* a day, undermasters and mistresses 1*s.* 'Swearing, lying or any other profaneness' brought expulsion. School was to be opened and closed with a psalm or hymn and a form of prayer was prepared. Scholars were to be a catechized. 'Children of the Established Church shall be grounded by the Masters in the Principles of the Church Catechism only.' Parents were expected to hear their children repeat their lessons at home during the week.[19]

The Manchester children were taught to read only, and from books and tracts of a strictly religious and improving nature. The Church of England children were provided with prayer books and the Dissenters with their approved substitute. Prizes were distributed for regular attendance and proficiency. The first chosen were Dr. Isaac Watts's 'Divine Songs for Children'. Some of its pieces were included in the Manchester Committee's school hymn-book. Next year the committee chose as prizes 'The Great Importance of a Religious Life', 'Serious Advice against Lying', and 'Serious Advice against Swearing'. Then 300 copies of Mrs. Trimmer's 'Servants' Friend' were printed to be given to 'those young persons who during their attendance in Sunday schools have behaved well and are going out to service'. But Manchester produced its own improving literature. In 1789 the following dialogue between two scholars, recited before school visitors, was published:

FIRST.   O! happy day, appointed for reproof
          Which brings our feet beneath this welcome roof,
          Where we may learn to read, to hear, and speak
          The paths of Virtue, which we ought to take:
          Where we can find instruction, and delight
          To pass in cheerful songs the sabbath night.

SECOND.   I too with joy this blessed day receive,
          And hope we shall assemble here at eve;
          Yea, gladly welcome ev'ry sabbath day—
          For we shou'd love the school more than our play.

FIRST.   It gives me pleasure much to find that we
          In these respects so happily agree;
          And children yonder playing in the street
          Had better here some useful task repeat.

SECOND.   I think so too; for though I love right well
          To play, I love to sing, and read, and spell:
          But play in school time we ought not indeed,
          For if we do, how shall we learn to read?
          To love our sport and not our books, at once
          Displays a hopeless child, a playful dunce.

FIRST.   Hopeless indeed: and we who better know,
          Shou'd thank the hands from whom our favours flow:
          For by their goodness we may here improve,
          And bless the worthy labours of their love.

SECOND.   Right, and I'll join you in this Christian part,
          To pay the tribute of a grateful heart.

BOTH.   Then as our thanks to all our friends are due,
         We give them now to *you*, to *you*, and *you*.[20]

To appreciate the setting we should remember that Sunday was the only day on which the children could either go to school or play. On weekdays they worked, either by night or day, twelve hours a day or more. The peculiar felicity of the arrangement was noted by Beilby Porteus, Bishop of Chester, when, in 1785, in a letter of encouragement to the Manchester Committee, he wrote:

The institution of Sunday schools I have always considered as one of the most probable means of diffusing sentiments of virtue and religion among the common people. They are more especially necessary in such populous manufacturing towns as Manchester, where the children are during the week days generally employed in work and on the Sunday are too apt to be idle, mischievous and vitious.[21]

In a letter to his clergy in the following year he enlarged on the theme:

The greater part of the children educated in the Sunday schools are not merely taught to be diligent and laborious by *words* and *precepts,* but what is far more useful and efficacious, they are actually trained up from their very childhood in *habits* of industry. They consist for the most part of such as are employed in trades, manufactures, or husbandry-work: to this they give up six days in the week, and on the remaining one (the Lord's day), they are instructed in the rudiments of Christian faith and practice.

By this wise expedient, that most desirable *union*, which has been so often wished for in Charity Schools, but which it has been generally found so difficult to introduce, is at length accomplished, the union of *manual labour* and *spiritual instruction.* These are by means of the Sunday schools both carried on together and the interests both of this life and the next so consulted, as not to interfere with or obstruct each other.[22]

And what made the arrangement especially satisfactory was that it was cheap. As the bishop noted: 'The whole expence of instructing twenty children, including books, rewards, and every other charge, will not amount to five pounds a year; a sum so trifling and so easy to be raised that it cannot create the smallest difficulty.'[23]

Manchester showed the same goodwill. After the first year the secretary of the schools exclaimed:

The improvement of these children in learning has been wonderful; in religious knowledge still more surprising; and, when they sing to the praise and glory of their maker, they appear a tribe of embryo-angels training for the skies. Every Christian heart glows with triumph; and heaven seems for a moment transplanted upon earth.[24]

Most comment, however, dwelt rather on the better behaviour of the children in the streets. In a few years Manchester came to have thirty-six schools and Salford six, with, in all, over 5,000 scholars on the books. The schools varied much in size. Many seem to have been rooms in houses and warehouses but some, with 200 or 300 scholars, were in factories, lent by the owners. Each district was under the supervision of its own 'visitors' (we might call them superintendents), with regular calls from the 'general visitors' of the central committee. Until 1788 all the visitors were men. Then the visitors were asked to 'sound the inclinations of their female friends' as to whether they would care to look after the girls' schools. In 1797 the committee proposed the appointment of a 'lady patroness' for each district to encourage the children by taking some under her particular notice. It was suggested that she should bring along with her some of her friends to hear the children catechized. This touch of feudalism was too much for the democratic spirit of the lady visitors; they protested and the committee hastily dropped the idea.

The schools were financed from two sources—annual subscriptions and church collections. The subscription list was long and representative; even the mule spinners' society contributed. The individual amounts were small, ranging mostly from 2 guineas to 5s. The collections were taken at all the places of worship in the town from the Collegiate Church to the 'Romish Chapel'. These 'anniversary services' ran on successive Sundays from September onwards. Between £900 and £1,100 a year was raised in roughly equal proportions from the two sources. The expenditure was mainly on teachers' wages, rent, firing, candles, books, and printing.

Discipline was pretty strict. The visitors had many things to watch, including the regrettable tendency of zealous teachers to break into extempore prayer, which was frowned upon.[25] No holidays were allowed in the schools and teachers who gave one were reprimanded. Another prohibition was against any 'Festival under the name of a Parting', presumably a leaving party. The committee spent a good deal of money on books, and in 1797 bought 2,000 'horn books'—a first reader covered with horn. A prize book in 1788 had the unappetizing title of 'The Sacrament explained to the Meanest Capacity'. Altogether the schools seem to have been conducted with both zeal and efficiency. The touch of coercion was not absent for the committee sought to have it made a condition that parents receiving poor relief should send their children to Sunday school.

The number of sermons preached bearing the title 'A Defence of Sunday Schools' reminds us that they had their opponents. We do not meet in Manchester any heretics like William Godwin who criticized them because 'the chief lessons that are taught are a superstitious veneration for the church of England, and to bow to every man in a handsome coat'.[26] The Manchester Committee in 1792 had to rebut the opposite charge, the same that had been brought against the charity schools:

The wit of man ... has not yet been able to contrive a mode of Charity, against which no plausible objection could be raised by avarice or perverseness.

Even against Sunday Schools we have sometimes heard it insinuated, that our exertions can do no real service (perhaps injury) to those who are the objects of this Charity: That it may refine and innervate, and consequently disqualify for the duties of an humble station. Suggestions these that must arise, if not from a worse motive, from ignorance of the nature and end of Sunday Schools. Refinement is not their object. The instructions bestowed are such as give strength and resolution to the heart. They call in a sense of religious obligation to the aid of industry.

Admittedly the streets were still full of youthful profligacy and disorder. But, the Manchester Committee pleaded, consider how much worse things might be if there were no schools![27]

The more serious and persistent criticism came from the extreme Evangelical side. If the Sunday schools were themselves the product of the new Puritanism, they were assailed by those who were still more Puritan. When the pains of Hell were a real prospect the precise limits of the Fourth Commandment became a matter of extreme moment. Indeed, it is a question Parliament has been unable to settle yet. The Manchester Committee was always strongly Sabbatarian. In 1785 it called on the Conductors of the Special Constables 'to take in rotation and patrole the streets on Sunday noon and evening to prevent Gambling and other Disorders that have prevailed on that day'. It protested in 1787 against the 'growing evil' of the Sunday work which was defeating the object of the schools. And from 1786 it set its face against the teaching of writing on Sunday: 'Resolved that no teacher shall be permitted to instruct any children belonging to the Sunday schools in writing on the Lord's day'. It was not that the Committee was against teaching writing as such for from 1794 it assisted schools which wished to teach writing to the children on Wednesday evenings. It provided the desks and inkstands, the other costs being borne by the visitors or perhaps from fees.

This question of Sunday writing was a bone of contention in the Sunday schools for two or three generations. It seemed such a natural thing to the keen educationist that if you could teach reading on Sunday you should also teach writing—if this was the only day the children were free to be taught. The extreme Sabbatarians were, however, already suspicious of the way reading was taught and feared that the attractions of school interfered with the children's church attendance. There was a lively and quite characteristic controversy in 1798 following on a published sermon by the parson of Mellor Chapel (near Stockport). He had inveighed against what he called the 'modern Sunday school'. The argument was:

Those Sunday schools are direct violations of the law of the Sabbath (1) where any kind of learning is taught during the season of public worship and made to serve instead of it, and (2) where any instructions are given, on any part of the day, which relate only to this world, and not immediately to the soul. In all such cases, both the teachers and the taught are employed in profaning the Lord's day, instead of keeping it holy, and improving it for the soul's spiritual advantage.

This was answered by Joseph Mayer, a teacher at the Stockport Sunday School, who contended that as the children had to go in relays to church, since there were so many of them, it was better to occupy them in writing than to turn them loose. More daring still, he justified the teaching of arithmetic. With naïve textual illustrations he pointed out that the Bible, especially the Pentateuch and the Prophets, could not be understood without some knowledge of arithmetic. What was more, 'It is by the knowledge of arithmetic that we obtain some of the best arguments in favour of the Christian religion. Indeed, without this science, we must give up some of its strongest foundations.' The parson of Ringway rejoined in another pamphlet that if writing could be taught why not knitting and sewing? It was absurd to try to reform mankind by a breach of the Fourth Commandment.[28]

The Church of England barred the teaching of writing on Sunday more often than did the Methodists or the Dissenters, but these were far from being united. Samuel Bamford describes with some bitterness how, while the newer Methodist societies accepted it, the main body decided against it.[29] This was by resolution of the Wesleyan Conference in 1814. Since, however, the connection of many of the schools with the Methodist societies was loose the prohibition was not wholly effective. It was not, indeed, until 1827 that the Conference brought the schools into the connectional machine and laid down rules for their governance. These reaffirmed the prohibition on the teaching of writing 'or any other merely secular branch of knowledge' on Sunday.[30] Others sects were less severe and some of the most successful and popular schools had quite a varied curriculum.[31]

After its first flush of enthusiasm in the 1780s the Sunday school movement fell away in many parts of the country. In the North it took vigorous root and, as we have seen, spread into the wider educational field. The Manchester Committee even ventured on the education of adults, though it is hard to say how extensively. It decided in 1788 'that a school be opened in each district for the instruction of grown up persons'. In April 1790, it decided that the 'evening schools for grown up young people' should be discontinued until September and the teachers be paid only sixpence an evening. (This was apparently an economy measure as funds were low.) Two schools for young men and two for young women were approved in 1792, and in 1795 one for young men and women 'as near as can be had to No. 31 John Street, Ancoats'. In 1794 it agreed that a school in Lever's Gates should be allowed a few shilling-books and also candles on Sunday evenings in order to instruct grown-up persons in reading. These must have been the first Manchester night-schools.

The interdenominational idyll lasted barely fifteen years. In Manchester, as in most other places, the Church of England took fright and decided to go its own way. In the charity school movement at the beginning of the century Dissent had parted company with Anglicanism because of the supposed taint of Jacobitism. Now it was the Anglicans who parted company with Dissent because it was supposed to be tainted with the subversive doctrines of the French Revolution on the one hand and of Methodism on the other. 'Schools of Jacobinical religion and Jacobinical politics abound in this country in the shape of charity schools and Sunday schools,' declared the Bishop of Rochester in 1800. In them the minds of 'the very lowest orders' were taught to despise religion and the laws of all subordination. His antidote was Sunday schools for the same class under clerical control.[32] In Manchester also the loyalty of Dissenters was looked on with some suspicion. They were, a colonel reported to the Home Office in 1792, 'all seditiously inclined'.[33]

This was nonsense, but passions ran high. The attitude towards 'Jacobinism'—the ideas of the French Revolution—was much like that towards Communism today, and the Manchester Committee on 7 January 1793 was firm on the dismissal of 'any teacher or assistant who shall be proved to be disaffected to the present Government'. The cause of the Manchester schism was, however, the Methodists. Or at least that is how it was described by the Anglican Committee in 1802:

about three years ago the Committee was disturbed by an Intimation, that the People called Methodists were exerting an undue Influence both in the Committee and in the Schools at large; that a large Proportion of the Visitors and Teachers were of that Persuasion; and that their ruling Object was to make Proselytes of the Children, and by every Artifice to draw them from the Church to the Conventicle.

The Clergy, as might reasonably be expected, took the alarm, and the event was, as might be expected also, that they and their Friends determined upon the Establishment of Sunday-Schools *to be appropriated to the use of the Established Church,* with which no order of Dissenters should interfere, but which, being supported by a distinct Fund, and governed by a distinct Committee, might hold forth a Security to the Public, that the Children would be preserved free from the taint of every evil Principle and Persuasion unfavourable to those in which they were intended to be educated.

The actual minutes of the committee present affairs less dramatically. The revolt was led by the parsons of St. James's and St. Mary's, Dr. Bayley and the Revd. C. P. Myddelton. There was a strong effort by the rest of the committee, Church as well as Dissent, to patch things up and alter the rules to suit them, but the two were obstinate and an amicable parting of the ways was agreed on. The trouble had been going on for two years and, as reflected in the minutes, mainly concerned the attendance of the children at church. In an effort at appeasement the committee strongly reaffirmed the rule of compulsory attendance, adding that it was from the consideration and under the persuasion that the *principal* use of the institution of Sunday schools is to habituate the children to a pious and orderly observance of the Sabbath day and of the duties to which it points; and that whatever advantages may be derived from learning to read it is a benefit of far higher importance and more essential concern to impress on young minds a devout sense of duty towards God and their neighbour, by introducing them early into habits of public and private worship, and thereby forming them to the love and practice of all Christian virtues.

From other resolutions it would seem that Church children had been straying (perhaps under the influence of Methodist visitors and teachers) to services outside the pale.

There is no open suggestion here that the Methodists were 'seditious' though there were many to believe it. The Ringway parson already quoted could hint that the Stockport teacher who had defended 'modern' Sunday schools was a Methodist who had 'a kind of disposition to turn Frenchman'. Actually the Methodist leaders went out of their way to show their loyalty to the government and to law and order. Thus in 1801, when the Duke of Portland was at the Home Office, Dr. Thomas Coke, the 'father of missions', kept up a flow of reports from his travels on the seditious organizations he heard talked about in Lancashire and Yorkshire. He confessed his sorrow that three Methodists had been arrested but, he added, 'on the strictest scrutiny and fullest satisfaction, I was happy enough to find that those men had been expelled the late Mr. Wesley's Society about five years ago solely for their Democratic sentiments.'[34]

But there was this amount of truth in the fear of Methodism, even if not of its conservative leaders—it appealed to the poor, and it was from the poor that the threat of revolution came. Some modern historians have plausibly argued that it was the Methodists who, by diverting the thoughts of the working classes towards Heaven and away from their miseries, saved England from revolution. The argument can be pressed too far, for Methodism was plainly subversive in the sense that it encouraged people to organize themselves outside clerical bonds.

What, however, probably troubled the Church party in Manchester most was the aggressiveness of Methodism. It was only in the 1790s that the Methodists had emerged as a distinct church. The 'Plan of Pacification', providing for the administration of the sacrament in Methodist chapels, did not come until 1795, and there were vigorous forces inside Methodism which demanded complete secession from the Church of England to which Wesley had kept it so ambiguously tied. The number of ministers had risen from 278 in 1790 to 442 in 1800, and the membership had grown by more than half. The hatred of Methodism in large sections of the Established Church was intense. Sydney Smith, a liberal-minded man, treated the Methodists, along with their evangelical Anglican counterparts, as part of 'one general conspiracy against common sense, and rational orthodox Christianity'. He poked fun at the more extravagant forms of their preaching, their substitution of providence for the mundane course of nature, and their hatred of pleasure and amusements. He warned the Church that it might lose the 'middling and lower classes', and though he had nothing very bold to suggest as counterweight, for he was all for toleration, he did think that: 'The greatest and best of all remedies, is perhaps the education of the poor;—we are astonished that the Established Church in England is not awake to this means of arresting the progress of Methodism.'[35] With that the Manchester churchmen, much as they might differ from Sydney Smith's Whiggery, would have agreed. But that education, they held, must be clerically controlled.

The Manchester division came on 5 May 1800. The schools were divided between the Anglicans and the Dissenters and the latter continued their group for a time as the Sunday Schools of All Denominations. Each side had to gather strength after the two years of confusion and lessened support. The Church divided itself into ten districts, each under the parish clergyman, with visitors and collectors. Funds had run low during the disruption and teachers' wages had had to be reduced and even withheld. At the same time sectarian discipline was tightened. Parents were warned that 'if they allow their children to attend schools of the opposite Party they must not expect to be admitted again into the schools belonging to the Established Church'. The ground lost was soon recovered, and though the funds had their ups and downs the schools grew in popularity. The organizers had, however, to face competition. The report of 1814 noted rather sadly that the eyes of the benevolent had been turned to the British and Foreign Bible Society and the missionary societies. It pleaded that 'in the eagerness to convert Gentiles abroad' it should not be forgotten that 'there are Gentiles at home'. The paragraph gave so much offence that a special meeting was held and more innocuous words were substituted.

The greatest stroke of the Church schools was to start the holding of the Whit-Monday processions. The children had always attended the charity sermons. Now they were to gather in St. Ann's Square and attend in a body a single sermon for the whole of Manchester and Salford. It was at first intended that they should go to St. Ann's but this was changed to the Collegiate Church. And on 6 May 1801, began one of the most famous of Manchester institutions.[36] The Dissenters also came to have their processions but never with the same united organization.

The number of Church of England scholars at the time of the disruption had fallen to under 3,000, but it soon doubled and stood at between 7,000 and 8,000 from 1810 to 1821. The number of Church schools fell from 24 in 1802 to 17 in 1810, largely because the smaller ones were given up. Special buildings came to be erected as the connection with the churches grew closer.[37]

Material on the history of the Nonconformist Sunday Schools is more fragmentary. There was a great increase in the number and variety of Dissenting chapels. In 1784 the Anglican places of worship outnumbered the Dissenters by almost three to one; by 1804 the Anglican churches were as three to four; by 1825 they were fewer than one to two; by 1836 fewer than one to three. Though many of the Dissenting chapels were small the changing balance of religious persuasion was reflected in the Sunday schools. In the minority in the 1790s, the Dissenting (including Roman Catholic) children slowly gained until by 1821 they were double the number of Anglican, and in the next decades increased their lead. In 1834–35 in the boroughs of Manchester and Salford there were 13,205 children on the books of Church Sunday schools, 25,432 on those of Protestant Dissenters and 4,493 on the Roman Catholic.[38] The immediate successors of the Dissenting section of the schism of 1800 were the Schools for All Denominations, which lasted for over two decades and came in the end to be mainly Methodist. Most other sects kept independent. By 1821 the 'Schools for All Denominations' accounted for only 3,947 of the 14,261 Protestant Dissenting children. All this, however, is a complicated story which deserves full investigation.

The character of the Sunday schools was changing, largely because of the disappearance of the paid teacher. In the early years he was universal; in 1797 a 'gratuitous teacher' was still such a rarity in Manchester that he was specially presented with a Bible. But as the parochial and congregational element was strengthened voluntary service became more general. The Manchester Church Committee in 1812 spoke with 'singular satisfaction' of 'a class of respectable persons who have kindly come forward with their services in the capacity of *gratuitous* teachers'; it hoped for more. 'The most flourishing and best-regulated schools,' it noted, 'are generally those in which the least money is paid to teachers for a given number of scholars, and where some of the regular visitors are *continually present* for the purpose of inspection.' In some Nonconformist schools voluntary teachers had always been present. Wesley had noted them at Bolton in 1787. The famous Stockport Sunday School, undenominational, was distinguished from the rest in having mostly voluntary teachers; it had begun in November 1784, as one of six schools conducted on a plan like that of Manchester, and still flourishes.[39] But in general the change took place in the early years of the nineteenth century, though some paid teachers lingered on until the seventies.[40]

We must not forget, however, that behind the panegyrics lay a very rudimentary sort of education. A return to the Select Committee of 1816 on Children in Manufactories estimated that only a quarter of the children in the Manchester and Salford schools could read and write; one-sixth were learning the alphabet; a third were learning to spell; one-sixth could read the Testament; one-twelfth could read the Bible.[41]

The history of Sunday schools in the nineteenth century lies outside the

scope of this paper but a word should be said of their place in the development of popular education. They had helped to bring about a marked
change in the attitude towards education. It could be complained in 1805
that the belief in education was carried 'to so violent a degree that ... the
man who should dispute the wisdom of Sunday schools would be considered as unworthy attention'.[42] The enthusiasm did not go far enough to
carry Whitbread's Bill of 1807 for a national system of education, but there
was enthusiasm, if also sectarian rancour, behind the great wrangle over
the Lancaster and Bell systems of education two or three years later. Here,
as in the Sunday schools, there was a simple and easy prescription. In the
1780s it had seemed that to take children off the streets on Sunday and
teach them to read the Bible and repeat the Catechism would make them
good and docile members of society. It was a short cut to the social
millennium, just as the spinning-frame and the steam-engine seemed short
cuts to a material millenium. Now, in the later years of the Napoleonic
wars, it seemed possible to transform society by applying the factory
system to education. Bell and Lancaster between them improved on the
Sunday schools. Those schools had up to forty children under a paid
teacher. One of the minor issues in the Manchester quarrel of 1799 had
been whether the classes ought not, for the sake of efficiency, to be reduced
to twenty-five children. Under the Bell and Lancaster systems the children
were set to teach each other. Lancaster wanted to cover England with
schools in each of which a thousand children should be taught in squads of
ten by a hundred monitors, at an annual cost of 5s. a head. Manchester
took up his plan in 1809 and the manifesto of the promoters (mostly Whigs
and Nonconformists) explained ecstatically how 'the Education of One
thousand ... can be accomplished by the superintendence of *one master*, and
the aid of *three books*, whilst in the common and general mode, it would
require, at least, twenty masters, and from one to two thousand books'.[43]

Manchester had its Lancasterian school and the Church followed with a
Bell school several years later.[44] But for the great mass of children the
Sunday school continued to be the only means of education. It is possible,
indeed, to argue that the Sunday schools became almost an impediment to
the emergence of a wider system of education, for they fixed the convention
that Sunday was the proper time for instruction and they entrenched the
sectarian interest in education. Certainly the promoters of the Lancasterian
school had to put in their appeal some carefully worded sentences about
co-operation with Sunday schools, and almost to suggest that week-day
education was supplementary to Sunday.

The survey of 1821 showed that in Manchester and Salford only 2,500
boys and girls were attending day schools (not counting private and dame
schools), and 23,000 were attending Sunday schools. In 1834 the report of
the Manchester Statistical Society showed that 10,000 attended day and even-

ing schools only, 10,000 attended day and Sunday schools, 23,000 attended Sunday schools only, and 17,000 had no instruction whatever. But the battle of the sects went on and nothing is more melancholy than to see how the meagre education provided by the Sunday schools was made a screen for bitter opposition to State aid for education. This is one of the least edifying chapters in the history of Nonconformity.

But this passionate attachment to the voluntary principle, which had such blighting effects, was also the expression of a great virtue. The Sunday school had become a vital part of religious organization and offered a field of warm personal service for the laity, especially for women, that did not exist in the indifferent eighteenth century. In the diary for 1816 of Benjamin Braidley, later Boroughreeve of Manchester, there is a passage characteristic of the new type of Sunday school worker. He was then a young man of twenty-four at St Clement's Sunday school:

My time is now occupied in this way: On the Sunday I am frequently at school during the whole day. On the Sunday evening I explain a chapter to as many scholars as choose to attend; after which we go to church. After church time (about eight o'clock) we come to school, and have a prayer, &c. meeting until about a quarter or half-past nine. On Monday evenings I attend the writing school. On Tuesday evenings we meet the scholars, &c. (boys and girls separate) for prayer, &c. On Wednesday evenings I often have to attend committees of the Church Missionary Society, Sunday Schools, &c. &c.; and there is also writing and accounts at the Sunday School. On Thursday evening I attend the writing, and on Friday evening I am generally at leisure, but we have accounts and writing at the school; and on Saturday evenings I am generally at school; so that I have very little leisure for other occupations. However, if my present employments bring glory to God, I am satisfied![45]

It was this kind of devoted, single-minded man and woman who made the Sunday schools so great a source of moral influence during the nineteenth century. Disraeli wrote, with doubtful truth, of the 'two nations' in English society. In the North and North Midlands, at any rate, rich and poor, master and man, met in the Sunday school. The mixture of social classes was freer there than perhaps in any other sphere of life. It was that, with their disinterested spirit, that gave them their unique social value in the harsh circumstances of the time.[46] There was something in the charge, which Canon Bardsley in 1877 felt it necessary to answer, that they were becoming 'mere courting institutions'![47] But that was a way of saying that in those days of more limited interests, less easy travel, few distracting amusements, they were the focus of the social lives of a great part of Lancashire's population. Just a century ago, the London *Morning Chronicle* sent a reporter to Manchester to study the condition of its people. In the midst of much gloom he had some suggestive things to say of what he called 'the Lancashire Sunday school system':[48]

The Lancashire Sunday-school system has already attained a European reputation. The muster of children collected in the Peel Park on the recent occasion of the royal visit to Manchester, and amounting, it is said, to more than 70,000, was a memorable proof of the perfection of the organisation which could call forth in such order and discipline so vast a juvenile army. Narrow, and often sectarian as is the education given by establishments of the kind, it has worked an incalculable deal of good. You often hear in the north, that Lancashire would have been a hell upon earth were it not for its Sunday-schools. Long before educational committees of the privy-council, and British and Foreign School Societies were heard of—long ere the days of Institutes and Athenaeums—the Lancashire Sunday-schools were at work, impregnating the people with the rudiments of an education—rude and fanatical, perhaps, but which long kept alive the glow of moral sentiment and popular intelligence.

The founders of the system still maintain a curious kind of local fame. Often will the visitors to Manchester observe, both in drawing-rooms and humble parlour-kitchens, little dingy portraits of soberly-clad, grave-looking men, whose names he has never heard of, and who yet will be pointed out to him as the greatest and most glorious of Englishmen. Of these the most renowed is an indefatigable worker in the cause of the name of Stott. For half a century, this gentleman was the foremost champion of the Lancashire Sunday-schools, and worked steadily on, although now accused of training up blood-thirsty young Jacobins, and again of organising an operative Jacquerie. The school to which he principally devoted himself opened with forty scholars. Its average number is now slightly under 3,000.[49]

Sunday-schools in Manchester are not only a vast educational instrument, but a great social fact. Nearly every school has its library, and many their benefit societies. At Whitsuntide, the yearly week of rest, every school has its country trip. Many of the richest men in Manchester will tell you, that to the Sunday-schools, which taught them to read and write, and inculcated habits of sobriety and honesty, they now owe their villas and their mills. Sunday-schools act also as powerful agents in binding different classes together. Men in the middle ranks of life very commonly act as teachers; and acquaintanceships formed in the school-room not unfrequently lead to life-long business connections. Families are for generations connected with the same school; a great proportion of the children, at any given time, are the offspring of old scholars; and a great proportion of the teachers were once scholars in the classes they subsequently instruct. The schools are elementary and religious. Scripture-reading and expounding, with instructions in psalmody, form the staple business of the meetings. Most schools have, however, their evening-classes, devoted to more secular instruction. For the working-day classes, small fees, varying from 2d. to 6d. per week, are paid. The Sunday education is entirely gratuitous. In general, the ages of the pupils vary from eight to twenty, and the girls commonly remain longer as scholars than the boys.

The Manchester Sunday-schools hold, not only in educational but in social organisation, from 40,000 to 50,000 children and young persons, controlled by 4,000 or 5,000 teachers, assistants, and inspecting-visitors. Of the whole number, about 25,000 may belong to the church-schools, of which there are about fifty. Of two Dissenting educational unions, the Manchester Union supports 28 schools, with a total of about 10,000 scholars; the Salford Union about 15, with a total of 6,000 or 7,000 scholars. There are also Calvinistic and Roman Catholic Sunday-schools, so that the educational provision in this respect is, if not ample, at least a great and constantly working moral engine.

That is not an unfair picture. As this observer of 1850 saw, the Sunday schools were a great civilizing influence in the raw, crude society which the Industrial Revolution created in Lancashire. They were begun as a form of police precaution imposed from above, and imbued with authoritarianism. They were transformed by the genius of ordinary people into a vital part of democratic society. They had the defects of that sectarian age. Educationally they were a makeshift, a miserable substitute for day-schooling. But, apart from their spiritual value, which is not here under discussion, they formed a point of social contact and sympathy in a confused and shifting community; they threw a bridge across the gulf between classes; they built up self-respect and individual responsibility; and they encouraged that spirit of voluntary service and voluntary organization which is, perhaps almost the best thing the nineteenth century bequeathed to us.

STATISTICAL NOTE

The following are figures of children on the books of the Manchester and Salford Schools.

Table 1. *Interdenominational Committee*

Year	Scholars	No. of Schools	
		Manchester	Salford
1784 (Sept.)	1800	25	—
1785 (Oct.)	2291		—
1786 (April)	2836	34	—
1788	5006	36	6
1791	4663	36	6
1792	4646	36	6
1793	4970	36	6
1794	4786	36	6
1795	5171	36	6
1796	5326	36	6
1797	5171	36	6

Table 2. *Established Church*

Year	Scholars	No. of Schools Manchester and Salford
1801	3157	24
1802	3651	
1803	4434	
1804	4765	
1805	5124	
1806	5360	
1807	5264	
1808	6657	
1809	6680	
1810	7424	17
1811	7634	
1812	7030	
1813	7015	
1814	7602	
1818	7272	
1819	7090	17
1821	7647	19
1825	8048	21
1834–35	13,025	34

Table 3. *Dissenters*

Year	Scholars	No. of Schools Manchester and Salford
1816 (*a*)	7040	
(*b*)	8092	
1821	14,261	39
1825	15,423	42
1834–35	25,432	72

Table 4. *Roman Catholics*

Year	Scholars	No. of Schools Manchester and Salford
1816 (*a*)	1000	3
(*b*)	674	
1821	1200	8
1825	2213	
1834–35	4493	11

Sources.

1. *Manchester Mercury*, 21 Sept. 1784, 14 Oct. 1788; J. Bennett, op. cit., 2 Oct. 1785; Minutes (1786); *Reports*.

2. *Reports; Manchester Guardian*, 6 May 1821; Baines, *Hist. Directory of Lancashire* (1825); Manchester Statistical Society's Report, 1834–5 (Wheeler, op. cit., pp. 386–8).

3. and 4. As above. For 1816 (*a*) *Minutes of Sel. Committee on Children in Manufactories*, p. 97; for 1816 (*b*) ibid., p. 388.

BIBLIOGRAPHICAL NOTE

Though there has been little further exploration of the social history of the Sunday School movement since Wadsworth wrote this essay, his approach to the education of working-class children in the late eighteenth and early nineteenth centuries has been followed up by a number of writers interested in the aims and character of working-class educational developments prior to the Education Act of 1870. Several of the essays in Brian Simon, *Studies in the History of Education, 1780–1870* (1960) deal explicitly with this theme, as, in a broader chronological context, does L. Stone's broad, though somewhat tentative article, 'Literacy and education in England, 1640–1900', in *Past and Present*, 42 (1969). M. W. Flinn, 'Social theory and the Industrial Revolution' in Tom Burns and S. B. Saul (eds.), *Social Theory and Economic Change* (1967), and Richard Johnson, 'Educational policy and social control in early Victorian England', *Past and Present*, 49 (1970), endeavour for different periods to place the provision of education for the working classes against the wider background of adjustment to industrialization. Harold Silver, *The Concept of Popular Education* (1965), though primarily concerned with Owenism, and Mary Sturt, *The Education of the People* (1965), perhaps the best general survey of educational history from the late eighteenth century onwards, both give some attention to the question of the social objectives of educational provision.

NOTES

1. *Manchester Mercury*, 8 Aug. 1786.
2. M. G. Jones, *The Charity School Movement* (1938), p. 3.
3. *Manchester Mercury*, 27 Jan. 1784.
4. *Considerations on the Fatal Effects to a Trading Nation of the Present Excess of Public Charity* (1763), p. 25. For this and similar quotations see E. S. Furniss, *The Position of the Laborer in a System of Nationalism* (1920), pp. 148–9.
5. Isaac Watts, *An Essay towards the Encouragement of Charity Schools* (1728), quoted Jones, op. cit. 74–5.
6. Alfred Gregory, *Robert Raikes, Journalist and Philanthropist* (1880 edn.), pp. 31–2.
7. Raikes to Richard Townley. First published *Manchester Mercury*, 6 Jan. 1784.
8. Gregory, op. cit. 68.
9. Richard Townley (1726–1802), the son of a Rochdale mercer. He had some literary pretensions, was a friend and patron of Tim Bobbin, and wrote intelligent letters on agriculture and other subjects to the Manchester papers.
10. *Manchester Mercury*, 6 Jan. 1784.
11. Ibid., 27 Jan. 1784. Raikes's letter to Townley was also printed in the *Gentleman's Magazine*, June 1784, as communicated by 'A Friend to Virtue', writing from Sheffield. This may be a misprint for Belfield and the writer Townley himself.
12. *Gentleman's Magazine*, 1784, i. 377, 410.
13. *Manchester Mercury* for these dates.
14. There is a useful list of Lancashire references (drawn from the *Mercury*) in C. W. Bardsley, *Memorials of St. Ann's Church, Manchester* (1877), pp. 120–1. The Manchester Committee took a census of schools in the Salford Hundreds in 1788 and the incomplete returns showed 6,598 scholars at 32 places outside Manchester and Salford, the largest being Bolton 950, Hey Chapel 445, Ringley 430, Rochdale 426, and Ashton-under-Lyne 406 (*Manchester Mercury*, 10 Sept. 1788).
15. W. B. Whitaker, *The Eighteenth Century English Sunday* (1940), 219. Its report of 1797 mentions that 37 Lancashire and 6 Cheshire schools had been assisted, but Manchester and Salford were apparently outside its scope. *Plan of a Society . . . for the Support and Encouragement of Sunday Schools* (1797).
16. e.g. *Manchester Mercury*, 10 Aug. 1784.
17. *Manchester Mercury*, 21 Sept. 1784.
18. Ibid., 28 Sept. 1784; Minutes (MS.) in Chetham Library.
19. Rules and Orders, *Manchester Mercury*, 11 Jan. 1785.
20. *Wheeler's Manchester Chronicle*, 11 Apr. 1789.
21. Minutes, 11 Aug. 1785.
22. *A Letter to the Clergy of the Diocese of Chester concerning Sunday Schools* (1786), p. 11.
23. Ibid., 8.
24. *The Advantages of Sunday Schools. A Sermon . . . by the Revd. J. Bennett* (1785), p. 4.
25. Minutes, 7 Mar. 1791. In the controversy of 1799 it was noted that the rules did not extend to 'absolute prohibition of extempore prayer'. The point was still troubling the Anglican Committee in 1815 when a meeting of subscribers rejected a proposed rule excluding 'all extemporaneous prayer and addresses upon any occasion, further than was necessary to the explanation of a word or a sentence, except such prayer or address should be uttered by a minister' (*Manchester Magazine*, 1815, p. 497).
26. *Enquiry Concerning Political Justice* (1797 edn.), ii. 299.
27. *Report*, 1 July 1792.
28. Revd. M. Ollerenshaw, *A Sermon on the Religious Education of Children and the Usefulness of Sunday Schools . . .* (1798); J. Mayer, *A Defence of the Sunday Schools: attempted in a series of letters addressed to the Rev. M. Ollerenshaw* (1798); T. Whitaker, *Four Letters to Mr. J. Mayer of Stockport on his Defence of the Sunday*

Schools (1798); J. Mayer, *Candid Animadversions on the Rev. Thomas Whitaker's Four Letters* (1798).

29. Samuel Bamford, *Early Days* (1849), p. 107.

30. H. E. Matthews, *Methodism and the Education of the People* (1949), pp. 41–2; W. B. Whitaker, *The Eighteenth Century English Sunday* (1940), pp. 229–30.

31. Cf. H. McLachlan, *The Methodist Unitarian Movement* (1919), p. 104.

32. Quoted Jones, op. cit. 153.

33. L. S. Marshall, *Development of Public Opinion in Manchester 1780–1820* (1946), pp. 120–1.

34. R. F. Wearmouth, *Methodism and the Working Class Movements of England* (1937), p. 61.

35. *Edinburgh Review*, 1808. *Works* (1859), i. 101.

36. See Bardsley, op. cit., for the history of the processions.

37. The interdenominational committee had had no special buildings. A legacy of £100 had been left to it and various sites were surveyed. As, however, the estate went into Chancery, the project dropped.

38. For the 1821 returns see *Manchester Guardian*, 6 May 1821, quoted S. E. Maltby, *Manchester and the Movement for National Education, 1800–1870* (1918), 129; for 1834–5 see J. Wheeler, *History of Manchester* (1836).

39. Interesting evidence on the Stockport 'gratuitous teachers' was given by Joseph Mayer in 1816 (*Minutes of Evidence, Sel. Comm. on State of Children employed in Manufactories*, 1816, p. 51).

40. Bardsley, op. cit. 133.

41. *Minutes of Evidence*, p. 389.

42. W. Playfair, quoted M. D. George, *London Life in the Eighteenth Century* (1925), p. 13.

43. *Wheeler's Manchester Chronicle*, 8 Apr. 1809.

44. The monitorial system was applied in 1812 in some Manchester Church Sunday schools.

45. *Memoir of Benjamin Braidley, Esq.* (1845), pp. 8–9. This school was later Bennett Street School, attached to St. Paul's, and famous as the biggest in Manchester. In 1812 it had 30 teachers, 40 monitors, and 1,820 scholars; in 1831 it had 2,700. Braidley gives an account of this remarkable school in his *Sunday School Memorials* (1831). It had had a sick society since 1812, a funeral society, and a writing school at which 250 children were taught. For details of this school in 1816 (including rules of its sick society) see *Mins. Sel. Com. Children in Manufactories* (1816), pp. 389, 394–9.

46. Cf. Unwin, G., *Samuel Oldknow and the Arkwrights* (1924), pp. 39–41.

47. Bardsley, op. cit. 138.

48. Summarized in Chambers's *Repository of Instructive and Amusing Tracts*, vol. i, no. 1, pp. 26–8.

49. The reference is to Bennett Street School and its founder David Stott.

6

The Myth of the Old Poor Law and the Making of the New*

M. BLAUG

No matter which authority we consult on the English Poor Laws in the nineteenth century the same conclusions emerge: the Old Poor Law demoralized the working class, promoted population growth, lowered wages, reduced rents, destroyed yeomanry, and compounded the burden on ratepayers; the more the Old Poor Law relieved poverty, the more it encouraged the poverty which it relieved; the problem of devising an efficient public relief system was finally solved with the passage of the 'harsh but salutary' Poor Law Amendment Act of 1834. So unanimous are both the indictment and the verdict of historians on this question that we may forgo the pleasure of citing 'chapter and verse'.

The bare facts are familiar enough. Until late in the eighteenth century, public relief was largely confined to those too young, too old, or too sick to work. But in 1782 Gilbert's Act sanctioned the principle of relieving the so-called 'able-bodied' without requiring them to enter the workhouse. Then, in 1795, the magistrates of Speenhamland in the county of Berkshire, responding to the exceptional rise in the price of wheat, decided to fix a 'minimum standard' by supplementing earned incomes in proportion to the price of wheaten bread and the size of worker's families. The idea was soon imitated in adjoining counties, and in the following year it was ratified by Parliament. The practice of making allowances-in-aid-of-wages was almost always associated with make-work schemes which rotated the unemployed among local farmers in accordance with the rated value of their property. By divorcing earnings from the productivity of labour, the Allowance system in conjunction with the Roundsman System sapped the initiative of agricultural workers and thus contributed to the unprecedented rise in poor-relief expenditures in the years before and after Waterloo. So ran the argument of the reformers of 1834 and so runs the consensus of modern opinion.

History repeats itself, says an ancient proverb—and historians repeat each

* From *Journal of Economic History*, 23 (1963), 151–84. Reprinted by permission of the author and the Economic History Association.

other. The standard analysis of the effects of the Old Poor Law is derived without qualification, from the *Poor Law Commissioners' Report of 1834*, that 'brilliant, influential, and wildly unhistorical document', as Tawney once described it. But it was a gross exaggeration that led the reformers of 1834 to characterize the Old Poor Law as 'a bounty on indolence and vice' and 'a universal system of pauperism'. Only an incomplete theoretical analysis of the working of the Speenhamland policy and a superficial examination of the facts could have produced so one-sided an interpretation. The continued endorsement of the *Report of 1834* has seriously distorted the history of the Industrial Revolution in Britain. The Old Poor Law tried to maintain the real income of workers by tying wages to the cost of living; it provided unemployment compensation together with a scheme to promote private employment; and it coupled both of these to a family endowment plan. It is not often realized that the kind of arguments which are used to condemn the Old Poor Law *per se* would equally condemn most modern welfare legislation. Perhaps this is the intention, but even 'left-wing' historians, such as the Webbs and the Hammonds, have attacked the Old Poor Law on the one hand, and, on the other, have argued that minimum-wage legislation accompanied by children-allowance payments would have been a preferable alternative to Speenhamland. But, in fact, their proposal amounts to nearly the same thing as the Old Poor Law.

The years between 1813 and the accession of Victoria have been aptly described as 'the blackest period of English farming'. When we put together everything we know about the causes of 'agricultural distress' in those years, we will have grounds more relative than maladministration of the Poor Laws to account for the growth of relief expenditures. This is not merely an academic question. In the Victorian era, the whole of what we would nowadays call 'social services' were reflected in poor-law expenditures. And the *Report of 1834*, with its strictures on 'the old system', was revered for three generations as a canonical book, teaching that all forms of dole, charity, and relief to the unemployed are suspect, because they only induce him to breed in idleness; that least relief is best relief; and that voluntary charity is always preferable to public aid because it is somehow capable of discriminating the 'deserving' poor from the 'undeserving'. Without the continued influence of 'the principles of 1834', Mrs. Jellyby is unthinkable.

I

Before looking at the empirical evidence, let us consider what results might be expected from a system of subsidizing wages, considered by itself. Most historians assume without question that the Allowance System must have depressed agricultural earnings: farmers could pay less than competitive rates because the parish officers were forced to make up the deficit. But what if the guaranteed subsidy made workers less willing to supply

effort? It is elementary economics that the short-run effect of a subsidy to
workers is to lessen the supply—the number of days per week offered by
men, women, and children; if the supply curve of labour is positively sloped
the result is that wages will *rise*. Of course, if the subsidy is tied to the size
of the family, it may promote earlier marriages and more children, so that,
within a decade or so, it does depress wages. To a generation drunk on
Malthusian wine, the population argument seemed irrefutable. But nowadays we are inclined to treat this type of reasoning with more scepticism,
particularly if the subsidy is modest in amount, increases less than proportionately with each additional child, and is continuously scaled down year
after year; as we shall see, all three things were true under the Old Poor Law.[1]

It is possible to argue, however, that the Allowance System depressed
wages even if it did not stimulate the growth of population. A subsidy that
varies inversely with earned wages, and that is what the Allowance System
amounted to, gives workers no incentive to supply genuine effort. And since
employers are not the only taxpayers, the system likewise deprives those
who hire labour of the incentive to exact a full day's work. In consequence,
productivity declines, output shrinks, and wages fall. This kind of reasoning,
which for present purposes we might label Benthamite rather than Malthusian, was very common in the days before 1834. It has a distinctly modern
ring: to divorce wages from their roots in the efficiency of labour must
lead to a misallocation of resources.

Applied to an underdeveloped country, however, this argument must be
severely qualified. The early stages of economic development are invariably
characterized by 'dualism': the high-wage industrial sector is largely independent of the low-wage agricultural sector. In contrast to manufacture,
labour in agriculture is typically hired on a day-to-day basis and the demand
for farm-workers varies sharply from season to season. Full employment
may be achieved during planting and harvesting, but during slack seasons,
which comprise from one-third to one-half of the calendar year, as much
as half the labour force may be idle. The gradual destruction of handicraft
industry due to the invasion of machine-made goods sometimes creates a
pool of chronically unemployed labour even during peak seasons. The automatic market forces which would eliminate such unemployment by driving
down wage rates fail to operate if wages are below the biological minimum,
implying that the food intake of workers is not sufficient to permit them
to supply their maximum effort per unit of time. The amount of work put
forth now depends on the wages paid, rather than the other way around:
lower wages would lower the consumption and hence the productivity of
workers. Under these circumstances, it will pay landlords and farmers to
maintain wages above competitive market-clearing levels and to devise a
special scheme to eliminate open unemployment. The standard method is
to disguise the manpower surplus by sharing the work out among all job-

seekers with each man putting forth less effort than he is capable of supplying. Since labour costs per unit of output are now lower than they would be if the unemployed were permitted to underbid going wage rates, such institutional arrangements lead to a greater total product than would otherwise be available.[2]

With 40 per cent of the gainfully occupied population in agriculture, England in 1815 must be counted among the underdeveloped countries, displaying all the familiar features of a 'dual' economy. Under the circumstances, a system of supplementing the earnings of agricultural workers so as to guarantee a 'living wage' must have pulled in opposite directions. On the one hand, it reduced mortalities, particularly infant mortalities, and so depressed wages by promoting population growth. It may also have slowed down emigration to the industrial sector with similar effects. On the other hand, in so far as it repaired nutritional deficiencies, it tended to raise wages by raising the effort-level of each worker. The family-endowment features of the Speenhamland policy pulled in one direction while the use of the bread scale to determine the amount of the wage subsidy pulled in the other.

The problem of deciding which of the two forces predominated is complicated by the fact that wheat was both the principal wage-good and, in some sections of the country, the principal product of farmers demanding labour. In years of drought, when the demand for agricultural labour fell off, tending to lower wages, the price of bread soared upwards and the subsidy increased. Conversely, in years of bumper crops, wages tended to rise and the subsidy would fall as the price of bread declined. One of the significant side effects of the Allowance System, as Malthus pointed out, was to render the demand for wheat insensitive to wheat prices by stabilizing the real income of agricultural workers who, if we are to believe Eden's budget studies, spent almost half of their income in wheaten bread. Thus, when wheat prices rose after a bad harvest, the total quantity of wheat sold declined less than proportionately and farmers enjoyed higher incomes than they had expected. On the other hand, a good harvest would lead to a decline both in the price of wheat and in the total receipts of farmers. So universal was this inverse association of the yield of the harvest and agricultural prosperity in this period that we may take it as a fact that the demand for wheat was then highly inelastic.

Since the poor rates were levied on the occupiers, not on the owners, of land and real estate, farmers themselves paid a major share of the rates used to finance wage subsidies. Owing to the inelastic demand for wheat, it was paradoxically true that they gained on the swings what they lost on the roundabout. Spending on relief rose when the harvest was poor, but at such times the income of farmers was at a maximum. Conversely, when they were squeezed by falling prices and rising wages in consequence of a good harvest, the pressure on the rates was at a minimum. In other words, poor-relief spending fluctuated with the income of farmers. No wonder we hear more complaints about 'the onerous burdens of the poor rates' in years when inclement weather produced 'agricultural prosperity'!

We must, however, take into account the possibility of a trend created by an excess of bad years over good. By putting a floor under the demand for wheat, the Old Poor Law kept up the price of bread in years of drought. In this way, a persistently unfavourable trend in rainfall or temperature could account for rising relief expenditures, irrespective of the effects of relief spending on population growth and work incentives.

To round out the analysis, we recall that allowances-in-aid-of-wages were almost always associated with the Roundsman System, modified by the use of the Labour Rate. The Poor Law authorities calculated the total wage bill of the parish and then levied the poor rate to cover this amount. Each ratepayer agreed to pay the allotted sum either in wages or in rates. By accepting his quota of the unemployed in proportion to the assessed value of his property, a farmer could be relieved of paying part of his rates. It was thought that this would encourage employment because farmers would prefer to employ more workers than they really needed rather than to pay the parish the deficiency in their allotted rates. In view of the existence of visible as well as invisible unemployment in rural districts at that time, the idea of the Labour Rate made good sense: as long as labour is in surplus, wasteful employment may well be cheaper than maintaining workers on the dole. But since employers of labour were not the only ratepayers, the system tended to discriminate against family farms and smallholders who employed little labour. We cannot say how much importance attaches to such consider- ations unless we know just how the rates were determined, how many workers in a parish were typically unemployed, and how far market wages stood below an acceptable minimum standard. It is time to turn to the evidence.

II

The first question is: How prevalent was the system of subsidizing wages out of the rates? To answer this question at all we must perforce over- simplify. Poor Law administration before 1834 differed widely in aims and methods from place to place and from time to time. Parliamentary legislation failed to produce a national Poor Law, and throughout this period there was only a casual connection between the statute books and the administrative practices of parish officers. The 15,000 parishes in England and Wales varied in area from thirty acres to thirty square miles, in population from a few dozen to tens of thousands, and in taxable capacity from a barren common to the built-up docks of the city of London. With a system so heterogeneous, any generalization is bound to be subject to serious qualification.

Moreover, we know next to nothing about the actual number of people relieved or about the proportions relieved inside and outside workhouses before 1834. Throughout this period, only two attempts were made to take a census of the poor. The first, in 1802, was the more thorough, showing about one million people on relief, including 300,000 children under the age of fifteen.[3] This implies that as much as 11 per cent of the population of England and Wales was then on relief, but we know that the census, unfortunately, counted more than once any 'pauper' who applied for relief at two or three separate occasions in the year, a common practice at the time. Of the total number receiving aid, only 8 per cent were residents of workhouses. This is not surprising, considering that there were almost 4,000 workhouses in the whole of the country, most of which were no larger than country cottages. Even where there was a workhouse in the parish, magistrates were frequently reluctant to 'offer the House' which was invariably an unsanitary and disorderly institution, herding together the young, the old, the sick, and the insane. The heavy reliance on outdoor relief, therefore, was as much due to a humane concern over the plight of the poor as to anything else. Even those reported to be 'disabled by permanent illness' were not always forced into the workhouse, as evidenced by the fact that their number in 1802 exceeded the number of workhouse residents. With more than 90 per cent of the pauper host receiving outdoor relief, about 55 per cent were said to be on 'permanent' relief, while 35 per cent were denoted as being relieved 'occasionally'. This does not tell us, however, how many were entirely dependent upon parish funds and how many had their wages supplemented 'permanently' or 'occasionally' by the Poor Law authorities. The next census, for 1812–14, was equally vague and, furthermore, it failed to count either children under fifteen on outdoor relief or non-residents of the parish.[4]

The prevailing belief at the time was that the Allowance System was confined to the agricultural counties of the South. The *Report of 1834* made no effort to verify this assumption. The Commissioner circulated questions in the rural districts, but not all parishes were visited, and it is impossible to tell whether the replies constitute anything like a representative sample. The Commissioners never attempted to summarize their findings, and in the *Report* itself they offered a few graphic examples of the Allowance System drawn from parishes in both the South and the North, thus conveying the impression that what they admittedly called 'the abuses of the South' were to be found throughout the country. Even the Webbs, in their definitive book on *The Old Poor Law*, say no more than that outdoor relief to the unemployed was 'adopted, in principle, at one time or another by practically every rural parish outside Northumberland', and was universal in rural districts south of the line that runs from the Severn to the Wash.[5]

The only worthwhile evidence we have is a neglected questionnaire circulated to the Poor Law authorities in 1824 by the *Select Committee on Labourers' Wages*, to which Clapham first drew attention in 1926.[6] Unfortunately, in the slapdash manner of the day, the Committee failed to indicate what proportion of the parishes responded to the questionnaire. The replies from the various counties were grouped in terms of 'hundreds' or wapentakes, and since these differed widely in population, it is difficult to weigh the

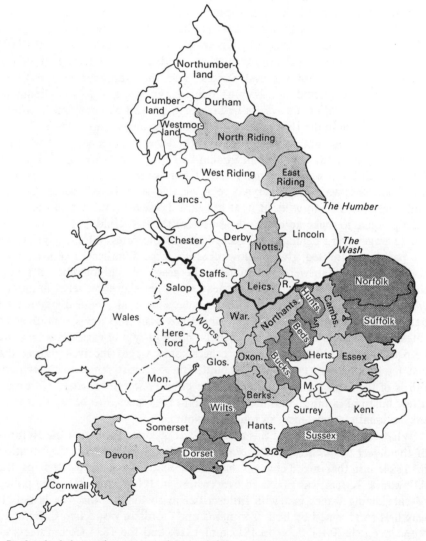

In the shaded counties, most parishes subsidized wages out of the poor rates in 1824. The system was particularly prevalent in the heavily shaded counties. The heavy line dissecting England separates the high-wage counties of the North from the low-wage counties of the South.

answers in order to arrive at an accurate picture of the spread of the Allowance System. The Committee itself concluded that the Speenhamland policy was pervasive in eight southern counties, but an examination of the returns shows that it was also fairly widespread in twelve others. The complex situation is conveniently summed up in the accompanying map.

Clapham provides a fair summary of the findings, which contain a few surprises worth noting. All the northern counties, with the exception of Yorkshire, categorically denied supplementing wages from the rates. But so did all the counties in Wales and in the Southwest, with the exception of some districts in Devon. Furthermore, even in the South and South-East, most of the parishes in Hampshire, Kent, and Surrey, at least half of the parishes in Essex, Suffolk, and Sussex, and the whole of Hertfordshire and Middlesex (including London) denied practising the Speenhamland policy. The spread of the system as far north as Nottinghamshire, however, and its adoption in the East and North Riding, is somewhat unexpected.

The Committee not only inquired whether wages were paid out of rates but also whether the Roundsman System was in use and whether allowances for extra children were customary. The Roundsman System in the form of a Labour Rate was found everywhere associated with the Allowance System and never resorted to without it. It appears, however, that it was not common practice to make an extra allowance for the first child, even in counties where wages were regularly subsidized out of the rates. At the same time, all parishes admitted giving allowances to large families as a matter of course. From the answers pertaining to the grant of outdoor relief, it seems that every parish followed its own rules: some parishes gave relief in money while others confined assistance to payments in kind; some distinguished between insufficient income due to unemployment and low-standard wage rates, but most did not; in some districts, no inquiry into earnings was made before granting outdoor relief; in others, only wages received during the last few weeks were taken into account. But we must remember that two-thirds of the Poor Law authorities in the country were concerned with only a few hundred families and, therefore, might be expected to be familiar with the personal circumstances of relief recipients.

What use can be made of this evidence? It is conceivable that the Returns of the *Select Committee on Labourers' Wages* correctly depict the situation in 1824, but that great changes had been made since 1795. Perhaps the Allowance System was practised everywhere in 1800 or in 1815. The policy of subsidizing wages met with little criticism so long as the war lasted. It was first condemned by both Commons and Lords in respective Committee Reports on the Poor Laws in 1817 and 1818, and the 1824 Committee was designed to add ammunition to the charge. We may suppose, therefore, that fewer parishes practised outdoor relief to the able-bodied in 1824 than in previous years, and that those who persisted in the policy in 1824 must surely have made use of it before it came under attack. In other words, the eighteen counties which we have found to be Speenhamland counties in 1824 may be described as the hard core of the problem. Whatever the harmful effects of the Old Poor Law, they should be revealed by a comparison of conditions in this group of counties with all others.

III

Before proceeding to the comparison, we must ask how generously wages were subsidized. Do we have any reason to believe that wages in agriculture were below subsistence standards before the Allowance System was introduced? The first piece of evidence we have is that of the bread scale devised by the Berkshire magistrates. The Berkshire scale began with the gallon loaf at a shilling and then increased with each rise of a penny up to 2*s*.: with the loaf selling at a shilling, a single man was guaranteed a minimum weekly income of 3*s*. with an additional 1*s*. 6*d*. for each dependent; with the loaf at 2*s*., the minimum weekly income of a single man rose to 5*s*. and the allowance for dependents to 2*s*. 6*d*. A gallon loaf of bread is 20 oz. of bread per day which was estimated, reasonably enough, to constitute a minimum ration for a man at work. The idea was that one-third of income was to be spent on bread, leaving a margin for rent, heat, clothing, and other food-stuffs. Thus, in cheap years, a family with three children was said to require an income of 9*s*. a week, spending 3*s*. on bread—a gallon loaf for the man and two loaves for his four dependents—and 6*s*. on other things. In dear years, with the gallon loaf at 2*s*., the bread allowance would double to 6*s*., leaving a margin of 9*s*. on the notion that the prices of things in general rise by 50 per cent when the price of bread doubles.

In 1795, a single man working full time in the Midlands or the southern counties would have earned about 8*s*. 6*d*. a week. Supplements in kind, which were common in rural districts, would bring this up to about 10*s*. a week. If he was unemployed, the scale allowed him 5*s*. in a dear year like 1795. If he married and had a child, his wife and he together might earn 15*s*. a week; out of work, the scale allowed him 10*s*. a week. This was hardly a temptation to marry and breed recklessly! Indeed, so modest was the Speenhamland scale that the Webbs calculated that it allowed a family with two children 'about one-half of what a parsimonious Board of Guardians would today [1926] regard as bare subsistence'.[7] Nevertheless, existing wage levels in agriculture frequently fell below the Speenhamland minimum. If a married man had a few children young enough to keep his wife at home, he could not possibly earn enough to support his family at the famine prices that prevailed during the Napoleonic wars. And this is precisely why the idea of a minimum-wage law as an alternative to the bread scale was rejected in 1795; if it took account of variations in the size of families, it implied a wage far in excess of prevailing rates.[8]

When the Allowance System came to be criticized in the closing years of the war, one reaction was simply to reduce the bread scale or to abandon it in favour of some loose index of food prices in general. An examination of the local scales in use in various parishes shows that they were indeed pared down everywhere, so that by 1825 they had dropped on the average by about one-third from their original level.[9] But money wages in agriculture were no higher on the average in 1825 than in 1795, and even in 1835 they still stood below the Speenhamland minimum. The Commissioners of 1834 found out to their surprise that the cost of maintaining workhouse inmates at a minimum diet sometimes exceeded the wages of agricultural workers in surrounding districts.[10]

It is clear then that the Allowance System subsidized what in fact were substandard wages. At the same time, the scale at which outdoor relief was given does not suggest that it could have devitalized the working class by offering an attractive alternative to gainful employment. Nevertheless, the bread scale tied the relief bill to the price of wheat, and its effect on the volume of relief spending shows up quite clearly: the peaks and troughs in the two series coincide almost perfectly (for sources see Appendices A and B).[11]

It is apparent from the variations in the gazette price of wheat that 1811–12, 1816–17, 1823–25, and 1828–31 were years of poor harvests when both relief spending and the price of wheat rose. As we might expect, the cry of 'agricultural distress' was loudest in the bumper-crop years of 1813–15, 1820–2, and 1832–5, all of which show falling Poor Law expenditures.

It will be noticed that 'real' relief in terms of wheat generally varied inversely with money relief up to 1834. This phenomenon might be taken as further evidence of the influence of the bread scales: the scales were so devised that they did not vary proportionately with the price of bread; hence, real relief fell in dear years and rose in cheap years. But this could well be an illusion. By itself, the inverse relationship between real and money relief tells us nothing more than that money expenditures on relief never rose or declined as fast as the price of wheat. It is easy to explain why the relief bill did not rise as fast as wheat prices: as the burden on the rates increased, the parish officers simply drew the strings tighter. It is not so obvious why the relief bill should have lagged behind falling wheat prices. But when one considers the inertia that characterized Poor Law administration in the period, the lag is not really surprising.

Total relief spending showed a sharp upward trend after 1795, reaching a peak in 1818, after which it declined again to a low point in 1823. In the latter part of the 1820s, the trend was upward once again. Earlier we hypothesized that the predominance of bad years over good leads to rising relief expenditures if the amount of relief given is tied to the price of wheat. We can now test this hypothesis. Out of the 25 years from 1793 to 1818 only

1796, 1814, and 1815 were years of abundant harvests, and as many as four-teen crops in this period were seriously deficient. In contrast, good harvests were prevalent in the decade after 1818; in particular, the yield and quality of the harvests of 1819, 1820, and 1821 were without precedent.[12] Thus, without resorting to additional considerations, it is possible to account for the sharp rise in poor relief expenditures up to 1818 and the decline there-after by 'long waves' in climatic conditions. This should serve to check hasty generalizations about the economic causes of a trend in the total relief bill.

Graph 1

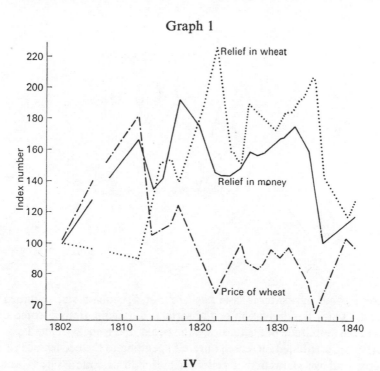

IV

The amount of poor relief per head was generally higher in the eighteen counties we have designated as Speenhamland counties than elsewhere. In 1802, it averaged 12s. in the Speenhamland counties and 8s. in the non-Speenhamland counties; by 1831, the average in the first group had risen to 13s. 8d. while the average in the second group had only increased to 8s. 7d. (see Appendix A). Such figures assume, of course, that there were no variations in the accuracy of population statistics between counties, an assumption which we know to be false. Nevertheless, the pattern is so pro-nounced that we may ignore the shortcomings of the data. Having said this much, it must be added that there appear to be no other significant differ-ences in the pattern of relief expenditures between the Speenhamland and the non-Speenhamland counties. For example, if we compare the rate of change of total expenditures in the two groups of counties, we discover that they varied with remarkable similarity (for sources see Appendix B).

In view of the fact that the Allowance System was almost entirely a rural problem in a particular part of the country, it is surprising to find so much coincidence between the two series. Would it make a difference if instead we grouped together the agricultural counties and contrasted their poor relief expenditures with the nonagricultural counties? It should make a difference: while all the Speenhamland counties fall into the agricultural

Graph 2

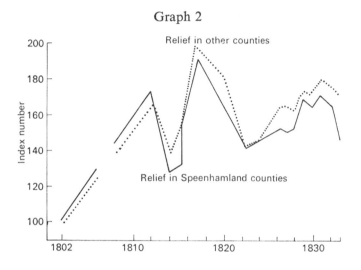

category, some agricultural counties are not Speenhamland counties (see Appendix C for the derivation of the series). But again, despite some differences in the amplitude of fluctuations, the peaks and troughs coincide.

Earlier we attributed increases in relief spending to the occurrence of poor harvests, and we showed that relief in agricultural counties rose and fell with the state of the harvest. But, in that case, what are we to make of the fact that relief in nonagricultural counties followed so closely upon the pattern in rural areas? The explanation lies in the fact that cycles in industrial activity in this period were closely geared to fluctuations in the harvest. A markedly deficient harvest called for an increase in grain imports which put pressure on the money market, leading to a reduction in investment and employment; owing to the inelastic demand for wheat, the rise in wheat prices redistributed income from consumers to farmers; since the marginal propensity to consume of farmers was lower than that of consumers in general, the result was to lower aggregate expenditures on consumption. Conversely, an abundant domestic harvest increased the level of effective demand throughout the economy.[13] Thus, despite differences in the administration of the Poor Laws, relief spending rose and fell more or less simultaneously in all counties.

What can we learn from a graphic comparison of the two series? It appears that relief rose faster than population in all counties up to 1812, and at a fairly uniform rate. It is tempting to credit this to lax administration of relief fostered by the emergency feelings of wartime. In 1803, Parliament ordered parish officers to give the wives and children of militiamen a weekly allowance equal to the current daily wage of agricultural labour; this added about 5–8 per cent to Poor Law expenditures in the years 1812–14.

Graph 3

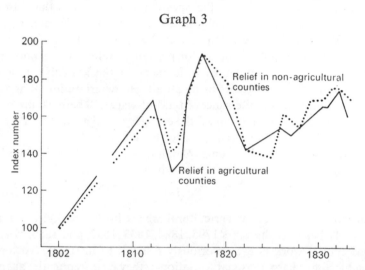

Nevertheless, such was the rise in prices during the war that the purchasing power of total relief was probably no higher in 1812 than in 1795. With the great break in wheat prices in 1813, relief expenditures were cut back everywhere, more successfully in rural than in industrial districts. The downward trend was short-lived, however. By 1816, the difficulties of conversion to peacetime production made new demands on the Poor Law authorities. In 1817 and 1818, the government found itself obliged to set the unemployed to work on road projects, financed by the sale of public bonds. With the improvement of conditions after 1818, the burden on the poor rates fell everywhere although in real terms the amount of relief given was still rising. The huge harvests of 1819–21 gave an edge to the agricultural counties where relief fell faster than in the industrial districts. Parliament's stern condemnation of the Allowance System in 1818, however, seems to have had some effect: the downward trend in relief spending is more pronounced in the Speenhamland than in the non-Speenhamland counties. The industrial boom of 1822–5 shows up in the stability of poor-relief expenditures in non-agricultural counties; in agriculture, these were not prosperous years. With the crash of 1825, relief spending in nonagricultural counties rose sharply, but thereafter the pattern in the industrial and agricultural areas did not differ significantly. The Poor Law officers in the Speenhamland counties, however, had come to heed the alarm at the rising burden on the rates: although the general trend was upwards from 1823–31, they prevented relief spending from increasing as fast in their parishes as it did in the country as a whole.

A comparison of index numbers cannot reveal differences that are present at the outset and that persist through time. We have noted that relief per head was consistently higher in the Speenhamland counties than elsewhere. It was also higher in the agricultural counties than in the nonagricultural counties. What we have just demonstrated is that whatever the reason for this pattern in the absolute amount of *per capita* relief, it was not seriously influenced before 1834 either by differences in the administration of the Poor Laws in different counties or by an alleged deterioration of agriculture under the influence of allowances-in-aid-of-wages. There is no evidence whatever of the most popular of all the charges levied at the Old Poor Law: the 'snow-ball effect' of outdoor relief to the ablebodied.

This still leaves us without an explanation of the higher absolute burden of the poor rates in certain counties, to which we now turn.

v

Trustworthy statistics for agricultural wages in this period are available on a county basis for the years 1795, 1824, 1833, 1837, and 1850. Wage data for agricultural workers are notoriously difficult to interpret. Not only are they subject to sharp seasonal variations; they are frequently augmented by money payments for task work and by payments in kind in the form of food, drink, fuel, and cheap rents. Although such supplements to cash earnings varied a good deal between counties in the nineteenth century, being higher oddly enough where money payments were higher, rural conservatism makes it plausible to assume that they did not vary radically from decade to decade. It appears that the ratio of total earnings to money wages changed little throughout the century, earnings generally exceeding wages by 15–20 per cent (see Appendix D). Thus, changes in the trend of money wages can be interpreted as reflecting changes in the trend of total earnings.

To test the effect of the Speenhamland policy, I have formed a composite index of the standard weekly money wage of agricultural workers in all counties which practised the Allowance System in 1814 (see Appendix E). The county is admittedly a poor unit over which to take an average of wages: in many counties, wages varied significantly from district to district. For example, the average wage in Middlesex, including as it does London, has little meaning. Still, we must make do with what we have. The comparison reveals the following:

	1795	1824	1833	1837	1850
Speenhamland Counties	100	100	124	106	104
Average for England and Wales	100	108	120	115	108

For Britain as a whole, the general picture is that of a rise from 1795 to about 1812 and a fall from 1813 to a low in 1824, but evidence about these years is very uncertain. Wages rose again in the latter half of the 1820s, varied little in the 1830s, and then moved down again in the 1840s. Given the rise in the price level during the war, agricultural workers were probably not much better off in 1824 than in 1795. But with the cost of living falling as much as 25 per cent between 1825 and 1850, real wages were much higher at the end of the period.

On the face of it, it seems that the Speenhamland policy depressed agricultural wages between 1795 and 1824. Strangely enough, however, in the decade before the passage of the Poor Law Amendment Act, wages in the Speenhamland counties recovered the ground lost during the war and immediate post-war years. We could attribute this result to stricter enforcement of the Poor Laws in the Speenhamland counties after 1824. But, in that case, why the rapid decline in the years 1833–50, after the Act of 1834 had crushed out the Allowance System?

In 1851, Caird drew a line through the middle of England to distinguish the high-wage counties of the North from the low-wage counties of the South. Above the Caird line, the money wages of agricultural workers averaged more than 10s. per week in 1824; below the line, they averaged less, except in Middlesex, Surrey, and Kent. If we hold with Clapham that 'the thoroughgoing adoption of the Speenhamland policy coupled with the working of poor law settlement tended to keep down the standard weekly money wage of agricultural labour', what accounts for the low wages of Wales and the whole of the South-west and West Midlands where the Allowance System was eschewed?[14] Moreover, agricultural wages in the North were not noticeably lower in the East and North Ridings, where wages were subsidized out of the poor rates, than in other northern counties where they were not. And in the northern Midlands, Nottinghamshire, and Leicestershire, both Speenhamland counties, paid wages about the national average. The fact that the Speenhamland counties were generally located below the Caird wage-line should not be submitted as evidence that subsidies depressed wages. On the contrary, the causal relationship seems to run the other way: wages were only subsidized when, for other reasons, they were too low to provide a minimum standard of living.

The picture of sharp wage differentials for equivalent kinds of labour between the North and the South—differentials which exceeded the real cost of transfer from one region to the other—dates back to the eighteenth century and persisted throughout the nineteenth century. In 1824, the range between the northern and southern counties was about 4s.; by the end of the century, it had risen to 5s.[15] Superimposed upon that pattern was another, which reflected the pull of rapidly growing towns upon the immediately surrounding countryside: in the South, the greater was the distance from London, the lower was the wage, and in the North the same thing was true of the Lancashire towns Manchester and Liverpool, and the Yorkshire towns Leeds and Sheffield. The internal migration of workers which accompanied the Industrial Revolution largely took the form of short-distance travel to the nearest factory town. The people who moved into the cotton towns came almost exclusively from Lancashire and Cheshire itself, or from Ireland. Migration into London came from the extra-metropolitan parts of Middlesex and Surrey, and to a lesser extent from the surrounding counties of Kent, Essex, Hertfordshire, and Berkshire. Similarly, migration into the Midland iron towns of Warwickshire came from the county itself or from Staffordshire and Worcestershire to the West.[16] The pull of these towns not only raised wages in the surrounding rural areas by reducing the supply of labour, but also increased the demand for labour by providing a dependable expanding market for agricultural produce. This accounts for the high level of agricultural wages in the North as well as the relatively higher wage levels in farm areas around London. We have already mentioned the fact that wages in Middlesex, Kent, and Surrey compared favourably with the North. Precisely for that reason, the parish officers did not resort to the Speenhamland policy in these counties. But even in East Anglia, where wages were supplemented by the Poor Law authorities, proximity to London produced wages higher than those in the South-West where wages were not subsidized. Again, in Sussex, the most notorious Speenhamland county, agricultural wages were higher than in any county in the South except those immediately around London.

We can hardly resist the conclusion that the parish officers only had recourse to the policy of subsidizing wages wherever the attraction of urban industry made itself felt too weakly, leaving a pool of surplus manpower and substandard wages.[17]

VI

It was a favourite doctrine of the Poor Law reformers of 1834 that the abolition of outdoor relief to the unemployed would soon dissipate 'the false and unreal appearance of surplus labour'; no labour surplus actually existed, they argued, apart from what had been artificially created by the operation of the Old Poor Law. They recommended emigration from the southern counties but only in the transition period from the old scheme to the new.[18] Nevertheless, the Assistant Commissioners found much evidence of structural unemployment in the Speenhamland counties of the South, and their testimony is particularly clear and detailed for the case of Sussex.[19] The natural periodicity of arable farming found in the wheat-growing counties threw workers entirely on the parish rates for three or four winter months. Seasonal unemployment was much less of a problem in the West, where no wheat was grown. This might explain why the Speenhamland policy was not adopted in the western counties.[20] The main wheat-growing area lay East of Cobden's famous line from 'Inverness to Southampton', and the bulk of the domestic wheat supply was produced on the stiff clay lands of eight South-Eastern counties. There is a striking coincidence, therefore, between the spread of Speenhamland and the production of wheat. Moreover, the wheat-producing counties were also areas of maximum recent enclosure.[21] Although it was mostly waste lands which were enclosed in this period, thus adding to employment opportunities, the enclosure movement increased the concentration on wheat, giving rise to the characteristic problem of winter unemployment.

Furthermore, the practice of boarding young unmarried farm-workers and guaranteeing them a fixed income irrespective of weather, which was still very common in the North, had by this time given way in the South to the day labourer hired at standard rates. Thus, seasonal unemployment became a social problem in southern agricultural counties which had to be dealt with by public action. The solution was the Roundsman System, which took up the slack by letting everyone work at low intensity; to have allowed wages to fall in order to clear the labour market would only have further reduced the productivity of labour via its depressing effect on the caloric value of the workers' diets.

In the nature of the case, it is very difficult to obtain direct evidence of disguised unemployment, and in practice it may be impossible to distinguish visible seasonal unemployment from invisible structural unemployment. Indeed, since the labour surplus is disguised by reducing the required effort of each worker, the situation gives the appearance of a labour deficit at low wage levels. At higher wages, the work done by each man would increase so rapidly that the deficit would be converted into a labour surplus. In other words, substandard wages, which are nevertheless above the level that automatic market forces would produce, are part of the mechanism which disguises a pool of surplus manpower in an underdeveloped country. Disguised unemployment may be said to exist when it is possible to release workers by means of a simple reorganization of production without significantly affecting output; but history rarely performs that decisive experiment, and so we must fall back on inference.

Apart from direct evidence of seasonal and technological unemployment in English agriculture, we have other reasons to believe that the countryside was overpopulated at this time. By 1834, manufacturing was already effectively concentrated in the large towns of Lancashire, Cheshire, and Yorkshire. Previously, it had been scattered throughout the country districts. The most famous example of the decay of local industry in this era is the migration of the woollen and worsted industry from East Anglia to the West Riding. But all through the South in, say, 1800 one would have found, here and there, malthouses and breweries; iron, paper, snuff, and flour mills; leather, parchment, and printing works; silk-spinning and silk-weaving factories; and various home industries making hose, ribbons, laces, strings, and cotton goods.[22] The gradual disappearance of this source of demand for labour in rural areas is rarely given its proper due in accounting for the increased burden of poor-relief expenditures. To be sure, the decay of rural industries was a very slow process which took place rapidly in the second rather than the first half of the nineteenth century. But in the second half of the century, the rate of emigration from rural districts was commensurate with the decline of employment opportunities in the countryside. It was the relative immobility of rural labour that made the decay of cottage industry a serious problem in the heyday of the Industrial Revolution.

The abolition of outdoor relief to the unemployed in 1834, at least in the agricultural counties of the South, did not by itself solve the problem of structural unemployment in the countryside. Even ten years later, when reliable figures about the number of people on relief first became available, the Speenhamland counties headed the list with 12–15 per cent of the population on relief, whereas the percentage in the non-Speenhamland counties was typically no more than 6–7 per cent.[23] What is more, in the 1891 census all the Speenhamland counties were found to be losing population to London or to the factory towns of the North—the only exception being Warwickshire, containing Birmingham.[24] This fact alone is indicative of rural overpopulation in the first half of the century.

VII

We bring our analysis of the Old Poor Law to a close by briefly considering the remaining items in the traditional bill of indictment: it promoted the growth of population; it lowered rents; it reduced 'yeomanry'; and, most general of all, it depressed agricultural output by destroying incentives.

It may be surprising that we have come so far without saying very much about the Malthusian objection to the Old Poor Law. It is simply that not much can be said. It is worth noting, of course, that the rate of population growth was no smaller in Scotland and Ireland, where earned incomes were never supplemented by the Poor Law authorities. Malthus himself added an appendix to the 1826 edition of his *Essay on the Principles of Population* which conceded that the Old Poor Law did not in fact 'greatly encourage population'.

The residence requirements of the Settlement Act, he argued, gave landlords a motive to pull down cottages on their estates; the scarcity of rural housing kept the Poor Laws from encouraging marriages. Be that as it may, estimates of birth and death rates for this period depend on the baptisms and burials entered in the parish registers and, as has been shown recently, there was a marked increase in the failure to register between 1780 and 1820; moreover the deficiencies in registration were not randomly distributed among the counties.[25] This renders suspect any quantitative statement about effects of the Old Poor Law on population growth.

Nevertheless, it has been argued that the death rate only became an important element in the 'population explosion' after 1820, not, as is usually alleged, after 1780. Between 1780 and 1820, it was the rising birth rate which enlarged the size of families, and this was due in part to the Old Poor Law.[26] Most of the Speenhamland counties had fertility ratios above the national average, and Sussex had the highest fertility ratio of any county in 1821. But the northern industrial counties also showed fertility ratios above the national average. After 1821, fertility ratios began to fall in the Speenhamland counties, either because of stricter administration of relief or because of the agricultural revival. But similarly, fertility ratios fell even faster in the North. A fertility *ratio*, however, is not the same thing as the fertility or crude birth *rate*, being defined as the number of children between zero and four years per 1,000 women between the ages of fifteen and forty-nine. High fertility ratios may be produced by a fall in infant mortality, swelling the number of births registered. In the Speenhamland counties, more generous relief may have worked to reduce the number of infant deaths and in this way increased registered births. To be sure, this implies that the Old Poor Law did promote population growth, but via the death rate rather than the birth rate.

It has also been argued that the family-endowment features of Speenhamland induced farmers to hire married men with children rather than single men as a method of lightening the rate burden, thus discouraging family limitation. This may have been an important consideration in small parishes where farmers knew the private circumstances of each hired hand. But in larger parishes, an expressed preference for married men must have encouraged workers to misrepresent their situation. On the whole, there is no persuasive evidence that, as the saying went at the time, 'population was raised by bounties'. Even the bastardy laws, which made it possible for unmarried mothers to claim support from a putative father, do not explain the increase in illegitimate births in the Speenhamland counties down to 1834. Illegitimacy was even higher in the northern industrial counties where the laws of bastardy were not stringently enforced. It seems that the Poor Laws, as Rickman said in the preamble to the census of 1821, were 'much less conducive to an Increase of Population than they are usually stated to be in Argument'.

Next, there is the contention that the Old Poor Law operated to depress rents. This argument depends entirely upon the way in which the poor rates were actually assessed. They were paid in the first instance by farmers and

other estate-dwellers, not by landlords. Assessments seem to have been based
on the annual value of lands and real estate occupied, but both the Poor
Law Commissioners of 1834 and Cannan, the modern historian of local
rating in England, were unable to determine the exact principle upon which
they were calculated prior to 1835.[27] It is clear that farmers bore the brunt
of the rates even in industrial districts, and when rates were rising they may
have pressed landlords for a reduction in rents. We recall, however, that the
relief bill varied in the same direction as the income of farmers. Hence, it is
far from obvious that rents were in fact reduced when the rates rose.

Wild charges about the poor rates 'eating up all rents' circulated during
and after the Napoleonic wars. The rates were set by the justices of the peace,
the wealthy landowners of the county, who paid rates only in so far as they
were occupiers of estates. The pressure on rents when rates were rising, if
it came at all, came only after a lapse of time, determined by the customary
length of tenant leases in the locality. With tenants-at-will, rentals might respond quickly to an upward trend in poor rates, but leases of seven to four-
teen years were not uncommon, and these must have been very insensitive
to increased overhead costs incurred by tenants. Thus, the link between rising
rates and falling rents made itself felt in different degrees in different counties, supposing, of course, that there really was such a link. The problem is
further complicated by the fact that a multitude of noneconomic considerations governed the relationship between landlord and tenant: landlords
with political ambitions were sometimes willing to charge lower rents to
favoured tenants. For the Speenhamland county of Warwickshire, the only
county in which this subject has been investigated, it proved impossible to
discover any connection between land rentals and rateable value as given in
the parochial assessments.[28] Nevertheless, it is theoretically plausible that the
incidence of the rates fell ultimately upon landlords, but we know so little
about the trend in land rentals after 1815, that it must be left an open
question.[29]

The idea of the disappearance of the 'yeomanry' in this period is dealt
with more quickly. Property-owners were not eligible for relief and so, it is
argued, the Old Poor Law discriminated against the cottage-proprietor seeking employment, as well as the smallholder who never used hired labour,
but had to pay his share of the rates. But if the 'yeomanry' or occupying
owner can ever be said to have disappeared from the land, it was in the
eighteenth and not the nineteenth century that he vanished.[30] There is evidence of some decline in the number of family farms after 1815, but it is
impossible to separate the burden of poor rates from the many other difficulties which afflicted smallholders in the years of deflation after Waterloo.

Nor is the alleged decline in the efficiency of agricultural workers under
the influence of the Old Poor Law discernible in statistics of production.
There are no reliable series of wheat, barley, and oats production in this

period, but isolated unofficial estimates all suggest a continued increase in output per acre during the first half of the nineteenth century. Despite the fact that population had doubled in those fifty years, imports of agricultural commodities never formed an important portion of the total supply, and contemporary observers were convinced that productivity in agriculture had risen.[31] In view of the failure of the money wages of agricultural workers to fall as fast as food prices through 1824–50, it is difficult to deny this conviction.

We have come to the end of our journey to find that hardly any of the dire effects ascribed to the Old Poor Law stand up in the light of available empirical knowledge. This is negative proof at best, but even in theory the weight of forces is not all in one direction. We have to remember that a system of local rating provides its own checks to excessive expenditures. The Allowance System, for example, added to the wages paid by farmers with one hand what it took from them in rates with the other; the link between taxpayer and beneficiary was much closer than it is with modern income-support programmes. Just as it is now realized that the Settlement Laws did not invariably work with the harsh and wasteful rigidity so often assumed,[32] so the Speenhamland policy was not always as imprudently administered as has been thought. And just as the extent to which 'paupers' were really transported by parish officers cannot be deduced from the statute books, so the actual effects of the Allowance System cannot be inferred from the purple passages of the *Poor Law Report of 1834*.

VIII

The Old Poor Law, with its use of outdoor relief to assist the underpaid and to relieve the unemployed was, in essence, a device for dealing with the problem of surplus labour in the lagging rural sector of a rapidly expanding but still underdeveloped economy. And considering the quality of social administration in the day, it was by no means an unenlightened policy. The Poor Law Commissioners of 1834 thought otherwise and deliberately selected the facts so as to impeach the existing administration on predetermined lines. Not only did they fail in any way to take account of the special problem of structural unemployment in the countryside, but what evidence they did present consisted of little more than picturesque ancedotes of maladministration. Even the elaborate questionnaire which they circulated among the parishes was never analysed or reduced to summary form. No attempt was made to make a census of the poor, and to this day we know more about the nature and composition of the pauper host in 1802 than in 1834. Anyone who has read the *Report of 1834* can testify to the overwhelming cumulative effect of the endless recital of ills from the mouths of squires, magistrates, overseers, and clergymen. But as evidence of a social malady it has little value, particularly on the ultimate question of the corrupting influence of lavish relief: in what age would it not be possible to collect complaints from the upper classes about the laziness of workers?

Nowhere in the *Report* is there any hint of a quantitative view of the problem. 'This ignoring of statistics,' as the Webbs remarked 'led, in the diagnosis, to disastrous errors in proportion; and made the suggested remedial measures lopsided and seriously imperfect.' For example, Nassau William Senior, who wrote 'the exposition of the evils of the old system' in the *Report*, surmised that 'the able-bodied paupers and their families now amount to a million'. Instead, the Webbs calculated that about 100,000 people were relieved indoors and 900,000 outdoors in 1834, of which perhaps 100,000 or at most 300,000 if we count all their dependants, were able-bodied workers.[33] In subsequent years, the Commissioners were to discover to their grief that the bulk of relief recipients were, indeed, not the able-bodied, but rather the helpless and dependent sick, aged, and infirm.[34] No wonder, the 'harsh but salutary Act' fell short, at nearly every point, of effecting a sweeping reform. Gradually, so gradually as to be almost imperceptible to contemporaries, the 'principles of 1834' were undermined in practice by the administration of successive governments, while competing public services increasingly took over the functions of the Poor Law.[35] The virtual abandonment of the Malthusian theory of population under the influence of the downward trend in births, the growing recognition of urban destitution caused by involuntary unemployment, the concern over sweated trades, all these contributed to 'the breaking-up of the Poor Law'. Nevertheless, the *Report of 1834* remained a force against which all changes had to make their way, and the public was still told by the Poor Law authorities that any abrogation of the 'principles of 1834' would give a spur to population and thus bring wages down. As late as 1893, Alfred Marshall remarked to the Royal Commission on the Aged Poor: 'It seems that whenever I read Poor Law literature of today I am taken back to the beginning of the century; everything that is said about economics has the flavour of that old time.'

Appendix A: *Poor Relief per Head, by Counties*

Speenhamland Counties	1802		1812		1821		1831	
	s.	*d.*	*s.*	*d.*	*s.*	*d.*	*s.*	*d.*
Sussex	22	7	33	1	23	8	19	4
Bucks	16	1	22	9	19	1	18	7
Wilts	13	11	24	5	15	8	16	9
Beds	11	9	17	6	16	6	16	11
Berks	15	1	27	1	17	0	15	9
Hunts	12	2	16	9	16	0	15	3
Suffolk	11	5	19	4	18	0	18	4
Norfolk	12	5	20	0	15	7	15	4
Dorset	11	4	17	5	13	3	11	5
Essex	12	1	24	7	20	0	17	2
Cambridge	12	1	17	0	14	9	13	8
Oxford	16	2	24	10	19	1	16	11
Northants	14	5	19	11	19	2	16	10
Leicester	12	4	14	8	16	6	11	7
Warwick	11	3	13	4	12	0	9	7
Devon	7	3	11	5	10	8	9	0
Notts	6	4	10	10	9	5	6	6
York, E. R.	7	6	12	6	13	0	11	11
York, N. R.	6	5	8	4	9	6	8	9
Average	12	3	18	8	16	4	13	8

Non-Speenhamland Counties	1802		1812		1821		1831	
	s.	*d.*	*s.*	*d.*	*s.*	*d.*	*s.*	*d.*
Kent	13	6	17	1	18	5	14	5
Hants	12	2	18	4	14	11	13	10
Surrey	10	0	13	6	13	11	10	11
Herts	11	5	13	10	15	1	13	2
Worcester	10	3	11	11	10	1	7	6
Rutland	10	1	13	8	12	3	9	1
Hereford	10	5	17	9	14	0	11	4
Lincoln	9	2	10	10	12	3	11	0
Somerset	8	11	12	3	9	11	8	10
Gloucester	8	8	11	7	9	10	8	8
York, W. R	6	6	9	11	8	2	5	7
Stafford	6	11	8	6	8	10	6	6
Chester	6	11	10	0	8	4	6	3
Cornwall	5	10	9	5	9	1	6	8
Derby	6	9	10	2	9	1	6	8
Durham	6	6	9	11	10	1	6	10
Salop	7	11	11	5	10	4	8	2
Northumberland	6	8	7	11	7	11	6	3
Cumberland	4	9	6	9	7	4	5	6
Westmorland	6	8	9	9	11	0	9	8
Lancaster	4	5	7	5	5	6	4	5
Middlesex	8	7	10	7	11	10	10	1
Monmouth	8	0	9	1	7	9	5	5
Wales	5	7	7	7	7	2	7	2
Average	8	4	11	4	10	2	8	7

Appendix A (*continued*)

    Select Towns

Manchester	4	7	9	8	3	9	—
Birmingham	6	2	9	6	7	11	—
Bristol	5	7	6	5	9	8	—
Liverpool	6	6	6	5	6	2	—

Sources. The counties are listed in each category roughly in order of average relief per head. The figures are obtained by dividing the 'annual expenditures for the poor' reported for each county by the county population as given by the census returns. Up to 1849, Poor Law Returns were reported annually for the year that ends at Lady Day (March 25). Hence, figures for, say, 1803, are here regarded as referring to 1802, and so forth. The available official returns up to 1830 are conveniently found in Marshall, *Digest of All the Accounts*, pp. 36–7. The figures for the towns are also derived from Marshall, ibid. 41. The returns for the year 1831–3 are given in *P.P.* 1835 (444), xlvii. The figures for county populations are derived from the decennial censuses of 1801, 1811, 1821, and 1831, as given by J. R. McCulloch, *Descriptive and Statistical Account of the British Empire*, ii, p. 400.

Andrew Ure in his *Philosophy of Manufactures* (1835), p. 477, gives figures for poor relief per head in what he calls 'factory counties' for 1801, 1811, 1821, and 1831, based, as he says, on the official returns. Since poor relief expenditures were not returned for the years 1801 and 1811, he probably applied a method similar to my own, dividing decennial census data on population into figures on relief spending for the years 1802 and 1812. His series generally agree with mine, except that they are all unaccountably lower for 1821.

Appendix B: *Total Poor-relief Expenditures in England and Wales*

Years	Total £000s	Index	Average Price of Wheat per Quarter s. d.	Index of Relief in Wheat	Relief in Speenhamland Counties £000s	Index	Relief in Other Counties £000s	Index
1802	4,078	100	69 10	100	1,782	100	2,296	100
1812	6,676	164	126 6	90	2,975	170	3,701	161
1813	6,295	154	109 9	98	2,672	145	3,623	160
1814	5,419	133	74 4	125	2,223	125	3,196	139
1815	5,725	140	65 7	149	2,279	130	3,447	150
1816	6,918	169	78 6	151	2,971	170	3,947	171
1817	7,890	193	96 11	139	3,374	190	4,516	197
1818	7,532	184	86 3	148	3,174	180	4,358	190
1819	7,330	180	74 6	168	3,069	172	4,261	185
1820	6,958	171	67 10	176	2,894	163	4,064	176
1821	6,359	156	56 1	194	2,673	150	3,686	160
1822	5,773	142	44 7	223	2,549	143	3,224	140
1823	5,734	141	53 4	185	2,473	139	3,261	142
1824	5,787	142	63 11	155	2,498	140	3,289	143
1825	5,929	145	68 6	148	2,579	145	3,350	146
1826	6,441	158	58 8	188	2,704	151	3,738	162
1827	6,298	154	58 6	184	2,616	147	3,716	162
1828	6,332	155	60 5	179	2,683	150	3,649	160
1829	6,829	167	66 3	170	2,937	165	3,892	169
1830	6,799	167	64 3	182	2,905	163	3,894	169
1831	7,037	173	66 4	182	2,997	170	4,040	176
1832	6,791	167	58 8	199	2,903	163	3,888	170
1833	6,317	155	52 11	204	2,596	146	3,721	169

Source. Average monthly gazette prices per quarter of wheat are given by Gayer, Rostow, Schwartz, *Fluctuations, Microfilm Supplement*, pp. 650–1. Since the poor-relief figures run from March 25 of one year to March 25 of the next, I have averaged annual wheat prices on the same basis.

Appendix C: *Poor-relief Expenditures in Agricultural and Nonagricultural Counties in England and Wales*

Years	Agricultural (£000s)	Index	Nonagricultural (£000s)	Index
1802	1,672	100	2,405	100
1812	2,822	169	3,835	160
1813	2,563	152	3,731	155
1814	2,137	128	3,281	137
1815	2,286	136	3,438	143
1816	2,839	170	4,072	170
1817	3,227	193	4,644	193
1818	3,028	181	4,489	187
1819	2,891	171	4,440	185
1820	2,748	164	4,211	175
1821	2,568	153	3,791	158
1822	2,370	140	3,402	142
1823	2,409	144	3,328	140
1824	2,443	146	3,344	140
1825	2,492	149	3,437	140
1826	2,582	153	3,859	161
1827	2,514	150	3,784	158
1828	2,594	154	3,739	155
1829	2,787	167	4,042	170
1830	2,789	167	4,010	170
1831	2,892	173	4,145	173
1832	2,766	166	4,025	170
1833	2,586	153	3,732	155
1834	2,295	140	2,232	136
1840	1,772	106	3,114	130
1850	1,723	103	3,239	134

Source. Gayer, Rostow, and Schwartz used decennial census figures on occupational distribution, by counties, to divide the counties into the two classes: ibid. 1678. Such counties as Devon, Kent, Somerset, Hampshire, Salop, and the East Riding were border-line cases and the decision had to be made on the basis of a qualitative judgement. Twenty-six counties and the West Riding were designated nonagricultural; the remaining fifteen counties, including East and North Riding, were designated agricultural counties. For a terse description of the character of economic activity in each of the counties in this period, see McCulloch, *Descriptive and Statistical Account*, i. 142–225.

Appendix D: *Weekly Money Wages of Agricultural Workers, by Counties*

Counties	1795 s. d.		1824 s. d.		1833 s. d.		1837 s. d.		1850 s. d.	
Middlesex	8	0	11	3	13	0	11	6	11	0
Surrey	10	6	10	8	12	0	10	6	9	6
Kent	10	6	11	9	13	1	12	0	11	6
Sussex	10	0	9	6	12	1	10	7	10	6
Hants	9	0	8	6	10	2	9	6	9	0
Berks	9	0	8	9	10	5	9	0	7	6
South-Eastern Average	9	6	10	1	11	10	10	6	9	10
Index number	100		107		126		111		104	

Counties	1795 s.	d.	1824 s.	d.	1833 s.	d.	1837 s.	d.	1850 s.	d.
Oxford	8	6	8	1	10	1	8	6	9	0
Herts	8	0	9	0	11	0	9	6	9	0
Bucks	8	0	8	3	10	2	9	6	8	6
Northants	7	0	8	0	10	3	9	0	9	0
Hunts	8	6	7	6	10	5	9	6	8	6
Beds	7	6	8	6	10	0	9	6	9	0
Cambridge	8	2	9	0	10	6	9	6	7	6
South Midlands Average	8	0	8	4	10	4	9	3	8	8
Index number	*100*		*105*		*129*		*114*		*109*	
Essex	9	0	9	4	10	3	10	4	8	0
Suffolk	10	6	8	3	9	11	10	4	7	0
Norfolk	9	0	9	2	10	9	10	4	8	6
Eastern Average	9	6	8	11	10	4	10	4	7	10
Index number	*100*		*94*		*109*		*109*		*83*	
Wilts	8	4	7	6	9	1	8	0	7	3
Dorset	8	0	6	11	8	2	7	6	7	6
Devon	7	0	7	6	9	0	8	0	8	6
Cornwall	8	6	8	3	8	11	8	9	8	8
Somerset	7	3	8	2	8	6	8	8	8	7
South-Western Average	7	10	7	8	8	9	8	2	8	1
Index number	*100*		*99*		*112*		*104*		*103*	
Gloucester	7	0	9	3	9	6	9	0	7	0
Hereford	8	0	7	0	8	1	8	0	8	5
Salop	7	6	8	10	9	2	9	0	7	3
Stafford	7	6	10	7	11	1	12	0	9	6
Worcester	8	6	8	2	9	6	9	6	7	8
Warwick	7	6	8	10	10	10	10	0	8	6
West Midlands Average	7	8	8	9	9	8	9	7	8	1
Index number	*100*		*115*		*126*		*124*		*107*	
Leicester	11	0	9	10	11	2	10	0	9	6
Rutland	9	0	—		12	2	—		—	
Lincoln	10	6	10	2	12	4	12	0	10	0
Notts	9	0	10	3	12	10	12	0	10	0
Derby	9	3	10	10	12	0	12	0	11	0
North Midlands Average	9	9	10	3	12	3	11	6	10	1
Index number	*100*		*106*		*127*		*120*		*105*	
Chester	9	0	10	8	9	10	13	0	12	0
Lancashire	13	6	12	5	12	2	12	8	13	6
York, W. R.	11	0	12	5	11	5	12	0	14	0
York, E. R.	11	3	11	8	11	0	12	0	12	0
York, N. R.	10	0	10	3	11	4	12	0	11	0
Durham	9	0	11	6	11	0	12	0	11	0
Northumberland	10	6	11	5	11	5	12	0	11	0
Cumberland	9	0	12	2	10	8	12	0	13	0
Westmorland	10	0	12	0	11	0	12	0	12	0
Northern Average	10	4	11	7	11	1	12	2	12	2
Index number	*100*		*113*		*105*		*118*		*118*	

Counties	1795 s. d.	1824 s. d.	1833 s. d.	1837 s. d.	1850 s. d.
Monmouth	9 0	10 0	10 8	10 6	19 8
Wales	6 8	8 0	8 2	7 6	6 11
General Average	8 11	9 7	10 8	10 3	9 6
Index number	*100*	*108*	*120*	*115*	*108*

Sources. The data are drawn from A. I. Bowley, 'The Statistics of Wages in the United Kingdom During the Last Hundred Years, Agricultural Wages', *Journal of the Royal Statistical Society* (Dec. 1898). The 1795 figures are derived from Eden and Young; the 1824 figures come from the same committee which circulated the questionnaire on the Allowance System; the 1833 and 1837 figures rest on returns from about 1,000 parishes collected by the Poor Law Commissioners; the 1851 figures are given by Caird. All of these represent the average of summer and winter wages; in those counties where free board or lodging was general, they include such payments in kind. The averages for the districts are simple arithmetic averages because no adequate weights were obtainable. Bowley's index numbers, based on 1892, have been reduced to 1795.

Slightly different figures, based on other authorities, are presented in A. L. Bowley, *Wages in the Nineteenth Century* (1900), chaps. 4–5, but the differences are negligible. These are reprinted in Lord Ernle, *English Farming*, Appendix IX, with comparable data down to 1926, giving an overview of trends throughout the whole of the nineteenth century.

After due reflection, Bowley concluded that index numbers found for wages can be adopted for earnings without alteration. See his Article 'The Statistics of Wages in the United Kingdom During the Last Hundred Years. Earnings and General Averages', *Journal of the Royal Statistical Society* (Sept. 1889), and his *Wages in the Nineteenth Century*, pp. 41–3. For a more sceptical view see O. R. McGregor, 'Introduction, Pt. 2: After 1815', to Lord Ernle, *English Farming*, pp. cxix–cxxi.

Appendix E: *Index of Weekly Earnings of Agricultural Workers, by Counties*
(*1795 = 100*)

Speenhamland Counties	1824	1833	1837	1850
Sussex	94	121	104	102
Bucks	105	130	120	105
Wilts	90	111	95	87
Beds	113	141	126	120
Berks	96	114	112	83
Hunts	88	139	112	100
Suffolk	80	90	99	80
Norfolk	101	120	113	93
Dorset	86	109	94	94
Essex	112	123	123	91
Cambridge	110	130	120	110
Oxford	96	121	103	107
Northants	114	150	128	128
Leicester	87	108	87	85
Warwick	120	145	132	115
Devon	108	130	111	123
Notts	115	141	133	110
York, E. R.	122	122	125	125
York, N. R.	103	112	120	109
Average	100	124	106	104

Appendix E (*continued*)

Non-Speenhamland Counties	1824	1833	1837	1850
Kent	112	126	115	109
Hants	85	104	92	90
Surrey	101	117	100	90
Herts	113	142	120	113
Worcester	96	120	111	90
Rutland	—	140	—	—
Hereford	88	111	112	105
Lincoln	99	138	115	96
Somerset	112	121	120	119
Gloucester	133	140	115	100
York, W. R.	107	111	101	124
Stafford	143	151	159	125
Chester	118	108	145	133
Cornwall	97	106	103	102
Derby	116	124	130	120
Durham	144	148	150	138
Salop	96	130	118	92
Northumberland	108	107	113	106
Cumberland	135	130	145	156
Westmorland	122	108	122	122
Lancaster	99	98	98	106
Middlesex	124	165	173	123
Monmouth	111	116	116	108
Wales	120	122	112	105
Average for England and Wales	108	120	115	108

BIBLIOGRAPHICAL NOTE

Professor Blaug followed up the essay reprinted here with a companion-piece on 'The Poor Law Report re-examined' in the *Journal of Economic History*, 24 (1964), which drew attention to the substantial disparity between the details of the data assembled by the Commission of Inquiry of 1832–4 in the form of replies to the extensive questionnaire circulated to upwards of 1,500 parishes and the conclusions ostensibly drawn by the Commission from them. From this it could be concluded that the reform proposed by the Commission which was quickly translated into the framework of the New Poor Law by the Poor Law Amendment Act of 1834 was based not on an accurate diagnosis of the malfunctioning of the Old Poor Law in its last years, but on the preconceptions and prejudices of the Commissioners. Disappointingly, Blaug's illuminating reconsideration of the practice of the Old Poor Law under the Overseers and Speenhamland system has not sparked off the extensive local research that such a re-appraisal calls for. One or two unpublished Ph.D. theses have made a start at county level, but their authors have not yet made their findings public in any major books or articles. J. D. Marshall, *The Old Poor Law, 1795–1834* (London, 1968) surveys the pre-Blaug literature and assesses critically, though for the most part favourably, the impact of Blaug's re-appraisal. J. S. Taylor, 'The mythology of the Old Poor Law', *Journal of Economic History*, 29 (1969) criticizes Blaug on a number of details without disputing any of his points of substance. James P. Huzel, 'Malthus, the Poor Law, and population in early nineteenth-century England', *Econ. Hist. Rev.*, 2nd ser. 22 (1969) reinforces some of Blaug's views by arguing that the allowance system under the Old Poor Law had little effect on either birth or death rates and hence did not promote population growth. G. W. Oxley, 'The permanent poor in south-west Lancashire under the Old Poor Law', in J. R. Harris (ed.), *Liverpool and Merseyside* (London, 1969), and J. R. Poynter's comprehensive study of *Society and Pauperism. English Ideas on Poor Relief, 1795–1834* (London, 1969) both produce evidence which broadly reinforces Blaug's conclusions. In contrast, Donald N. McCloskey, 'New perspectives on the Old Poor Law', *Explorations in Economic History*, 10 (1973), while seeming to attack Blaug's economic analysis rather fiercely, actually leaves the central elements of his interpretation unscathed, perhaps because the analysis is conducted on a purely theoretical level without reference to contemporary sources. Eric Hobsbawm and George Rudé, too, in *Captain Swing* (London, 1968), argue that Blaug's 'welfare state economics' approach is too narrow, and seek to view the Speenhamland system against the background of the structure of rural society and the beliefs of the landed interests of the day.

NOTES

1. Alfred Marshall, testifying in 1893 before the Royal Commission on the Aged Poor, deplored the persistence of Malthusian thinking among laymen and illustrated the evolution of professional economic opinion in the nineteenth century in these words: 'Suppose you could conceive a Mad Emperor of China to give to every English working man a half-a-crown for nothing: according to the current notions, as far as I have been able to ascertain them, that would lower wages, because it would enable people to work for less. I think that nine economists out of ten at the beginning of the century would have said that that would lower wages. Well, of course, it might increase population and that might bring down wages; but unless it did increase population, the effect according to the modern school would be to raise wages because the increased wealth of the working classes would lead to better living, more vigorous and better educated people with greater earning power, and so wages would rise. That is the centre of the difference.' *Official Papers* (London, 1926), p. 249.

2. For theoretical analysis of the phenomenon of disguised unemployment, see H. Leibenstein, 'The Theory of Underemployment in Backward Economies', *Journal of Political Economy*, 65 (Apr. 1957); and P. Wonnacott, 'Disguised and Overt Unemployment in Underdeveloped Economies', *Quarterly Journal of Economics*, 76 (May 1962).

3. *P.P.* 1803–1804 (175), xiii. The returns of the census are also found in J. Marshall, *A Digest of All the Accounts* (1833), pp. 33, 38.

4. Ibid., 34.

5. S. and B. Webb, *English Poor Law History: Part I: The Old Poor Law* (London, 1927), pp. 181, 185, 188–9, 400–1.

6. J. Clapham, *The Economic History of Modern Britain. The Railway Age* (2nd edn.; Cambridge, 1939), pp. 123–5. The Webbs dismissed this piece of evidence in a footnote in *English Poor Law History: Part II: The Last Hundred Years* (London, 1929), i. 61 n.

7. *Poor Law History*, p. 182.

8. See ibid., 170–3.

9. See ibid., 182–3; J. L. and B. Hammond, *The Village Labourer* (4th end., London, 1927). E. M. Hampson, *The Treatment of Poverty in Cambridgeshire, 1579–1834* (Cambridge, 1934), pp. 195–6.

10. See S. E. Finer, *The Life and Times of Sir Edwin Chadwick* (London, 1952).

11. There are no official figures available for total relief expenditures in the years 1785–1801 and 1803–11.

12. T. Tooke, *History of Prices* (1857), vi, App. 6.

13. See A. D. Gayer, W. W. Rostow, A. J. Schwartz, *Economic Fluctuations in the British Economy, 1790–1850* (Oxford, 1953), ii. 563–4, 793, 854; R. C. O. Matthews, *A Study in Trade-Cycle History* (Cambridge, 1954), chap. 4.

14. Clapham, *The Railway Age*, p. 125. He cited a few Speenhamland counties which show a fall of wages between 1795 and 1824, but does not mention Buckinghamshire, Bedfordshire, Norfolk, Essex, Cambridge, Northamptonshire, Warwick, and Devon —all Speenhamland counties—where wages were higher in 1824 than in 1795.

15. See C. S. Orwin, B. I. Felton, 'A Century of Wages and Earnings in Agriculture,' *Journal of the Royal Agricultural Society*, 92 (1931).

16. See A. Redford, *Labour Migration in England, 1800–1850* (Manchester, 1926), chap. 11, and Appendices.

17. Another explanation suggests itself. The *Report of 1834* presented some evidence to show that small parishes, measured in terms of population per acre, granted more relief per head than large parishes, the reason being that the intimate personal connections between magistrates and farm hands in small parishes invited prodigality. If this were so, the high rates of relief per head in southern rural counties might be due to the fact that most of the 1,000 parishes under 50 inhabitants and most of the 6,000 under 300 inhabitants were located in southern agricultural districts. To test this hypothesis, we would have to examine the size distribution of parishes among counties, a question which cannot be entered into here; but see my 'The Poor Law Report reexamined', *Journal of Economic History*, 24 (1964), Appendix.

18. In the years 1835–7, they arranged for the migration of about 5,000 workers to the northern factory districts. In the same period, some 6,500 Poor Law emigrants went overseas, and in both cases about half the migrants came from the East Anglian counties of Norfolk and Suffolk. Redford, *Labour Migration*, p. 94.

19. For a review of the evidence, see N. Gash, 'Rural Unemployment, 1815–1834', *Econ. Hist. Rev.* 6, no. 1 (Oct. 1935). The records of the Emigration Inquiry of 1826–7 supply additional evidence of redundant labour in the southern rural counties: See Clapham, *The Railway Age*, pp. 64–5.

20. G. C. Fussell, M. Compton, 'Agricultural Adjustments after the Napoleonic Wars', *Economic History* (Feb. 1939), show that it was the grain-growing areas which were hit hardest in the post-war years.

21. Clapham, *The Railway Age*, pp. 19–22, 124, 467.

22. See Lord Ernle, *English Farming, Past and Present* (6th edn., London, 1961), pp. 308–12.

23. The official returns for the year 1844 are found in J. R. McCulloch, *A Descriptive and Statistical Account of the British Empire* (1854), ii. 670.

24. Redford, *Labour Migration*, Appendix 1, Map A.

25. J. T. Krause, 'Changes in English Fertility and Mortality, 1781–1850'. *Econ. Hist. Rev.*, 2nd series, 9 (Aug. 1958).

26. Ibid., and T. H. Marshall, 'The Population Problem During the Industrial Revolution: A Note on the Present State of the Controversy', *Economic History* (1929), reprinted in *Essays in Economic History*, ed. E. M. Carus-Wilson (London, 1954), i.

27. E. Cannan, *The History of Local Rates in England* (4th edn., London, 1927), p. 80.

28. A. W. Ashby, *One Hundred Years of Poor Law Administration in a Warwickshire Village. Oxford Studies in Social and Legal History*, ed. P. Vinogradoff (Oxford, 1912), iii. 57–8.

29. For the available evidence, see Gayer, *et al., Economic Fluctuations*, pp. 927–9.

30. Clapham, *The Railway Age*, pp. 98–105, 430–2. E. Davies, 'The Small Land-

owners, 1780–1832, in The Light of the Land Tax Assessments,' *Econ. Hist. Rev.* 1927, reprinted in *Essays in Economic History*, i; J. D. Chambers, 'Enclosure and the Small Landowner', *Econ. Hist. Rev.* x, no. 2 (Nov. 1940); J. D. Chambers, 'Enclosure and Labor Supply in the Industrial Revolution,' *Econ. Hist. Rev.* 2nd Ser., 5, no. 3 (1953).

31. See M. Blaug, *Ricardian Economics. A Historical Study* (New Haven, Conn., 1958), pp. 183–4.

32. See D. Marshall, 'The Old Poor Law, 1662–1795,' *Econ. Hist. Rev.* 1937, reprinted in *Essays in Economic History*, i.

33. Webbs, *Old Poor Law History*, p. 88 n.

34. This fact was carefully, and perhaps intentionally, hidden from the public. Throughout the remainder of the century, the Poor Law authorities displayed an incredible reluctance to supply any quantitative information about the body of people relieved, other than the ratio of outdoor to indoor relief recipients. Since some children and old people received outdoor relief, while a proportion of the ablebodied did enter the workhouse, we have no way of knowing just how many of the ablebodied received unemployment compensation; the 'ablebodied' were not even defined by the Act of 1834 for purposes of administration. See M. Dessauer, 'Unemployment Records, 1848–1859,' *Econ. Hist. Rev.* 9, no. 1 (Feb. 1940).

35. See H. L. Beales, 'The New Poor Law,' *History*, 1931, reprinted in *Essays in Economic History*, ed. E. M. Carus-Wilson (London: Edward Arnold, 1962), III.

7

The Language of 'Class' in Early Nineteenth-Century England*

ASA BRIGGS

THE concept of social 'class' with all its attendant terminology was a product of large-scale economic and social changes of the late eighteenth and early nineteenth centuries. Before the rise of modern industry[1] writers on society spoke of 'ranks', 'orders', and 'degrees' or, when they wished to direct attention to particular economic groupings, of 'interests'. The world 'class' was reserved for a number of people banded together for educational purposes[2] or more generally with reference to subdivisions in schemes of 'classification'.[3] Thus the 1824 edition of the *Encyclopædia Britannica* spoke of 'classes of quadrupeds, birds, fishes and so forth, which are again subdivided into series or orders and these last into genera'. It directed its readers to articles on 'Animal Kingdom' and 'Botany'. By 1824, however, the world 'class' had already established itself as a social label, and ten years later John Stuart Mill was to remark:

> They revolve in their eternal circle of landlords, capitalists and labourers, until they seem to think of the distinction of society into those three classes as if it were one of God's ordinances not man's, and as little under human control as the division of day or night. Scarcely any one of them seems to have proposed to himself as a subject of inquiry, what changes the relations of those classes to one another are likely to undergo in the progress of society.[4]

The word 'class' has figured so prominently in the subsequent development of the socialist—and of other social—vocabularies that a study of the origins and early use of the term in Britain is not simply an academic exercise in semantics. There was no dearth of social conflicts in pre-industrial society, but they were not conceived of at the time in straight class terms. The change in nomenclature in the late eighteenth and early nineteenth centuries reflected a basic change not only in men's ways of viewing society but in society itself. It is with the relationship between words and movements—in an English context—that this essay is concerned.

* From *Essays in Labour History*, ed. A. Briggs and J. Saville (London, 1967), pp. 43–73. Reprinted by permission of Macmillan, London and Basingstoke.

I

Eighteenth-century English society was hierarchical, and was often conceived of in terms of a pyramid with the 'common people', those without rank or 'dignity' at the base. The 'meer labouring people who depend upon their hands', as Defoe called them, were never without defenders[5] but social orthodoxy had little use for 'the gross and inconsistent notion' of equality.[6] Skilled artisans had their own grades of 'superiority' and 'inferiority',[7] while between the 'nobility' and the 'commonalty' were the growing numbers of 'middling people' or 'middling sorts' whose praises were frequently sung in an age of increasing wealth and mercantile expansion. The most successful of them were easily absorbed into the 'gentry', that most English of social groupings, and chapter 24 of Defoe's *Complete English Tradesman* (1726) was entitled 'Extracts from the genealogies of several illustrious families of our English nobility, some of which owe their rise to trade, and others their descent and fortunes to prudent alliances with the families of citizens'.[8]

The element of mobility in the social system—based on what Adam Smith and Malthus after him called 'the natural effort of every individual to better his own condition'[9]—was often stressed by social commentators, particularly those who drew a sharp distinction between England and the continent. There were two other very different elements, however, which were given equal attention and were especially emphasized by the first generation of writers to condemn the social disintegration' consequent upon the rise of factory industry. The first of them was what Cobbett called 'the chain of connection' between the rich and the poor[10] and the second was what Southey described as 'the bond of attachment'.[11] The use of the nouns 'chain' and 'bond' is as eloquent (in retrospect) as the choice of 'connection' and 'attachment', but Cobbett and Southey in their different ways were praising the past in order to condemn the present. 'Connection' was associated not only with a network of social obligation but with gentle slopes of social gradation. It implied that every man had his place within an order, but that the order allowed for declensions of status as well as bold contrasts. To those who were willing to disturb that order Cobbett exclaimed, 'You are for reducing the community to two classes: Masters and Slaves.'[12] 'Attachment' was directly associated both with 'duty'—the 'duty' appropriate to 'rank'—and with dependence, and thereby with 'charity', 'deference', and 'subordination'. 'The bond of attachment is broken,' wrote Southey in 1829, 'there is no longer the generous bounty which calls forth a grateful and honest and confiding dependence.'[13]

Before the Industrial Revolution of the 1780s there were many signs of tension and contradiction both in society and in contemporary writings about it. The growth of population, the problem of 'indigence', the enclosure movement in the villages, the increase in home and foreign trade, and the emergence of 'radical' ideas in politics preceded the development of the steam-engine. It was the steam-engine, however, which was the 'principal factor in accelerating urban concentration' and 'generalizing' the labour force.[14] It was the steam-engine also which inspired both the optimistic panegyrics of man's 'conquest of Nature' and the critical analyses of the contradictions and conflicts of the new society. The extent of the contradictions and the conflicts was clearly appreciated before the term 'industrial revolution' was coined. John Wade, the author of the *History of the Middle and Working Classes* (1833), one of the first attempts to put the facts of the recent past into historical perspective, wrote as follows:

The physical order of communities, in which the production of the necessaries of subsistence is the first want and chief occupation, has in our case been rapidly inverted, and in lieu of agricultural supremacy, a vast and overtopping superstructure of manufacturing wealth and population has been substituted.... To this extraordinary revolution, I doubt not, may be traced much of the bane and many of the blessings incidental to our condition—the growth of an opulent commercial and a numerous, restless and intelligent operative class; sudden alternations of prosperity and depression—of internal quiet and violent political excitement; extremes of opulence and destitution; the increase of crime; conflicting claims of capital and industry; the spread of an imperfect knowledge, that agitates and unsettles the old without having definitely settled the new foundations; clashing and independent opinions on most public questions, with other anomalies peculiar to our existing but changeful social existence.[15]

The use of the word 'class' and the sense of class that made the use increasingly meaningful must be related to what Wade called both 'the bane' and 'the blessings' of the new society. The development of factory industry often broke 'the bond of attachment', substituting for it what Carlyle was to call a 'cash nexus'.[16] The continued existence of factory paternalism checked but did not reverse this process. At the same time with the breaking of the bond there was increasing pressure to secure 'union' among the workers themselves. The demand not only for union at the factory or the local level but for 'general union', the story of which has been told by Professor Cole,[17] was directly related to the story of the emergence of a self-conscious 'working class'. Cobbett, who was one of the most forthright advocates of the old social system operating in an ideal form, saw clearly that once that system had been destroyed, 'classes' would be ranged against each other:

They [working men] combine to effect a rise in wages. The masters combine against them. One side complains of the other; but neither knows the *cause* of the turmoil, and the turmoil goes on. The different trades combine, and call their combination a GENERAL UNION. So that here is one class of society united to oppose another class.[18]

The same consequence followed on the growth of industrial cities, where the 'masses' were segregated and left to their own devices. A few years before Disraeli used the phrase 'two nations', a distinguished preacher spoke in very similar terms at a chapel in Boston across the Atlantic:

It is the unhappiness of most large cities that, instead of inspiring union and sympathy among different 'conditions of men', they consist of different ranks, so widely separated indeed as to form different communities. In most large cities there may be said to be two nations, understanding as little of one another, having as little intercourse, as if they lived in different lands.... This estrangement of men from men, of class from class, is one of the saddest features of a great city.[19]

It was a theme which was to be taken up frequently in nineteenth-century argument, and which dominated Engels's picture of Manchester in the 1840s. 'We know well enough,' Engels wrote, 'that [the] isolation of the individual ... is everywhere the fundamental principle of modern society. But nowhere is this selfish egotism so blatantly evident as in the frantic bustle of the great city.'[20] But the 'disintegration of society into individuals' was accompanied by the carving out of classes. 'The cities first saw the rise of the workers and the middle classes into opposing social groups.'[21]

Forty years before Engels, Charles Hall had stressed the snapping of 'the chain of continuity' in society and stated clearly for the first time the central proposition of a class theory of society:

The people in a civilised state may be divided into different orders; but for the purpose of investigating the manner in which they enjoy or are deprived of the requisites to support the health of their bodies and minds, they need only be divided into two classes, viz. the rich and the poor.[22]

The sharp contrasts of industrialism encouraged the restatement of theories of society in these terms. In one sense 'class' was a more indefinite word than 'rank' and this may have been among the reasons for its introduction.[23] In another sense, however, employment of the word 'class' allowed for a sharper and more generalized picture of society, which could be provided with a historical and economic underpinning. Conservatives continued to prefer to talk of 'ranks' and 'orders'—as they still did in the middle of the nineteenth century[24]—and the old language coexisted with the new, as it did in the words of the preacher quoted above, but analysts of the distribution of the national income[25] and social critics alike talked increasingly in class terms. So too did politicians, particularly as new social forces were given political expression. The stormiest political decade of early nineteenth-century English history, that which began with the financial crisis of 1836 and the economic crisis of 1837, was the decade when class terms were most generally used and 'middle classes' and 'working classes' alike did not hesitate to relate politics directly to class antagonisms.

There was, however, an influential social cross-current which directed attention not to the contrasting fortunes and purposes of 'middle classes' and 'working classes' but to a different division in industrial society, that between 'the industrious classes' and the rest. Those writers who were more impressed by the productive possibilities of large-scale industry than afraid of social 'disintegration' dwelt on this second division. Saint-Simon's demand for unity of 'the productive classes' against parasitic 'non-producers'[26] had many parallels as well as echoes inside England. Patrick Colquhoun, whose statistical tables were used by Robert Owen and John Gray,[27] attempted to divide industrial society into a productive class whose labour increased the national income and a 'diminishing class' which produced no 'new property'. When he argued that 'it is by the labour of the people, employed in various branches of industry, that all ranks of the community in every condition of life annually subsist',[28] he was not stating, as Gray later did, that manual labour created all wealth. Owen, who occasionally wrote in what were coming to be regarded as conventional terms of the 'upper', the 'middle' and the 'working classes', more usually conceived of society in the same terms as Colquhoun:

> There will be, therefore, at no distant period, a union of the government, aristocracy, and non-producers on the one part and the Industrious Classes, the body of the people generally, on the other part; and the two most formidable powers for good or evil are thus forming.[29]

The same conception influenced radical politics. The *Extraordinary Black Book*, also borrowing from Colquhoun and mixing up the language of 'class' and 'orders', maintained that

> The industrious orders may be compared to the soil, out of which every thing is evolved and produced; the other classes to the trees, tares, weeds and vegetables drawing their nutriment, supported and maintained on its surface.... When mankind attain a state of greater perfectibility ... [the useful classes] ought to exist in a perfect state. The other classes have mostly originated in our vices and ignorance ... having no employment, their name and office will cease in the social state.[30]

Thomas Attwood, who in favourable social and economic circumstances in Birmingham, tried to unite 'middle' and 'working classes' in a single Political Union,[31] also believed that what he called 'the industrious classes' should secure political power. 'The ox is muzzled that treadeth the corn.'[32] It was only after the Reform Bill of 1832 had failed to satisfy his hopes—and only then for a short period of time—that he claimed that 'in a great cause, he was content to stand or fall with the workmen alone' even if the middle classes, to which he belonged, were against him.[33]

II

Before turning to 'working-class' critics of both Owen and Attwood and to the statement of class theory in specifically working-class perspectives, the terms 'upper class' and 'middle class' require more careful and detailed examination. The phrase 'higher classes' was used for the first time by Burke in his *Thoughts on French Affairs* in 1791, significantly only when the position of the 'higher classes' seemed to be threatened not only in France but in England. It was an exhortatory phrase in much of the Evangelical literature of the last decade of the century. When the French Revolution challenged the power of artistocracies and in England traditional duties seemed to be in disrepair, there was a need to re-define them. It was in this mood that Thomas Gisborne, clergyman friend of Wilberforce, published his *Enquiry into the Duties of Men in the Higher Rank and Middle Classes of Society in Great Britain* in 1795. There was much literature of this kind in the 1790s. Hannah More, Cobbett's 'old bishop in petticoats',[34] was an indefatigable supporter of 'the old order', and her tracts, some of which were specially addressed to 'Persons of the Middle Ranks', 'were bought by the gentry and middling classes full as much as by the common people'.[35]

The phrase 'middle classes', which antedates the phrase 'working classes',[36] was a product, however, not of exhortation but of conscious pride. As early as the 1780s attempts had been made to create new organizations which would uphold the claims of the new manufacturers. Pitt's commercial policy goaded manufacturers to set up the General Chamber of Manufacturers in 1785:

> Common danger having at length brought together a number of Manufacturers in various branches, and from various places, and their having felt the advantages resulting to each from unreserved conferences and mutual assistance, they are now persuaded, that the prosperity of the Manufacturers of this kingdom, and of course that of the kingdom itself, will be promoted by the formation of a general bond of union, whereby the influence and experience of the whole being collected at one common centre, they will be the better enabled to effect any useful purposes for their general benefit.

In eighteenth-century terms this was the mobilization of a new economic 'interest', an interest which failed to maintain its unity in the immediate future. It was something more than that, however. 'The manufacturers of Great Britain', their statement began, 'constitute a very large, if not a principal part of the community; and their industry, ingenuity and wealth, have contributed no small share towards raising this kingdom to the distinguished and envied rank which she bears among the European nations.'[37] The word 'class' was not used, as it was used freely and unashamedly by the Anti-Corn Law League half a century later, but what was whispered in private in the 1780s was shouted on the platform in the 1840s.

There were several factors encouraging the development of a sense of middle-class unity where hitherto there had been a recognition of (imperfect) mutual interest. First in time was the imposition of Pitt's income tax, which entailed the common treatment of a group of diverse 'interests' by the government. Second was the impact of the Napoleonic Wars as a whole, which laid emphasis on the incidence of 'burdens', burdens which seemed to be of unequal weight for the owners of land and the owners of capital. Adam Smith had already distinguished clearly between these two 'interests' or 'orders' as he called them (and, indeed, a third 'interest', that 'of those who live by wages' as well), but he did not concede the claims of the merchants and 'master manufacturers': in his opinion they were more concerned with their own affairs than with the affairs of society as a whole. 'Their superiority over the country gentleman is, not so much in their knowledge of the public interest, as in their having a better knowledge of their own interest than he has of his.'[38] Between 1776 and 1815, however, the numbers and wealth of the 'owners of capital' increased, and both their public grievances and their public claims were advocated with energy and persistence.

It is not surprising that a sense of grievance stimulated talk of 'class', and there are many expressions of it in the periodicals of the day. 'Why rejoice in the midst of rivers of blood,' asked a writer in the *Monthly Repository* in 1809, 'while the burden of taxation presses so heavily on the middle classes of society, so as to leave the best part of the community little to hope and everything to fear?'[39] Four years later the same magazine demanded immediate peace 'for the relief of those privations and burdens, which now oppress every class in the community, including the poor and middle classes'.[40] The *Oxford English Dictionary* gives 1812 as the first occasion on which the phrase 'middle class' was used—in the *Examiner* of the August of that year —and in the twentieth century the example has a very familiar ring—'such of the Middle Class of Society who have fallen upon evil days'.

By 1815, however, statements about the 'middle classes' or the still popular term 'middle ranks' often drew attention not to grievances but first to the special role of the middle classes in society as a strategic and 'progressive' group and second to their common economic interests.

As early as 1798 the *Monthly Magazine* sang the praises of 'the middle ranks' in whom 'the great mass of information, and of public and private virtues reside'.[41] In 1807 the *Athenaeum* eulogized 'those persons whom the wisest politicians have always counted the most valuable, because the least corrupted members of society, the middle ranks of people'.[42] Such magazine comments had an element of editorial flattery about them, but beneath the flattery was a keen awareness of social trends. The growing reading public included large numbers of people who belonged to the 'middle classes',[43] and their views were considered to be the main expression of the new 'public opinion'. It was not difficult, indeed, to argue, as James Mill did in his *Essay on Government*, that 'the class which is universally described as both the most wise and the most virtuous part of the community, the middle rank' was the main opinion-making group in a dynamic society and would control politics 'if the basis of representation were extended'.[44] In the diffusion of Utilitarian ideas in the 1820s this case was frequently argued. The middle classes, 'the class who will really approve endeavours in favour of good government, and of the happiness and intelligence of men', had to unite to bring pressure upon the aristocracy. Their philosophy, like their wealth, depended on 'individualism', but their social action had to be concerted. 'Public opinion operates in various ways upon the aristocratical classes, partly by contagion, partly by conviction, and partly by intimidation: and the principal strength of that current is derived from the greatness of the mass by which it is swelled.'[45]

Politicians could not remain indifferent to this language, particularly when it was backed by wealth and increasing economic authority. One of the first to appreciate the need to win the support of the 'middle classes' was Henry Brougham. While the Luddites were engaged in what Engels later called 'the first organized resistance of the workers, as a class, to the bourgeoisie',[46] the 'middle classes' were being mobilized in a campaign to abolish the Orders-in-Council. Brougham, 'the life and soul' of the agitation, was later in his life to produce his celebrated equation of the 'middle classes' and 'the People'. 'By the people, I mean the middle classes, the wealth and intelligence of the country, the glory of the British name.'[47] During the Reform Bill agitation of 1830–2 many similar statements were made by Whig leaders who were anxious, in Durham's phrase, 'to attach numbers to property and good order'.[48] Even the aristocratic Grey, who feared the Political Unions with their propaganda for unity between the middle classes and the working classes, chose to appeal 'to the middle classes who form the real and efficient mass of public opinion and without whom the power of the gentry is nothing'.[49] The Whigs wished to hitch the middle classes to the constitution to prevent a revolution: a section of the extreme radicals wanted to associate them with the working classes to secure revolution. In the tense atmosphere of the years 1830–2 it was not surprising that advocates of cautious change insisted that 'any plan [of Reform] must be objectionable which, by keeping the Franchise very high and exclusive, fails to give satisfaction to the middle and respectable ranks of society, and drives them to a union, founded on dissatisfaction, with the lower orders. It is of the utmost importance to associate the middle with the higher orders of society in the love and support of the institutions and government of the country.'[50] The language as much as the content of this statement reflects a traditionalist view not only of politics but of society.

The relationship between 'public opinion' and the growing strength of the 'middle classes' was recognized even when there was an absence of political crisis. Sir James Graham, at that time an independent but later a member both of the Whig committee which drafted the Reform Bill and of the Conservative cabinet which proposed the repeal of the corn laws, remarked in 1826:

I know no bound but public opinion. The seat of public opinion is in the middle ranks of life—in that numerous class, removed from the wants of labour and the cravings of ambition, enjoying the advantages of leisure, and possessing intelligence sufficient for the formation of a sound judgement, neither warped by interest nor obscured by passion.[51]

The remark echoes Aristotle rather than Mill,[52] but it was one version of an extended argument. Another, more cogent, was set out in a historically important but neglected treatise *On the Rise, Progress, and Present State of Public Opinion in Great Britain and Other Parts of the World* (1828). Its author, W. A. Mackinnon, generalized from recent experience.[53] His book began with a 'definition' of the 'classes of society' and went on to describe how the rise of the 'middle classes' led to the growth of wealth and freedom:

> The extent or power of public opinion ... resolves itself into the question whether ... a community is possessed of an extensive middle class of society, when compared to a lower class; for the advantages called requisites for public opinion, cannot exist without forming a proportionate middle class. ... In every community or state where public opinion becomes powerful or has influence, it appears that the form of government becomes liberal in the exact proportion as the power of public opinion increases.[54]

Mackinnon related the recent rise of the 'middle classes' to what was later called 'the industrial revolution':

> Machinery creates wealth, which augments the middle class, which gives strength to public opinion; consequently, to allude to the extension of machinery is to account for the increase of the middle class of society.[55]

In a footnote to this passage he drew attention to the magnitude of the changes in his own lifetime:

> That the results arising from the improvement of machinery and its increase, are almost beyond the grasp of the human mind to define, may seem probable from the change that has and is daily taking place in the world.

Finally, he pegged class divisions to the distribution of property:

> The only means by which the classes of society can be defined, in a community where the laws are equal, is from the amount of property, either real or personal, possessed by individuals. As long as freedom and civilisation exist, property is so entirely the only power that no other means, or choice is left of distinguishing the several classes, than by the amount of property belonging to the individuals of which they are formed.[56]

Not only the amount of property was relevant in shaping class consciousness after 1815, but the kind. The prolonged but intermittent battle for the repeal of the corn laws encouraged social analysis in class terms: at the same time, particularly in its last stages, it sharpened middle-class consciousness and gave it highly organized means of expression.

The kind of social analysis set out in T. Perronet Thompson's *Catechism on the Corn Laws* (1826) was immediately popular for its content as much as for its style of exposition. The theory of rent was used to drive a wedge between the 'landlords' and the rest of the community, often with as much force as the labour theory of value was used in working-class arguments. Rent was defined as 'the superfluity of price, or that part of it which is not necessary to pay for the production with a living profit'. Adam Smith's argument that 'the landed interest', unlike the manufacturing interest, had a direct concern in 'the affairs of society as a whole' was turned on its head. The landlords were described by the repealers as selfish monopolists, who used the corn laws to protect their own selfish interest against the interests of the community. No vituperation was spared. There were two other particularly interesting questions and answers in the *Catechism*. '*Q*. That we must reconcile conflicting interests. *A*. There can be no conflict on a wrong. When the question is of a purse unjustly given, it is a fallacy to say we must reconcile conflicting interests, and give the taker half. *Q*. That the relation between the landlords and others, arising out of the Corn Laws is a source of kindly feelings and mutual virtues. *A*. Exactly the same was said of slavery.'[57]

Between the publication of the *Catechism* and the formation of the Anti-Corn Law League in 1839 there was a lull in the agitation. The League, however, was a uniquely powerful instrument in the forging of middle-class consciousness. 'We were a middle-class set of agitators', Cobden admitted, and the League was administered 'by those means by which the middle class usually carries on its movements'.[58] When the battle for repeal had been won Cobden asked Peel directly—'do you shrink from the post of governing through the *bona fide* representatives of the middle class? Look at the facts, and can the country be otherwise ruled at all? There must be an end of the juggle of parties, the mere representatives of tradition, and some man must of necessity rule the state through its governing class. The Reform Bill decreed it: the passing of the Corn Bill has realized it.'[59] Such a bold statement demonstrates that by 1846, not only had the phrase 'middle class' established itself as a political concept, but those people who considered themselves as representatives of the middle classes were prepared to assert in the strongest possible language their claim to political leadership.

Behind the League was middle-class wealth and what Disraeli in *Coningsby* (1844) called 'the pride of an order'.[60] There was also what had recently been called 'a strong belief in the nobility and dignity of industry and commerce', a kind of businessmen's romantic movement: '... trade has now a chivalry of its own; a chivalry whose stars are radiant with the more benignant lustre of justice, happiness and religion, and whose titles will outlive the barbarous nomenclature of Charlemagne.'[61]

This kind of rhetoric was usually accompanied by attacks on 'aristocratic tyranny', 'hereditary opulence' and 'social injustice', and by the declaration that 'trade shall no longer pay a tribute to the soil'. At the same time, it was necessary to supplement it—for political purposes—by an appeal to the 'working classes' ('joint victims' of the 'monopolists') and by an attempt to win over tenant farmers and to draw 'a broad distinction ... between the landed and the agricultural interest'.[62] The case for repeal had to be stated in different terms from those employed in Manchester in 1815, when the narrow economic interests of the manufacturers were the main staple of the published argument.[63] In Morley's famous words, 'class-interest widened into the consciousness of a commanding national interest'.[64] The argument was radically different in its tone and its implications from that advanced by the General Chamber of Manufacturers in the 1780s. Again Morley has caught the mood as the Leaguers themselves liked to interpret it:

Moral ideas of the relations of class to class in this country, and of the relations of country to country in the civilized world, lay behind the contention of the hour, and in the course of that contention came into new light. The promptings of a commercial shrewdness were gradually enlarged into enthusiasm for a far-reaching principle, and the hard-headed man of business gradually felt himself touched with the generous glow of the patriot and the deliverer.[65]

III

The glow was not always infectious, and although the League had some success in attracting the support of 'the working classes of the more respectable sort',[66] it was confronted in the provinces with the first large-scale self-consciously 'working' movement, Chartism. Relations between Chartists and Leaguers often demonstrated straight class antagonism. Mark Hovell quotes the story of the relations between the two groups in Sunderland. The Leaguers asked the local Chartist leaders, moderate men who agreed that the corn laws were an intolerable evil, to join them in their agitation. They replied that they could not co-operate merely on the merits of the question:

What is our present relation to you as a section of the middle class?—they went on—It is one of violent opposition. You are the holders of power, participation in which you refuse us; for demanding which you persecute us with a malignity paralleled only by the ruffian Tories. We are therefore surprised that you should ask us to co-operate with you.[67]

This attitude was not shared by all Chartists in all parts of the country— actual class relations, as distinct from theories of class, varied from place to place—but it was strong enough and sufficiently persistent to ensure that Chartists and Leaguers were as violently opposed to each other as both were to the government. Indeed, middle-class claims both of the rhetorical and of the economic kind helped to sharpen working-class consciousness, while fear of independent working-class action, tinged as it was with fear of violence, gave middle-class opinion a new edge. To men like Ebenezer Elliott, the Corn Law Rhymer, who believed—as part of the same programme—in repeal, suffrage extension, and class concilation, the 'middle classes' were being assailed on two sides. On the one side was 'the tyranny of aristocracy': one the other was 'the foolish insolence of the Chartists, which has exasperated into madness the un-natural hatred which the have-somethings bear to the have-nothings'.[68]

Chartist theories of class and expressions of class consciousness have recently been scrutinized.[69] In this essay more attention will be paid to the concept of a 'working class' before it was proclaimed in eloquent language by William Lovett and the London Working Men's Association in 1836.

Adam Smith often showed considerable sympathy in his writings for the 'workman', but the sympathy was frequently accompanied by statements about the workman's powerlessness. 'Many workmen could not subsist a week, few could subsist a month, and scarce any a year without employment.' Nor did their 'tumultuous combinations' do them much good. 'The interposition of the civil magistrate', 'the superior steadiness of the masters', and 'the necessity which the greater part of the workmen are under of submitting for the sake of the present subsistence' were handicaps to concerted action.[70] In addition Smith was impressed by the limitations on the effectiveness of political action on the part of the 'labourer':

Though the interest of the labourer is strictly connected with that of the society, he is incapable either of comprehending that interest, or of understanding its connection with his own. His condition leaves him no time to receive the necessary information, and his education and habits are commonly such as to render him unfit to judge even though he was fully informed. In the public deliberations, therefore, his voice is little heard and less regarded, except upon some particular occasions, when his clamour is animated, set on, and supported by his employers, not for his, but their own particular purposes.[71]

Between 1776 and 1836 such a diagnosis, warmed as it was by human sympathy, began to be increasingly unrealistic. The combined effect of the French and industrial revolutions was to direct attention not to the powerlessness of the labourer but to the potential power of the 'working classes', whether hitched to the 'middle classes' or, more ominously, relying on their own leaders. In the early 1830s, when political radicalism was often blended with labour economics in a lively brew, critics of 'working class' claims, like Peter Gaskell, talked of the dangers of the growth of a dual society hopelessly torn apart:

Since the Steam Engine has concentrated men into particular localities—has drawn together the population into dense masses—and since an imperfect education has enlarged, and to some degree distorted their views, union is become easy and from being so closely packed, simultaneous action is readily excited. The organisation of these [working-class] societies is now so complete that they form an 'imperium in imperio' of the most obnoxious description.... Labour and Capital are coming into collision—the operative and the master are at issue, and the peace, and well-being of the Kingdom are at stake.[72]

The same case was argued in Henry Tufnell's extremely interesting study, *The Character, Objects and Effects of Trades Unions* (1834), which expressed horrified alarm at the ramifications of a secret and hidden system of trade-union authority, based on its own laws with 'no reference to the laws of the land'. Like Gaskell, Tufnell argued that:

Where combinations have been most frequent and powerful, a complete separation of feeling seems to have taken place between masters and men. Each party looks upon the other as an enemy, and suspicion and distrust have driven out the mutual sentiments of kindness and goodwill, by which their intercourse was previously marked.[73]

Leaving on one side the merits of Tufnell's assessment of earlier industrial relations,[74] there has been a marked shift of emphasis since *The Wealth of Nations*. The shift was marked even in the far shorter period between the end of the Napoleonic Wars and the Reform Bill crisis. James Mill, who in his *Essay on Government* stated categorically that 'the opinions of that class of the people, who are below the middle rank, are formed, and their minds are directed by that intelligent and virtuous rank, who come the most immediately in contact with them ... to whom they fly for advice and assistance in all their numerous difficulties, upon whom they feel an immediate and daily dependence',[75] was bemoaning in 1831 the spread of 'dangerous doctrines' among 'the common people' which would lead to a 'subversion of civilised society, worse than the overwhelming deluge of Huns and Tartars'. In a letter to Brougham he exclaimed:

Nothing can be conceived more mischievous than the doctrines which have been preached to the common people. The illicit cheap publications, in which the doctrine of the right of the labouring people, who say they are the only producers, to all that is produced, is very generally preached, are superseding the Sunday newspapers and every other channel through which the people might get better information.[76]

A pamphlet published by an 'approved source', the Society for the Diffusion of Useful Knowledge, warned that such doctrines, apparently 'harmless as abstract propositions', would end in 'maddening passion, drunken frenzy, unappeasable tumult, plunder, fire, and blood'.[77]

While James Mill was finishing off his *Essay on Government*, there had already been published what seems to be one of the first English working-class manifestos to talk straight language of 'class'. *The Gorgon*, published in London in November 1818, set out a series of four objections to an argument which was being frequently employed at that time that 'workmen must be expected to share the difficulties of their employers and the general distress of the times'. The language of eighteenth and nineteenth centuries overlaps in the statement of their second objection, as it does in much of the socialist literature of the 1820s:

To abridge the necessary means of subsistence of the working classes, is to degrade, consequently to demoralise them; and when the largest and most valuable portion of any community is thus degraded and demoralised, ages may pass away before society recovers its former character of virtue and happiness.[78]

Their other objections—the last of them related to the lack of political representation—were frequently reiterated by later working-class organizations. What Mill most complained of in 1831—the spread of the doctrine of the right of the labouring people to the whole produce of labour—still needs a more systematic examination than historians have given it. The story of the development of formal labour economics in the 1820s is relatively well charted,[79] but the story of popular social radicalism is as yet only partly explored. The two stories are related, but they are not the same. Cobbett's post-war demand for the restoration of the dignity of labour in a changing society[80] merged with Owen's demand for an end to 'the depreciation of human labour',[81] and theories of radical reform of parliament and economic co-operation were often seen not as alternative ways to working-class emancipation but as pointers to complementary areas of working-class action. As early as 1826 a speaker in Manchester claimed that 'the purpose of parliamentary reform was to secure to the labourer the fruits of his own labour ... and to every British subject a full participation in all the privileges and advantages of British citizens.'[82] John Doherty and his supporters in industrial Lancashire continued to argue that 'universal suffrage means nothing more than a power given to every man to protect his own labour from being devoured by others' and urged that parliamentary reform would be of little value to the masses of the population unless it was accompanied by social action to guarantee to the workmen 'the whole produce of their labour'.[83] The same views were being canvassed in the London Rotunda in 1831 and 1832 and were often expressed in the pages of the *Poor Man's Guardian.*[84] During the agitation for the Reform Bill the National Union of the Working Classes, founded in 1831, identified political oppression and social injustice:

Why were the laws not made to protect industry, but property or capital? Because the law-makers were compounded of fund and landholders, possessors of property, and the laws were made to suit their own purposes, being utterly regardless of the sources from which the property arose.... Had the producers of wealth been the makers of laws, would they have left those who made the country rich to perish by starvation?[85]

As far as the leaders and members of the National Union of the Working Classes were concerned—numerically they were extremely small, and on many points they were divided[86]—it did not need disillusionment with the results of the Reform Bill of 1832 to make them distinguish clearly between the interests of the 'middle classes' and the 'working classes'. The distinction was made on economic grounds before 1832. The 'working classes', the argument ran, were victims of the industrial system, yet they constituted a majority in society. They did not receive that to which they were legitimately entitled: the rights of property were the wrongs of the poor.[87] They could only secure their proper place in society, however, by concerted action, what was called in the language of the day—with both economic and political reference—'union'. History could be employed to support their claims,[88] but the claims could be understood without difficulty in their immediate context, an industrial system founded on 'competition' instead of 'co-operation'. There was an urgent need for 'the elite of the working classes'[89] to communicate their ideas and solutions to the rest. As one popular lecturer on co-operation in Lancashire put it:

> About one third of our working population ... consists of weavers and labourers, whose average earnings do not amount to a sum sufficient to bring up and maintain their families without parochial assistance. ... It is to this class of poor fellow creatures, in particular, that I desire to recommend the system of co-operation, as the only means which at present, seem calculated to diminish the evils under which they live.[90]

Owen might be suspicious of the mixing of his doctrines with those of popular radical reformers[91] and continue to talk of the need to create an ideal class of 'producers' which included both workmen and employers, but the social and political situation was beyond his control. It was not only the National Union of Working Classes which talked in class terms. As the third Co-operative Congress held at the Institution of the Industrious Classes in London in 1832 several speakers described operatives and employers as separate and hostile forces,[92] while in the pages of the *Pioneer*, which first appeared in September 1833, there were many signs of differences of opinion between the editor, James Morrison, and Owen on questions of class. The first number of the *Pioneer* had a 'correct' Owenite editorial,[93] but Morrison soon proclaimed the independence of the 'working class' from the 'middle men'.[94] In one striking passage he declared:

> Trust none who is a grade above our class, and does not back us in the hour of trial. ... Orphans we are, and bastards of society.[95]

In writing the detailed history of working-class movements of the 1830s, culminating in Chartism, it is necessary to separate out different strands.[96] For the purposes of this essay, however, emphasis must be placed on the element of class consciousness which in various forms was common to them all. Bronterre O'Brien, who was identified with three of the main movements—the struggle for Reform in 1831 and 1832, trade unionism, and Chartism—described this element as follows:

> A spirit of combination had grown up among the working classes, of which there has been no example in former times. ... The object of it is the sublimest that can be conceived, namely—to establish for the productive classes a complete dominion over the fruits of their own industry. ... Reports show that an entire change in society—a change amounting to a complete subversion of the existing 'order of the world'—is contemplated by the working classes. They

aspire to be at the top instead of at the bottom of society—or rather that there should be no bottom or top at all.[97]

In the bitter rivalry between Chartists and Leaguers there was class consciousness on both sides, although a section of the Chartists came to the conclusion that they would be able to accomplish nothing without middle-class support and the Leaguers were always compelled to look for working-class allies. Tory traditionalists disliked the language of 'class' from whichever quarter of society it came. Peel, prime minister in the critical years of the century, would have nothing to do with it. During the middle years of the century, the language of class was softened as much as social antagonisms themselves, but it burst out again in many different places in the years which led up to the second Reform Bill of 1867.

IV

There were some affinities, on the surface at least, between eighteenth-century views of society and those most frequently canvassed in the 1850s and 1860s. Attention was paid not to the broad contours of class division, but to an almost endless series of social gradations. The role of deference even in an industrial society was stressed, and the idea of a 'gentleman', one of the most powerful of mid-Victorian ideas but an extremely complicated one both to define and to disentangle, was scrutinized by novelists as much as by pamphleteers. The case for inequality was as much a part of social orthodoxy as it had been a hundred years before. 'Almost everybody in England has a hard word for social equality', wrote Matthew Arnold in 1878.[98] The language of 'interests' enjoyed a new vogue both in the world of politics and outside. It was perhaps a sign of the times that the Amalgamated Society of Engineers, founded in 1851, did not claim that it was its duty to secure the objects of a 'class' but rather 'to exercise the same control over that in which we have a vested interest, as the physician who holds his diploma, or the author who is protected by his copyright'.[99] The term 'labour interest' figured prominently in political discussion at all levels. A distinction was drawn even by radical politicians between the articulate 'labour interest' and the 'residuum', the great mass of the working-class population. The concept of the 'residuum', indeed, was useful to writers who wished to write off the 'condition of England question' of the 1840s as something dead and done with.

Against this background, 'class' came to be thought of as a rather naughty word with unpleasant associations. *The Times* in 1861 remarked that 'the word "class", when employed as an adjective, is too often intended to convey some reproach. We speak of "class prejudices" and "class legislation", and inveigh against the selfishness of class interest.'[100] One of the most influential of the people who inveighed was Herbert Spencer. In a chapter with the significant title 'The Class Bias' he wrote:

The egoism of individuals leads to an egoism of the class they form; and besides the separate efforts, generates a joint effort to get an undue share of the aggregate proceeds of social activity. The aggressive tendency of each class thus produced has to be balanced by like aggressive tendencies of other classes.[101]

The word 'balance' was one of the key words of the period both in relation to politics and to society.

It is not surprising that during these years three main points were made about 'class' in England. First, England was a country where there was a marked degree of individual mobility and this made class divisions tolerable. Second, the dividing lines between classes were extremely difficult to draw. Third, there were significant divisions *inside* what were conventionally regarded as classes, and these divisions were often more significant than divisions *between* the classes. Taken together these three points constituted a description rather than an analysis. The description was compared, however, with descriptions of the state of affairs in other countries, the United States or France, for example, or even India.[102] Whereas during the 1840s both middle-class and working-class politicians (and most writers on society) had argued about 'class' in general terms, relating what was happening in England to what was happening in other countries,[103] during the middle years of the century most of the arguments were designed to show that England was a favoured special case.

The 'facts' of individual mobility were stated eloquently and forcefully by Palmerston in his famous speech during the Don Pacifico debate in the House of Commons in 1850:

We have shown the example of a nation, in which every class in society accepts with cheerfulness the lot which Providence has assigned to it; while at the same time every individual of each class is constantly striving to raise himself in the social scale—not by injustice and wrong, not by violence and illegality, but by preserving good conduct, and by the steady and energetic execution of the moral and intellectual faculties with which his Creator endowed him.[104]

Only two years after the revolutions of 1848 and the waning of Chartism the language of politics was changing. The values were the same as those described by Beatrice Webb at the beginning of *My Apprenticeship*:

It was the bounden duty of every citizen to better his social status; to ignore those beneath him, and to aim steadily at the top rung of the ladder. Only by this persistent pursuits by each individual of his own and his family's interest would the highest general level of civilisation be attained.[105]

The rungs of the ladder did not move: it was individuals who were expected to do so. 'Individuals may rise and fall by special excellence or defects', wrote Edward Thring, the famous public school headmaster, 'but the classes cannot change places.'[106]

The metaphor of 'ladders' and 'rungs' proved inadequate for the many writers who wished to emphasize the blurring of class dividing-lines in mid-

Victorian England. 'Take any class of Englishmen, from the highest to the lowest,' wrote the young Dicey in a stimulating essay, 'and it will be found to mix, by imperceptible degrees, with the class below it. Who can say where the upper class ends, or where the middle class begins?'[107] Arnold, who was quick to catch the 'stock notions' of his age, some of which he believed in himself, referred in *Friendship's Garland* to 'the rich diversity of our English life ... the happy blending of classes and character'.[108] Other writers described 'intermediate classes' bridging the chasms of class antagonism.

Finally, divisions within classes—the presence of what were sometimes called 'sub-classes'—were stressed. The 'middle classes', which Cobden had struggled to pull together during the 1840s, separated out into diverging elements after 1846, and the plans of the more daring spirits of the Manchester School to carry through a 'middle-class revolution' were never realized.[109] To cross the 'moral and intellectual' gulf between the skilled workers and unskilled, wrote Henry Mayhew, was to reach 'a new level ... among another race'.[110] In some respects, at least, dividing lines seemed to be sharper at the base of the social pyramid than towards the apex.

The political debate which followed the death of Palmerston in 1865 and ended with the passing of the Second Reform Bill two years later led to a revival of interest in the problems and terminology of 'class'.[111] It was the change in economic circumstances in the 1870s and 1880s, however, and the disturbance of the mid-Victorian social balance which shifted the debate on to a wider front. An understanding of the new phase which was opening during the late Victorian years depends on a thorough examination of the phrase 'working classes' in a context of socialism. Whatever else may be said of the new phase, one development is incontrovertible. The language of 'ranks', 'orders', and 'degrees', which had survived the Industrial Revolution,[112] was finally cast into limbo. The language of class, like the facts of class, remained.

BIBLIOGRAPHICAL NOTE

Two remarkable books have been written, from very different standpoints, on the theme of changing perceptions of class and class structure of Britain in the period with which this article deals: E. P. Thompson, *The Making of the English Working Class* (London, 1964) and Harold Perkin, *The Origins of Modern English Society, 1780–1880* (London, 1969). Patricia Hollis, *Class and Conflict in Nineteenth-Century England 1815–1850* (London, 1973) is a book of documents admirably illustrating the changing 'language of class' in the period. See also D. Thompson, *The Early Chartists* (London, 1971), a similar work on a narrower front, and B. Harrison and P. Hollis, 'Chartism, liberalism and the life of Robert Lowery'. *Eng. Hist. Rev.* 82 (1967) which suggests a modification of the traditional emphasis on class conflict in the 1840s. Plainly, the theme also ties in with John Foster's article reprinted below (chap. 8), and the second paragraph of the Bibliographical Note following that article is also relevant here.

NOTES

1. In its modern sense the word 'industry', used with reference not to a particular human attribute, but to a complex of manufacturing and productive institutions, was itself a new word in the late eighteenth century. See R. Williams, *Culture and Society* (1958), p. xv. Adam Smith was on of the first writers to use the word in this way: he did not use the word 'class' in the sense discussed in this essay.

2. It was later used by the Methodists to refer to 'class' meetings, a usage which was later borrowed by early nineteenth-century 'Political Protestants' and Chartists.

3. Daniel Defoe, who usually wrote in terms of 'orders', 'ranks', and 'degrees', on a few occasions used 'class' in contexts where he was referring to social classification. See, for instance, *Review*, 14 Apr. 1705, 21 June 1709. Smith also referred (incidentally) to 'classes of people' in his account of 'the three great orders of society' in his *The Wealth of Nations*, bk. i, chap. 11.

4. *Monthly Repository* (1834), p. 320.

5. For one of the most important strands in the defence, see C. Hill, 'The Norman Yoke' in J. Saville (ed.), *Democracy and the Labour Movement* (1954).

6. For an early eighteenth-century criticism of it and an alternative analysis of society, see D. Defoe, *Of Royall Educacion* (written 1728–9).

7. Francis Place complained in the early nineteenth century of the indiscriminate jumbling together of 'the most skilled and the most prudent workmen with the most ignorant and imprudent labourers and paupers' when the term 'lower orders' was used. 'The difference is great indeed,' he went on, 'and in many cases will scarce admit of comparison.' Place Papers, British Museum, Add. MSS. 27,834, f. 45.

8. Cp. P. J. Grosley, *A Tour of London, II* (1772): 'The mixture and confusion ... between the nobility and the mercantile part of the nation, is an inexhaustible source of wealth to the state, the nobility having acquired an accession of wealth by marriage, the tradesmen make up for their loss by their eager endeavours to make a fortune, and the gentry conspire to the same end by their efforts to raise such an estate as shall procure a peerage for themselves or their children.' For nineteenth-century statements of a similar point of view, see above, p. 171.

9. *The Wealth of Nations* (1776), bk. iv, chap. 9.

10. *Political Register*, 14 April 1821.

11. R. Southey, *Sir Thomas More: or, Colloquies on the Progress and Prospects of Society* (1829), p. 47.

12. *Political Register*, loc. cit.

13. *Sir Thomas More*, loc. cit.

14. For the social impact of the change from water power to steam power, see G. D. H. Cole, *Studies in Class Structure* (1955), pp. 28–30. Marx, *Capital,* i, pt. IV, chap. 13, quoted A. Redgrave, a factory inspector, who argued that 'the steam-engine is the parent of manufacturing towns'. (Everyman edition, 1930, i. 398.)

15. J. Wade, *History of the Middle and Working Classes* (1842 edn.), Preface, p. 1.

16. This phrase, which was used by Disraeli, the authors of the *Communist Manifesto,* and many of the novelists and reviewers of the 1840s, was first used by Carlyle. As early as 1829 he wrote in his essay *Signs of the Times* that 'Cash Payment' was becoming the 'sole nexus' between man and man. Later, the shorter term became something of a slogan.

17. *Attempts at General Union* (1953), originally published in 1939 in the *International Review for Social History.*

18. *Political Register*, 27 Aug. 1825.

19. W. E. Channing, *A Discourse on the Life and Character of Rev. Joseph Tuckerman* (Boston, Mass., 1841), pp. 7–8.

20. *The Condition of the Working Class in England* (tr. W. O. Henderson and W. H. Chaloner, 1958), p. 31.

21. Ibid., 203.

22. C. Hall, *The Effects of Civilisation on the People in European States* (1805), p. 3.

23. Williams, op. cit. xv.

24. The *Quarterly Review*, which continued to refer to 'attachment' and 'continuity' in many of its articles on the social system even in the second half of the nineteenth century, referred in 1869 (vol. 126, p. 450) to 'lower-middle class', adding hastily, 'We must apologize for using this painful nomenclature, but really there is no choice.'

25. Writers on the national income were among the first to have to consider how best to describe the various sections of the population. 'Political arithmetic' and social classification went together.

26. See G. D. H. Cole, *Socialist Thought, The Forerunners, 1789–1850*, pp. 42–3, for the distinction between *les industriels* and *les oisifs*. The word 'industry' itself had a special significance for Saint-Simon (see his *L'Industrie* (1817)), and there were socialist undertones beneath many of the words derived from it. See the fascinating, pioneer article by A. E. Bestor, 'The Evolution of the Socialist Vocabulary', in the *Journal of the History of Ideas*, 9 (June 1948).

27. Owen constructed visual aids to illustrate Colquhoun's tables, a set of eight cubes exhibiting a 'General View of Society', the working classes being represented at the base by a large cube whilst the apex was formed by a small cube, representing the royal family and the aristocracy. See F. Podmore, *Robert Owen* (1906), pp. 255–6. John Gray's *A Lecture on Human Happiness* (1825) set out the case that Labour received only one-fifth of its produce, the rest being appropriated by the 'unproductive' classes.

28. *A Treatise on the Wealth, Power and Resources of the British Empire* (1814). Colquhoun's attempt—in his own words—'to show how ... New Property ... is distributed among the different Classes of the Community'—had socialist implications which he did not draw out. He believed that poverty was necessary in society, that Malthus's population doctrine was sound, and that improved 'social police' would hold society together. Yet just as Ricardian economics were used to develop a socialist theory of value, so Colquhoun's statistics were used to propound a socialist analysis of distribution, behind both Ricardo and Colquhoun was Adam Smith. For Smith's account of 'productive' and 'unproductive' labour, see *The Wealth of Nations*, bk. ii, chap. 3.

29. 'Address to the Sovereign', printed in *The Crisis*, 4 Aug. 1832.

30. *The Extraordinary Black Book* (1831 edn.), pp. 217–18. Colquhoun was described as 'a bold, but, as experience had proved, a very shrewd calculator'. (ibid. 216.)

31. For the significance of his thought and work against a European background, see my article, 'Social Structure and Politics in Birmingham and Lyons' (1825–48) in the *British Journal of Sociology*, i (Mar. 1950).

32. *Report of the Proceedings* of the *Birmingham Political Union*, 25 Jan. 1830. The Declaration of the Union drawn up on this occasion claimed that the House of Commons 'in its present state' was 'too far removed in habits, wealth and station, from the wants and interests of the lower and middle classes of the people to have any just views respecting them, or any close identity of feeling with them'. It went on to complain of the over-representation of the 'great aristocratical interests', only nominally counter-balanced by the presence of a few 'rich and retired capitalists'. The National Political Union, founded in London in 1831, also proclaimed as one of its purposes, 'to watch over and promote the interests, and to better the condition of the INDUSTRIOUS AND WORKING CLASSES'. (Place Papers, Add. MSS. 27,791, f. 184.)

33. *Birmingham Journal*, 17 Jan. 1836.

34. *Political Register*, 20 Apr. 1822.

35. Letter to Zachary Macaulay, 6 Jan. 1796, quoted by M. G. Jones, *Hannah More* (1952), p. 144. These tracts were regarded as 'antidotes to Tom Paine', 'Burke for Beginners'.

36. Gisborne's *Enquiry* was certainly one of the first publications to use the term

'middle classes'. In 1797 the *Monthly Magaine*, founded by Richard Phillips and John Aikin to 'propagate liberal principles', spoke of 'the middle and industrious classes of society' (p. 397). The phrase 'working classes' seems to have been used for the first time by Robert Owen in 1813 in his *Essays on the Formation of Character*, later reprinted under the more familiar title *A New View of Society*, but it was a descriptive rather than an analytical term ('the poor and working classes of Great Britain and Ireland have been found to exceed 12 millions of persons'). He used the term frequently in letters to the newspapers in 1817 and in 1818 he published *Two Memorials on Behalf of the Working Classes*.

37. *Sketch of a Plan of the General Chamber of Manufacturers of Great Britain* (1785).

38. Smith's general account of the division of the 'annual produce' of land and labour is given at the end of the last chapter (11) of bk. i of *The Wealth of Nations*. For Smith's view of the 'labourer', see above, p. 165.

39. *Monthly Repository* (1809), p. 501.

40. Ibid. (1813), p. 65.

41. *Monthly Magazine* (1798), p. 1. It referred to the 'ignorant apathy' of the 'lowest classes'.

42. *Athenaeum* (1807), p. 124.

43. See R. D. Altick, *The English Common Reader* (Chicago, 1957), p. 41.

44. *An Essay on Government* (ed. E. Barker, 1937), pp. 71–2. The essay was completed in 1820. There is a remarkable and significant contrast between the method and style of Mill's argument and the form of his dogmatic and defiant concluding sentence. 'It is altogether futile with regard to the foundation of good government to say that this or the other portion of the people, may at this, or the other time, depart from the wisdom of the middle rank. It is enough that the great majority of the people never cease to be guided by that rank; and we may with some confidence, challenge the adversaries of the people to produce a single instance to the contrary in the history of the world.' (Ibid., 73.)

45. James Mill in the *Westminster Review*, 1, Oct. 1824.

46. Engels, op. cit. 243.

47. This quotation is given in the *Oxford English Dictionary*. In introducing the Reform Bill Lord John Russell talked of changing the House of Commons from 'an assembly of representatives of small classes and particular interests' into 'a body of men who represent the people'.

48. Quoted by N. Gash, *Politics in the Age of Peel* (1953), p. 16.

49. Grey made this remark outside Parliament. See Henry, Earl Grey (ed.), *The Correspondence of the Late Earl Grey with His Majesty King William IV* (1867), i. 376.

50. H. Cockburn, *Letters on Affairs of Scotland*, quoted by Gash, op. cit. 15.

51. Sir James Graham, *Corn and Currency* (1826), p. 9. Graham appealed to the landed proprietors to unite as 'the manufacturing and commercial body' had done, and to frame their actions in accordance with 'public opinion' and 'the interest of the community'.

52. It also recalls a passage in Defoe's *Robinson Crusoe*—'Mine was the middle state or what might be called the upper station of low life ... not exposed to the Labour and sufferings of the Mechanick part of Mankind, and not embarrassed with the Pride, Luxury, Ambition and Envy of the Upper Part of Mankind.'

53. William Mackinnon was a Member of Parliament almost continuously from 1830 to 1865. His book on public opinion was rewritten in 1846 as a *History of Civilisation*. Mackinnon was one of the first writers to relate the rise of the 'middle classes' to the 'progress of civilization'.

54. *On the Rise, Progress, and Present State of Public Opinion* (1828), pp. 6–7.

55. Ibid., 10.

56. *On the Rise, Progress, and Present State of Public Opinion* (1828), p. 2.

57. For the background of the *Catechism* and its importance in the struggle for repeal, see L. G. Johnson, *General T. Perronet Thompson* (1957), chap. 8, and D. G. Barnes, *A History of the English Corn Laws* (1930), pp. 210–12.

58. J. Morley, *The Life of Richard Cobden* (1903 edn.), i. 249.

59. Ibid., 390–7. In his reply Peel was careful to avoid all reference to 'class'.

60. Disraeli also referred to 'classes'. When Coningsby went to Manchester, 'the great Metropolis of Labour', he 'perceived that [industrial] wealth was rapidly developing classes whose power was imperfectly recognized in the constitutional scheme, and whose duties in the social system seemed altogether omitted'. (bk. iv, chap. 2.) In conversing with Milbank he had already 'heard for the first time of influential classes in the country, who were not noble, and yet were determined to acquire power'. (bk. ii, chap. 6.) He referred to 'the various classes of this country [being] arrayed against each other'. (bk. iv, chap. 12.)

61. H. Dunckley, *The Charter of the Nations* (1854), p. 25. Quoted by N. McCord, *The Anti-Corn Law League* (1958), p. 24.

62. A phrase of Cobden, quoted ibid., p. 145.

63. The early advocates of free trade in 1815 'took the untenable and unpopular ground that it was necessary to have cheap bread in order to reduce the English vote of wages to the continental level, and so long as they persisted in this blunder, the cause of free trade made little progress'. W. Cooke Taylor, *The Life and Times of Sir Robert Peel* (1842), p. 111.

64. Morley, op. cit. i. 180.

65. Ibid., 182.

66. A phrase used in a letter from a repealer in Carlisle, quoted by N. McCord, op. cit., p. 97. There was strong working-class support in Carlisle for Julian Harney, who preached a very different gospel to that of the League. See A. R. Schoyen, *The Chartist Challenge* (1958), p. 72.

67. Quoted by M. Hovell, *The Chartist Movement* (1925 edn.), pp. 215–16.

68. Quoted by Johnson, op. cit., p. 233.

69. See Schoyen, op. cit.; A. Briggs (ed.) *Chartist Studies* (1959), chap. 9.

70. *Wealth of Nations*, bk. i, chap. 8.

71. Ibid., bk. i, chap. 9.

72. Gaskell to Lord Melbourne, 16 April 1834 (Home Office Papers 40/32). Gaskell, whose book *The Manufacturing Population of England* (1833) was freely used by Engels, had a diametrically opposed view of the correct answer to the 'social problem'.

73. H. Tufnell, *The Character, Objects and Effects of Trades Unions* (1834), pp. 2, 97.

74. Gaskell shared his tendency to idealize social relations before the industrial revolution. 'The distinctions of rank, which are the safest guarantee for the performance of the relative duties of classes, were at this time in full force' (op. cit., p. 20). Engels, who did not make use of this sentence, borrowed direct from Gaskell in the 'Historical Introduction' which forms the first chapter of his book, and thereby overrated 'patriarchal relationships' and 'idyllic simplicity'. He broke sharply with Gaskell, however, in his conclusion. Workers before the rise of steam-power 'know nothing of the great events that were taking place in the outside world.... The Industrial Revolution ... forced the workers to think for themselves and to demand a fuller life in human society' (op. cit., p. 12).

75. *Essay on Government*, p. 72. He added the words 'to whom their children look up as models for their imitation, whose opinions they hear daily repeated, and account it their honour to adopt'.

76. Quoted by A. Bain, *James Mill* (1882), p. 365.

77. 'The Rights of Industry' (1831), *passim*.

78. The statement in *The Gorgon* (28 Nov. 1818) is printed in full in G. D. H. Cole and A. W. Filson, *British Working-Class Movements, Select Documents, 1789–1875* (1951), p. 159.

79. The road leads back before Adam Smith, but Ricardo's *Principles of Economics* (1817) was the greatest single milestone. Smith used the phrase 'the whole produce of labour' (bk. i, chap. 8), but claimed that the labourer had only been able to secure it in a primitive society and economy, 'the original state of things'. Ricardo (with important qualifications) based his general theory of value on 'the quantity of labour

realised in commodities'. William Thompson (*An Inquiry into the Principles of the Distribution of Wealth, most Conducive to Human Happiness* [1824]) and Thomas Hodgskin (*Labour Defended* [1825]) anticipated Marx in using the theory as part of a socialist analysis.

80. *Political Register*, 2 Nov. 1816. 'The real strength and all the resources of a country, ever have sprung and ever must spring, from the *labour* of its people.'

81. See 'Labour, the Source of All Value' in *A Report to the County of Lanark* (1820). Owenism has been studied far less than Owen.

82. *Wheeler's Manchester Chronicle*, 28 Oct. 1826.

83. Home Office 52/18. A letter from a Preston correspondent to the Home Secretary encloses a pamphlet, *A Letter from one of the 3730 Electors of Preston to his Fellow Countrymen*. See also Doherty's pamphlet, *A Letter to the Members of the National Association for the Protection of Labour* (1831).

84. E.g. 16 Feb. 1833. 'Universal suffrage would give the power to those who produce the wealth to enjoy it.'

85. Ibid., 24 Dec. 1831.

86. For the division between 'Huntites' and 'Owenites', see ibid., 4 Feb. 1832.

87. Ibid., 26 Jan. 1833.

88. The old Saxon/Norman theme (see note 5 above) was still raised. In a London debate in 1833 on the notion that 'until the laws of property are properly discussed, explored, and understood by the producers of all property the wretched condition of the working classes can never be improved', more than one spectator referred to 'the misappropriation' of the Norman Conquest and its aftermath. (Ibid., 18 May 1833.)

89. This phrase, which has often been used with reference to the London Working Men's Association, was employed in the *Poor Man's Guardian*. Describing the fourth Co-operative Congress, the newspaper reporter said that it was comprised of 'plain but intelligent workmen ... the very elite of the working classes'. (Ibid., 19 Oct. 1833.)

90. F. Baker, *First Lecture on Co-operation* (Bolton, 1830), p. 2.

91. He sharply condemned 'a party of Owenites of the Rotunda or desperadoes' and said that he had never been to the London Rotunda (*Union*, 17 Dec. 1831).

92. See *the Crisis*, 28 Apr. 1832.

93. 'The Union [the Grand National Consolidated Trade Union] is a well-organized body of working men, bound together by wise and discreet laws, and by one common interest. Its object is to affect the general amelioration of the producers of wealth, and the welfare of the whole community. Its members do not desire to be at war with any class, neither will they suffer any class to usurp their rights.' (*Pioneer*, 7 Sept. 1833.)

94. Ibid., 21 June 1834. 'The capitalist,' he wrote (21 Dec. 1833), 'merely as a property man, has no power at all, and labour ... regulated by intelligence, will in a very few years, be the only existent power in this and in all highly civilized countries.'

95. Ibid., 22 Mar. 1834.

96. See for the various strands, *Chartist Studies*, especially chap. 1, 'The Local Background of Chartism'. It is important to note that at the local level many working-class activists joined several movements, caring less about doctrinal differences than leaders or writers.

97. *Poor Man's Guardian*, 19 Oct. 1833.

98. Essay on 'Equality' in *Mixed Essays* (1878), p. 49.

99. Quoted in J. B. Jefferys (ed.), *Labour's Formative Years* (1948), p. 30.

100. *The Times*, 10 Aug. 1861.

101. H. Spencer, *Principles of Sociology* (1873), p. 242.

102. See, for instance, Walter Bagehot's essay on Sterne and Thackeray reprinted in *Literary Studies* (1873), where he distinguished between social systems founded upon caste and those founded upon equality. The English system of 'removable inequalities' was preferable to both.

103. The leaders of the London Working Men's Association, for example, had clearly stated in addresses to working men in America, Belgium, and Poland that there were

common interests among 'the productive millions' in all parts of the world and that it was 'our ignorance of society and of government—our prejudices, our disunion and distrust' which was one of the biggest obstacles to the dissolution of the 'unholy compact of despotism'. See W. Lovett, *Life and Struggles* (1876), p. 152.

104. Quoted in J. Joll (ed.), *Britain and Europe, Pitt to Churchill* (1950), pp. 124–5.

105. B. Webb, *My Apprenticeship* (1950 edn.), p. 13.

106. Rev. E. Thring, *Education and School* (1864), p. 5.

107. *Essays on Reform* (1867), p. 74. Dicey added that 'in criticizing a theory of class representation, the words "classes", "orders", or "interests", must be constantly employed.' Such employment, in his view, gave an undue advantage to the view criticized, for 'the very basis on which this view rests is not firm enough to support the conclusions grounded upon it.' For a parallel question of a later date about the social position of 'working men' see C. Booth, *Life and Labour of the People, East London* (1889), p. 99.

108. *Friendship's Garland* (1897 edn.), pp. 49–50. One aspect of the blending, which deserves an essay to itself, was the association of the industrial and agricultural 'interests'. 'Protection,' wrote a shrewd observer, Bernard Cracroft, 'was the only wall of separation between land and trade. That wall removed, the material interests of the two classes have become and tend to become every day more indissolubly connected and inseparably blended.' (*Essays on Reform*, p. 110.)

109. Cobden himself came to believe in the 1860s that 'feudalism is every day more and more in the ascendant in political and social life.... Manufacturers and merchants as a rule seem only to desire riches that they may be enabled to prostitute themselves at the feet of feudalism.' (Quoted by Morley, op. cit. ii, chap. 25.) He was very critical of the alliance of the industrial and the landed 'interest', and on one occasion in 1861 wrote to a friend, 'I wonder the working people are so quiet under the taunts and insults offered to them. Have they no Spartacus among them to head a revolt of the slave class against their political tormentors?' (quoted ibid. ii, chap. 30).

110. H. Mayhew, *London Labour and the London Poor*, i (1862), 6–7. Cp. T. Wright, *Our New Masters* (1873): 'Between the artisan and the unskilled a gulf is fixed. While the former resents the spirit in which he believes the followers of "genteel occupations" look down upon him, he in his turn looks down upon the labourers.' (p. 5.)

111. A. Briggs and J. Saville (eds.), *Essays in Labour History* (1959), p. 220. See the remarkable letter written by Professor Beesly on the day Palmerston died.

112. Traditionalists employed the old language in some of the mid-century debates about education, e.g., P. Peace, *An Address on the Improvement of the Condition of the Labouring Poor* (Shaftesbury, 1852), p. 15. 'Children must be instructed according to their different ranks and the station they will probably fill in the graduated scale of society.' A similar thought was expressed quite differently by Sir Charles Adderley in 1874. 'The educating by the artificial stimulus of large public expenditure, a particular class, out of instead of in the condition of life in which they naturally fill an important part of the community, must upset the social equilibrium.' (*A Few Thoughts on National Education and Punishment*, p. 11.)

8

Nineteenth-century Towns : A Class Dimension*

J. FOSTER

'It must always be kept in mind that the social war is avowedly raging in England; and that whereas it is in the interest of the bourgeoisie to conduct this war hypocritically under the disguise of peace and philanthropy, the only help for the workingmen consists in laying bare the true state of things.'

ENGELS 1845[1]

'It is however to be considered ... whether the state of Oldham is likely ... to be at any future time better able to do without a military force than at present; and also whether, it being deemed advisable that such a force should be kept there, it is not highly expedient that that force should be such a one as under any possible circumstance would be able to act in an efficient manner and act at all events to protect itself against such a body of people as might in the event of serious excitement be poured upon it.... The force now in Oldham I look upon as totally inadequate.... Two companies of infantry never exceeding 120 men would be placed in a very trying and dangerous predicament in such a town.'

MAJ.-GEN. BOUVERIE, 'The defence of Oldham', report to Home Secretary,
21 July 1834[2]

A WAY OF COMPARING TOWNS AS A WHOLE

This paper puts forward a method of comparing nineteenth-century English towns; comparing them in terms of the class consciousness of their inhabitants. This, it will be argued, provides a way of comparing them as a whole —not just bits of them (birth rate, street-plan, council composition). *As a whole* (or nearly so) because the degree to which labour was politically and socially united very largely determined a community's mass social structure —housing and marriage, language and politics. *As a whole* because class consciousness or labour fragmentation refers to a community reaction to the essential nature of contemporary English society; a reaction to it as a structured, politically endorsed system of economic inequalities.

A comparison on these lines must involve working out the local implications of the country's total social make-up; and coming to grips with the

* From *The Study of Urban History*, ed. H. J. Dyos (London, 1968), pp. 281–99. Reprinted by permission of the author and Edward Arnold Ltd.

incompleteness of the town as a social community. To start with, then, it is worth restating the basic characteristics of nineteenth-century England. English society was organized along class lines: in other words, there was a gross 'unfairness' in the way opportunities of social success were distributed—with the country's underlying economic organization placing the real interests of the privileged and the non-privileged in long-term opposition. More particularly, the underlying organization was capitalist: so the structural unfairness involved the inheritance of accumulated capital (or the means of production). In addition, English capitalism was imperialist: the continuation of an industrial economy depended one way or another on the subordination of other economies (thus introducing a critical inhibition into any mass movement produced by the class situation).

Wherever a man lived, and whatever the particular economic make-up of his community, this was the overriding political reality he had to face. And, equally, though social reactions differed, they were all designed to solve in some way the problem of having to live in a capitalist society. Anyone without capital had to come to terms with the knowledge that socially he counted for nothing; and even more difficult that there was nothing he could do—at least within the law—that would make the slightest difference. Success meant capital: to the worker obviously because it meant physical well being; to the men with capital (and the power that went with it) because they had to justify their authority *socially*. But the essence of the system—the inheritance of accumulated capital—meant that socially (in the rewards it held out) capitalism contradicted itself. Society, to use R. K. Merton's term, was 'anomic'—there was a 'disjunction between culturally defined goals and means'.[3] Or, as people said more forcefully at the time, capitalism turned men into 'things'; in terms of capitalist society labour could have no meaningful social (or human) existence.

This was the basic social organization—all too fixed and solid. In contrast, the ways people reacted differed a great deal. And attempts to accommodate and live with social 'unfairness' (and the variants of behaviour this entailed) were, of course, quite as much the product of a class society as labour solidarity and class consciousness. The grouping of such reactions into some sort of typology has been a major preoccupation of social scientists (both non-Marxist and Marxist) for the past generation; developing a dimension of community reactions from total accommodation to total rejection—isolating the variables that disposed a community to a particular place along the dimension. The results provide the historian with what is potentially a very powerful comparative tool.

The way people reacted (labour fragmentation or solidarity—in effect, the community's social structure) depended on their social consciousness; and it is important to stress its straight political content. When and where there seemed a strong chance of overthrowing the whole system (which

could only be very infrequently), labour had good reason to become conscious of itself as a class, and act politically as such. More usually, when
capitalism seemed immovably permanent, class consciousness became irrelevant, and labour was socially fragmented.

Before going on to look at class formation in particular towns, it would
be useful to examine the reaction to capitalist permanence (as the typical
capitalist social structure) in slightly more detail. It was described by Engels
as 'the social division of society into innumerable gradations, each recog-
nised without question, each with its own pride but also its inborn respect
for its "betters" and "superiors".'[4] This type of reaction (sometimes called a
'status system' to distinguish it from the 'caste system' developed by the
unfree labour of feudal-serf societies) protected people from irrelevance
within society at large by allowing them to build up smaller subcultures
with their own small-scale versions of success. Consequently, to avoid dis-
ruptive comparisons, the members of each subgroup had to have roughly
the same life-chance, and, thus, the same type of job, income, and pattern
of expenditure. Place in society (or social function) fixed each group's
identity—an identity in terms of the existing order. Each group had its
'pride' but also its 'respect'. The church-and-king labourers carried their
branches of oak; the sailors their 'loyal standard'; the clerks their paper
collar of 'gentility'. Each group also defined itself *against* other subgroups
—particularly groups with lower incomes or those prevented by race from
properly identifying themselves in terms of the existing order.

The immediate task of this paper is to suggest reasons for the diversity
of community reactions within mid-nineteenth-century England; and
methods of measurement. The following section will sketch the backgrounds
to labour politics in three very different towns; and the last section will
discuss variables and their measurement.

LABOUR IN THREE MID-NINETEENTH-CENTURY TOWNS

1. *Oldham*

Oldham parliamentary borough was formed in 1832 out of four industrialized Pennine townships six miles east of Manchester: Oldham, Chadder-
ton, Crompton, and Royton. The area's population ran: 4,000 (1714), 13,000
(1789), 21,000 (1801), 50,000 (1831), 72,000 (1851). Industrialization went
back to the mid-eighteenth century when weak apprenticeship and rapid
population-growth made it profitable for merchants to promote outwork production successively in wool, hatting, and cotton. The area also had coal.

By 1851, two-thirds of the borough's 40,000 labour force was employed in
cotton, coal, and engineering. All three industries had been fairly fully
capitalized, and control was concentrated in the hands of a small number
of families—most of whom combined interests in more than one industry.

Over three-quarters of the cotton-workers were employed by 60 firms with over a hundred hands (mean labour force 240); 80 per cent of the engineering workers by three big firms; and almost all coalminers by one combine or the subsidiaries of cotton firms. This structure ruled out any chance of a man working his way into the employer group; and there was certainly no chance of marrying in. Nor was there much mobility during the period of factory-building: a survey of early firms shows only one manual worker coming up—the rest, predictably, were small landowners switching over from outwork manufacturing. In fact, land- and (critically) coal-ownership restricted large-scale operations to the tight group of families who, as yeomen manufacturers, had been in at the mid-eighteenth-century beginning.

Thus at mid-century there were 12,000 worker families selling their labour to 70 capitalist families. The capitalist families were very rich—annual incomes ranged between £3,000 and £10,000—and most owned estates in other parts of the country. Incomes of worker *families* ranged from £50 to £100—insufficient to keep any but the top 15 per cent of high-paid craft workers *permanently* out of primary poverty.[5] One worker child in five died before its first birthday. One female mill-worker in seven died while in the age group 25–34 (mostly of TB). One miner in every five could expect to be killed during a normal working life. Up to 1850 mill hours were never much below 12 a day, 6 days a week. Nor could the system guarantee even this minimal existence. There were regular periods of mass unemployment— sending the proportion of families in primary poverty at *any one time* well over 40 per cent. This was the class situation with which people had to come to terms.[6] For the first 50 years of the century their reaction was to fight it.

It is not easy to give a satisfactory assessment of class formation in the small space available. Probably the best thing is to document the success of working-class leaders in getting hold of local government—an operation that manifestly demanded mass organization, and, in terms of union control of poor relief and police (especially during strikes), was of critical importance for working-class living standards; and also brought headlong conflict with the state.

The working-class leaders ought first to be defined—they were something more than plain trade-unionists or friends of the poor. Right through from the 1790s to the 1840s Oldham possessed a coherent and stable group of social revolutionaries, linked to a succession of national organizations, frequently in prison and working for the overthrow of the existing pattern of ownership and production. These were the people who directed the 'social war' in the Oldham area and whose activities in 1834 ultimately forced Bouverie to evacuate. In the early 1790s these revolutionaries were a minority and could be persecuted.[7] The military and economic disasters from 1795 on reversed the position and by 1801 gave them a mass following.[8] By 1812 they had captured control of Oldham vestry, and at least by 1816 of the subsidiary northern township of Royton; and thus got their hands on police and poor relief (which, with expenditure running at around £5,000 a year, was a useful source of political influence).[9] Similar trends in the country at large provoked the 1818 Vestry Act imposing cumulative voting by rateable value and the 1819 Act requiring poor relief to be managed either directly by magistrates or by select vestry.[10] Neither act shook working-class control in Oldham.[11] In 1821 the crown revived its right to dispense with vestry elections and appoint constables direct through the hundred court leet.[12] This gave the authorities nominal control over the police, but left them unable to prevent the vestry blocking funds. In 1825–6 a local act was put through parliament enabling commissioners to levy a police rate—and fixing the minimum commissioner qualification of £60 rateable value.[13] This 'police commission' functioned as intended for five years, and then the work-class (using large-scale intimidation) again got control, and cut the town police down to size.[14] In 1832 the caucus was able to put Fielden and Cobbett in parliament without much trouble.[15]

The 1830s saw the crest of the wave. The police were neutralized and the experience of the military (especially in 1820, 1826, and 1834) made commanders reluctant to commit any but impossibly large detachments to garrison duty. As a result, there was no help nearer than Manchester or Rochdale, and the unions could safely act as 'schools of war'; wage-rates from the 1820s were significantly higher in Oldham than Manchester.[16] In 1838 the caucus felt confident enough to appoint the secretary of the spinners' union as secretary of the poor-relief fund (a man who had been an organizer of the 1812 fighting and was held on treason charges in 1817 and 1819).[17]

From then on, however, working-class power declined—the Whig 'reforms' were beginning to take effect. In March 1841 police recruited under the 1839 County Constabulary Act (and controlled by the Lord Lieutenant) were brought in to break a colliers' strike.[18] The Act of 1842 transferred all police to the control of the magistrates, and the same year a permanent military garrison was established.[19] 1842 also saw 33 local leaders arrested on sedition charges.[20] In 1847 the new Poor Law was finally introduced with its cumulative voting, secret ballot and *ex officio* magistrate guardians (the new secretary to the board was also, neatly, secretary to the cotton employers' association).[21] That year for the first time the working-class failed to carry the parliamentary elections. In 1849 the supersession of the 'corrupt' police commission by a corporation did away with the last stronghold of popular government.[22]

To make sense, the sketch needs to be filled out a bit. First, how did the working-class get hold of local government? Right through, voting was restricted to property-owners; which in Oldham largely meant shopkeepers. These shopkeepers were dependent on working-class custom, and 'exclusive dealing' or blacklisting was the method used to bring them to heel. Three quotations will show this worked. The first comes from the preface to the 1832 poll book. 'When this trust was conferred upon them [our electors] it was unjustly withheld from you who possess superior claims to it—who are they who do not earn their bread by the sweat of their brow? ... We are well aware it is in the interest of the shopkeepers to uphold the cause of the working-classes—but the question is, are they resolved to do this? ... The great majority of this portion of society ranked themselves on the side of tyranny. What guarantee have we for their future better behaviour? I'll tell you ...' And the writer goes on to list shops to be blacked.[23] The second quotation comes from an 1834 military report. When the vestry disallowed barrack expenses, Bouverie inquired whether the 'delegates of the class of shopkeeper voted this way out of hostility to the presence of the military, the answer was "they darst not vote otherwise".'[24] And the third dates from 20 years after the breaking of Oldham's working-class when Platt (the M.P. owner of the largest machine works) still felt frightened enough to speak out for the secret ballot. 'For many years the small shopkeepers, for fear of violence, had had to place in the windows of their houses the names of the candidates for whom they intended to vote, and sometimes pickets were actually stationed to stop customers.... This was what was done by those turbulent and unscrupulous men who formed the minority of operatives ... and who were at the bottom of all strikes.... He believed the Ballot would have a conservative influence because it would ... take away the power possessed by small sections of the working classes.'[25] All this nicely reveals both the strength and weakness of the Oldham working class. The method used to influence elections provides a foolproof demonstration of careful direction and organized *mass* allegiance. But the power had to be gained by proxy and used within the legal forms. In the same way that local trade unionists had to keep their demands within 'competitive reason', so the politicians had to operate inside the system. And their efforts to break the system (intensified during the ruling-class counter-attack of the late 1830s and 1840s) were hamstrung by the contradictions of national leadership and policy that could not, in the broader circumstances, be avoided.[26]

So Oldham's working class cannot be seen as a properly mature class movement. But it came very near. Certainly it was a great deal more than short-term political trade unionism or just plain municipal corruption. The feeling of class is unmistakable. A frightened coal-owner of 1817 describes a mass meeting of colliers and cotton-workers—making their point with a timeless menace that could come as much from twelfth-century France or 1925 China. A journeyman mechanic had got hold of a loyalty declaration by the 'principal inhabitants'. 'The signatures he read over one by one with a considerable pause betwixt each of them. This pause was filled up by some sort of indecent remark accompanied by a characteristic gesticulation

... all the most respectable people in the town for character and property were made the subject of public derision.'[27] When people laugh off a lifetime of caste and subjection, they risk a great deal, and will only do so when the old sanctions seem to have failed altogether. The essential precondition of class consciousness is that people *think* it possible to change things. Though all the national movements failed, and had to fail, they can only be understood while it is remembered that for fifty years people believed themselves on the brink of a new age. 'The people are in a most insubordinate state, and set the law at defiance. Out of 92 summons issued for 17th July [1819] only three of the parties appeared—they damned the constables and told them that in three weeks their day would be over.'[28] An old Oldham cotton-worker remembered 1848. 'The near prospect was that of the monarch dethroned and all her dependents and followers ... in headlong flight to escape the vengeance of an oppressed and vindictive people. This is no fancy sketch; it is a fair picture of the wandering daydreams of the whole body of what were called the working classes forty years ago.'[29]

In this sense, even though national revolution had repeatedly to be cried off, it remained a reality. And locally the explosion of popular consciousness that this sustained produced a critique of capitalism that cut pretty near the bone. Here is the Oldham's spinners' secretary in 1834. 'Your employers seem to know no way of meeting a declining market but that of getting more work out of you and paying less wages.... It is high time for all English workmen to awake ... and no longer be driven along the road to ruin by their blind employers.... We must learn to look beyond the improvement of our own particular branch of business.... and improve the whole body of English labourers.... With this view we ought to ascertain the *intrinsic* value of labour; for until we have learned that it is impossible to ascertain to what extent we are robbed of the fruit of our labour.'[30] And four years later the following resolutions were passed at a mass meeting of Oldham workers. 'That labour is the source of all property; without a surplus of labour has been performed and property produced no accumulation of capital can take place.... That it is an indisputable fact that the various classes of capitalists have the whole power of making and administering the laws, which is almost uniformly done for their own benefit.... That the time has now arrived when Englishmen must learn to act instead of talk.'[31] It would be easy to go on—'the working classes should form a nation apart and govern themselves'[32] and so forth. But the point to be made is obvious. The analysis of the Oldham workers was in terms of class; they were asking what was wrong with the community, and not how an interest group could better itself. Looking at Oldham, they saw the basic contradiction as capital and its inheritance. And they defined themselves as Labour—in an analysis that could only make sense in terms of conflict and change.

This leads to the last and, from the historian's angle, the most important aspect of Oldham's class consciousness. Working-class power depended on a solidarity that stretched to all sections of the labour force. The power, and the terrorism and blacklisting that went with it, was real enough. But it needed organizing. Keeping hold of local government and fighting off the employers meant something near semi-permanent mobilization. The network of control had to penetrate every corner of working-class life—union, factory, shop, and beerhouse; and, to maintain it, the solidarity slogan had to be banged out incessantly. The great, traditional divisions of an English working population were, for the moment, suspended. In 1834 a mass meeting demanded the elimination of wage differentials and the levelling up of labourers' pay.[33] The year before there had been a call for an end to coercion in Ireland.[34] And throughout the period a predominantly English population was willing to accept Irishmen among its leaders. The very fact of class formation meant that the controlling spell of the ruling-class had been broken, and with it, the sub-group system by which people accommodated social 'unfairness'. Substituted was another system, just as coercive, but working in the opposite direction.

The effect is best appreciated comparatively. In the 1850s, after the breakdown of the organized working-class, there was a rapid expansion of Orange lodges; in 1861 serious Anglo-Irish riots; and from then on mass politics in Oldham largely hinged on the existence of two racial communities.[35] Again, broadening the comparison to our other two towns, marriages between the families of labourers and high-paid craftsmen were far more frequent in Oldham than in Shields (which had no class conflict) and slightly more frequent than in Northampton (where class conflict was very partial).[36] The other side of the social distance coin tells the same story. Shields possessed a highly developed hierarchy of occupational neighbourhoods; in Oldham this segregation and subgrouping does not appear to have existed at all.[37] For more than a generation, the social structure of Oldham's very diversified labour force—clerks, labourers, engineers, schoolteachers, spinners, and small shopkeepers—seems to have remained significantly open.

2. Northampton

At the beginning of the century the town had two functions: supplying fine living for the county's landowner aristocracy, and an interim market for farm produce. By 1830 a third function had been added. The crisis of rural overpopulation flooded the town with cheap labour (the population jumped from 10,000 to 26,000 between 1821 and 1851) and provided the basis for an industrial sector. By 1851 almost half the labour force was in the shoe industry. Production, requiring no fixed capital, was organized on garret-sweatshop lines, and London merchants mostly supplied the credit and made the profits.

As a community, therefore, Northampton had none of the tight completeness of Oldham: ultimately almost everyone's boss lived over the horizon. Nor had it the simplicity. The three sectors produced Tory hoteliers and lawyers (together the pre-1835 corporation); Whig-Dissenter corn and wool dealers; and radical garret-masters. Along these lines élite politics were set rigid. The lack of a real bourgeoisie and the three-way split in the town economy also had its effect on class. Northampton was not without poverty: the proportion in primary poverty was, if anything, higher than in Oldham; the death rate from TB almost as bad, and from typhus and scrofula worse; life expectation for males at the age of five was identical. But class formation was slight, and what there was had a tame, sheet-lightning quality about it.

'Working-class' leaders there were—duly in contact with a succession of the national associations: London Working Men's Association, the Charter Association, the Reform League; then, right a bit, to Bradlaugh; and finally back left to the Social Democratic Federation. But their influence was restricted to one ward: the West. This had the lowest proportion of households with votes or servants, and the highest proportion of shoemakers, multi-generation families and country immigrants. Even here, the population was by no means solid, and there was never any attempt to practise exclusive dealing.

The language of this 'working class' reflects its unfortunate background. There was no critique of capital; many leaders were garret-masters and small employers. Targets were the aristocracy, the establishment, and the Church; or, when the mob broke out of the West ward slums, just the rich. In a sense, Northampton's 'working-class' politics remained those of an occupational subgroup—not of labour as a whole. The ruling class never lost its grip (the town had a barracks and the surrounding countryside was thick with aristocrats); as a result the 'status' system held up. Workers in the other two sectors—shopmen, coachwrights, furniture-makers, and brewery-workers (mostly better-paid anyway)—remained deferent, anglican, and hostile.

And even within the shoemaker sub-group it would certainly be arguable that the politics were largely irrelevant to the immediate situation. Most shoemakers had come in from the surrounding countryside—forced out by unemployment and poverty. Here, in the closed, authoritarian villages, the realities of the class situation bit deep (1830 and the burnings and killings of 1843–4 were one answer). The men that ran the system were clergymen —many doubling the job with landowning; and, not surprisingly, most Northampton shoemakers clenched their fists when they saw a priest.

All these problems and pre-occupations are conveniently summed up in a note from the secretary of the Northampton WMA to the 1839 Chartist convention:

We are struggling hard against many obstacles from the combined influence of whigs, tories, sham radicals aided by all the power of the priests who ... have hung the terrors of the world to come before the view of their deluded votaries to prevent them co-operating with us.[38]

3. *South Shields*

As in Northampton, the men who commissioned the work lived outside. Half the labour force was organized round shifting coal to London for the profit of Durham landowners: a quarter were seamen; 10 per cent ship-builders; and as many again keelmen, dockers, provisioners, and sailmakers. But there were two important differences. First, there was no permanent economic split in the town élite; largely as a result of the way the shipping was owned. There were 200 ships (mostly 300-tonners carrying crews of six or so) distributed among 150 owners: small men—tradesmen, provisioners, shipbuilders—who had invested their savings. This, for a start, gave almost all Shields' trade a common overlap. But interests were tied even closer by the half-a-dozen interlocking insurance and broking clubs that formed a kind of unofficial town senate. This background effectively prevented the rigidity that marked Northampton's élite politics; and political, and even religious, allegiances were notoriously short-term. The structure of shipping owner-ship also meant that admission to the town's élite (small-time and thread-bare though it was) was comparatively easy.

The second big difference (taking in Oldham as well as Northampton) was the absence of work for women and children. In the other towns additions to family income from this source largely made up for pay differentials between men. In Shields the difference between the way a shipwright and a labourer could afford to live stood out sharply—in fact, labourer's families had little chance of ever rising above the poverty line (with all that this meant in terms of total pauperization).

Consequently the development of working-class consciousness had small scope in Shields. There was no resident bourgeoisie, admission to the town élite seemed easy and the labour force was socially fragmented. There were certainly bad strikes (keelmen, shipwrights, seamen); but the conflict re-mained strictly economic. Neither delegate nor national rent was sent to the 1839 Chartist convention. During 1839, 1842, and 1848 Shields, in con-trast to the surrounding mining areas, remained quiet. What 'working-class' activity there was took two forms: Chartist rallies organized from New-castle which brought out the whole town (including the shopkeeper-ship-owners)—and to which O'Connor predictably talked about the union of the middle and working classes.[39] Or the sectarian activities of a small group meeting in a waterside pub, and never getting much more for their pains than a couple of inches in the *Northern Star*.[40]

The three communities just examined all formed part of the same capitalist society; and did so in roughly the same way—as medium-size industrial towns. Yet their 'social structures' were strikingly different: extreme class consciousness in Oldham; extreme fragmentation in Shields; with Northampton somewhere in between. The previous section was intended as descriptive—sketching in the contexts of these different responses. But the business of description inevitably also involved some degree of explanation, and two general factors have already emerged: the structure of the élite; and the occupational make-up of labour. This section will attempt to pinpoint these factors more precisely; explain why they, particularly, should be important; and suggest methods of measurement. To do this, it is first necessary to make a rough examination of how capitalism in general maintained its social equilibrium, and the ways in which this equilibrium could be disturbed.

1. *Capitalist equilibrium; authority and crisis*

As a social system, capitalism ultimately rested on the military power of the state: the defence of property and the enforcement of contract. In addition, capitalism could also claim the more immediate sanction of being the going economic concern on which everyone depended. Together these gave capitalism its apparent dead-weight permanence. But there were also powerful factors working the other way. Socially, capitalism contradicted itself: it operated to the long-term benefit of only a minute proportion of the population, and denied the rest meaningful social existence. Economically as well, capitalism had its contradictions—the most important probably being its imperialist dependence on other economies, and its consequent vulnerability to military defeat. What was the precise *social* manifestation of these conflicting forces? How did the ruling class sustain its authority within the community? What was the nature of the working-class challenge?

First, ruling-class authority. The most important instrument of mass control seems to have been provided by the subgrouping process itself. Subgrouping was, in essence, the way people accommodated social 'unfairness' —by creating small-scale success systems of their own. From the angle of social control, subgrouping also had a more strictly political side. Subgroups, to start with, had to define themselves within the existing order— partly in terms of economic function and partly by how far their members could afford to imitate ruling-class spending and behaviour. Subgroups, in addition, had institutions and leaders, and the men with authority held it fairly directly from the ruling-class: either directly by legal or political arrangement, or because they could claim successful bargaining 'influence'. The subgroup leaders acted, then, as link-men in the over-all political system; and the subgrouping process, besides allowing people to accommodate deprivation, functioned as an authority system by which labour could be tied politically to the ruling class.

The working-class challenge also derived structurally from capitalism's social contradictions—but more directly. Some people experienced social 'unfairness' in a way that made accommodation impossible: men who had suffered long unemployment; men whose families had suffered class injustice; men who had succeeded within the 'peer system' at school, and then found themselves irrevocably classed as labour in a capitalist economy. Men like this would remain inescapably class-conscious, and would find it very difficult to acquiesce in the acceptance of ruling-class values which subgrouping involved. For them, to use Merton's terminology, the only meaningful social existence would be 'rebellion' or 'realistic conflict'—not 'ritualism' or 'withdrawal'.[41] This group formed the social base of the 'working-class challenge'. So long, however, as capitalism seemed secure and permanent (and the mass social relevance of subgrouping remained), the political position of this working class could only be marginal. In favourable circumstances, they might hope to direct mass economic conflict in which the interests of capital and labour were visibly opposed—but over-all their influence would remain strictly industrial. *Socially*, they were committed to spotlight precisely those social contradictions that people generally were trying to avoid; and *politically* to a policy demanding some sort of class confrontation that was immediately unrealistic.

The real threat to ruling-class authority came from ouside the social structure—though not from outside the system as a whole. Economically, capitalism was prone to instability and crisis. Long-term instability concentrated attention on economic issues in which the conflict between capital and labour was obvious, and gave 'working-class' leaders the chance to seize initiative within labour subcultures. Crisis (economic collapse or military defeat) could bring even more dramatic change. On the one hand, defeat or collapse discredited the ruling class (and, with it, the subgroup proxies); and, on the other, broke the 'inevitability' spell of the whole system. At such times, class unity might replace subgrouping (or labour fragmentation) as the socially relevant mass response—producing a 'revolutionary situation'.[42]

Socially, then, this was the pattern of conflict. There was the 'normal' equilibrium in which the working-class group was insulated from mass influence by the subgroup authority system. Against this, there was the historical dimension of economic change and crisis that could produce a meaningful context for working-class action. With this rough model of capitalist equilibrium in mind, it may be easier to talk about the purely local factors in the equation. Why did class consciousness develop in some English towns and not in others? What factors in a town's economic make-up could prevent working-class leaders taking full advantage of a particular historical situation?

2. *Local context: labour's occupational make-up*

From the earlier descriptions of the three towns it seemed that the differences in occupational make-up had considerable impact on 'working-class' influence. This purely occupational factor seems to have been given its political relevance by the way it affected a town's subgroup structure—by whether or not it made for one or more than one labour subculture. A 'single subculture' town might develop in a number of situations: where there was only one basic occupation (the isolated mining town, for instance); where the over-all differential between male earnings was small; or where (when there was a larger differential) there was also work for women and children—which allowed semi-skilled and labourer families to level up their incomes. Communities like this presented one way in which a 'working-class' group might acquire *social* influence. With just one subculture covering the whole labour force, it was much easier to identify it on some issues *against* capital, and give the working-class critique a social (and not just industrial) foothold. When, on the other hand, the community had a number of labour subgroups—each defining itself against the others—it would be very difficult to identify one subculture in particular with conflict phrased in terms of labour as a whole. In this way, a town's occupational make-up could partially predetermine the political success of its working-class leaders.[43]

What methods are available for measuring this? The first step might be to compare differences in life experience among the general spread of labour families: family structure; housing; poverty—which can fairly easily be done by a punched-card sample of census schedules (used in conjunction, if possible, with rate-books, and wage and employment data). This, taken comparatively with results from other towns, should show which towns were most *likely* to have an unfragmented labour subculture. A census sample, however, cannot show whether a town did, in fact have a socially less fragmented labour force than its neighbours; nor whether this was the result of occupational make-up or of purely political factors.

Luckily, complete information survives for all English towns from the 1840s on the two most important aspects of social distance: who married whom, and who lived next to whom (this potentially very exciting material has so far hardly been used at all). The marriage frequencies between occupations provide a way of discovering whether labour was, in fact, socially fragmented. Marriage within stable capitalist societies takes place within subgroups. If a town's labour force was split (by occupation) into a number of subgroups, the town would show up by having a lower frequency of marriages between 'top' and 'bottom' occupations (e.g. between craft and labour) than one where this was not so.[44]

The big problem, however, is the second one. How far was subgroup structure, at a particular historical moment, the simple result of occupational make-up, and how far is one also measuring (as one very probably is in Oldham) the social results of political solidarity—the effect of class consciousness itself? The most helpful solution here is to compare the frequency of *marriage* between occupation with the frequency with which these

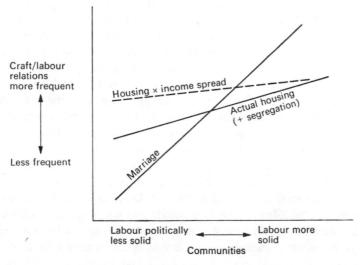

Fig. 1. *Marriage and neighbouring relations between craft and labourer families.* Graph of postulated association between two types of relationship within more and less class-conscious communities

occupations lived together as *neighbours*. Housing-neighbour frequencies (conditioned by the spread of housing rents) would take into account family income differences. Thus, in a politically class-conscious, non-subgrouped community (where there was no additional element of segregation) the neighbour frequencies would stand for the absolute rock-bottom basis to labour's social structure. An inter-town survey would then show whether marriages between labour occupations were, or were not, more frequent than neighbouring relations where labour was politically solid. In the case ·of the three towns it is interesting, for instance, that it is Oldham which reveals the *smallest* difference between the rates of craft–labourer inter-marriage and neighbouring intermarriage. In both Northampton and Shields marriage was considerably more segregated in occupational terms than the distribution of housing.[45] This, in effect, would make it possible to see if mass class consciousness did have actual *social* results (at least locally); and thus make it possible to isolate the social contribution of a town's occupational makeup (see Fig. 1).

3. Local context: élite structure

Élite structure, like occupational make-up, also takes its political relevance from the impact it had on the 'working-class' bid for mass support. Élite structure could, it seems, increase or diminish the local plausibility of the working-class social critique—simply because social 'unfairness' was less obvious in some towns than others. The usual reason was that the people who owned the capital and made the profit lived out of sight. Engels developed his concept of a 'resident bourgeoisie' to account (in part) for the differing reactions of workers in Manchester and Birmingham: militant in the former and passive in the latter. Manchester had a resident bourgeoisie because the social distribution of wealth was a fair reflection of the distribution for the economic nation; in Birmingham it was not.[46] Of the three towns examined, the two with the strongest subgrouping and the least labour solidarity seem also to have had the most primary poverty. But while mid-century Shields and Northampton each had less than a dozen men who would leave more than £25,000 personalty, Oldham had over seventy; and many of these would leave a great deal more than £25,000. In Shields and Northampton several men who passed as influential at mid-century had started out in a small way; in contemporary Oldham none. If a town's top people were not 'well-bred' men of property but garret-masters who started out (and remained) working-men, then a man's picture of his own chance would not be so unfavourable (to society or himself) as it might be otherwise.

The distinction between élite and bourgeoisie (comprehending as it does the completeness of the local community and its relation to the larger structure of the national economy) is plainly very important. By itself, of course, the presence or absence of a bourgeoisie could not make the difference between labour fragmentation or solidarity. But where the bourgeoisie was absent the logic of subgrouping could be made much more credible: 'success' *within* the community plainly could not derive directly from the critical capital-inheritance contradiction of capitalist society. Still more important possibly, the absence of a bourgeoisie broke the immediate, visible dependence of wealth on labour.

Finding out whether a town possessed a 'resident bourgeoisie' (or just a holding company for somebody else) presents its problems. And there seems no easier solution than a fairly intensive study of the ownership, markets, and profits of the main industries and a sample of the town élite running to several hundred individuals. The sample is especially difficult.

In the absence of any census of wealth, the only sure way of getting all the wealthy families is to spread the net very wide: industrial and merchant firms, professional men, tradesmen, magistrates, and guardians—even, perhaps, every census household with two or more resident servants. Once the sample has been set up, there remains the still more painful task of collecting the facts. The first thing, probably, is to identify the rich and the not-so-rich: probate, rates, and company records; then to examine social mobility to see precisely how industrial structure affected life-chance; and then social distance (frequency of marriage between élite occupations) to see whether or not there actually existed a capital-owning group that cut itself off from the rest of the community. This, given the facts, should be enough to establish the existence or non-existence of a bourgeoisie.

After all this, however, the proof of the pudding must still be in the eating. Did the people show themselves conscious of their class interests? Was the town, like Oldham, unable 'to do without a military force'? Or did it show all the signs of 'accommodated deprivation': race riots, 'model' unionists, and poverty churches? Here, the evidence can only be documentary: Home Office papers, poll books and pamphlets, the working-class press, diocesan visitations, trade-union, and local government records.[47]

Together, analysis and plain description should make it possible to put most towns somewhere on the class dimension. But it ought to be remembered that the casual factors can vary in time within towns as much as between towns, and that towns can change their characters. In the early 1790s, while Oldham employers could still hire thugs to break up working-class meetings, the people of Shields were planting the Liberty Tree. And at the beginning of the twentieth century, when the Tory-imperialist Churchill was M.P. for Oldham, the SDF were winning local elections in Northampton.

BIBLIOGRAPHICAL NOTE

Information on current British work on urban history can be found in *The Study of Urban History* (ed. H. J. Dyos, London, 1968) and the *Urban History Newsletter*, now supplemented by the *Urban History Yearbook* (Leicester). Comparable American research is reviewed in S. Thernstrom (ed.), *Nineteenth Century Cities* (New Haven, Conn., 1969) with the articles by Joan Scott, C. Griffen, and S. Blumin, particularly concerned with the problem of class consciousness. *The Victorian City: Images and Realities*, ed. H. J. Dyos and Michael Wolff (London, 1973) contains several relevant essays. E. Wrigley (ed.), *Nineteenth Century Society* (Cambridge, 1972) provides a comprehensive guide to the main demographic sources and the techniques available for their use. For methodology, see also W. A. Armstrong, 'Social structure from the early census returns', in E. Wrigley (ed.), *English Historical Demography* (London, 1966). However, M. Anderson, *The Family in Nineteenth-Century Lancashire* (Cambridge, 1971) is the only major study so far published to have used such techniques in any systematic fashion.

On class consciousness G. Stedman Jones, *Outcast London* (Oxford, 1972) and D. Jones, *Before Rebecca: Popular Protests in Wales 1793–1835* (London, 1973) both shed important new light on developments among urban workers in nineteenth-century Britain. See R. S. Neale, *Class and Ideology in the Nineteenth Century* (London, 1972), especially chap. 1, 'Three classes or five', for a different view on class in nineteenth-century urban society.

NOTES

1. *Marx & Engels on Britain* (Moscow, 1962), p. 248.
2. Bouverie—Home Office, 21 July 1834 (HO 40/32/214–25).
3. R. K. Merton, *Social Theory and Social Structure* (New York, 1965 edn.), pp. 131 et seq.
4. Engels–Sorge, 7 Dec. 1889 (*On Britain*, p. 568).
5. Poverty survey: earning potential and consumption minima (1851 census schedules) with variable wages, prices, and employment simulated for 'normal' times (Summer 1849) and 'bad' times (Spring 1847)—using the Rowntree poverty line as modified by Bowley (A. L. Bowley, *Livelihood and Poverty*, 1915). No account is taken of secondary poverty.
6. It is obviously not possible to list in detail the sources used in this and following analyses the most important are discussed in the last section of the paper. Any doubts about the social consequences of Victorian capitalism can be quickly set at rest by a glance at contemporary estimates of national income distribution: at actuarial tables giving workers half the life expectancy of a 'gentleman'; or just at the annual reports of the Registrar-General—which (looked at in human terms) have something of the enormity of mass graves.
7. Rowbottom Diary (Oldham Public Library) especially 4 Jan. 1793 and 21 Apr. 1794. Samuel Bamford, *Early Days* (1849), pp. 45–8.
8. Rowbottom, 29 May 1797, 20 May 1800, 3 May 1801. Hay–Pelham, 7 June 1801 (HO 42/62): captured papers show Oldham United Englishmen with a paid-up membership (including Lees) of 426—also enclosed is a fragment of the Crompton subscription list.
9. Chippendale–Fletcher, 23 Apr. 1812 (HO 40/1/1). Fletcher–Becket, 14 Sept. 1816 (HO 42/153). Chippendale–Fletcher, 23 Mar. 1818 (HO 42/175).
10. 58 Geo III c. 69 (3 June 1818). 59 Geo III c. 12 (31 March 1819). At a mass meeting in Ashton-under-Lyne on 15 May 1818 the proposed 1818 bill was attacked as 'a death-blow to their rights and privileges—that now what was called a gentleman would gain no less than six votes'. Thackeray–Fletcher, 16 May 1818 (HO 42/177).
11. To avoid magistrate control of relief a select vestry was formed in April 1820. The unionists still controlled the annual elections. *Manchester Guardian,* 20 Oct. 1821. First Report, Royal Commission on the Poor Laws, 1834, *Parl. Papers*, 1834, xxviii, Appendix A, Part I [*Reports from assistant commissioners*], pp. 909a–19a.
12. *Manchester Guardian*, 20 Oct. 1821. The inhabitants appealed to King's Bench without success. *MG* 24 Nov. and 1 Dec. 1821.
13. 7 Geo IV c. 117 (26 May 1826). Hobhouse–Collinge & Lancashire (cotton manufacturers), 26 February 1827 (HO 41/7): 'Mr. Peel is glad to find that the workmen have again returned to their labours and particularly that the provisions of the New Police Act have had so good an effect in accelerating that desirable event.'
14. *Voice of the People*, 19 Feb. 1831.
15. The caucus maintained a fairly close supervision over its M.P.s. See especially Knight (secretary to both the Oldham spinners and the Oldham Political Union)—John Fielden, 21 Jan. 1835 (I am indebted to the late Professor David Owen, Harvard, for transcripts of this and other letters).
16. Eckersley–Hobhouse, 19 Sept. 1826 (HO 40/21/523).

17. *Manchester Advertiser*, 31 Mar. 1838.

18. 2 & 3 Vict c. 93. Butterworth Diary (Oldham Public Library), 5 Mar. 1841.

19 Arbuthnot–HO, 12 Dec. 1842 (HO 45/268). Barker–Graham, 29 June 1843 (HO 45/350). Parish Constables Act, 5 & 6 Vict c. 109.

20. The arrests continued spasmodically all autumn. *Manchester Advertiser*, from 27 Aug. to 19 Nov. 1842.

21. R. versus Overseers of Oldham (10 QB 700), 29 May 1847. Oldham Poor Law Union Minute Book 1847–50, 22 Sept. 1847 (Lancs. Record Office).

22. PRO PC 1/851, 852, 853, 855.

23. *William Spier, Member of Oldham Political Association, A List of the Voters in the Borough* (n.d.) (OPL).

24. Bouverie–Phillips, 11 Aug. 1834 (HO 40/32/234).

25. *Hansard*, ccvii, c. 612 (26 June 1871).

26. Fielden was especially aware of these contradictions—the difficulty of reconciling his own demand for the state regulation of industry (wages and investment as well as hours) with the country's dependence on foreign markets and commodities. See his important speech *Hansard*, xlvi, c. 805 (18 March 1839).

27. Chippendale–Sidmouth, 10 Feb. 1817 (HO 40/10).

28. Chetwode (Ashton-under-Lyne recorder)–Sidmouth, 17 July 1819 (HO 42/189). The 'three weeks' doomsday was headed off by Peterloo.

29. Benjamin Grime, *Memory Sketches* (Oldham, 1887), pp. 1, 81.

30. John Knight reported in *Herald of the Rights of Industry*, 1 Apr. 1834.

31. *Northern Star*, 17 Mar. 1838.

32. Benjamin Harrop at Tolpuddle protest meeting. Butterworth, 27 Mar. 1834.

33. Butterworth, 27 Mar. 1834.

34. Butterworth, 21 Feb. 1833.

35. *Oldham Chronicle*, 15 July 1854; 8 June 1861; 13 July 1861.

36. Marriage certificate analysis: all marriages taking place within the registration districts of Oldham, Northampton, and South Shields between 1846 and 1856.

37. Reply to Royal Commission on Health of Towns (1842) questionnaire (draft at back of South Shields Improvement Act Letter Book 1829–48—Town Clerk's Office, South Shields).

38. James Robertson, 9 Apr. 1839. Chartist Convention Minutes, Vol. I, f. 225 (BM Add. MSS. 34, 245A).

39. *Northern Star*, 26 July 1839.

40. *Northern Star*, 20 Nov. 1841.

41. Merton, loc. cit.

42. Cp. for a dynamic relation of politics and social structure J. H. Goldthorpe and D. Lockwood, 'Affluence and the British class structure', *Sociological Review* (July 1963).

43. Erik Allardt, 'Patterns of class conflict', *Trans. Westermarck Soc.* (1964). N. Dennis, F. Henriques, and C. Slaughter, *Coal is our Life* (1957). K. Newton, 'British Communism: sociology of a radical political party', Cambridge Ph.D. dissertation, 1965 (on Welsh mining towns).

44. The calculation follows (in reverse) the procedure used by J. Berent in D. V. Glass (ed.), *Social Mobility in Britain* (1954), pp. 321 et seq. For the three towns the index of association between craft and labouring occupations stands at 80 in Oldham (5,500 marriages used); 77 in Northampton (3,100 marriages); and 69 in Shields (3,100 marriages) (100 = unity). Similar use of marriage material has been made by T. Geiger, 'Soziale Umschichtungen', *Acta Jutlandica*, 1951; and by Charles Tilly, *The Vendée* (1964), pp. 93–9.

45. The index of association for neighbouring relations between craft and labourer families (calculated from the 1851 census schedules) stands at 104 for Northampton, 88 for Oldham, and 80 for Shields. For present-day populations there has been a good deal of research on the relationship between neighbouring and occupation. Perhaps the most immediately relevant is that by J. Musil, 'Development of Prague's ecological structure', *Readings in Urban Sociology* (ed. R. Pahl, 1969). This relates Prague's

declining rate of occupational segregation in housing to the development of working-class consciousness in the period of the Czech socialist revolution of 1948.

46. *On Britain*, p. 233.

47. The relation between relative deprivation and ethnic conflict is examined, among others, by J. H. Robb, *Working-class Anti-Semite* (1954). Marx's analysis of the ethnic split in the English working class can be found in Marx–Meyer, 9 Apr. 1870 (and following letters) *On Britain*, pp. 500 et seq. Relevant studies of ethnic subculture are made by John Dollard, *Caste and Class in a Southern Town* (Newhaven, Conn., 1937) and elsewhere. For labour subculture, there are interesting descriptions of modern American textile communities in Liston Pope, *Millhands and Preachers* (Newhaven, Conn., 1942); J. K. Morland, *Millways of Kent* (New York, 1958); and Robert Blauner, *Alienation and Freedom* (Chicago, 1965).

9

Nineteenth-century Social Reform:
a Tory Interpretation of History*

JENIFER HART

EVERY schoolchild is now taught as an article of dogmatic faith that 'the Whig interpretation of history' is false. Is the Tory interpretation any better? I propose here to examine certain manifestations of it in relation to nine-teenth-century English history. The historians I shall be chiefly concerned with are Dr. Kitson Clark, Dr. Oliver MacDonagh, Mr. David Roberts, Prof. W. L. Burn, and Dr. R. J. Lambert.

According to its critics, a Whig interpretation requires human heroes and villains in the story. What do the Tories put in their place? In explaining progress in nineteenth-century England, they belittle the role of men and ideas, especially the role of the Benthamites; they consider that opinion, often moved by a Christian conscience, was generally humanitarian; that social evils were therefore attacked and dealt with when people felt them to be intolerable; that many changes were not premeditated or in some sense planned, but were the result of 'the historical process' or of 'blind forces'. The implication is that social progress will in the future, as in the past, take place without human effort; all will turn out for the best if we just drift in an Oakeshottian boat.

I

I will start by examining their denigration of the Benthamites, since from this much else follows.

As a result of his studies of emigrant traffic, MacDonagh concluded that its regulation developed 'without the faintest spur from Benthamism', and he suggested that this might tell us something about the general revolution in administration during the nineteenth century.[1] This point was developed in his famous article in the *Historical Journal* on 'The Nineteenth-Century Revolution in Government'[2] in which he provided what he calls a 'model' of what happened in other spheres, and in the course of doing this criticized

* From *Past and Present, a journal of historical studies*, 31 (1965), 39–61. World copyright The Past and Present Society, Corpus Christi College, Oxford. Reprinted by permission of the author and the society.

the notion that Benthamism was the operative force in most instances. Instead of seeing the useful, rational, and centralizing changes of the nineteenth century as Benthamic in origin, we should, he says, see them as 'natural' answers to concrete day-to-day problems. An 'independent historical process' was in operation to which Benthamism was extraneous and at points antagonistic.

The same line was taken by Roberts in an article in *Victorian Studies*[3] offering what he regards as support for it on a wide front; and it was repeated by Kitson Clark in fairly general terms in his Ford Lectures[4] where Mac-Donagh's 'model' article is described as 'very revealing'. Roberts had called it 'brilliant'. On a smaller field Lambert has shown that compulsory vaccination did not derive in any essential sense from Benthamism;[5] and while in his more recent life of Sir John Simon, Lambert says that Benthamism inspired the practical action of many of Simon's generation and that the development of health legislation and administration does not in his case exactly fit MacDonagh's model, he nevertheless writes warmly of Mac-Donagh's article and seems in general to believe in its thesis.[6] Another writer, R. M. Gutchen, offers support for the idea in connection with some aspects of local improvements and centralization.[7] Others also praise the article: for instance Burn in *The Age of Equipoise* calls it 'courageous and helpful'.[8]

The only note of dissent in print that seems to have appeared is to be found in an article by H. Parris.[9] In this he makes some sound points which have not received enough attention. Some authors when praising Mac-Donagh's or Roberts's articles add 'But see Parris', without apparently themselves accepting the validity of his answer; others do not even mention Parris; they just jump on to the bandwagon. It is important therefore to examine this latest orthodoxy before it becomes part of the historian's gospel. I wish here to make four points about it.

(1) MacDonagh generalizes unwarrantably from the facts about emigrant regulation. His thesis is clearly correct in this field: he has shown that it is possible to account for the development of this branch of central administration without considering the influence or at any rate the direct influence of the Benthamites. But he has not shown that other branches developed in a similar way: he does not substantiate his claim that his detailed studies of passenger regulation demonstrate 'truths about the "administrative revolution" as a whole',[10] and his move from one field to his model is not explained. He is admittedly at times fairly guarded himself about how often his model applies: thus he writes of it as 'not always present', and as 'rarely present'; he says there are deviations from it; he calls it a hypothesis. But whatever he himself meant by a model as a historical tool, others have taken it to describe what actually happened or at any rate usually happened. For instance Kitson Clark says 'MacDonagh describes the various stages by

which public services were built up', and after referring to MacDonagh's 'very important article' writes wholly as if he were on *terra firma* and not dealing with a hypothesis about how things may have happened.[11] Burn does the same thing: 'MacDonagh has delineated the course of action which usually followed upon the discovery that something existed which was "intolerable" '.[12]

(2) Some of the anti-Benthamites, as they may be called, bring forward specific examples to try to show that the model works. Thus Roberts moves boldly into many fields: factories, prisons, education, poor law, health, etc. He argues that 'the ideal of central inspection was a commonplace' and not a new device of the Benthamites.[13] He seems here to be making three separate points: (*a*) that central inspection existed before the eighteen-thirties; (*b*) that its extension was recommended by others besides the Benthamites; and (*c*) that it was as a result of their efforts and not as a result of those of the Benthamites that its use was extended.

On point (*a*), the examples of inspectors in England cited by Roberts are not convincing. If by 'Police Commissioners' he means the Metropolitan Police Commissioners, they were the people who were actually in charge of the Metropolitan police and not inspectors of some service run by others. As to excise surveyors, these were a locally based inspectorate supervising the excisemen in their divisions. It is true that in the process of doing this they also surveyed in detail the processes of manufacture of exciseable goods, and to this extent they resembled the later factory inspectors. But they had none of the authority over local government which was a leading characteristic of post-Bentham inspection. Indeed all the surveying and inspectorial powers of the Revenue Boards generally were concerned with securing the Crown's revenue, and only trenched on private interests to protect income accruing to the Crown. As to the Metropolitan Commissioners in Lunacy, it seems unlikely that any analogy was drawn between the management of madmen and the supervision of the sane.

On points (*b*) and (*c*), as regards factories, Roberts asks whether Bentham's idea of central inspection 'defined the Factory Act of 1833', and answers his question by saying that the Benthamites on the Factory Commission of 1833 'did not initiate the reforms' contained in the Act and that these 'had their origin in the agitation of Evangelicals and Tories like Lord Ashley and R. Oastler, to whom Benthamism was an anathema'.[14] As far as central inspection is concerned, Roberts appears to be simply wrong. Thus neither of the two bills (Sadler's and Ashley's) which were introduced in 1832 and 1833, before the Government bill of 1833, contained any provision for inspection:[15] they were to be enforced by the Justices of the Peace assisted by registers which were to be kept by the factory managers. Many of the reformers saw that enforcement was the important problem, but they did not suggest inspection as a remedy; and in Parliament in 1832 a spirit of fatalism existed as regards the enforcement of any regulations. On the other hand the Royal Commission of 1833 whose composition was wholly Benthamite (members: Chadwick, Tooke, and Southwood Smith; secretary: James Wilson) recommended the appointment of inspectors on the typically Benthamite ground that the restrictions proposed were 'not directly conducive to the immediate interests either of the master manufacturers, or of the operatives, or of any powerful class, and are not therefore likely to receive continuous voluntary support'.[16] In fact the idea seems to have been wholly Chadwick's,[17] and it was the Government which decided to include inspection in their bill. Oastler and the reformers in the factory districts on the other hand were sceptical about the value of inspection and got no vestige of satisfaction from the Act of 1833. When the inspectors started work they met considerable hostility from operatives as well as from masters.[18]

On the Poor Law, Roberts admits that Chadwick's influence was profound on the growth of the central government, but suggests that his ideas were not inspired by Bentham. It is true that the new law may have departed in certain minor respects from Bentham's ideas (e.g. the cost of poor relief was not to be borne by pauper labour), but in all important respects the Commission's report, on which the Act of 1834 and its administration were based, was full of Benthamite ideas: for instance, to give one example from the many possible, that the private interests of the distributors of the rates were commonly at variance with their public duties. 'Every man ought ... to distrust his own judgement and his own actions in the affairs of others in proportion as his interests and affections are concerned.'[19] Roberts also makes the point that the new Poor Law reflected many commonly accepted notions and economic interests, besides some Benthamite suggestions. Of course it did, in the sense that many people besides Benthamites were extremely worried about the cost of the old Poor Law and wanted strict workhouse relief; but the important fact is, as indeed Roberts himself admits, that no one had been able to think of administrative machinery which would produce the desired results. When a solution was proposed by the Commission, others accepted the logic of its arguments. We can agree that the new Poor Law had its origin in the 'administrative necessities of the time', but who saw clearly what was necessary, except the Benthamites?

On Public Health, Roberts rests his case on the fact that Chadwick did not play much part in actually framing the Act of 1848, and that the Act was a compromise. It nevertheless remains true, as indeed Roberts shows, that the first exposure of unhealthy conditions in towns came from Benthamites (Chadwick, Southwood Smith and Kay), that Chadwick's report of 1842 made a deep impression on influential public opinion, and that its findings were corroborated by the Buccleuch Commission on whose recommendations the Act of 1848 was based. As to the fact that the Act was a compromise, in order to prove Benthamite influence, one does not have to prove that they got all they wanted.

On prisons, Roberts says that the Act of 1835, which first provided for government inspection of prisons, arose not from the ratiocinations of Benthamites, but that it owed its origins to a few peers and to the Evangelicals of the Prison Discipline Society. Roberts seems here to admit that Benthamites had advocated the inspection of prisons, so that I shall not prove that this was so by quoting passages from their works e.g. Bentham's Constitutional Code, and James Mill's article of 1824 on 'Prisons and Prison Discipline'.[20] There were certainly many prison reformers who were not Benthamites and it seems correct to say that the immediate cause of the Act was the initiative of some peers; but this is not incompatible with the view that Benthamite propaganda contributed in part to the passing of the act: the Benthamites had taken a deep interest in punishment generally, and it seems at least likely that they had helped to clear people's minds about the purposes of punishment and the means to secure the ends intended. At any rate Roberts does not prove this is not true. Indeed one of the three sources he refers to to support his contention does not do so: for the Revd. W. L. Clay in his *Memoir of John Clay* says the doctrines of Bentham were already by 1812 exercising vast influence in the field of criminal law reform and its inevitable corollary prison reform, and he emphasizes the part played by the Benthamites, as well as by the Evangelicals and others, in support of this cause.[21]

On the central inspection issue generally, admittedly other factors such as the example of foreign practice may have been of some importance (e.g. on school inspection), but the Benthamites were the only consistent and systematic advocates of inspection in some form or other. MacDonagh's 'model' article requires that officers should be appointed because men had learnt from experience. But why did they learn from experience in the eighteen-thirties and eighteen-forties and not before then? They had had some experience before of acts passed but not enforced, especially factory acts and prison acts, but they did not apparently learn from experience or at any rate they did not act effectively on it. Whereas after about 1830, central inspection started in several fields. The obvious way to account for this seems to be by attributing it to the accumulated influence of arguments used by the Benthamites, and, more important, to the fact that they got into positions of influence and power on commissions of inquiry and in office. The result was that, more and more, men did not wait to learn slowly from experience in each field, but appointed enforcement officers simultaneously with the first legislative incursion into a new field, e.g. railways in 1840, mines in 1842, steamships in 1846, public health in 1848, and police in 1856.

(3) The anti-Benthamites maintain (i) that a man's ideas can only affect

the course of events through those who have read his works, or at least heard his name—indeed Roberts regards having read the *Constitutional Code* as *the* test; and (ii) that many officials who were responsible for administrative and other changes had probably never heard of Bentham, much less read his works. But as to (i), it is surely nearer the truth to hold that ideas can influence people who are unconscious of their origin, by becoming part of the general climate of opinion, than that they cannot. If they cannot, there would be few thinkers who could be shown to have had any practical influence at all. The criteria of 'reading the works', or of 'hearing the name' are therefore improper criteria by which to assess influence. However, although it is not necessary for our case to show that many important officials and politicians had heard of Bentham and read his works, it is relevant to point out that Bentham talked to a great many persons during his long life, as did also his disciples, and that both he and they were extremely active in pressing their ideas on important people. For example Bentham talked and corresponded with Peel on a number of different matters connected with the administration of justice from at least 1826 onwards.[22]

Much of the recent attack on the Benthamites has been based on the notion that they were 'mere philosophers', doctrinaires who proceeded from *a priori* principles and who dealt only with theories. This is contrasted with practical men, full of common sense, who met and solved problems as they occurred. Thus MacDonagh writes that 'In short, Benthamism was in certain respects none the less *a priori*, generalised and abstract for believing itself to be nothing of the kind.' The officials responsible for emigration regulation, he says, were not spurred to action by 'Benthamism or any other *a priori* influence'. They were 'innocent of doctrinaire intention'. 'Without the slightest spur from doctrinaires or any other *a priori* influence, experience and the brute facts of the situation forced those who were concerned with emigration ... towards the sort of state we recognise as modern.'[23] And Roberts constantly makes the point that the determining factor in producing administrative and social reforms was the 'actual conditions', 'the urgent problems of an industrial age', and not the ideals or ratiocinations of a philosopher.[24] These charges against Benthamism are based on certain confusions, make very little sense, and are not in accordance with the facts. For actual conditions alone constitute no problem; before there can be a problem, there must be an attitude to actual conditions. People must be dissatisfied with actual conditions. And before one knows what one wants to do about the conditions, one must have some principle, or standard, or good, by reference to which the conditions are judged intolerable. The Benthamites provided just such principles, standards, goods. Moral principles are always general and must be so if they are to be useful. Bentham always thought of his greatest happiness principle as the most general of all —as the one principle applying to all situations; but this does not mean that he dealt only in theory: on the contrary he got down to tremendous and indeed tedious detail. In fact he combined in an extraordinary way an interest in practical detail with boldness and rashness in generalization. Moreover he thought the criticism of existing institutions unaccompanied by demonstrably practical alternatives worthless. For criticism like all else was to be judged by its utility. The same conclusion is reached if we take the Benthamites as a whole: quite as important as their statement of the greatest happiness principle was its detailed working out in relation to law and institutions. Thus James Mill pointed out that it had been shown that jailers and justices often managed prisons very badly; indeed it was in their interest to manage them badly; there was no guarantee a man would seek the happiness of others (as he will his own) if you leave him to himself; therefore the actions of every public functionary must be open to public inspection to supply him with a strong motive to perform well the duties of his station.[25]

To sum up: we can agree with the critics in so far as what they are saying is that the Benthamites had what one could call a theoretical framework, viz. the criterion of utility, which they used when judging the institutions of society. What should be emphasized however is:

(*a*) that some such framework, i.e. a principle or standard, is necessary if one is to form any judgement about how things are, and suggest how they should be. There is no learning from experience except by reference to some such principle or standard, though the principle or standard may be latent, implicit, unexpressed, even unrecognized;

(*b*) that the critics do not prove that new theories and doctrines were not an important factor in determining the new standards by reference to which conditions were judged intolerable. Even if they could show that the new theories 'caught on' only because 'actual conditions' changed, they would not have shown that new theories and doctrines were not an important factor determining the new standards;

(*c*) that the Benthamites did not confine themselves to stating a principle. They made empirical studies often of a novel kind and found out what actually happened, and then proposed specific remedies for what they considered evils, e.g. pieces of machinery like inspection, or a preventative police.

(4) The anti-Benthamites' case rests partly on their views about Benthamism and *laissez-faire*. Many writers have identified Benthamism with 'individualism' and *laissez-faire*; they have observed encroachments on these principles in the sphere of government in nineteenth-century England; and so they have concluded that the Benthamites cannot have been influential. But the Benthamites were not doctrinaire advocates of *laissez-faire*. The main principle of utilitarianism was that the test of policy should be its effect on human happiness. The application of this principle led to consider-

able extensions of both *laissez-faire* and of state intervention. This has been shown conclusively by Lionel Robbins in a book to which insufficient attention is paid.[26] Thus, writing of Bentham's views on the economic functions of the state, Robbins says that although there is an explicit presumption that, over a wide field, interference is inadvisable, there is no suggestion that it is ruled out *a priori* by some system of natural rights. 'According to the principle of utility . . . the expediency of any act of government must be judged solely by its consequences and not regarded as ruled out in advance by some metaphysical system of rights.' If Bentham's work is considered as a whole, it will be seen that he was 'continually seeking all along the line to erect a structure of institutions, thought out in great detail, within which action is so limited and coordinated as to create the good society'.

It may be asked how such a gross error as identifying Benthamism with *laissez-faire* can have arisen. The answer would seem to be that insufficient attention has been paid to the fact that, while it is true that the Benthamites believed that people always acted in what they conceived to be their interests, of which they were the best judges, they did not think such actions always added up to the greatest happiness of the greatest number: the pursuit of self interest might not result in social benefits e.g. public health: in such cases it was necessary for the state to intervene. In Roberts' case the error is due partly to incomplete quotation from Bentham. He refers to Bentham's view that 'in itself Government is one vast evil',[27] but he does not point out that Bentham after writing this went on to say that 'whenever, by evil thus produced, greater evil is excluded, the balance takes the nature, shape, and name of good; and government is justified in the production of it'.[28] Roberts thus ties himself in knots seeing contradictions in Bentham—contradictions between a belief in natural economic laws, and the usefulness of positive legislation and administrative centralization—which in reality do not exist.

II

The second idea I wish to examine is that opinion in nineteenth-century England was generally humanitarian, and that social evils were attacked and dealt with when people felt them to be intolerable.

MacDonagh in his 'model' article says that 'throughout and even before the Victorian years "intolerability" was the master card. No wall of either doctrine or interest could permanently withstand that single trumpet cry, all the more so as governments grew ever more responsive to public sentiment, and public sentiment ever more humane.' He repeats the same idea in his book. 'It was very likely that legislation to stamp out the "intolerable" miseries and mortalities of the Atlantic passage would sooner or later be enacted: "intolerability" would sooner or later open any door.'[29] (Note incidentally the use of 'it was likely that' when writing history. It is a frequent phrase of Kitson Clark's too, and it is also used by Burn. It seems to mean

'It is not remarkable to us that ...', or 'We can see why, given x, y followed.' But it is ambiguous, because it may suggest not this, but that something seemed likely to happen to contemporaries, or that contemporaries did not think it odd that something had happened.) Burn in a review of MacDonagh's book[30] repeats the same point about 'intolerability' without analysis: the case against individualism, he says, was always more difficult to prove than the case against collectivism, but the public were moved by an 'intolerable' situation such as the conditions of emigration. He says much the same in his own book: 'As "evils" came to light they were dealt with.'[31] Roberts says something similar, i.e. that it was sufficient 'to describe the chaotic administration of the poor law, the exploitation of children, the disgraceful state of prisons, the increasing crime, the unhealthiness of slums, and the profound ignorance of the working classes to convince of the need for reform.'[32]

But does this idea get us anywhere? It purports to be an explanation of why certain things happened, but it is not really an explanation at all. It is a tautology. For what else does one mean when one says the public found something 'intolerable' than that they took steps, or supported steps, to change it or to eradicate it? Moreover even if the alleged explanation is not so interpreted as to escape condemnation as a tautology, it is open to at least two other objections. Firstly there was no agreement as to what was intolerable, since there was agreement neither as to the criteria of what was or was not intolerable, nor even as to the bare facts. For example the hours worked in factories seemed in the 1830s intolerable to many workers, whereas to Nassau Senior the long hours were practicable because of the extraordinary lightness of the labour. Edward Baines and others too in the forties insisted that the work was light. Bright and Cobden thought in 1846 that the philanthropists would pamper the people. And as late as the sixties and seventies, after exhaustive, impartial inquiries had taken place into many industries, several M.P.s said that the evils had been much exaggerated. Similarly the miners felt they could only tolerate the physical and mental strain and the extreme unpleasantness of their work if they confined their working week to five or five and a half days; but Tremenheere, the first mines inspector, thought it was wrong for them to take two days off each week, even though they earned less by doing so. Nor was there agreement as to whether work in mines was prejudicial to the health of children; Ashley and other philanthropists of course thought it was, whereas the mineowners considered it was not. Nor did this attitude obtain only in the forties when the subject was new: it was still in evidence in the sixties and seventies. Indeed as late as 1892, the general manager of some collieries, referring to labour in the mines generally, said before the Royal Commission on Labour: 'Coal mining is not an unhealthy occupation. The atmosphere in which the miner works is temperate, and of necessity fresh and comparatively pure. The coal miner is not liable to ... wet and dry ... He is liable to accidents of various descriptions,' but he added that there was a considerable number of workmen between the ages of fifty-five and seventy still following their occupations.[33] For many people this would not have been the criterion of tolerability. Even on public health—a field in which most people by 1848 were convinced something should be done—there was a good deal of disagreement about the facts: thus it was said that the Health of Towns Association and the various Commissions of Inquiry had exaggerated the evils, though no doubt few went so far as the vestry which in 1849 said cholera was a weak invention of the enemy—cholera which had killed 80,000–90,000 persons in Great Britain in 1848–9. This kind of thing shows the extreme difficulty in getting agreement on the facts or on the criteria by which one should judge them.

A second objection to the 'intolerability' thesis is that it is so elastic it can never be proved false. Its proponents talk of a 'trumpet cry which could not be permanently withstood' and say it would 'sooner or later open any door'. This is rather like Marx's theory of the inevitability of revolution, or Toynbee's declining civilizations. Neither of them commits himself to a time schedule and thus cannot be proved wrong by the argument that what they have predicted or postulated has not yet happened. Moreover the time necessary for the removal of an 'intolerable' state of affairs might be very great. Even the field studied by MacDonagh supports this: it took fifty years to secure tolerable conditions in emigrant ships. Many people in the early 1840s thought it intolerable to employ boys under the age of thirteen underground, but this continued until 1900 when it was forbidden by statute. Similarly many people from the forties onwards thought the accident rate in mines intolerable and reducible, but very little improvement was effected until the last decade of the century.

As to humanitarianism, Kitson Clark considers there was a general tendency towards humanitarianism and reform in most classes in the country throughout the reign of Queen Victoria; he writes of 'the conscience ... of the nineteenth century' and of a 'strong sense of social responsibility'.[34] MacDonagh says that opinion was 'sensitive and generally humanitarian'; to believe that action was necessary was the normal reaction to suffering and mortality when the facts were disclosed. One of the sources of social reform was 'a public opinion sensitive to inhumanity'.[35] Burn considers the age (1852–67) was 'sensitive ... to the condition of those who never could or never would get on'.[36] Roberts writes of 'a deep humanitarianism' and of 'the humanitarianism of the period'.[37]

These phrases are objectionable because either they are so vague as to be useless, or, if they are taken to mean something, namely that most people or most important people were humanitarian, they are false or at any rate misleading. Of course there were some humanitarians in nineteenth-century England, some philanthropists, some people with a social conscience; but the important question is how many? How widespread was humanitarian feeling? One of the ways of throwing light on this is to look at the arguments used against the reformers and at the obstacles they met. Burn warns us against assuming that the opponents of reasonable improvements 'were necessarily selfish or callous or blind'. Clearly one should not accept this as true without looking at the evidence. If it is shown to be correct, it is no longer an assumption.

Take factories for example: no one could deny that there were some philanthropists in this field, but there were also many employers who would not comply with the safety measures prescribed by the law. Numerous deaths and accidents were caused every year by unfenced shafts, though a simple, inexpensive precaution would have prevented these accidents. The long battles the inspectors had with employers on this issue can leave no doubt that many employers were extremely callous. It was no answer, in the inspectors' view, to say, as the employers did, that people were careless: death or mutilation were too severe punishments for heedlessness and indiscretion. And anyway it was precisely because people were careless that one should protect them.

Or take mines: the inspectors attributed accidents in the fifties largely to the faults of the proprietors and managers. The proprietors (they said) were ignorant of conditions of work; the managers were entirely reckless about safety and lacked all sense of humanity. They did not seem interested in preserving their fellow men from unnecessary danger. Profit and loss were the only considerations. It was no good appealing to the higher feelings of the managers, as they had none. The only possible approach seemed to be through self-interest: to point out that the sacrifice of labour must in the long run increase the average cost. During the three years 1851–4, about three thousand deaths had occurred in the mines, but no compensation had been paid to any widows or children; all the interests in an area were arrayed against the survivors, e.g. solicitors would not act against colliery owners. Twenty years later, in the seventies, one of the inspectors was still very depressed: the safety of the men was little thought of when it stood in the way of a few shillings more profit, e.g. proper pit-props were often not provided because of the expense. In the light of the inspectors' reports, it is misleading not to take the matter any further than MacDonagh does, for, when writing of safety devices in the mines, he says that once they had been clearly proved, the corresponding regulations passed effortlessly into law.[38]

Nor does the treatment of poverty suggest a great advance in the sentiment and practice of humanity, although many of the people concerned with it conceived they were thinking about the best interests of the recipients. For they were more worried about the allegedly corrupting effects of distributing even very small amounts in charity than about the existence of poverty and the hardships suffered by the sick, the old or the workless. Charity properly bestowed should never be given until some calamity had overtaken a man, or he had made every attempt to escape it. A woman deserted by her husband was not to receive outdoor relief during the first year after desertion. If a widow had several small children, some of them should be sent to the workhouse rather than the widow be given relief.[39] Does this show sensitiveness to the feelings of a woman for her children which are normally particularly strong after losing her husband? Roberts shows in an article called 'How cruel was the Victorian Poor Law?'[40] that *The Times* and various pamphleteers got some of their facts wrong when they alleged considerable cruelty in workhouses. He also shows that some cruelties in workhouses were not ordered by the Commissioners, but were due to the parsimony of the local administrators. But this article does not really require one to make a substantial change of verdict on the treatment of the poor, partly because Roberts only deals with the poor in workhouses and not with those outside who suffered through loss of outdoor relief, and partly because of an ambiguity in his use of the word 'law': he proves that the law itself was not cruel; we can agree with that, but the fact remains that its administration caused gross hardship.

The tendency to think of the nineteenth century as more humanitarian than it was may be partly explained by identifying a concern for morality with a concern for happiness. Thus Tremenheere considered he was a humanitarian, but in fact he was really a moralist. He was not shocked by the hardness and unpleasantness of the labour of miners, or by the accident rate: what shocked him was their drunkenness, sensuality, laziness, extravagance, and lack of respect for their masters. It seems odd to think of a man as a humanitarian who did not wish even by 1854 to raise the minimum age for work in the mines from ten to twelve. Nor is there any evidence among his many reports that he wanted to make people good in order to make them less miserable. Another example of the same kind of thing is provided by the image of Sir Charles Trevelyan which has been conjured up by his descendants. Thus G. M. Trevelyan writes of his grandfather as living in a philanthropic and evangelical society, and suggests that he inherited some of 'the philanthropic zeal of Evangelicalism'.[41] But Charles Trevelyan was not a philanthropist in the ordinary sense of that word: neither during the Irish famine nor later was he primarily anxious to relieve suffering. He thought much more about the demoralizing effects of charity than about the diminution of pain; dependence on others was a moral disease. We can agree that he inherited something from Evangelicalism, but this was its distrust of pleasure and ease, and high valuation of work and effort, rather than its humanitarian strain.

Overstress on humanitarianism can also be explained by misconceptions about the doctrines of the churches and the effect generally of religion in the nineteenth century. It is often said that the influence of religion was in support of social progress. Thus Kitson Clark considers that the sanctions of religion were probably more important than Benthamism, and he seems to suggest that because the Anti-Corn Law League modelled itself from the point of view of organization on the anti-slavery movement, the evangelical revival was somehow behind the Anti-Corn Law League. He makes the same kind of point in his introduction to Shannon's book on Gladstone and the Bulgarian agitation, where he says that the attack on the corn laws 'was in its way a religious movement'; that the arguments used against the corn laws and in other movements were moral arguments; and that many causes and movements in the nineteenth century were always conceived of as religious. He is insistent that the second Evangelical revival of the late fifties has been wrongly neglected, and that religion was very important in the history of the country in the nineteenth century. He sees the revivalist movements as the response of Christians to the challenge of conditions, giving shape and meaning to many lives. In other passages he says that the revival of religion gave impetus to political changes after 1867 and that it gave support to the move for democracy; that it was almost as dynamic as the Industrial Revolution and the increase in the population; and that the revival of religion contributed towards humanitarianism. Christianity was 'unavoidable and all intrusive'.[42] Burn considers that religion, which was pervasive, 'lowered class barriers, occasionally even levelled them to the ground'. 'Acceptance of the will of God was by no means synonymous with apathy towards life'.[43] Roberts says that 'the humanitarianism of the period, so important in inspiring men to press for social reform, had deep roots in England's Christian faith, pre-eminently in the evangelical movement inspired by John Wesley.'[44]

Statements of the kind quoted above are misleading on various counts, viz:

(i) Some causes may appear superficially to have been religiously inspired, but were not;
(ii) many Christians were not interested in social or political problems at all;
(iii) the influence of religion was often hostile rather than conducive to social progress.

As to point (i), even when the anti-slavery agitation formed the model on matters of organization, it does not follow that all those taking up the cause were religious, or that they all conceived of it as a religious cause. This can be illustrated from the anti-corn law movement. Admittedly many Nonconformists supported repeal, and thought, or at any rate said, that God was on their side. But it would be absolutely wrong to see the League as the product wholly or even mainly of religious faith: others besides

Christians can feel strongly and evince moral indignation. The League was in origin the product of many forces: e.g. the desire of radicals (many of whom were anti-religious) to take up a cause against the Whigs; the desire of manufacturers to strike a blow at the political and social control of the aristocracy; and the desire of the Dissenters to attack parsons' tithes. Admittedly many supporters of the League were inspired by humanitarian motives and gave prominence to religious and humanitarian arguments against the corn laws. But much of the propaganda of the League was based on economic theories. The arguments were not all moral arguments as Kitson Clark says they were, and many supporters of the cause did not conceive of it as a religious cause. The leaders of the movement may all have been Christians and humane men; but too much should not be made of this. For instance it does not follow that because Cobden was a Christian, he took up the anti-corn law movement on Christian grounds. The significance of the 700 Dissenting ministers at the conference of 1841 should not be exaggerated: many of them were not sent by their congregations, and the conference was in a sense rigged by the League.[45] Admittedly faith in free trade after 1846 became to some extent blind and dogmatic; in this way it resembles religious faith, but this does not prove that the attack on the corn laws was mainly inspired by religious motives, or that it was a religious movement.

As to point (ii), there were of course individual Christians and groups of Christians who took up or supported some causes, often it may be added because they were acquiring new standards as a result of secular ideals and secular philosophies. As examples of this one can cite Evangelicals and the anti-slavery movement, northern Anglicans and factory reform in the thirties and forties, Quakers and prison reform, Christian socialists in the mid-century; and from the eighties onwards all the churches were influenced to some extent by discussion of 'the social problem'. But there were also many individual Christians and groups of Christians who were not interested in social matters at all; for instance many rural Anglican parsons, the Oxford Movement, many Nonconformists apart from their support of the Anti-Corn Law League, the revivalists of the fifties and sixties, and the later Evangelicals. It is therefore a great mistake to think, as some writers seem to, that all Christians during the nineteenth century modelled themselves on the Clapham sect. Throughout the century a great many Christians were interested in things other than social problems: e.g. theology, liturgy, ritual, agnosticism, relations with the state, disestablishment, attracting the working classes to religion, saving souls, not bodies. Thus spiritual not material salvation was the main concern of the revivalists Spurgeon, Sankey and Moody, and the Salvation Army, who are so much stressed by Kitson Clark. What worried these people was lack of religious faith among the poor. It is true that in 1890 General Booth turned almost in despair towards social reform, but in the long run the only realities for Booth were sin and salvation, hell and heaven, the devil and the Lord. In fact far from the Evangelicals being leaders in this field, the hard core of resistance to social radicalism was to be found among them, whichever church they were in.[46]

As to point (iii), the influence of religion was not just neutral: there are good grounds for thinking that it retarded social progress perhaps very considerably. It is difficult to assess the extent of the influence of the social doctrines preached by clergymen; but that those of the Church of England at least were often socially unprogressive, there can be little doubt. Many examples can be found among the sermons and pamphlets produced by Anglican clergymen to show that it was very common, specially in the middle years of the century (1830–70), to hold publicly that poverty was ordained by God, that afflictions, even cholera and the plague, were good for people, that the poor should simply trust in God and take a long term view of their miseries. Disease of all kinds was sent by God as a punishment and to teach people to be less sinful. Even in 1866 the cattle plague was thought to be sent by God as a judgement on sin.[47] Such doctrines can hardly have assisted the efforts which were being made in many quarters to study disease and public health in a scientific way. In one important instance at any rate—the Irish famine—this kind of view actually affected government policy: for the chief person in charge of government relief-measures (Sir Charles Trevelyan) believed the famine was the judgement of God on an indolent and un-self-reliant people; and as God had sent the calamity to teach the Irish a lesson, that calamity must not be too much mitigated. Similarly high prices were, in Trevelyan's view, a check imposed by God and nature when there was scarcity.[48]

In the field of education, while it is true that many Christians, both through their churches and individually, started and maintained schools and taught in them, a strong case can be made out to show that on balance Christianity was the chief force retarding the advent of a national system of education in England; and this not only because of inter-church squabbles, but because some Christians were against education altogether on the ground it would encourage discontent with one's lot and a disbelief in religion.

III

Finally I wish to turn to the wider views thrown out by these Tory historians. For their study of nineteenth-century English history has led them to make certain generalizations about how things happen: viz. that somehow they happen all by themselves, as a result of chance, of 'the historical process', or of 'blind forces', and that they are not planned or even the result of human agency. Thus MacDonagh refers in his 'model' article to 'the independent historical process in operation'; he says 'a genuine historical process was involved'; the same phrase is repeated in his book: 'a genuine historical process was at work, moulding men and ideas'; 'it was not, [he says] in absolute terms, an inevitable process: there are no inevitable processes in history ... In absolute terms none of this had to happen ... [but it was] inherently probable in the circumstances of the early and mid-nineteenth century'. We should not seek to explain the change in the role of the state in the nineteenth century almost exclusively 'in terms of the great individuals and ideas and events', though we should not fall into the opposite error of regarding it as due to social, political, or economic forces. As the adjustment to what was needed in the field of passenger regulation was unplanned, not premeditated or well recognized, so the same kind of explanation should be presumed to be the correct one in all spheres of government activity. 'An explanation in terms of natural inclination and momentum is precedent to one which predicates an artefact.'[49]

Kitson Clark writes similarly. 'Unnoticed, unplanned, and certainly as far as most men were concerned absolutely undesired, the modern state ... was beginning to take shape'. State control and officials were 'largely unwanted, altogether unplanned'. He constantly sees 'blind forces' at work. In these he includes the Industrial Revolution, the increase in population, and the increase in wealth. He suggests that evil is often caused by 'chance' or by 'impersonal historical forces which possibly no man can control', and indeed he criticizes historians and others for conceiving in a facile way that evil has been caused by the misbehaviour of people. It follows of course from this view that we should not judge the Industrial Revolution from a moral standpoint: 'it probably should be considered as nearly void of moral significance as a change in the weather'.[50]

Roberts in one of his articles stresses that social legislation was a necessity, and 'explains' its enactment by in effect saying 'it had to be passed'. In his book he goes further and implies that things happened in spite of what people wanted or intended. Thus Parliament established departments 'in almost absence of mind ... The Victorians did not want the central government to manage local affairs, or even to tell local officials what to do.' 'With no conscious intent to do so, they [the Inspectors] helped lay the basis for the administrative state.'[51]

Lambert as always does not go quite so far as the others, but he makes the same kind of point. Thus writing of vaccination, he says it 'exhibits those "spontaneous developments in administration" which Dr. MacDonagh has recently brought to our attention. Once the state had become loosely associated with the subject, a certain spontaneous momentum of growth developed ... Vaccination administration developed a certain dynamic of its own to which the administrators naturally contributed, but by which they were in turn partly driven.' He admits that the personalities of Simon and Seaton made some difference to what happened, but he emphasizes 'the existence of an inherent dynamism in the process of vaccination administration itself'. After studying the whole career of Simon in great detail, Lambert is more willing to admit that the influence of an individual can be important, but he still clings nevertheless to the MacDonagh model. For in his book on Simon he still thinks in terms of 'the administrative process' and of 'an inherent momentum of administration' 'based on sheer ineluctable (or empirical) necessity'; this is the so to speak 'natural' course of events, but sometimes large personalities such as Simon's impede or divert natural tendencies. Then, after a period in control of affairs, what Simon desires appears to become the natural thing to happen, and when his wishes are frustrated, Lambert has to explain the situation by saying that Simon's plans 'were certainly not foredoomed to failure'; this was due to certain accidents. But Lambert cannot for long keep away from the notion of inevitability, for in the next paragraph we are told that 'it is ... certain that, as it turned out, disaster was inevitable', and that Simon's resignation was inevitable.[52]

All these views are misleading and indeed dangerous in their implications. They are misleading because they conceal certain ambiguities. For instance when Kitson Clark talks of 'man' ('possibly no man can control' impersonal historical forces), it is not clear whether he means one man, or men in general. Many things, e.g. social conditions in towns, are admittedly not controllable by one man, or even by a small number of men, but are in principle controllable by men in general, as contrasted with some things that are not so controllable at a given level of technical knowledge, e.g. physical phenomena such as the weather or earthquakes. Moreover MacDonagh's language encourages one to forget that there were men behind the abstractions, behind his inherent structures, patterns of development, administrative processes, historical processes, inner momentums. Similarly when Roberts says 'The Victorians did not want the central government to manage local affairs', this obscures the fact that some Victorians did want it to, in the sense that they saw it was necessary if they were to get certain other things which they wanted, such as better public health or adequate policing. Lambert's phrases, too, obscure the fact that decisions are ultimately made by people. 'It was not so much Simon's intention as inescapable necessity [the protracted refusal of the medical schools] which entailed the perpetuation of the State's exclusive educational system.'[53] But in the end Simon willed the action taken, although he may not have wanted it earlier. Similarly Lambert's 'dynamic' and 'inherent dynamism' would be less misleading if he abandoned these abstractions and talked about the actual people, i.e. administrators rather than administration. It is true of course that what happens may be affected by the machinery of administration which exists (e.g. a system of inspection and reports), but ultimately that machinery is created by men, and worked by men, and what happens is due to people making decisions, even if only decisions not to alter the machinery.

These views are dangerous when applied to evil happenings because they encourage what Sir Isaiah Berlin calls 'the great alibis'.[54] The social effects of the Industrial Revolution were caused in the final analysis by men, by men's inventiveness, by men's decisions to build factories, by men's desires to make profits. Kitson Clark has probably been led to his views by the fact that these men did not desire or intend the social evils which appeared. But it does not follow from this that they did not cause them. Maybe we should not pass moral judgements on them if they did not intend evil; but we should not go on from there to say that the evils were not caused by people. Moreover in some instances the action taken by men so much aggravated the effects of an already existing evil that it comes very near to men intending evil. For instance, take tenement housing: the increase in population in the nineteenth century created possibilities of making money out of housing the working classes which had not existed earlier. A house would be converted into numerous dwellings, and when new buildings were erected the same plan was copied. The people who built tenements were not blind: they did it consciously in order to make money. Kitson Clark considers we should not say that the conditions of the Industrial Revolution caused men to become callous and ruthless; we should see them at the mercy of 'impersonal historical forces'.[55] It is not clear whether he is arguing against all moral judgements, or only against moral judgements on the past. Should we for instance not have condemned Stalin (when he was alive) for some of his actions because he was just a leaf being blown in the wind, swept along by blind historical forces? I imagine Kitson Clark would have called Stalin callous and ruthless and would not have wished to exonerate him from all responsibility for his actions. There are of course greater problems of evidence which arise in connection with the past than with the present, but the issue is not in principle different, and historians who suggest that it is confuse issues and are liable to do harm by undermining notions of responsibility.

Moreover these views are dangerous because they lead imperceptibly to the notion that it is better not to plan: because so much was achieved unplanned, the process can and should be repeated. Unplanned changes are spoken of as 'natural', a praise word. Social progress, it is implied, will take place in the future as in the past without human effort as a result of 'the historical process'. The role of men and of ideas (whether for good or for bad) is belittled: we are, as it were, just drifting at the mercy of chance and of blind forces; but all will turn out for the best because of a generally diffused humanitarianism. The only way of testing the validity of this advice is empirically by examining the evidence offered by the past. And in so far as social reform in nineteenth-century England is concerned, the evidence seems to suggest that most social evils were not removed without fierce battles against absurd arguments, vested interests, obscurantism, and timidity, and that their removal required considerable effort and determination on the part of men (even if only of obscure men) who realized that it was worthwhile making a conscious effort to control events. And in this enterprise many of them were assisted, whether they knew it or not, by Benthamism in spite of all its shortcomings, in the sense not so much of practical and ingenious answers to particular problems (though these were important), but in the sense of the humanist notion that the diminution of misery is in itself a sufficient justification for action, and that reforms need not be justified on the ground they improve the morality of the sufferer.

BIBLIOGRAPHICAL NOTE

The debate on the origins of nineteenth-century social reforms, closely interlinked with discussions about the influence of *laissez-faire* and interventionist ideologies, may be said to have been revived in the post-war period by J. B. Brebner in his 1948 article in the *Journal of Economic History*. Debate turned to controversy in O. MacDonagh's 1958 article in *Hist. Journal*, but has continued to be productive of thoughtful, if conflicting, reinterpretations. The most useful to be published since 1965 are V. Cromwell, 'Interpretations of nineteenth-century administration: an analysis', *Victorian Studies*, 9 (1966); Eric Midwinter, 'A Tory interpretation of History: some comments', *Past and Present*, 34 (1966); W. O. Aydelotte, 'The Conservative and Radical interpretations of early Victorian social legislation', *Victorian Studies*, 11 (1967); L. J. Hume, 'Jeremy Bentham and the nineteenth-century revolution in government', *Hist. Journal*, 10 (1967); G. H. Himmelfarb, 'Bentham scholarship and the Bentham problem', *Journal of Modern History*, 41 (1969); H. W. Parris, *Constitutional Bureaucracy: the Development of British Central Administration since the 18th Century* (London, 1969); W. C. Lubenow, *The Politics of Government Growth: early Victorian Attitudes towards State Intervention, 1833–1848* (Newton Abbot, 1971); and chapters by Finer and Ryan in G. Sutherland (ed.), *Studies in the Growth of Nineteenth-Century Government* (London, 1972). A number of these are critical of Mrs. Hart's interpretation. A. J. Taylor, *Laissez-faire and State Intervention in Nineteenth-Century Britain* (London, 1972) is a cautious, balanced survey of the whole field and includes a good, annotated bibliography.

NOTES

1. O. MacDonagh, 'Emigration and the State, 1833–55: an essay in Administrative History', *Trans. Roy. Hist. Soc.*, 5th ser., 5 (1955), 133–59; and 'The Regulation of emigrant traffic from the United Kingdom, 1842–55', *Irish Hist. Studies*, 9 (1954), 162–89.
2. O. MacDonagh, 'The Nineteenth-century Revolution in Government: A reappraisal', *Hist. Journal* 1 (1958), 52–67.
3. D. Roberts, 'Jeremy Bentham and the Victorian Administrative State', *Victorian Studies*, 2 (1959), 193–210.

4. G. Kitson Clark, *The Making of Victorian England* (London, 1962), p. 19.

5. R. J. Lambert, 'A Victorian National Health Service—State Vaccination, 1855–71', *Hist. Journal* 5 (1962), 1–18.

6. Royston Lambert, *Sir John Simon, 1816–1904, and English Social Administration* (London, 1963). See pp. 33 and 168–9, esp. footnote 63, p. 169.

7. Robert M. Gutchen, 'Local Improvements and Centralisation in Nineteenth-century England', *Hist. Journal* 4 (1961), 85–96.

8. W. L. Burn, *The Age of Equipoise* (London, 1964), p. 224.

9. H. Parris, 'The Nineteenth-century Revolution in Government: A Reappraisal Reappraised', *Hist. Journal* 3 (1960), 17–37.

10. MacDonagh, *Irish Hist. Studies*, as above, p. 172.

11. G. Kitson Clark, 'Statesmen in Disguise', *Hist. Journal* 2 (1959), 19–39.

12. Burn, *The Age of Equipoise*, p. 224.

13. Roberts, *Victorian Studies*, as above, p. 199.

14. Ibid., 198.

15. *P.P.* 1831–2, II, and *P.P.* 1833, II.

16. *P.P.* 1833, XX, p. 68.

17. S. E. Finer, *The Life and Times of Sir Edwin Chadwick* (London, 1952), p. 58.

18. See J. T. Ward, *The Factory Movement, 1830–1855* (London, 1962), especially pp. 111, 115, and 127–8; and C. H. Driver, *Tory Radical, the life of Richard Oastler* (New York, 1946), p. 246. Roberts refers to the latter to support his case, but it does not seem to.

19. *Report of Commissioners on inquiry into Poor Laws* (1834), p. 288.

20. *Encyclopaedia Britannica*, Supplement, 1824.

21. The Revd. W. L. Clay, *The Prison Chaplain: a Memoir of John Clay* (Cambridge, 1861), pp. 89–90.

22. N. Gash, *Mr. Secretary Peel* (London, 1961), pp. 312 and 331–4.

23. MacDonagh, *Hist. Journal*, as above, p. 66; *Irish Hist. Studies*, as above, p. 163; *Trans. Roy. Hist. Soc.*, as above, p. 133; and *A Pattern of Government Growth, 1800–1860. The Passenger Acts and their Enforcement* (London, 1961), p. 17.

24. D. Roberts, *Victorian Origins of the British Welfare State* (New Haven, Conn., 1960), pp. 73–4; and article in *Victorian Studies*, as above, pp. 204 and 206.

25. *Encyclopaedia Britannica*, Supplement, 1824.

26. Lionel Robbins, *The Theory of Economic Policy in English Classical Political Economy* (London, 1952), see esp. pp. 40–2.

27. Roberts, *Victorian Origins*, p. 26.

28. *The Works of J. Bentham*, ed. J. Bowring (Edinburgh, 1838–43), vol. ix, p. 24.

29. MacDonagh, *Hist. Journal*, as above, p. 58; and MacDonagh, *A Pattern of Government Growth*, p. 9.

30. W. L. Burn. *Hist. Journal* 6 (1963), 140–3.

31. Burn, *The Age of Equipoise*, p. 217.

32. Roberts, *Victorian Origins*, pp. 33–4.

33. *P.P.* 1892, XXXVI, Part i, p. 166.

34. Kitson Clark, *The Making of Victorian England*, pp. 282, 195, and 177.

35. MacDonagh, *A Pattern of Government Growth*, pp. 17, 58; and *Irish Hist. Studies*, as above, p. 172.

36. Burn, *The Age of Equipoise*, p. 128.

37. Roberts, *Victorian Origins*, p. 103.

38. MacDonagh, *Hist. Journal*, as above, p. 61.

39. Instructions of Local Government Board, 1871.

40. Roberts, *Hist. Journal* 6 (1963), 97–107.

41. G. M. Trevelyan, *Sir George Otto Trevelyan, a Memoir* (London, 1932), pp. 6, 13.

42. Kitson Clark, *The Making of Victorian England*; see esp. pp. 20–1, 22–5, 146–7, 191, 196, 283–4; and Introduction to R. T. Shannon, *Gladstone and the Bulgarian Agitation, 1876* (London etc., 1963), pp. xv and xvi.

43. Burn, *The Age of Equipoise*, pp. 7, 46, 47. Burn in general thinks well of *The Making of Victorian England*: see *The Age of Equipoise*, p. 228, note 52.

44. Roberts, *Victorian Origins*, p. 103.

45. See N. McCord, *The Anti-Corn Law League, 1838–1846* (London, 1958), esp. pp. 103–4 and 147.

46. See K. S. Inglis, *The Churches and the Working Classes in Victorian England* (London and Toronto, 1963).

47. This passage is based on a study of the pamphlet collection in Pusey House, Oxford. The material there is representative of most sides of the church.

48. See my article on 'Sir Charles Trevelyan at the Treasury', *Eng. Hist. Rev.* 75 (1960), 99.

49. MacDonagh, *Hist. Journal*, as above, p. 67; and *A pattern of Government Growth*, pp. 16, 346, 348.

50. These views are expressed in many passages in *The Making of Victorian England*, but see esp. pp. 64, 89, 91, 93, 108, 109, 278–81, 289.

51. Roberts, *Victorian Studies*, as above. See in particular, pp. 209–10; and *Victorian Origins*, pp. 179, 318.

52. Lambert, *Hist. Journal*, as above, p. 17; and *Sir John Simon*, pp. 225, 271, 460, and note 95 on p. 460.

53. Lambert, *Hist. Journal*, as above, p. 17.

54. Isaiah Berlin, *Historical Inevitability* (London, 1954), p. 78.

55. The present brand of Tory historians are not on the whole romantic about the past in the G. M. Trevelyan tradition, though there are occasional exceptions to this: e.g. Burn considers that the old-fashioned tramp offers a 'picturesque contrast to the sleek beneficiaries of the Welfare State', though he does go on to warn us against endowing him and his predecessors with virtues they are unlikely to possess (*The Age of Equipoise*, p. 169).

10

Reasons for the Decline of Mortality in England and Wales during the Nineteenth Century*

T. MCKEOWN and R. G. RECORD

INTRODUCTION

OUR object in this and a previous communication[1] has been to assess the relative importance of the major influences which affected the growth of the population of England and Wales between 1770 and 1900, with special reference to medical evidence. The reason for starting at 1770 is, of course, that the modern rise of population began at about that time, and the reason for ending at 1900 is that from the beginning of the twentieth century the issues become considerably more complex because of extension of the public medical service and the introduction of some effective forms of therapy. To anticipate a conclusion we shall later have to justify, we believe, that with the notable exception of vaccination against smallpox, specific preventive or curative measures could have had no significant influence on mortality before the twentieth century, and that we must look elsewhere for the explanation of the rise of population.

The period referred to can be divided into two intervals in which the issues with which we are confronted are different. From 1770 to 1837 national birth rates and death rates were not recorded, and our first task is to decide whether a rise of the birth rate or a decline of mortality was the more important influence on the growth of population. And because no data are available which put the answer beyond dispute, the acceptability of either hypothesis turns upon the credibility of the explanation we can give. In this interval we are therefore concerned with reasons for changes in the two rates, and with their relative effectiveness in bringing about a rise in population. After 1837 the birth rate and death rate are not in doubt, and it is evident that the continued growth of population was due in part to the excess of births over deaths established by 1837, and in part to a further decline of mortality. Our main task in the second interval is therefore to assess the reasons for the decline of mortality.

* From *Population Studies* 16 (1963), 94–122. Reprinted by permission of the authors and the editor of the journal.

The earlier communication considered the rise of population during the eighteenth century. (It might indeed have been preferable to have continued the examination to 1837, but we refer briefly to the first third of the nineteenth century in the present report.) It was concluded that the most important influence was a decline of mortality, probably attributable to improvements in the environment. Many economic historians are not at present prepared to say that on balance the economic and social changes associated with the Industrial Revolution in the eighteenth century were favourable, and some find such a conclusion quite unacceptable. Our reasons for accepting it, at least in relation to health, are those given in another context by Sherlock Holmes: *When we have eliminated the impossible, whatever remains, however improbable, must be the truth.* We gave reasons for regarding as unacceptable the alternatives: (*a*) that medical effort had a significant effect on mortality or (*b*) that the marked and sustained decline of the infectious diseases (the diseases almost exclusively affected) could be attributable wholly to a change in the balance between the virulence of infective organisms and the immunity of the hosts. What remains after elimination of these 'impossibilities' is the 'improbability' that the environment improved. This improvement could have resulted in a decline of mortality (by reducing the incidence and fatality of the infectious diseases) or in a rise in the birth rate (brought about mainly by a reduction in age at marriage). Our reasons for preferring the first of these explanations were essentially (*a*) because at the prevailing high level of both rates, a decline in the death rate is intrinsically a more likely response to an improvement in the environment than a rise in the birth rate, and (*b*) because a decline in the death rate would have a marked effect on growth of population, whereas the effect of an independent increase in the birth rate would have been relatively small.

Our object in the present communication is to consider reasons for the decline of mortality during the nineteenth century. A great deal has been written about this subject and we shall begin by summarizing the evidence and indicating the ways in which it is considered to be deficient. There have been three main lines of enquiry:

(*a*) *Consideration of the diseases associated with the decline of mortality*

Cause of death has been registered in England and Wales since 1837, and at first sight it might be thought that whatever the difficulties before that date, it would be a relatively simple matter to follow the subsequent trend of mortality attributable to a specific disease. Difficulty arises because of vagueness and inaccuracy of diagnosis and changes in nomenclature. Gross examples are the confusion between scarlet fever and diphtheria until 1855, the identification of typhus with typhoid until 1869, and the uncertainty about a diagnosis such as tuberculosis at a time when it was not possible to X-ray the chest or recognize the infective organism. Even the less exacting task—which has a particular relevance to the present discussion—of separating infectious from non-infectious causes of death presents difficulties. For example, deaths attributed to diseases of the heart and nervous system include a considerable but unknown number due to infectious diseases such as rheumatic fever, syphilis, and meningitis.

In spite of these difficulties several attempts have been made to determine which diseases contributed to the decline of mortality during the second half of the nineteenth century. Longstaff[2] examined the trend between 1861–70 and 1876–80 and later extended the examination to 1888. He concluded that the decline during this period was due mainly to reduced mortality from typhus and tuberculosis, and to a lesser extent from scarlet fever, smallpox, diarrhoeal diseases, diphtheria, and measles. Phillips[3] conducted a similar inquiry for the period 1851 to 1905, and again underlined the diminished mortality from typhus, smallpox, whooping cough, typhoid, scarlet fever, tuberculosis, and diphtheria. A much later paper by Gale[4] was concerned with mortality under the age of 15 between 1841 and 1943. But the most comprehensive investigation was that of Logan[5] who examined in considerable detail the changes in causes of death between 1848 and 1947. His data for 1848–72 and 1901–10 cover approximately the period in which we are interested.

Although these reports have varied in their objectives and in the period covered, they leave no doubt about the predominant contribution of the infectious diseases to the decline of mortality. What they do not attempt is a more precise assessment of the contribution of specific diseases or of any group of diseases such as the infections.

(b) Examination of reasons for the decline of mortality from specific diseases

The present status of opinion on this subject can be summarized most readily by considering in turn each of the main diseases. Those discussed below were, with certain ill-defined causes of death, the ones associated with the decline of mortality during the nineteenth century.

Tuberculosis: Mortality attributed to tuberculosis has declined at least since the time that causes of death were first registered. Almost everyone who has considered reasons for the decline has agreed (i) that until recently, and certainly during the nineteenth century, specific preventive or curative therapy had no effect, (ii) that there is little evidence of a change in the character of the tubercle bacillus, and (iii) that an important influence was the progressive improvement in the standard of living.[6] The point on which there has been some difference of opinion is the effect of selection. Burnet considered that the elimination of susceptible individuals must have had a profound influence on the history of the disease, whereas Springett attached less importance to it.

Typhus: Long before there was any knowledge of its origin or means of spread, it was known that typhus occurred in association with war and famine. The new knowledge which followed the discovery that the body louse was the vector has not disturbed the conclusion which was evident for centuries: that the most effective means of preventing the disease was avoidance of a low standard of living. Since there is no reason to suppose that the character of the disease changed, or that specific treatment was effective, it has been concluded that the virtual elimination of typhus from England and Wales was due to an improvement in the standard of living.[7]

Typhoid: There has been no serious difference of opinion about the reasons for the decline of typhoid. It is attributed to improvements in water supply and other sanitary measures such as efficient sewage disposal and protection of food.[8]

Scarlet Fever: It is widely accepted that the most important influence, perhaps the only important influence, was a change in the nature of scarlet fever, due to a reduction in the virulence of the organism or an increase in the resistance of the host, or, possibly, to both.[9] The main reason for this unanimity of opinion is that the character of the disease changed dramatically during relatively short periods of time. The rapidity of the changes, their independence of specific measures, and their inconsistent relationship to environmental progress has all been considered to suggest that variation in the virulence of the infective organism and of resistance to it, were the only important reasons for the decline of scarlet fever as a cause of mortality since the third quarter of the nineteenth century.

Cholera: Experience of cholera was different from that of the other diseases which we have been considering, for although it was an important cause of death in the nineteenth century, the mortality was limited to pandemics which spread to Europe from India. The interpretation of the epidemiology of cholera is complex in those areas where it is endemic, but there is less difficulty in explaining its disappearance from Western Europe. (The last two world-wide pandemics in the nineteenth century did not reach the West.) The elimination of cholera as of typhoid, is attributed confidently to improvements in water supply and other sanitary measures.[10]

Smallpox: Because of the controversy concerning the efficacy of vaccination, smallpox has possibly been discussed more in this context than any other single disease. Opinions about vaccination have differed widely. Creighton[11] thought that it made no contribution, whereas Edwardes[12] regarded it as almost the sole reason for the decline of mortality. Most writers have accepted neither of these extreme views: they have accorded to vaccination a large part in the disappearance of smallpox, but have concluded that some other influence, probably a change in the character of the disease itself, must also have contributed substantially.[13]

(c) *Assessment of the relative importance of influences which may have affected mortality*

Interpretation of the contribution of different influences to the decline of mortality has been impeded hitherto by: exaggeration of the part played by preventive and curative therapy; the practice of grouping together as 'medical advances' such different elements as specific therapy and the environmental measures introduced under the sanitary revolution; and failure to consider separately trends in the nineteenth and early twentieth centuries.

(i) Since Talbot Griffith's assessment[14] of the importance of medical measures in the eighteenth century was widely accepted until recently, it is scarcely surprising that they should also have been judged effective in the nineteenth. Indeed, if one were prepared to accept increase of medical knowledge as evidence of public benefit, the grounds for doing so are incomparably stronger. It was in the nineteenth century that disease processes began to be understood, first because of the work of the morbid anatomists, and later through recognition of the bacterial origin of infectious diseases. The discovery of anaesthesia greatly increased the possibilities of surgery and knowledge of antisepsis added to its safety. But there could be no better indication of the interval between discovery and application of medical knowledge than the fact that in the golden age of bacteriology, and many years after the identification of the first infective organism, vaccination against smallpox was still the only effective procedure in general use. Reasons will be given for believing it to be the only therapeutic measure which made any contribution to the control of infectious disease in the nineteenth century. And since the improvement was wholly in respect of the infections, it was also the only therapeutic measure which made any significant impact on mortality.

(ii) The practice of grouping as 'medical advances' both therapy and environmental measures is undesirable not only because the latter were by no means exclusively the work of medical men. These two classes of influence differ grossly in their nature and effectiveness, and for interpretation of trends in the nineteenth century it is essential that they should be considered separately.

(iii) When discussing reasons for the decline of mortality most writers have examined the interval between registration (or shortly after) and the time at which they were writing. Hence they have usually been concerned with influences in both the nineteenth and twentieth centuries. The disadvantages of this approach are self-evident. The task of interpretation becomes incomparably more complex after 1900 when social and personal health services were introduced and some forms of effective therapy became available. It therefore seems essential to clarify our ideas about events in the nineteenth century before considering the still more complex problems presented by the twentieth.

In the first part of the discussion which follows we examine the trend of the death rate during the nineteenth century, and in the second part we assess the relative importance of the different diseases which contributed to the decline. In the third section we discuss reasons for the reduction of mortality from the most significant diseases. Finally we attempt to relate the considerable amount that is known about the diseases which declined and the reasons for their decline to the much less conclusive evidence concerning the nature and timing of improvements in the environment in the nineteenth century.

(1) THE TREND OF MORTALITY

Our knowledge of the birth rate and death rate in the first four decades of the nineteenth century is in the same unsatisfactory state as in the eighteenth century. All that can be said with certainty is that the population was rising, and that the increase was attributable in large part to an excess of births over deaths established before 1800 and maintained thereafter. Whether this excess was due primarily to a rise in the birth rate or a decline in the death rate is still regarded as an open question. McKeown and Brown[15] gave reasons for believing the death rate to have been the more important influence. It should perhaps be stressed that this view did not rest on evaluation of statistical data. Indeed, a recent full discussion[16] of the period 1781–1850 makes us more than ever doubtful whether the trend of mortality and natality before registration can be settled by consideration of numerical evidence. The data are so treacherous that they can be interpreted to fit any hypothesis, and it seems preferable to rely on assessment of the sensitivity of birth rate and death rate, and their relative effectiveness in promoting population growth, in a period when both rates were high. We shall not attempt to discuss further the trend of mortality in the pre-registration years.

Since 1837 knowledge of the birth rate and the death rate of England and Wales has been available from national sources. Although registration was incomplete in the early years, the data leave no doubt that until the eighth decade, the growth of population was due to the excess of births over deaths established before 1837 (that is to say there was no marked change in either rate) and that from about 1880, when the birth rate began to fall, the continued increase in population was attributable chiefly to a further decline of mortality. These data have been readily accessible for more than half a century, and we shall refer only to features which provide an essential background for the discussion which follows.

Fig. 1 shows the trend of mortality in England and Wales in the last six decades of the nineteenth century, as indicated by (*a*) the crude death rate, and (*b*) the death rate standardized to correspond with the age structure of the population of 1901. The fact that the decline is more marked for the

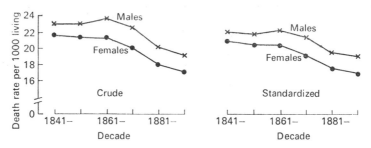

Fig. 1. *Mean Annual Death Rates in England and Wales (1841–1900)*

crude than for the standardized rate shows that part of the reduction in the crude death rate is attributable to a change in the age structure of the population. (Mainly because of the fall of the birth rate, the population in the last two decades was older than that in the first four. And since mortality was high at the youngest age groups, correction for age reduces the estimate of mortality in the early decades.) Nevertheless, in the present context it would be misleading to refer only to the age-standardized rates, since the change in age structure of the population is one of the considerations which must be kept in view. Both the crude and the standardized rates show two features which concern us here: after registration of births and deaths mortality did not begin to decline until the eighth decade; and mortality was consistently higher for males than for females.

The only other point with which we are concerned in this section is the relationship between mortality and age. From 1841 mortality rates are available for ten-year age groups, but because of the significance of mortality in infancy it seems desirable to examine the first five years separately. Infant mortality is recorded from 1841, but the rates at ages 1, 2, 3, and 4 are not given before 1861, presumably because the census returns for these ages were not reliable. (In fact there are errors throughout the nineteenth century in these age groups; for example, the number of children aged 2 is shown as consistently greater than the number aged 1.) However, the number of deaths at ages 1, 2, 3, and 4 is given, and we have estimated the related populations for the decades 1841–50 and 1851–60 graphically by interpolation from census data.

Fig. 2 shows (*a*) that in certain age groups (approximately from ages 3 to 34) mortality had begun to decline before the eighth decade (this fact is obscured when all ages are considered together), and (*b*) the reduction of mortality between 1841–50 and 1891–1900 was greatest at ages at which mortality was lowest in 1841–50. There was no improvement in infant mortality, or in mortality at ages 45–74. (We have not included data for ages over 75, which do show a slight decline of mortality, probably attributable to errors in registration at late ages.)

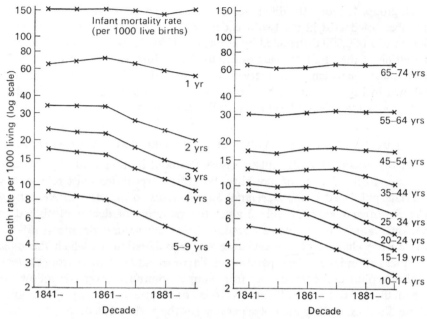

Fig. 2. *Mean Annual Death Rates according to Age (1841–1900)*

Fig. 2 is on a logarithmic scale, and does not, of course, show the relative contribution of different age groups to the total decline of mortality. The contribution of an age group is determined by three things: the number of individuals in it, the level of mortality, and the rate of decline of mortality.

Table I. *Mortality in 1841–50 and 1891–1900 based on a population of 1,000,000 distributed by age as the 1891–1900 population*

Age	Number alive	Mean annual number of deaths		Difference a–b	Percentage distribution of difference
		1841–50 (a)	1891–1900 (b)		
0–	118,520	7,822	6,839	983	27·8
5–	112,289	1,016	487	529	15·0
10–	107,071	566	269	297	8·4
15–	100,800	754	376	378	10·7
20–	93,525	869	443	426	12·1
25–	156,097	1,608	999	609	17·2
35–	118,688	1,531	1,246	285	8·1
45–	87,609	1,489	1,471	18	0·5
55–	58,396	1,746	1,839	−93	−2·6
65–	33,622	2,138	2,185	−47	−1·3
75 and over	13,383	2,185	2,037	148	4·2
Total	1,000,000	21,724	18,191	3,533	100·0

Table 1 gives a more accurate impression of the number of lives saved in each group. It shows the difference at various ages between the mean annual numbers of deaths in the two decades 1841–50 and 1891–1900, in a population of 1,000,000 distributed by age as the 1891–1900 population. The contribution of the first five years of life to the decline was greater than that of any subsequent ten-year interval, because although the rate of decline (shown in Fig. 2 by the use of a log scale) was not as marked as in older age groups the original level of mortality was much higher.

(2) DISEASES ASSOCIATED WITH THE DECLINE OF MORTALITY

In this section we attempt to assess the contribution made by different diseases to the decline of mortality. For this purpose we must rely mainly on data published in the *Decennial Supplements to the Annual Reports of the Registrar General*. Table 2 gives the numbers of deaths attributed to various causes in successive decades. After the second decade (1861–70) there were changes of nomenclature and classification, of which the most obvious examples are the separation of diarrhoea and dysentery from cholera, and of typhus and enteric fever from simple continued fever. To follow the trend throughout the half-century it is, of course, necessary to combine these diseases, as they are not separable for the earlier decades.

The chief difficulty in interpreting these data is due to uncertainty about the reliability of death certification. It is particularly serious because during the period understanding of the nature of infectious disease—with which we shall be almost exclusively concerned—was revolutionized by the work of the bacteriologists. Nevertheless, the significance of this work in relation to diagnosis between 1851–60, when little was known, and 1891–1900, when a good deal was known, is not as great as might be thought. Many of the infectious diseases—e.g. smallpox, scarlet fever, whooping cough—were fairly clearly identified on clinical grounds, and medical experience of them was then much greater than it is today. And in a disease such as tuberculosis, which was less sharply differentiated by clinical assessment, the methods of examination (radiology and identification of the tubercle bacillus) which were later to prove invaluable were not in general use during the nineteenth century. No useful purpose would be served by full discussion of the limitations of the data in Table 2, and we shall reserve our comment to a later stage, and restrict it to diseases found to be significant in the present context.

(a) Diseases which declined

Fig. 3 shows the trend of mortality attributable to (i) certain infectious diseases: smallpox; measles; scarlet fever; diphtheria; whooping cough; diarrhoea, dysentery, and cholera; typhus, enteric fever, and simple continued fever; and all forms of tuberculosis, and (ii) other causes. Under (i) are in-

Table 2. *Mean annual crude mortality rates (per 1,000,000 living) from certain causes in successive decennia, 1851–1900*

Cause (applicable to 1851–70)	1851–	1861–	1871–	1881–	1891–	Cause (applicable to 1871–1900)
Smallpox	222	163	240	45	13	Smallpox
Measles	412	440	380	440	414	Measles
Scarlet fever	876	971	720	334	158	Scarlet fever
Diphtheria	109	184	120	163	263	Diphtheria
Whooping cough	504	528	510	450	377	Whooping cough
Diarrhoea and Dysentery } Cholera }	1,080	1,076	940 { 910 { 30	674 { 659 { 15	738 { 713 { 25	Diarrhoea and Dysentery Cholera
Typhus } Enteric fever } Simple continued fever }	908	885	490 ⎰ 60 | 320 | 110	235 { 14 | 196 | 25	182 { 2 | 174 | 6	Typhus Enteric fever Simple continued fever
Tuberculosis— respiratory	2,679	2,475	2,126	1,731	1,391	Tuberculosis—respiratory
Tuberculosis— other forms	789	767	753	701	621	Tuberculosis—other forms
Diseases of the brain	2,740	2,785	2,770	2,592	2,171	Diseases of nervous system
Dropsy and diseases of the heart	1,247	1,349	1,310	1,576	1,657	Diseases of circulatory system
Diseases of the lungs	3,020	3,365	3,760	3,729	3,409	Diseases of respiratory system
Diseases of the stomach and liver	1,004	981	980	1,104	1,193	Diseases of digestive system
Diseases of the kidneys	214	298	390	435	461	Diseases of urinary system
Other causes	6,361	6,148	5,781	4,871	5,146	Other causes
Total	22,165	22,415	21,270	19,080	18,194	

Source: Tuberculosis statistics from data published in the *Report of the Ministry of Health for the Year ended 31st March, 1949* (Cmd. 7910), H.M.S.O.

All other statistics from successive *Decennial Supplements* to the *Annual Reports of the Registrar General of Births, Deaths and Marriages in England*.

cluded all infections which can be identified in Table 2; under (ii) are un-doubtedly some deaths from infections such as syphilis, rheumatic fever, and tuberculosis in which the primary cause of death was not certified. Nevertheless, it seems unquestionable that the decline of mortality between 1851–60 and 1891–1900 was attributable almost exclusively to a reduction in the frequency of death from infectious disease, and we shall not go far wrong if we base our investigation on the recognized infections listed under (i). To allow for changes in age structure of the population the mean annual mortality rates shown in Fig. 3 were standardized in relation to the 1901 population.

Fig. 4 shows the secular trend of mortality attributed to each of the eight

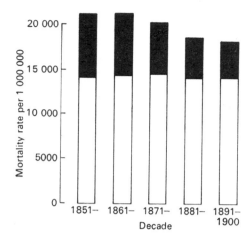

Fig. 3. *Mean Annual Mortality Rates, Standardized to Age and Sex Distribution of the 1901 Population* (Shaded areas represent deaths due to certain communicable diseases (specified in Fig. 4); unshaded areas represent deaths due to other causes)

specified infections or groups of infections. The data are again age-standard-ized. They leave no doubt that much the largest contribution to the reduction of mortality was made by tuberculosis, and that the decline was almost restricted to five of the eight disease groups. There was little reduction in deaths due to whooping cough, none in deaths due to measles, and an appreciable rise in those attributed to diphtheria.

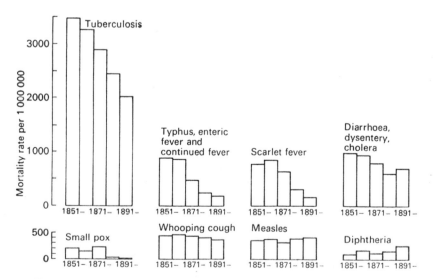

Fig. 4. *Mean Annual Mortality Rates due to certain communicable Diseases* (Standardized to Age and Sex Distribution of 1901 Population)

We have attempted to give more meaning to these estimates by a comparison of the mean annual mortality rates (per million of population) in the decades 1851–60 and 1891–1900 (Table 3). Of the lives saved the proportions attributable to each of the major diseases (or groups of diseases) were as follows: tuberculosis (all forms), 47·2 per cent; typhus, enteric fever, and simple continued fever, 22·9 per cent; scarlet fever, 20·3 per cent; diarrhoea, dysentery, and cholera, 8·9 per cent; smallpox, 6·1 per cent; and whooping cough 2·3 per cent.

Table 3. *Mean annual mortality rates per 1,000,000 living (standardized*) due to certain communicable diseases in decennia 1851–60 and 1891–1900*

Cause	1851–60 (a)	1891–1900 (b)	Difference (a)–(b)	Difference per cent of total difference (a–b) 100 / 3085
Tuberculosis—respiratory	2,772	1,418	1,354	43·9 } 47·2
Tuberculosis—other forms	706	603	103	3·3
Typhus, enteric fever, simple continued fever	891	184	707	22·9
Scarlet fever	779	152	627	20·3
Diarrhoea, Dysentery, Cholera	990	715	275	8·9
Smallpox	202	13	189	6·1
Whooping cough	433	363	70	2·3
Measles	357	398	−41	−1·3
Diphtheria	99	254	−155	−5·0
Other causes	13,980	14,024	−44	−1·4
Total	21,209	18,124	3,085	100

* Standardized to age and sex distribution of 1901 population.

In the remainder of this discussion we shall restrict attention to the first five of these disease groups, excluding whooping cough from which the contribution to the total reduction of mortality was trivial.

(b) Contribution of specified communicable diseases to reduction of mortality at different ages

Fig. 5 shows the contribution of the five groups of communicable diseases (those which contributed substantially to the decline of mortality) to the trend of mortality (1851–60 to 1891–1900) at different ages. To simplify the presentation the data are given in four age-periods within each of which the trend is reasonably consistent. In the first period (0–4 years) there was a substantial reduction in mortality from the infections and a much smaller reduction in the death rate from other causes. Results in the second period (5–34 years) are similar but the number of deaths in 1851–60 (and hence the contribution to the total reduction in mortality) was very much smaller than in the younger age group. In the third period (35–54 years) mortality from the communicable diseases decreased but this was largely offset by an increase in deaths due to other causes. In the last age period (55 years and over) mortality from infections also decreased but a substantial increase in other deaths resulted in an over-all increase of mortality in the age group.

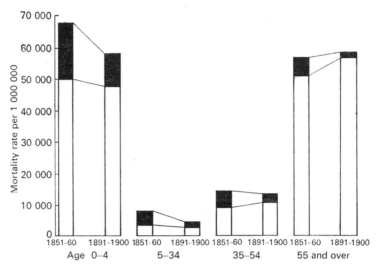

Fig. 5. *Standardized Mortality Rates in different Age Groups distinguishing between certain communicable Diseases* (shaded) and Other Causes (unshaded): 1851–60 and 1891–1900*

* Tuberculosis, Typhus, Enteric Fever, Scarlet Fever, Diarrhoea, Dysentery, Cholera, and Smallpox

In Fig. 6 the examination is restricted to the five groups of communicable diseases for which the trend of mortality between 1851–60 and 1891–1900 is shown separately according to age. Here it has been considered desirable to use a finer age grouping than in Fig. 5. The most notable features are: (*a*) the substantial reduction of mortality in all age groups from tuberculosis and from the typhus enteric group of fevers; (*b*) the substantial reduction of mortality in childhood from scarlet fever; (*c*) the reduction of mortality from the diarrhoeal diseases in the older age groups but not in young children (aged 0–4 years) for whom it remained a very important cause of death; and (*d*) the decline of mortality from smallpox, most marked at ages 0–4 and 5–9 (inevitably, for the death rate from the disease was highest at these ages in 1851–60).

(c) *Reliability of death certification*

We must now inquire whether it is likely that these estimates are much influenced by changes in death certification. The question is most serious in the case of tuberculosis, because of its large contribution to the reduction of mortality. The most likely possibility is a transfer of deaths, attributed in the earlier decades to respiratory tuberculosis, to other forms of respiratory disease. The figures exhibited in Table 2 make it unlikely that this could explain more than a small part of the total reduction. Between 1851–60 and 1891–1900 the deaths per million from other forms of respiratory disease increased by approximately 400; in the same period the deaths from respir-

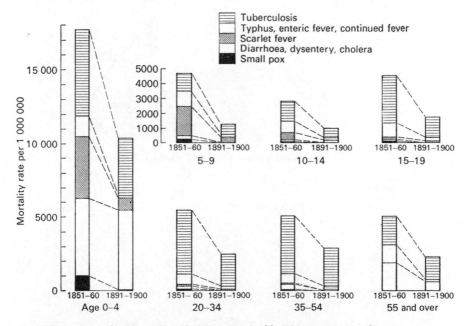

Fig. 6. *Contribution of Specified Communicable Diseases to Mortality Rates at Different Ages in 1851–60 and 1891–1900*

atory tuberculosis fell by 1,300. Even if the whole of the increase were attributable to false certification, it could account for less than one-third of the reduction of tuberculosis mortality.

Further suggestive evidence is available from a comparison of age-specific mortality due to tuberculosis (all forms) in 1851–60 and 1891–1900 (Figs. 7 and 8). If there had been a substantial transfer of deaths to other causes of respiratory death, a considerable reduction of mortality in middle and late life might have been expected (because the disease with which tuberculosis is readily confused—chronic bronchitis—is most common in these age groups). In fact the most marked reduction of mortality in both sexes was in the twenties and early thirties.

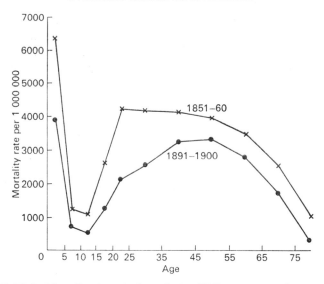

Fig. 7. *Male Mortality from Tuberculosis (All Forms) According to Age*

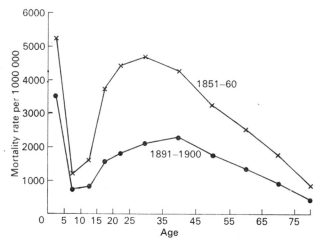

Fig. 8. *Female Mortality from Tuberculosis (All Forms) According to Age*

(3) REASONS FOR THE DECLINE OF MORTALITY FROM SPECIFIC DISEASES

We must now consider reasons for the decline of mortality from the five diseases, or in two cases disease groups, shown to be responsible for the improvement during the second half of the nineteenth century. They will be discussed in order of relative importance. The first disease   tuberculosis— accounted for nearly half of the reduction of the death rate between 1851 and 1900 and the first three—tuberculosis, the typhoid–typhus group, and scarlet fever—accounted for about nine-tenths.

TUBERCULOSIS

In an interpretation of the decline of mortality in the nineteenth century, tuberculosis is even more significant than its large contribution would inevitably make it. For while we can be fairly confident about the time of onset and cause of the decline of the other important infectious diseases (discussed below), in the case of tuberculosis both are in doubt. Moreover, interpretation of the behaviour of tuberculosis raises again the central questions related to eighteenth-century population growth. On balance, were the changes associated with the early phases of the Industrial Revolution favourable to health? Or can the decline of mortality be attributed wholly to a fortuitous shift in the precarious balance between the virulence of infective organisms and the defences of the human host? It is not too much to say that the reason for the decline of mortality from tuberculosis is one of the most important issues in respect of the improvement in health and rise of population before the twentieth century.

(a) The trend of mortality

Mortality from tuberculosis declined from about the time when cause of death was first registered. The consistent trend after 1851 was exhibited in Fig. 4, but Fig. 9 (based on deaths from respiratory tuberculosis) shows that it was already well established in the fifth decade when mortality fell by about one-quarter. There can therefore be no serious doubt that the decline began at least thirty years earlier than in the case of other major infectious diseases.

Experience of tuberculosis in the pre-registration period is much less certain. From literary evidence, as well as from the slender statistical data, it has been concluded that mortality from the disease was consistently high for several centuries, and attempts have been made to assess the trend from the early seventeenth century when causes of death were first given in the London Bills of Mortality.[17] The main grounds for reservation in accepting this evidence are:

(i) Cause of death was based on the opinion of non-medical observers (particularly in the early years), or of medical observers even less well informed than in the nineteenth century. Other wasting diseases must often have been included and the Bills have been criticized for overstating the number of tuberculous deaths.

(ii) Related populations from which the deaths were drawn were unknown, and it was necessary to express deaths from tuberculosis as a proportion of all deaths. This procedure makes no allowance for age changes in the related population or for variation in the incidence of other causes of death.

(iii) The London data given in the Bills cannot be assumed to reflect experience of the disease in the country as a whole.

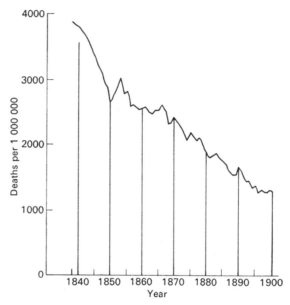

Fig. 9. *Secular Trend in Mortality from Consumption or Phthisis*

It is hardly surprising that different conclusions have been drawn from this evidence. Farr believed that the relative importance of tuberculosis increased until 1810, but that the death rate from the disease declined. Brownlee thought that mortality increased during the eighteenth century and considered that there had been 'a long epidemic wave of phthisis which reached a maximum in the early years of the nineteenth century'. Greenwood concluded 'that no great changes of mortality from phthisis occurred between the end of the Stuart period and the beginning of the nineteenth century—certainly no improvement'. Our own view is that there can be no serious doubt that mortality from tuberculosis was very high during the seventeenth and eighteenth centuries but the evidence—which is unlikely to become any better—does not justify a firm opinion about variation within this period. In particular, there are no adequate grounds for the concept of an epidemic wave.

We are on slightly firmer ground in concluding that mortality from tuberculosis decreased in the first third of the nineteenth century. The fact that it did so as early as the fifth decade (Fig. 9) is suggestive, but it is possible, for reasons discussed below, that the first national registration of causes of death roughly coincided with the beginning of a reduction of the death rate. However, the exact time at which mortality from tuberculosis began to decline is not essential in the present context (fortunately, for it is unlikely that it will ever be known). The important point is that it declined from about the time when registration began, at least three decades earlier than in the case of the other causes of death which contributed substantially to the total reduction in mortality during the nineteenth century.

(b) Reasons for the decline of mortality

We shall consider the possible causes of a decline in mortality from the infectious diseases under the three headings: specific preventive or curative therapy; a change in the balance between the virulence of the infective organism and the resistance of the host; and improvements in the environment. It will be easier to assess the relative importance of these influences in the case of tuberculosis, if we first give the dates of the most significant advances in methods related to the disease:

1882   Identification of the tubercle bacillus.
1922   The first Ministry of Health Order concerned with pasteurization of milk.
1947   Introduction of chemotherapy.
1954   Substantial use of vaccination in England and Wales.

It is clear that specific therapy contributed nothing to the decline of mortality from tuberculosis during the nineteenth century. Even the therapeutic measures introduced about 1920 (collapse therapy) were of little value and it was not until the middle of the present century that effective methods (chemotherapy and B.C.G. vaccination) came into general use. Our main task is therefore to assess the importance of the second and third of the three groups of causes listed above.

Is it likely that much of the decline of mortality during the early nineteenth century was due to a change in the virulence of the tubercle bacillus or of man's response to it? Before attempting to answer this question let us consider some relevant points about which there would be little dispute.

(1) The relationship between an infective organism and its host is a changing one which reflects the influence of nature and nurture on both.

(2) The stability of the relationship varies considerably between different organisms. It is relatively much more stable in the case of the tubercle bacillus than in that of the haemolytic streptococcus.

(3) The effects of the tubercle bacillus on populations not previously exposed to the disease, as well as tests on experimental animals, provide no evidence of a reduction in its virulence during the period in which it has been examined critically.

(4) The main question is therefore whether the decline of mortality was due to an increase in man's genetic resistance to the bacillus.

Both twin evidence and the response of populations not previously exposed leave no doubt that susceptibility to tuberculosis is in a considerable degree genetically determined. But it does not follow that the trend of mortality during the nineteenth century was due to genetic selection. As Brownlee[18] and Springett[19] have noted, the effect of selection is maximal after first exposure, and it is not easy to see how it could account for a dramatic change in a population which had been exposed to the disease for several centuries. Theoretically, however, there are two ways in which selection might have contributed.

(i) The break-up of isolates. This possibility was discussed by Dahlberg:[20]

If susceptibility to tuberculosis is conditioned by recessive genes, the break-up of isolates should cause the disease to become more infrequent, since the frequency of allelic genes in duplicate doses thereby decreases. Another way of expressing the same thing is to say that the break-up of isolates decreases the frequency of consanguineous marriages, and thereby also the frequency of homozygotes.

Such a mechanism must clearly have played some part, particularly in countries with a more highly developed and extensive industry where cities have grown at the expense of the rural population.

While the break-up of isolates may have made some contribution to the reduction of mortality from rare conditions, it seems very unlikely to have had much effect in a disease as common as tuberculosis. Indeed, if the dispersal of rural populations was significant, it is the second possibility which must be considered more seriously.

(ii) The effect of selection in rural populations not previously exposed. Is it conceivable that although tuberculosis was common in England and Wales during the seventeenth and eighteenth centuries, a large part of the rural population had not been exposed to the disease and that the decline of mortality during the nineteenth century largely reflected the effects of selection in those meeting the disease for the first time? This explanation rests on three assumptions:

(1) That until the Industrial Revolution a substantial proportion of the rural population had not been exposed to the disease. There is no evidence on this point.

(2) That improved communications and the movement into the towns resulted in first exposure and death of many susceptible individuals. The movement into towns was not at the right time nor of sufficient magnitude to be consistent with this interpretation. Approximately from the beginning of registration of cause of death the decline of mortality from tuberculosis was very rapid; it fell by one-quarter in the fifth decade. To have contributed

largely to this change selection would have had to operate in respect of almost the whole population at least thirty years earlier. Yet by 1801 only 16·9 per cent (by 1831, 25 per cent) of the population of England and Wales were living in towns with 20,000 or more people.

(3) That mortality from the disease increased sharply in the late eighteenth and early nineteenth centuries. Again, the statistical data are quite inadequate. But to have had a selective effect of the requisite dimensions the rise in mortality would have to have been very great indeed. Moreover, its subsequent decline would be only in respect of the newly exposed population and would certainly not be expected to continue to or below the level of the early eighteenth century (the level determined by that part of the population which had been exposed to the disease for centuries).

We therefore conclude that genetic selection is most unlikely to have been the main reason for the trend of mortality from tuberculosis in the nineteenth century.

There are also general considerations which seem to us to point to the same conclusion. Our assessment of reasons for the decline of mortality of the other four major disease groups (discussed below) suggests that only in the case of smallpox, and therefore to a small extent, did therapy make any contribution. In the typhus and cholera groups the improvement was due chiefly to the specific measures of environmental control introduced in the mid-nineteenth century and effective from the eighth decade, and in scarlet fever it resulted from a change in relationship between the infective organism and the human host. This means that if the trend of mortality from tuberculosis is also attributed to this last cause, two-thirds of the reduction of the death rate in the nineteenth century (the proportion for which tuberculosis and scarlet fever were together responsible) was due to a shift in the balance between virulence of infective organisms and man's resistance. And this shift must have been either independent of environmental change (as in the case of scarlet fever it appears to have been) or a by-product of the worsening conditions created by the Industrial Revolution (if the trend in tuberculosis was due to selection which followed increased exposure of the rural population). Hence if we accept the premiss, we are forced to the conclusion that wholly until 1870, and largely until 1900, the decline of mortality from infectious disease, which we believe to have been the reason for the rise of population in the eighteenth century as it undoubtedly was in the nineteenth, was independent of the profound environmental changes brought about by the Industrial Revolution, or was a most improbable consequence of its worst features. These considerations seem to us to provide further support for the view that genetic selection was not the main reason for the decline of mortality from tuberculosis.

We have so far considered grounds for not accepting genetic selection as the main cause of the decline of mortality from tuberculosis. Let us now inquire whether improvements in the environment were more important. Enough is known about the disease to suggest that there are only a few features of the environment which could be expected to have much influence. They are: conditions of exposure to the infection; diet; and—more doubt-fully—physical and mental stress. We can be fairly confident that in a period when mortality from tuberculosis was very high, a substantial im-provement in at least the first two of these features would result in a decline of mortality.

Before considering these possibilities we must examine more critically the behaviour of tuberculosis mortality in the years following registration. Two questions are particularly relevant: Was mortality falling when registra-tion began? And could the remarkable decline during the fifth decade be due largely to changes in death certification?

Table 4 gives the annual mortality rates attributable to various forms of respiratory disease. (Populations for each year were obtained by interpolation from the 1831, 1841, and 1851 censuses.) The unfortunate gap in the death records from 1843 to 1846 makes interpretation more difficult. But the figures

Table 4. *Mortality from respiratory diseases in the years following registration (crude death rates per million, England and Wales)*

	1838	1839	1840	1841	1842	1843–46	1847	1848	1849	1850
Phthisis	3,856	3,840	3,831	3,745	3,678	—	3,114	2,983	2,869	2,629
Bronchitis	135	107	131	142	163	—	964	863	846	824
Hydrothorax	151	139	149	143	132	—	—	—	—	—
Pleurisy	38	38	45	42	45	—	69	59	55	49
Pneumonia	1,176	1,170	1,183	1,131	1,181	—	1,370	1,263	1,208	1,145
Asthma	375	334	368	376	349	—	377	226	235	258
Other lung diseases	168	164	174	175	183	—	162	153	149	136
Scrofula	73	74	84	75	80	—	140	136	156	140
Tabes mesenterica	47	46	66	67	80	—	268	252	253	226

show no decline in mortality from phthisis in the first three years, and only a small one before 1842. Moreover, in this period deaths from other causes with which the disease might be confused were reasonably constant. Be-tween 1842 and 1847 phthisis mortality fell from 3,678 deaths per million to 3,114; but deaths attributed to bronchitis increased by an even greater amount. On this evidence, therefore, we cannot say confidently that the death rate from respiratory tuberculosis fell before 1847. But after this date the facts are not in doubt. Mortality declined to 2,629 in 1850 and in the pre-ceding four years death rates from bronchitis (and other forms of respiratory disease) were also falling.

So far as they go the data suggest: (i) that mortality from tuberculosis fell only slightly between 1838 and 1842; (ii) that the apparent decline between 1842 and 1847 may have been due largely to changes in certification (especially from tuberculosis to bronchitis); and (iii) that the reduction between 1847 and 1850 was probably genuine. The best judgement we can make on this treacherous evidence is therefore that mortality was falling, certainly from 1847, and possibly from 1840. The fact that the statistics do not show that it was doing so in three previous years should make us cautious in acepting a decline in the earlier years of the nineteenth century.

Against this background we can now attempt to assess the importance of the four features of the environment to which we referred. In spite of vast clinical experience the significance of physical and mental stress in tuberculosis is still in doubt. Rest has long been a feature of treatment but there is no evidence of its effectiveness which would meet present-day standards. There is, moreover, good evidence that in afebrile patients given antibiotics, rest has little influence on the results of treatment.[21] But whatever the effect of physical and mental stress on the course of the disease there is no reason to suppose that they were greatly reduced during the nineteenth century. It therefore seems permissible to conclude that changes in these elements of the environment are unlikely to have contributed substantially to the decline of mortality.

Frequency and amount of exposure to infection are of first-rate importance and the only question is whether they changed significantly. Infection occurs mainly at home or at work and is determined, not by general hygienic conditions, such as water supply and sewage disposal, but by crowding. New building of houses did little more than keep pace with the increase in the size of the population, and the number of persons per house decreased only slightly (from 5·6 in 1801 to 5·3 in 1871).[22] Exposure to infection at work must have increased during the first half of the nineteenth century[23] and it is unlikely that it was reduced significantly before its end.

In discussing the trend of mortality from tuberculosis Newsholme[24] also concluded that improvements in housing were unimportant but he attached considerable significance to segregation of patients in sanatoria. While this may well have been significant in the twentieth century, it can hardly have been so in the nineteenth. By 1900 only a few sanatoria had been provided under voluntary auspices or by progressive local authorities, and most patients were still admitted to the beds of the Poor Law infirmaries. This is scarcely surprising when we recall that the infectious nature of the disease was not established until 1882.

Even on the significance of the fourth feature of the environment to which we have referred, opinion is by no means unanimous. Burnet[25] states that 'the importance of adequate nutrition in the prevention and cure of tuberculosis has probably been grossly overstated in the past', whereas Greenwood[26] concluded 'that a principal determinant of mortality from tuberculosis is nutrition'. For although there is general agreement that standard of living has a profound influence on the behaviour of the disease, the precise features which are most important are still in doubt. We can do no more than express a preference (or prejudice) and give grounds for it.

A sharp rise in tuberculosis mortality was associated with both world wars and there is reason to believe that this was due largely to inadequate diet. In Holland during the last war this was the only obvious feature of the environment which deteriorated greatly. Moreover, mortality fell rapidly after the war when the diet improved and while other elements such as housing were unchanged. Data for mental hospitals during the first world war are also impressive. Mortality rose in the absence of any increase in the total hospital population, so that crowding—the other obvious possibility—appears to be eliminated. An investigation during the years 1921–3, showed that mortality from tuberculosis was considerably higher in mental hospitals with dietaries of lowest calorie value than in those with dietaries of highest calorie value.[27]

There is one component of diet—milk—which requires separate consideration in relation to tuberculosis. We can be quite confident that the milk supply was heavily infected throughout the nineteenth century[28] and any considerable increase in consumption would have affected the trend of mortality: (a) by causing more early deaths from the bovine form of the disease; and (b) by affording some degree of protection to those who survived early infection. We must therefore inquire whether there was any considerable increase in milk consumption and in mortality from bovine infection.

Unfortunately the data in respect of the first part of this question are inconclusive.[29] But it is possible to examine the trend of mortality from scrofula and tabes mesenterica, two forms of the disease which are often of bovine origin.[30] Between 1838 and 1850 mortality attributed to scrofula doubled, and in tabes mesenterica the increase was about five-fold (Table 4). Of itself this increase could not account for a very large part of the reduction of the death rate from phthisis in the same period. But the effect of protection afforded to those who survived early bovine infection might well be more substantial. Hence the data suggest that some part of the reduction of phthisis mortality may have been associated with the consumption of infected milk.

Incomplete as it is, the evidence for the nineteenth century is at least consistent with the view that diet was the most significant environmental influence in relation to the trend of mortality from tuberculosis. We cannot be confident that mortality was declining before the fifth decade, and economic historians are divided in their assessment of the standard of living before this time. But there is no serious doubt that conditions had improved considerably by 1850,[31] and a notable feature of the improvement must have been a better diet. The fact that mortality fell rapidly from the time when nutrition improved, and when there is no reason to believe that exposure to infection was reduced, seems to us to provide good grounds for regarding diet as an important influence.

To sum up: tuberculosis accounted for nearly half of the reduction of the death rate in the nineteenth century. Mortality from the disease began to fall in the fifth decade, at least thirty years earlier than in the case of the other major infectious diseases. Experience of the pre-registration period is less certain, although there is no serious doubt that mortality from tuberculosis was very high during the previous three centuries.

It is quite certain that specific therapy, preventive or curative, made no contribution to the course of the disease before the twentieth century. In the case of an infectious disease it is never possible to be confident that there has been no change in the balance between the virulence of the organism and the resistance of the host. But there is reason to believe that there has been no significant variation in the tubercle bacillus. Man's resistance to it is a more difficult issue. The fact that the population has been heavily exposed to the infection for several centuries makes it unlikely that genetic selection could explain the favourable trend in the nineteenth century, unless it resulted from contact with the disease for the first time by a large part of the rural population which had not been exposed previously. The movement into the towns was too late to be consistent with this possibility, which in any case could not have been expected to have so profound and prolonged an effect on the death rate.

Having excluded therapy confidently and genetic selection with reservations (we have concluded only that it is very unlikely to have been the main influence), we are left with changes in the environment as the most acceptable reason for the trend of mortality from tuberculosis. There are four features of the environment to be considered—conditions of exposure to the disease, diet, physical, and mental stress—and in the circumstances of the nineteenth century only the first two of them need be considered seriously. Exposure to infection is determined mainly by crowding at home or at work; it must have increased in the first half of the nineteenth century and was not significantly reduced before its close.

The evidence in respect of diet seems to us to be highly suggestive. The increase in tuberculosis mortality in both world wars is most plausibly attributed to a deterioration of nutrition. And in the nineteenth century the time at which we can be fairly confident that mortality began to decline rapidly—the fifth decade—is also the time when we can be reasonably certain that the standard of living began to improve. But although a better diet is not the only consequence of a higher standard of living, as there was no significant reduction in crowding at home or at work, it is probably the one which is relevant in this context. We conclude that improvement in diet was probably the main cause of the decline of mortality from tuberculosis during the nineteenth century.

TYPHUS, ENTERIC, AND SIMPLE CONTINUED FEVER

Because they were not separated in national statistics before 1871, these ill-assorted diseases which accounted for about 22 per cent of the reduction of mortality in the second half of the nineteenth century were grouped together in our examination of the trend of mortality. But the data are given separately for the last three decades (Table 2). In this period mortality from enteric fever was reduced by about a half and the other two causes of death almost disappeared.

Interpretation of the behaviour of typhus is complicated by the fact that its prevalence varied greatly at different periods, and it is impossible to say to what extent this was attributable to environmental or genetic change. Nevertheless, it is generally agreed that the disappearance of the disease from the British Isles, many years before identification of the body louse as the vector,[32] was due largely to an improved standard of living. But although a good deal is now known about the nature of the disease and the way in which it is spread, it is still difficult to assess the relative importance of various features of the environment affected by the standard of living. It seems probable, however, that the two main influences were: (i) improved hygienic standards—particularly an improved water supply and better personal cleanliness—which prevented infection by reducing contact with the louse; and (ii) better diet,[33] which affected the response to infection. The first of these influences would have begun to operate in the eighth decade, and the second somewhat earlier.

Little need be added to the views concerning typhoid fever referred to in the introduction. The spread of the disease is due to defective sanitary arrangements, and the rapid reduction of mortality during the last third of the nineteenth century can be attributed confidently to the specific measures—particularly the improved water supply—introduced at that time.

Continued fever still appears in the international classification, where it refers to pyrexias of unknown origin. In the nineteenth century they must have comprised a very mixed group, including undiagnosed respiratory infections such as tuberculosis, as well as other fevers in which a rash was either absent or unrecognized. In view of the fact that they were not shown separately before 1871 we can only guess about their earlier behaviour. But since the whole group (typhus, enteric, and continued fever) began to decline sharply in the eighth decade, perhaps the most reasonable guess is that the trend was due to the specific hygienic measures which were also responsible for the reduction of mortality from typhus and enteric fever.

SCARLET FEVER

Scarlet fever was responsible for about 19 per cent of the reduction of mortality during the second half of the nineteenth century. Views concerning interpretation of the trend of mortality to which we referred in the introduction, are perhaps more consistent than in the case of any other infectious disease. No specific measures of prevention or treatment were available in the nineteenth century, and the only possibilities are environmental improvement or a change in the nature of the disease.

Scarlet fever was described by Sydenham in 1676 when it was a mild disease. It has since exhibited at least four cycles of severity followed by remission.[34] It was very serious in the late eighteenth century and again in the mid-nineteenth century, when it was at its worst at about 1863. The rapid reduction of mortality in the next forty years is shown in Table 2 but it was still a relatively important cause of death at the beginning of the present century. It has declined progressively, and is today a mild disease.

These changes in the behaviour of scarlet fever appear to have been largely independent of the environmental changes which we have been discussing in relation to the other infections, and there is no reason to differ from the general opinion that they have resulted from a change in the nature of the disease. This change was probably due mainly to variation in the virulence of the haemolytic streptococcus rather than to modification of man's response to it.

CHOLERA, DYSENTERY, AND DIARRHOEA

The bowel infections accounted for about 8 per cent of the reduction of mortality in the second half of the nineteenth century. Although they were grouped in national statistics before 1871 (Table 2), cholera must be distinguished from the endemic diseases referred to as diarrhoea and dysentery. Cholera was not endemic in the British Isles, and was introduced from the continent of Europe at least five times during the nineteenth century,[35] but apparently not before. It is therefore not possible to speak of the reasons for its disappearance with quite the same confidence as in the case of the other causes of death.

But with this reservation there is little doubt about the main reasons for the rapid reduction of mortality from the bowel infections in the late nineteenth century. These diseases are spread mainly by infected water and food, and their decline began in the eighth decade when substantial improvement in hygienic conditions also began. There are no grounds for thinking that either therapy or (with a possible reservation in the case of cholera) modification of the nature of the disease made any impact. We therefore conclude that the reduction of mortality attributable to the decline of bowel infection resulted from the specific measures introduced under the sanitary revolution.

SMALLPOX

The contribution of smallpox (about 6 per cent) to the reduction of mortality during the second half of the nineteenth century was small and the reasons for it are therefore of secondary importance in interpretation of the causes of the total decline. This is the one disease in which a specific measure—vaccination—appears to have made a substantial contribution and the only difficulty is to decide how large it was. Vaccination was made compulsory in 1854 but the law was not enforced until 1871. From that time until 1898 when the conscientious objector's clause was introduced, almost all infants were vaccinated. Over the same period mortality fell sharply (Table 2). However, it must be remembered that there had been considerable variation in mortality from smallpox before 1871, and indeed before the nineteenth century. Nevertheless, the fact that the disease, present for several centuries, virtually disappeared from the time when vaccination became compulsory suggests that this was the main reason for its decline.

DISCUSSION

At first sight the task of accounting for the decline of mortality seems formidable, and it might be doubted whether it is possible to go further than the usual generalizations concerning the combined effects of genetic selection, therapy, sanitary science, and a rising standard of living. The problem becomes somewhat more tractable if attention is restricted to the nineteenth century. In this way we can exclude any contribution from the public social and personal medical services, and from specific therapy other than vaccination against smallpox. And since smallpox was responsible for only a very small part of the reduction of mortality between registration and the end of the century, our task can be narrowed to evaluation of the relative importance of genetic and environmental influences (other than therapy) in that period.

We have examined (Fig. 1) the trend of the death rate in the last six decades, correcting by standardization for the rapidly changing age structure of the population. For the population as a whole the decline began in the eighth decade, but experience was quite different in different age periods. There was no improvement in infant mortality or in mortality at ages over 45 (Fig. 2). But for those aged 3 to 34 the decline had begun before 1870.

We have approached the assessment of reasons for the decline of mortality by considering the contribution of different diseases. Here the chief difficulties are the grouping of certain causes of death in national statistics (which makes it necessary to examine them in groups) and the inevitable doubts about the reliability of diagnosis in a period when knowledge and methods were so limited. The possibility of mistaken diagnosis is most serious in tuberculosis, because of its large contribution to the decline. But so far as we can judge from the limited evidence, a substantial transfer of deaths from tuberculosis to other forms of respiratory disease (the most obvious way in which erroneous diagnosis might have resulted in the appearance of a decline) might have occurred only in the period 1842–7. We have concluded that five diseases or groups of diseases accounted for almost the whole of the reduction of the death rate between 1851–60 and 1891–1900: tuberculosis (45 per cent); typhus, typhoid, and continued fever (22 per cent); scarlet fever (19 per cent); cholera, dysentery, and diarrhoea (8 per cent); and smallpox (6 per cent).[36] Each of these diseases has been considered in turn and we shall now try to bring together our conclusions about the main influences.

Some part of the decline was undoubtedly due to an alteration of the balance between the virulence of the infectious organisms and man's resistance to them. The relationship between an infective agent and its host is a changing one, although the rate of change varies greatly in different diseases. At any time in human history an assessment of the trend of mortality from infections would probably have revealed that in some it was increasing, in others decreasing and in still others more or less constant; the total effect on the death rate at any time depending upon the balance between these trends. Can we estimate with any degree of accuracy the contribution of this effect to the decline of the death rate in the nineteenth century?

In respect of the five disease groups with which we are concerned this task is perhaps less difficult than might be expected. We can be fairly confident that a change in the agent–host relationship was the main, perhaps the only influence in scarlet fever; that it had little part in the trend of the typhus–typhoid[37] and cholera–dysentery groups (for which other more convincing explanations are available); that it may have contributed to the behaviour of smallpox, but the contribution of this disease to the total decline was so small that in this context the issue is of secondary importance. The only real uncertainty is in respect of tuberculosis, and we have discussed at length reasons for believing that a change in the tubercle bacillus or in man's response to it is unlikely to have been a very significant influence in a population which had been exposed to the disease for centuries. It therefore seems permissible to conclude that a change in the character of these infectious diseases, essentially independent of human intervention, may have been responsible for not less than one-fifth of the total improvement and—as a very rough estimate—for not more than one-third. The remainder must be attributed to environmental change.

In evaluating the relative importance of different types of environmental influence we must distinguish broadly between changes associated with a rising standard of living and those which resulted from the work of sanitary reformers. They differed greatly in respect of the motives which led to them, their character and their timing. The former were initiated for economic and social rather than health reasons and would have occurred even if they had led to no improvement in health; they were unspecific in the sense that while their collective influence on health was great, it is not possible to estimate the precise effects of any single feature; and the improvement began certainly by 1850 and, in the opinion of some economic historians, considerably earlier. The measures introduced by the sanitary reformers were for the purpose of preventing disease; in the light of present knowledge there is no doubt about their specificity; and their effects were delayed until the eighth decade, at least thirty years after the beginning of a substantial rise in the standard of living.

Against this background we can be fairly confident that it is to sanitary reform that we owe the decline of mortality in the typhus–typhoid and cholera groups.[38] This interpretation is consistent both with what we now know about the nature and means of spread of these diseases, and with the fact that their decline coincided with the introduction of the specific measures which would be effective. There are no grounds for thinking that the same measures would have had a significant influence on mortality from tuberculosis; they would not have had much effect on frequency or intensity of exposure or on the response of those exposed. These considerations suggest that the specific changes introduced by the sanitary reformers were responsible for about a quarter of the total decline of mortality in the second half of the nineteenth century.

The remainder of the improvement, mainly associated with tuberculosis,[39] must be attributed to a rise in the standard of living brought about by the Industrial Revolution. In this discussion we have come to this conclusion by eliminating other possibilities, but in our earlier assessment of tuberculosis the same conclusion was drawn more directly. If we are satisfied, as we are, that genetic selection was not a major influence on the trend of this disease, the effect must be attributed to the environment. The number of agents to be considered is not large. Diet was probably the most important of them, since there are no grounds for believing that frequency of exposure to infection— the other potentially important influence—was much reduced during the nineteenth century. Hence we conclude that the rising standard of living was the other main influence which accounted for perhaps half of the total reduction of mortality.

To sum up: In order of their relative importance the influences responsible for the decline of mortality in the second half of the nineteenth century were: (*a*) a rising standard of living, of which the most significant feature was improved diet (responsible mainly for the decline of tuberculosis and less certainly, and to a lesser extent, of typhus); (*b*) the hygienic changes introduced by the sanitary reformers (responsible for the decline of the typhus–typhoid and cholera groups); and (*c*) a favourable trend in the relationship between infectious agent and the human host (which accounted for the decline of mortality from scarlet fever and may have contributed to that from tuberculosis, typhus, and cholera). The effect of therapy was restricted to smallpox and hence had only a trivial effect on the total reduction of the death rate.

Finally we must consider whether these conclusions about the second half of the nineteenth century have any bearing on the questions concerning the relationship between economic developments and population growth in the late eighteenth and early nineteenth centuries. In particular, do they help us to decide whether improved economic and social conditions led to a rise in population and, if so, whether an increase in the birth rate or a decline of the death rate was the more significant influence?

The nineteenth-century data suggest that theoretically at least these questions are answerable, that the relationships between population growth and economic change and between birth rate and death rate were not such that it is meaningless to try to separate them. In the period after registration the rise of population was due primarily to the decline of mortality and the most important reason for the decline was an improvement in economic and social conditions.

The difficulty before registration is, of course, that the same data are not available, and valuable as the studies of parish registers are, it is hard to believe that they will provide an adequate substitute. In these circumstances we must resist the temptation to put too fine a point on our interpretation; to comment on the relative importance of infant and adult mortality when we cannot be sure of the death rate; or to speak confidently about the trend of the major epidemic infections in a period for which we do not really know the causes of death. All that we can attempt is a judgement on the main issues in the light of knowledge derived from a later period when interpretation is less difficult.

Our conclusions about the second half of the nineteenth century can be stated briefly. In part the reduction of mortality was due to a change in the relationship between the infective organism and the human host, most notably in the case of scarlet fever. But more important were the rising standard of living and, later, an improvement in hygienic conditions. In the late eighteenth and early nineteenth centuries there is no reason to believe that there were advances in hygiene, and we need assess only the contribution of the other two causes.

In making this assessment it is helpful to have in mind the concept of a constant high level of mortality from endemic infections, itself subject to fluctuations in response to changes in virulence and resistance (as in scarlet fever). Superimposed on this, and much more variable, was mortality from epidemic infections such as plague.

Confronted with a continuous rise of population in a period for which birth rate, death rate, and cause of death are unknown we can only ask ourselves for how long we could reasonably attribute the trend wholly to changes of this kind, not essentially different from those which operated in previous centuries. No precise answer can be given; but the fact that the size of the population was trebled between 1700 and 1851 strongly suggests that some other influence was at work well before the middle of the nineteenth century. And even in the late eighteenth century, by comparison with earlier experience, the rate and duration of growth seems greater than can be accounted for by 'natural' changes in the behaviour of infectious diseases. If we accept this view, and if we are satisfied that specific medical measures made no significant contribution to the death rate, we must conclude that the main reason for the rise of population in the late eighteenth and early nineteenth centuries was an improvement in economic and social conditions. We drew attention to the fact that his conclusion follows whether we attribute more importance to the response of the birth rate or death rate.[40] We have given reasons for attaching more importance to the death rate; but in either case the answer to the question whether the Industrial Revolution created its own labour force is the same.

BIBLIOGRAPHICAL NOTE

Surprisingly, the challenging conclusions of this article have not so far stimulated further research either into the social and medical developments underlying the reductions in mortality from various causes analysed here, or into the continuation of the decline of mortality after 1901. The only comparable work remains W. P. D. Logan's article on 'Mortality in England and Wales from 1848 to 1947', *Population Studies*, 4 (1950–1), though more recently M. W. Beaver has offered some interesting hypotheses in an article 'Population, infant mortality and milk', in *Population Studies*, 27 (1973) to explain the decline of infant mortality, an aspect of the mortality decline not explored by McKeown and Record since it is a phenomenon entirely of the twentieth century. Professor McKeown and his colleagues have more recently integrated their work on the decline of mortality into a broader interpretation of the growth of European population in modern times in Thomas McKeown, R. G. Brown, and R. G. Record, 'An interpretation of the rise of population in Europe', *Population Studies*, 26 (1972).

NOTES

1. Thomas McKeown and R. G. Brown, 'Medical evidence related to English population changes in the Eighteenth Century,' *Population Studies*, 9 (1955), 119–41.

2. G. B. Longstaff, 'The recent decline in the English death rate considered in connection with the cause of death', *Jour. Stat. Soc.*, 47 (1884), 221–58.

3. S. Phillips, 'A review of mortality statistics during the last half century', *Clinical Journal*, 30 (1908), 55–61, 73–80.

4. A. H. Gale, 'Variations in the mortality and incidence of the common infectious diseases of childhood over a century', *Proceedings of the Royal Society of Medicine*, 36 (1943), 97–103.

5. W. P. D. Logan, 'Mortality in England and Wales from 1848 to 1947', *Population Studies*, 4 (1950), 132–78.

6. Sir Arthur Newsholme, *The Elements of Vital Statistics*, (London, 1923), chap. 38. M. Greenwood, *Epidemics and Crowd Diseases* (London, 1935), pt. ii, chap. 14. Sir Stanley Woodwark, 'The rise and fall of certain diseases concurrently with the progress of hygiene and sanitation', *Journal of the Royal Institute of Public Health and Hygiene*, 1 (1938), 897–910. V. H. Springett, 'An interpretation of statistical trends in tuberculosis', *Lancet*, 1 (1952), 521, 575. Sir Macfarlane Burnet, *Natural History of Infectious Disease* (Cambridge, 1953), chap. 21.

7. C. Creighton, *A History of Epidemics in Britain*, 2 (Cambridge, 1894), chap. 1. A. Newsholme, 'Relation of vital statistics to sanitary reform', *Medical Magazine*, 11 (1902), 360. Greenwood, op. cit., pt. ii, chap 3. Woodwark, loc. cit. D. Thompson, 'The ebb and flow of infection', *Monthly Bulletin of the Ministry of Health*, 14 (1955), 106–16.

8. Newsholme (1902), loc. cit. Woodwark, loc. cit. Burnet, op. cit., p. 16. Thomson, loc. cit.

9. Phillips, loc. cit. Newsholme, op. cit., chap. 37. Greenwood, op. cit., pt. ii, chap. 6. A. H. Gale, 'A century of change in the mortality and incidence of the principal infections of childhood', *Archives of Diseases of Childhood*, 20 (1945), 2–21. Thomson, loc. cit.

10. Burnett, op. cit., p. 16.

11. Creighton, op. cit., chap. 4.

12. E. J. Edwardes, *A Concise History of Smallpox and Vaccination in Europe* (London, 1902).

13. J. C. McVail, chapter in *A Treatise on Public Health* by Stevenson and Murphy, vol. ii (London, 1893). Newsholme, op. cit., chap. 35. Greenwood, op. cit., pt. ii, chap. 9. Gale, loc. cit., Burnet, op. cit., p. 215.

14. G. T. Griffith, *Population Problems of the Age of Malthus* (Cambridge, 1926).

15. McKeown and Brown, loc. cit.

16. J. T. Krause, 'Changes in English Fertility and Mortality, 1781–1850', *Econ. Hist. Rev.* 2nd ser. 11 (1958), 52–70.

17. W. Woolcombe, *The Frequency and Fatality of Different Diseases, particularly on the Progressive Increase of Consumption* (1808). W. Farr, cited by Greenwood, op. cit. 345. J. Brownlee, *An Investigation into the Epidemiology of Phthisis in Great Britain and Ireland*, Medical Research Committee Special Report Series no. 18 (1917), pp. 38–44.

18. J. Brownlee, *An Investigation into the Epidemiology of Phthisis in Great Britain and Ireland, Part III*, Medical Research Committee Special Report Series no. 46 (1918), p. 26.

19. Springett, 1952, loc. cit.

20. G. Dahlberg, 'Mortality from tuberculosis in some countries', *British Journal of Social Medicine* 3 (1949), 220–7.

21. J. A. Weir, R. L. Taylor, and R. S. Fraser, 'The ambulatory treatment of patients hospitalised with pulmonary tuberculosis', *Ann. Intern. Med.* 47 (1957) 762–3; N. Wynn-Williams and R. D. Young, 'How much rest in pulmonary tuberculosis?' *Tubercle*, London, 38 (1957), 333–9; Tuberculosis Chemotherapy Centre, Madras, 'A concurrent comparison of home and sanatorium treatment of pulmonary tuberculosis in South India', *Bull. of the W.H.O.*, 21 (1959), 51–144; Tuberculosis Society of Scotland, 'The Treatment of pulmonary tuberculosis at work: a controlled trial'. *Tubercle*, London, 41 (1960), 161–70.

22. W. M. Fraser, *A History of English Public Health* (London, 1950), p. 99.

23. R. and J. Dubos refer to tuberculosis as 'the social disease of the nineteenth century, perhaps the first penalty that capitalist society had to pay for the ruthless exploitation of labour', *The White Plague* (London, 1953), p. 207.

24. Newsholme, 1923, op. cit. 452–62.

25. Burnet, op. cit. 298.

26. Greenwood, op. cit. 342.

27. *Report of the Departmental Committee Appointed to Inquire into Certain Matters Relating to the Diet of Patients in County and Borough Mental Hospitals* (H.M.S.O., London, 1924), p. 14.

28. A survey in 1897–9 showed that in some counties 50 per cent of cows showed evidence of tuberculous infection. Examination of milk for tubercle bacilli was not extensively done until the 1920s; in many areas 10 per cent or more of samples were found to be infected (*Principles and Practice of Preventive Medicine*, edited by C. W. Hutt and H. H. Thomson (London, 1935), pp. 686–9).

29. It seems reasonable to suppose, however, that milk consumption in the towns was greatly stimulated by the provision, about the middle of the century, of good railway links between town and country.

30. See Topley and Wilson's *Principles of Bacteriology and Immunity,* ii (London, 1946), 1310–11.

31. According to Hartwell they did so 'slowly during the war, more quickly after 1815 and rapidly after 1850' (*Econ. Hist. Rev.* 2nd ser. 13 (1961), 412).

32. In 1909.

33. Malnutrition is generally regarded as an important contributory influence—see Creighton, op. cit. 215; Greenwood, op. cit. 178; A. H. Gale, *Epidemic Diseases* (London, 1959), p. 75.

34. H. S. Banks, *The Common Infectious Diseases* (London, 1949), p. 52.

35. In 1831, 1848, 1853, 1866, and 1893. The last introduction was not followed by a widespread epidemic.

36. The figures give the percentage contribution of the disease or disease group to the reduction of mortality for which collectively they were responsible.

37. Consideration of the agent–host relationship in the case of typhus is complicated by the role of the intermediate host. Burnet believes that typhus is an ancient disease of rats and mice but that the louse-borne disease is a relatively recent development. 'The mild disease of the rat passes accidentally to man, it finds a new vector in the louse, and under circumstances of war and famine spreads widely and fatally, but where circumstances allow its easy spread in a stationary population, it eventually develops the character of a typical relatively mild endemic infection.' loc cit. 183.

38. Our only reservation here is in respect of mortality from typhus and cholera, which fluctuated greatly before 1870. But for reasons which we have discussed earlier it seems reasonable to attribute their virtual disappearance from the British Isles to hygienic measures.

39. Typhus is the other disease to whose decline the rise of the standard of living may have contributed.

40. McKeown and Brown, op. cit. 140.

11

Trade Unions and Free Labour : The Background to the Taff Vale Decision*

J. SAVILLE

IT is a commonplace that public sympathy for the cause of the strikers was an important factor in the dockers' victory in the late summer of 1899.[1] What is not so well appreciated is that this sympathy was already beginning to waste away during the last weeks of the strike[2] and public opinion in general very quickly turned to outright opposition in the months that followed. Through all the decade of the nineties and well into the new century, a hostility developed towards trade unionism in general and new unionism in particular that bordered at times on the hysterical. It finds various expressions in the contemporary press, in the employment of large police and military forces during trade disputes, and in increasingly adverse judgements against the unions in the courts. This whole period after 1889 is one of a developing counter-attack by the propertied classes against the industrial organizations of the working people. The final breakthrough is reached in 1901 when, as the result of the Taff Vale case and the decision in *Quinn* v. *Leathem*, the trade unions found themselves stripped of the legal rights that had been written into the Statute Book by the legislation of the 1870s.

It was the special characteristics of new unionism that made it the immediate target of ruling-class fury. Recent research has modified the picture of new unionism that has been generally accepted, and today it is recognized that 1889 was less of a break with the past than was formerly believed.[3] There were stirrings, and organization, among the unskilled workers half a dozen years before 1889,[4] and, on the other hand, the old skilled unions were in some respects less conservative than is usually believed. Nevertheless, when all the necessary qualifications have been added to the traditional interpretation of old and new unionism, it is important not to underestimate the climacteric of 1889. The economic problems of the unskilled and semi-skilled trade unionists were very different from those of the skilled workers,

* From *Essays in Labour History*, ed. A. Briggs and J. Saville (London, 1960), pp. 317–50. Reprinted by permission of Macmillan, London and Basingstoke.

and their industrial methods and tactics were perforce also different. While the old unions were able to rely upon the skill of their members as a crucial bargaining weapon, the new unionists were at all times, even in the years of good trade, subject to the pressures of an overstocked labour market. Picketing, for instance, was rarely a major problem in the strike action of many sections of skilled workers. The Webbs noted that among the cotton-spinners of Lancashire, or the boilermakers of the north-east coast, or the coalminers in well-organized districts, both sides to an industrial dispute knew that when work was resumed the same men would have to be taken on.[5] The problem of scab labour did not, therefore, arise in the virulent form that occurred in the casual and semi-skilled trades. 'Picketing, in fact, is a mark not of Trade Unionism, but of its imperfection.' So the Webbs wrote in 1896.[6] The position was very different, for example, in the ports employing dock labour, where only a proportion of those applying for work on any one day would be accepted[7] and where much of the work could be performed by agricultural labour or casual labour drafted in from outside. In such circumstances, and these were familiar in many other industries, it was immensely more difficult to make a strike solid or to achieve stable trade unions. Outside the highly skilled trades, to win even an approximation to the closed shop or to ensure that blackleg labour did not swamp a strike, militant tactics were demanded which the older unionists had pioneered decades before but which, by the end of the 1880s, they believed they no longer needed. The employers, too, in the semi- and unskilled trades were more uncompromising than their fellows in industries where unionism had long been established; and their first, and for men of property not unnatural, reaction was to smash these new upstart organizations rather than attempt to meet them on common ground.

Trade unionists in the newly organized trades like dockers and gas-workers were rarely more than a minority of the labour force, and to achieve their main objectives of higher wages, shorter hours, and union recognition, with or without a strike, brought them right up against the prejudice, ignorance, and apathy of important groups in their own class who were not prepared to accept the need for, or the decisions of, the unions. It was this clash between unionists and what was nicely called 'free' labour that provided much of the drama of the industrial struggles of the early 1890s, and it was this aspect of trade-union activity that public opinion mainly seized upon. *The Economist* noted in 1891 when commenting on the setting up of the *R.C. on Labour* that 'the general labour controversy is going largely to turn upon the respective rights and duties of free labourers and unionists'[8]— free labourers being defined as all those who wished to make their own independent contract with their employers regardless of the trade-union position. If the union members came out on strike, that was not necessarily any concern to those who were not union members; and to insist that all shall stop work at the behest of a minority of trade unionists, was not this a new form of 'corporate tyranny' as oppressive as those forms of monopoly that Adam Smith, at the very beginning of the modern era, sought to destroy with the publication of *The Wealth of Nations*? Thus *The Times*,[9] never slow to recognize 'tyranny' in working-class dress.

Besides their industrial tactics, the attitude of the new unionists towards state intervention, symbolized by the slogan of the Eight-Hour Day, was a further cause for anxiety on the part of the propertied classes. Intervention-ism and socialism were for many indistinguishable terms, and the identifi-cation of new unionism, state intervention, and socialism was increasingly made. The opposition to the eight-hour day and to any increase in state intervention came from expected quarters: from business circles whose mouthpiece was *The Economist*; from social philosophers like Herbert Spencer; and from old-style trade unionists who had accepted much of middle-class ideology. For Herbert Spencer, in the introduction to a widely circulated volume of essays, published in 1891, whose title, significantly, was *A Plea for Liberty*, society has only the choice between freedom of contract and coercive status, and any infringement of the former can only lead to an extension of the latter.[10] George Howell, representing the lib–lab trade union-ist, said the same things in more homely language.[11]

It is difficult for the mid-twentieth century to appreciate fully the hor-ror with which the upper classes at this time regarded every new step towards a curtailment of *laissez-faire*. No doubt for those like Spencer, who regarded any intervention as a step along the road to serfdom, *laissez-faire* was still the only untried Utopia. What is relevant here is the way resistance was built up to some of the elementary demands of social justice. Against the background of Ireland, the growth of socialist movements on the Continent, and the dreadful example of labour legis-lation in Australia, the good bourgeois found that it was indeed time to cry halt.[12] When the demands of the new unionists found expression in the industrial militancy and the wave of disputes that followed the great Dock Strike, the stage was set for struggle. The old unions were reason-able; the new, impossible.

The older Unions, presided over by men having some knowledge of political economy and of the conditions of trade, have a defined policy. They desire, when it is possible, to improve the position of the working man; in times of commer-cial prosperity they will insist, using his obedience to them as a weapon, that he shall have what they consider his fair share of that prosperity; in times of commercial depression they will help him and, in effect, they perform many of the functions of a friendly society. Admission to such Unions is a privilege not lightly to be obtained. This policy is stigmatised as degenerate by the secre-tary of the new Union. His policy and that of his Union is that of the daughter of the horseleech;[13] it is a policy of continual importunity. The new Union cares not whether men are ill or well paid; it is ever ready with a fresh demand.

Concession does but whet its appetite; it claims for labour the whole of the
profits made by labour and capital combined; it aims to be the absolute dictator
of the conditions of toil; to say who shall work and how much he shall receive.
... The principle which underlies the militant Union is the principle of socialism. In the first place, the individual is subordinated to the class; in the second
place, the class desires to obtain the whole of the profits which are derived from
capital and labour combined. In other words, it desires to confiscate capital.[14]

There was, clearly, only one thing to be done with the offspring of the
horse-leech.

I

The change in the temper of public opinion towards New Unionism is
noticeable already in the closing stages of the 1889 Dock Strike from a
reading of the editorial columns of *The Times*. Prior to 28 August the
leader writers had been fairly sympathetic to the dock labourers; but on
that day, in a tougher-minded editorial, *The Times* warned that 'evidence
is accumulating that intimidation is playing an appreciable, if not an
important, part in this strike'. Moreover, while it was no doubt 'natural'
that the dockers should turn for leadership to the 'professional agitators',
public sympathy was given 'not for the sake of, but in spite of such leaders.
This sympathy is as yet a young and delicate plant. It may wither if they
indulge in excesses or persist in immoderate demands.' By early September
the leader writers had discovered that intimidation 'is playing a very definite
part in the maintenance of the strike'.[15] If the strike continues, the editorial of
2 September went on, 'it must be conducted with a proper regard for personal freedom', by which *The Times* meant that blackleg labour must not
be interfered with; and the police were warned that it was their elementary
duty to see that 'the game was played fairly' and that men who wished to
exercise their right to work must be 'thoroughly protected'. By the end of the
strike, in mid-September, the 'sympathy' of *The Times* had been thoroughly
dissipated; and thenceforward *The Times* was at the head of all those who
attacked new unionism. In an extraordinary leader on Christmas Eve 1889
The Times exhorted employers to take the lead in encouraging and organizing an anti-union labour force in their own industry, and once again re-
proved the police for passivity in the face of mass picketing and intimidation.
Referring to free labour, *The Times* wrote:

Why should they suffer themselves to be intimidated by a set of loud-voiced
bullies, whose skins, we venture to say, are quite as tender as those of the
honest men they coerce? The difference lies, we believe, in discipline and organisation. The bullies organise themselves, having nothing else to do, while the
workers feel themselves isolated and undisciplined. Surely there is a function
here for employers to discharge. They ought to take the lead in organising,
disciplining, and encouraging men who wish to work. If picketing is legal, as
seems to be the theory of the police, then it must also be legal to picket the

pickets. If a union can lawfully beset all the roads to a manufactory with paid bullies, why cannot employers take a leaf out of their book? Sauce for the goose is sauce for the gander, and if goose and gander came to blows at least the fight would be fair, and it might even expand the intelligence of the police authorities and enlarge their conceptions of duty.[16]

The employers were not slow to follow this advice. The famous strike at the South Metropolitan Gasworks, whose chairman was George Livesey, one of the best known of the union-baiters of the nineties, was already proceeding; and the strike was eventually broken by the large-scale importation of free labour under heavy police escort and protection. For once *The Times* was satisfied.[17] The most concerted effort on the part of the employers, and the beginning of a sustained war against new unionism on the waterfront, came exactly a year after the Dock Strike, when the shipping owners established the Shipping Federation.[18] 'From the first,' wrote the author of the Federation's official history, 'the Federation was founded as a fighting machine to counter the strike weapon, and it made no secret of the fact.'[19] The Shipping Federation, which united seven-eighths of all British tonnage, immediately began an offensive against the seamen's and dockers' unions, by establishing offices at all the main ports at which seamen must register before they could be employed; and then, early in 1891, it introduced its own ticket which pledged the holder to work with union and non-union men alike, and without which in many firms it was impossible to get work.

There was already in existence a United Labour Council of the Port of London which had been formed at the end of the Dock Strike and which embraced most of the waterside unions; and there were in addition a number of unions catering for seamen and firemen, of which the most important was that organized by J. Havelock Wilson. Faced with the opposition of the Shipping Federation all these bodies affiliated to a new Federation of Trade and Labour Unions connected with the Shipping, Carrying, and other Industries.[20] Its secretary was Clem Edwards,[21] and by the time Edwards gave evidence before the *R.C. on Labour* in November 1891 some 25 or 26 unions were affiliated.[22]

The industrial war which now began between the employers' and workers' federations was only a continuation on a larger scale of guerrilla actions that had been taking place ever since the Mansion House agreement brought the great strike of 1889 to a close. Despite the face that Tillett and others reported to the *R.C. on Labour* that for the first twelve months after the 1889 strike relations between capital and labour were fairly good,[23] strikes were in fact frequent in some of the docks.[24] Among the early strikes in the provinces that showed the emerging pattern were those at Southampton and Plymouth in the autumn of 1890. Port conditions at Southampton were said to be among the worst in the country.[25] The Dockers' Union had begun organization among the labourers in the spring of 1890, and both wages and hours of work had somewhat improved by the later summer. The strike at Southampton began over the question of union recognition on Monday 7 September. Troops were called in on the second day and small sympathetic strikes began among other groups of labourers. The strike was solid, the spirit of the strikers good, but for reasons which are still unclear, the union executive were unwilling to recognize the strike and no strike pay was given. The strike ended five days later on the following Saturday. Will Sprow, a roving organizer of the Dockers' Union who led the strike, was later sentenced to three months' imprisonment for intimidation and stated on his release that had the strike continued, the men would have won. The results of the strike were disastrous for dock unionism in Southampton. A Free Labour Association was formed in the month following this strike, the honorary secretary of which was also the vice-president of the Chamber of Commerce.[26] Tom McCarthy admitted in January 1892 that the present position of the union 'is very low indeed',[27] and he also admitted that in this case the union was not broken initially by the employers or the Free Labour Association but as a result of differences between the local branch and the national executive.[28]

In October 1890 a strike developed over the free labour issue in Plymouth. It was broken after nearly a fortnight and was the familiar story of heavy police protection for blackleg labour. A Free Labour Association was established, the honorary secretary this time being the secretary of the Coal Merchants' Association. Trade-union influence was 'most materially' diminished.[29]

With the establishment of the Shipping Federation in the autumn of 1890, strike-breaking along the waterfront became more organized. In the complicated strike in the London docks which originated with the Wade's Arms Manifesto on 5 December 1890[30] and which lasted through until the end of February 1891, the Shipping Federation introduced free labour into the docks on a very extensive scale. A depot ship, the *Scotland*, was provided for accommodation for blacklegs who were given three months' agreements with food and lodgings. The metropolitan police were 'introduced' into the docks with most effective results. At the conclusion of the strike the Shipping Federation established a free labour office on the Albert Dock, and George Laws, the general manager of the Federation, spoke of the strike as having been 'utterly defeated'.[31] His evidence before the *R.C. on Labour* on the organization of strike-breaking is worth study.[32] Before this London strike had concluded, another against the Shipping Federation had broken out at Cardiff. In the previous August (1890) a committee of the Cardiff Shipowners' Association had passed a resolution affirming 'the right of free labour'—a statement which all knew was a declaration of war on the unions. On 5 February 1891 a gang of coal-tippers, at the instance of the Amalgamated Sailor's and Firemen's Union, refused to service a boat whose crew